'A memorable and acutely observed portrait of one summer of cricket from an award-winning sports writer who has watched – and loved – cricket since he was a boy, it is essential reading for anyone who cares about the English game.'

Yorkshire Evening Post

'Hamilton writes skilfully and with enthusiasm about the players he admires.'

Times Literary Supplement

'Beautifully written ... Hamilton is sharply and thoughtfully observant, giving a wealth of perceptive vignettes.'

Guardian

'Quite brilliant. There's a reason that Hamilton wins a heap of awards and it's that he's a great writer with a stirring turn of phrase. You'll be moved by this.'

Sport

'A tour de force ... an addition to the uppermost shelf of contemporary literature.'

Yorkshire Post

'The title ... which is about the convulsions of the 2009 season, captures well this tone of fragility and of something being lost.'

Evening Standard

'It is something of a treat for cricket followers that after his Brian Clough biography and forensically researched account of Harold Larwood's life, Duncan Hamilton should turn to chronicling an English cricket season in full, from the ICC World Twenty20 and Ashes Tests to the village green ... [When] Hamilton reflects on the past here, he uses telling detail to bring it to life. There's no lazy nostalgia; there is though, a certain wistfulness and from the title down, there is a suggestion that something is on the verge of disappearing for good.'

Spin

Duncan Hamilton's *Provided You Don't Kiss Me* won the William Hill Sports Book of the Year for 2007 and a British Sports Book Award in 2008. In 2009, he was awarded the William Hill, again, for *Harold Larwood*, as well as winning the prestigious Wisden Book of the Year for 2009 and biography of the year at the 2010 British Sports Book Awards. He lives in West Yorkshire.

'Hamilton's mix of reportage, observation, history and anecdote never fails to hold the reader's interest. The quality of his writing, so evident in his previous works, shines again.'

Mike Atherton, *The Times*

'It is full of well-chosen anecdotes, choice descriptions, pertinent observations and allusions that come from wonderfully diverse sources. I would not be at all surprised if this was his third William Hill winner.'

Daily Telegraph

'*A Last English Summer*, set to the beat of the 2009 season, is a ... personal and contemplative read, which escapes woolly romanticism by the style of its delivery, every bit as crisp as the sound of a new leather ball on a willow bat ... [It] captures all the flavours of a summer's cricket: the grounds, the crowds, the players, the shots and the echoes of history. And it does so memorably, with an eye for the finest detail.'

Spectator

'[A] must-read for those who love the game ... his comparisons are sharp and his longing for the eroded joys of the county game shrewdly expressed.'

Wisden

'Hamilton's erudite and unhurried writing, as lush as an outfield in April, is a constant pleasure.'

Financial Times

'Beautifully crafted ... written with intense feeling for an age that's sliding away.'

Independent

'Combining old-fashioned journalism, beautifully observed writing and his own recollections, he recounts the story of a single season's cricket from a personal perspective ... Even non-cricket fans will be enthralled by this quality book. ★★★★★'

News of the World

A LAST ENGLISH SUMMER

DUNCAN HAMILTON

Quercus

First published in Great Britain in 2010 by Quercus
This paperback edition published in 2011 by

Quercus
21 Bloomsbury Square
London
WC1A 2NS

A CIP catalogue record for this book is available
from the British Library

ISBN 978 0 85738 148 4

Design and typesetting: Jane McKenna

Printed and bound in Great Britain by Clays Ltd. St Ives plc

To my grandfather, alive on every page,
who taught me to love two things: cricket and libraries.
I am forever grateful.

CONTENTS

*Trent Bridge, which Neville Cardus called a 'lotus land'
for batsmen and 'fit for Heaven itself'.*

A GOLDEN AGE SORT
OF A CHAP

Duncan Hamilton and his grandfather –
taken only a few weeks before his grandfather died.

The man who taught me to love cricket was born in 1889, one year before its Golden Age began – those glorious summers of W. G. Grace and Archie MacLaren, F. S. Jackson and C. B. Fry. He was christened John, but everyone called him Jack.

He was my grandfather.

As a boy, I admired him above anyone else. If I had known the full truth – and been mature enough to understand his story properly – I would have admired him even more. He usually wore a brown suit, a grey wool cap, rather in the style of the Australian Baggy Green, and segged black shoes, which he polished to mirrored perfection. At all times he carried a silver pocket watch.

We are naturally pulled into the orbit of those who dote on us, and we stay in it as a consequence. And it's true that my grandfather doted on me. We walked together in our separate but shared silences. I had a stammer, so bad that the words got stuck on my tongue to the extent that I couldn't pronounce my own name without the hard rat-a-tat of overstretched syllables accompanying terrible facial grimaces and contortions. For a long time I decided I would be better off saying nothing unless it was absolutely necessary.

My grandfather was almost completely deaf and wore the heavy contraption of the hard of hearing: a battery-powered pack, which he clipped to the band of his trousers, and a round earpiece, which was connected to the pack by a barley-twist cord. The pack, the cord and the earpiece were the bright, shining flesh colour of a doll's face. Sometimes, if my grandfather turned the volume up too loud, the pack whistled like a boiling kettle. The loss of his hearing pared down his speech. There was no point in asking a question if you had to strain to catch the answer. So we were locked together – the young boy who couldn't speak, the old man who couldn't hear.

My grandfather returned with his condition from the Great War and came home to unimaginable misery, swapping one horror for another. He found his wife had died in childbirth; and that his baby had died too. My grandmother's first husband had died in the same acreage of churned mud occupied by my grandfather in France. The two of them – alone, confused and partly broken – met and married. Like two refugees from the fighting, and marked for ever by it, the couple began to rebuild their lives and shape a future entirely dictated for them by a past neither wanted to remember. That my grandparents each had two wedding rings was our shut-away family secret. I learned about it only several years after my grandfather had died.

There was always a dignified stoicism about him. He never spoke about the war, or what had happened to him during it. He never spoke about the things he'd seen or felt there and the sadness of hopes unfulfilled, or the friends, including his brother, who became carved names on stone memorials. He never complained and never explained, which only in retrospect I recognise as demonstrating bravery of a quite different kind.

This brief account of my grandfather and his history is necessary because the book you're holding wouldn't exist without him or it. He is the undertow of the book, the strong current dragging me from spring into summer and on into autumn. The two gifts he left me profoundly moulded my own life. He gave me a love of cricket and of libraries.

Home from France, and back to work as one of the 'poor drudges underground, blackened to the eyes' as he hewed tubs of coal, my grandfather took refuge by living a deliberately uneventful life. He sought nothing purely for himself except peace of mind. After the vast, bloody landscape of the fighting he scaled down and consciously shrank his world into a small, manageable size. Survivors of the Great War concealed a gutted soul, fury and bewilderment, bottled-up grief and shards of guilt at being alive when tens of thousands of others were dead. The nature of Fate troubled them, and each coped in his own way with it. My grandfather found his comfort in, and his took convalescence from, long walks and the groomed greenery of the cricket field. (He did so, ironically and coincidentally, in those same years that Neville Cardus also benefited from cricket's restorative powers to recover from a nervous breakdown at the *Manchester Guardian*. In this, if nothing else, my two heroes – the miner and the writer – were no different from one another.)

To say the least, we were an impecunious family. There was not much money for high days and holidays. Our yearly fortnight was spent in my grandfather's council house close to the north-east coast. He would travel back with us to Nottingham for two or three weeks more. All of us see life more sharply as the past recedes. Looking back, I recognise those summer weeks as a blessing. Without them I'd never have got to really know him. He was a reader, especially fond of stories of the Wild West, which he borrowed from the library at the rate of seven per week. All the books had bright, custard-coloured covers. He took me with him and organised the first library card I ever owned.

From Monday to Friday we read together. On Saturday we went to watch village cricket. By then I was already entranced by the game. In fact, it was love at first sight. On our minuscule TV screen, no more than an oversized full stop embedded in a huge teak cabinet, I watched Derek Underwood against Australia as he jagged the ball off The Oval pitch and made it climb at John Inverarity like a leaping hare. The black-and-white picture was so dusky and indistinct that both Underwood and the fielders, packed so tightly around Inverarity as to induce claustrophobia before his fatal lapse, which gave England victory, shimmered like ghosts. Inverarity was outnumbered, like Custer in one of my grandfather's Westerns.

I had no idea of the significance of the game; no notion of how cricket was truly played either. What hooked me was its drama. Nothing felt so vital and intense. I wanted to learn more about it. My grandfather taught me because my father, a Scot, had no interest in, or experience of, cricket. He was raised on the sweat of football and the blood of boxing. There was no cricket pitch within four 'country miles' of the mining village in which he grew up. No one had a bat, ball or stumps. You played football in the street or boxed with bare knuckles. Compared to what happened within the roped ring or between the lime markings of a football pitch, my father at first regarded cricket as slow, dull and effeminate. Men in white – unless striding under the banner of Real Madrid or Leeds United – always looked slightly ridiculous to him. This only changed later on.

Instead of talking about the war, or those it had claimed with bullets, shells and shrapnel, my grandfather talked to me about 'his cricketers' – the men of another, richer vintage: Herbert Sutcliffe and Percy Holmes, Walter Hammond and Denis Compton, Frank Tyson and Ray Lindwall. He spoke of Keith Miller's swept-back hair and matinee-idol flourishes, Don Bradman's relentless pursuit of runs and the casual ticking-off of his big scores, Jack Hobbs' deft touches and the aching sadness of Hedley Verity, who made the poetry of bowling flesh before a different war claimed him. My grandfather would re-enact Hobbs' strokes with a swish of his muscled arms and miner's callused hands. 'There is a beauty about cricket,' he said.

He'd seen this beauty himself in the 1920s during coach journeys to the Scarborough Festival – setting off in dawn's pale shadow and returning to the soft blackness of early autumn. For the rest of the season he followed the first-class game with his obsessive reading and memorising of the morning newspapers. Although he didn't play much himself, he taught me the fundamentals: the grip of the bat, the stance, the set of the field with its curiously named positions, the basic way to hold the ball when bowling. He cut a thin bat out of boxwood and bowled at me with a tennis ball in the concrete passageway next to the coal bunker. It was rudimentary coaching, and the closeness of the walls made me feel rather as Inverarity must have done when England's fielders hemmed him in at The Oval. But it was a start.

The village cricket ground's pavilion doubled as the Working Men's Institutive, where my grandfather went to meet friends who had served in, but didn't discuss either, the war. These were men who rolled thin cigarettes (cheaper than packets of Woodbines or Capstan Full Strength) or jammed pinches of tobacco into the bowl of their pipes with knotted, nicotine-stained fingers. They read the *Daily Mirror* and rattled dominoes across scarred oak tables. On Saturday afternoons I saw them in smart suits, dressed as if going to a wedding, sitting on the slatted benches just beyond the boundary rope. The ground was beside the plain, dark stone of the squat Methodist chapel where my parents were married and I was baptised. Whenever I think of it now, I feel the overwhelming nostalgic pull and affection of place and people. This is where cricket started for me. Instantly I liked the paraphernalia of the game: the thick, V-necked, cable-knit sweaters, the boots and pads that required Blanco, the stiff peaked caps, the obligation to coat bats in linseed oil, and the pungent scent of that oil in the air. I liked the fact each match was fashioned like a mystery play. The outcome was not always obvious. I liked the shape it took and how it often progressed, very slowly like nature, to reveal itself to me in complicated ways. I liked its arcane rituals of lunch and tea, the toss of the coin, the marking-out of the pitch and the use of the creaking roller with its pale-grey wood handle. Odd though it seems to say it, I even liked rain-spotted days when play just might be possible. I was able to read in between the showers.

Later, during the same summer, my grandfather took me to Trent Bridge to watch 'real cricket'. He was nearly eighty years old. Without thinking about his worn, stiff joints, I told him I wanted to sit on the wide expanse of grass between the lip of the Parr Stand and the boundary, and he guided me there by resting a huge, steady hand on my right shoulder. Somehow, and without complaint, he crouched down beside me on the dewy turf, ran his fingers against the rough, thick rope and pulled his cap further over his creased face to shield it from the sun. It was one of those marvellously clear afternoons when the sky seems higher and wider and stretched to its very limit. The sharp details of the match have faded. The years have rubbed them away as easily as soft pencil marks on a page. I can only recall that we had gone specifically to watch Garry Sobers, who did not play, and that Nottinghamshire were batting and Leicestershire stood in the field. I cannot remember who scored runs or took wickets, and I have always held in check the temptation to take an archaeological dig into *Wisden* to find out. Long ago I realised that to go looking for the evidence risked shaking loose the memories I already had; and possibly losing some of them as a consequence. So the important fragments of that day remain intact, shut and airtight in my mind, as if sealed in a jar. The scorecard my grandfather bought me – and filled in with a silver ballpoint pen – is long gone too. I have nothing that preserves our time together there except for the dozen or so still, square images which I can slide in a private show across my mind. These keep alive its broad outline, which is sufficient. The bold statistics don't matter anyway. What does matter is the imprint our journey to Trent Bridge left on me. It's evident in this book, which is also part-payment of an outstanding debt to my grandfather which I can never fully repay.

Exactly forty summers have gone by since he took me to see those first matches and, no matter how much fashionable change occurs, my perception of cricket is irrevocably bound up in them. As the 2009 English season came closer, it struck me that cricket could be embarking on the most significant and rapid period of its development since the Packer Revolution of 1977. Much of what had drawn me to cricket in the first place seemed in danger of being dismantled. The County Championship limped along and struggled to define itself anew as a consequence of the introduction of central contracts, which restricted the domestic workload of Test players. Technology and the referral system challenged the mettle and authority of umpires. Most of all, there was Twenty20, altering the contours of the whole summer and shifting the calendar of the entire year. The traditional weave of the game was being unpicked and rearranged for the modern, global age.

   Cricket always seems to be on the brink of radicalism of one sort or another in an effort to make it relevant. As far back as 1971 John Arlott felt it necessary to offer the opinion that: 'It may be true that English cricket as we know it is dying.' When he wrote that sentence the fixture list was stable and ordered, like a good filing system; everything sensibly arranged and in its own neat place. Now matches are scattered everywhere, as if picked up and carried by a gale and then strewn across each corner of the cricket playing world. So many matches are arranged – most inconsequential and instantly forgettable – that it is impossible to keep track of them.

I grew up with the BBC covering Tests in a didactic but avuncular manner. Now an Ashes series can only be viewed with a satellite dish and a set-top box. In the past even the best cricketers were paid shamefully pitiful sums and regarded as glorified chattel. Now the best can become financially secure for life in a handful of summers. No one wants to condemn them to near penury again, but fatter salaries have created a degree of detachment between the modern player and the modern cricket watcher.

I can't entirely camouflage the fact that I am always measuring today against yesterday. I know there are times when it makes me sound one hundred years old, as though I belong in the steam age. Perhaps I do. In defence we often best record what's been lost by detailing, however nit-pickingly, what remains. This was the premise and spirit of *English Journey*, which J. B. Priestley wrote in 1933. He caught England at a pivotal moment. It was shaking off, albeit briefly, the consequence of the Great War and then the Depression, and heading towards yet another conflict in the middle distance. Priestley embalmed his homeland in black ink. With it and him in mind I set off with the aim of preserving this single – possibly seminal – summer in the belief that cricket's own pivotal moment was looming too.

Priestley took with him the essential accoutrements of his trade: notebooks, paper clips, pencils, erasers and a portable typewriter. He also wedged into his over-large black bag a copy of *Muirhead's Blue Guide to England* and began from Southampton, amid the oily black smoke of ships' funnels and the long, slow drone of the hooter, because, he reckoned, it was 'where a man might well first land'. (Today, of course, he'd be obliged to push, shove and queue his way through Heathrow airport's congested terminals.) I took the modern equivalent of Priestley's paraphernalia: a leather notebook and loose sheets of A5 paper, an assortment of pens, a miniature tape recorder and the indispensable laptop. Into my over-large satchel went the 146th edition of *Wisden*, a copy of *Playfair* and *The Cricketers' Who's Who*. I began at Lord's – the only appropriate place to start. A week or so before setting off I met Priestley's son Tom, explained what I was doing and talked through the influence of his father's book on me. 'He'd have come with you,' he explained. 'He thought cricket was a part of England and part of English character. Losing it would have diminished England somehow.' As his son unhesitatingly conceded, Priestley, despite his gruff reputation, was a romantic and 'very much a Golden Age sort of a chap'. It's why he wrote of cricket: 'I cannot believe there is another game in the world that releases so many floods of nostalgic reminiscence.'

I know it to be true because I experienced the same thing. Everywhere I went I remembered things long past; but chiefly I remembered my grandfather.

Wherever I went, he came too, which became the real point of everything. The more I travelled, the more I understood it; and the more grateful I became for the love of cricket he gave me.

CHAPTER ONE

WHY DON'T YOU COME BACK WHEN IT'S LESS BUSY?

Michael Vaughan contemplates the 'uncertain glory of an April day' as another shower disrupts the start of the 2009 season at Lord's.

The all-rounder turned writer-poet R. C. Robertson-Glasgow always believed that 'by foot' was the best and most respectful way to approach Lord's. It enables you, he said, to 'drink the slow, deep draught of anticipation'. He was right, and never more so than on the opening day of the season. For there are certain rules and rituals which rigorously apply to it, and the first is the obligatory walk, which became so familiar to Robertson-Glasgow from the moment he became chief correspondent of the *Morning Post* in 1933. It owes everything to history and – if done properly – the journey ought really to begin from Dorset Square beside an unobtrusive brown plaque with a peculiar arrangement of capital letters. It declares that:

THOMAS LORD
laid out his original
CRICKET GROUND
on this site in 1787

To start here is akin to bowing in deference to him. His portrait, which hangs in its gold frame in the Long Room, makes Lord look an unattractive, plain figure: balding with combed tufts of frosty hair, heavy eyebrows hooding the inky dots of his eyes, a long blade of a nose and thin, tight lips that suppress a half-smile. He wears a high, white starched shirt and a coal-black coat. Without Lord and his entrepreneurial acumen, there would be no Lord's. When Dorset Fields was just an untidy scrap of land, Lord fenced it, built a wood hut to store bat, ball and stumps and let the high-falutin' gentlemen of the White Conduit Club preen themselves within its rough boundary before the creation of the MCC. To set off from the Georgian elegance of Dorset Square today, with early blossom clinging to the branches of its trees, is to stroll with benign ghosts in breeches. Here, Alexander, Duke of Hamilton (sadly, no relation), once drove the ball so hard and high that it travelled one hundred and thirty-two yards.

Beyond Dorset Square is the rust-coloured brick-and-glass-canopied entrance of Marylebone Station, which John Betjeman described as the 'most gracious' of terminals. He thought he always heard birdsong on the platforms. There's no birdsong today; just the rattle of fully loaded lorries, the din of revving engines and the impatient hooting of horns from black cabs. Any bird has to splutter a tune through exhaust fumes.

Eventually the road turns into Lisson Grove. On his route, which he described in 1951, Robertson-Glasgow picked out the 'cigarette shop', which had 'not changed', a boy pulling a boat on a string along Regent's Canal and the anglers dotted on its banks. The cigarette shop is now Tesco Express with glowing signage. The canal's chocolate-brown water is still and the banks are bare. Halfway along Lisson Grove is a second, grander plaque crested with the MCC's neat insignia. As a Yorkshireman, who always kept a gimlet eye on his wallet, Lord refused to pay increased rent on Dorset Fields. When his lease expired, he rolled up his turf and carried it here instead. The plaque – a pale, fading blue – commemorates the site of: 'The second Lord's Cricket Ground 1811–1813'. It sat on what is now the charmless, low grey sprawl of a housing estate. With an extension to the Regent's Canal threatening to slice off most of his outfield, Lord soon pocketed £4,000 in compensation and moved gratefully for the third and last time.

Sometimes to travel hopefully is a better thing than to arrive; but not in this case. At the top of Lisson Grove, between the choking traffic, is Lord's at last. Posters advertising today's fixture are attached to its outer wall. The blood-red font is quaintly old-fashioned, as though still belonging to the polite, sepia age when Jack Hobbs and Herbert Sutcliffe were paired on the scorecard. Those of us who have already arrived – it is 9.30 a.m. – won't be allowed inside for another half an hour. A dozen pairs of eyes peer pleadingly through the lofty magnificence of the Grace Gates, as if expecting the green-jacketed stewards to show some pity. The gates are a finely ornate example of Bromsgrove ironwork. The stone pillar, with its tribute to W. G. worn by the weather, is so grand that it wouldn't look out of place in Highgate Cemetery with the good doctor's bones buried beneath it.

I'm relieved to be early, and mindful of the advice J. M. Kilburn – one of Robertson-Glasgow's contemporaries in the press box – once gave about coming to Lord's: 'To arrive breathless and dishevelled at the main gate would be an offence almost beyond forgiveness.' As the most patrician of writers, deferential to the MCC and its traditions, Kilburn expected what he wrote about it to be taken seriously. None of us loitering on the pavement, repeatedly glancing at our watches in the forlorn hope that doing so might hurry time along, is dishevelled; and we are only breathless for the beginning of the match. Our numbers slowly grow. There is pole-thin man in a blue windcheater and jeans who mournfully reports that he's recently been made redundant from his job – 'another victim of the recession', he says – and will be watching 'more cricket than usual'. He clutches a Lord's cushion against his chest. There is a trim gent with a prominent nose, shaped like a fin, and protuberant cheekbones, the reddish skin pulled tight across them. His veins are like marks in marble. He is wearing a deerstalker and a tweed jacket, as if dressed for an afternoon's shooting on the moors. There are two elderly couples, who greet one another in the fulsome, short sentences of Hirst greeting Spooner in Harold Pinter's *No Man's Land*. 'Ah,' says the woman, offering her left cheek for a kiss. 'The South Africans last summer. Smith and McKenzie. Hundreds for both. Lovely day. How are you?' The reply is sucked away on the stiffish breeze.

Those of us who aren't MCC members are told to buy our £15 ticket from a wooden, padlocked door set into the wall. Soon a young, sallow attendant appears clutching a set of keys. The door, rusted over the winter, refuses to budge without a heave, which threatens to take it off at the hinges. When it does open, the attendant reaches for strips of plasticene, rolls them into several tight balls and produces an oblong notice which he fastens on to the wall. 'PLAY IS NOT GUARANTEED', it says, like the warning small print of a contract. 'REFUNDS WILL NOT BE GIVEN'. Play certainly isn't guaranteed this morning. The proof that we live on a small, damp island is all around us. The sky is the colour of slate. Spots of rain are falling. The wind – gathering in strength – cuts like a scythe. On one hand it is ridiculous to be playing a showpiece game so prematurely when low fronts and powerful gusts roll in from the Atlantic like a punishment. If not thoroughly drenched, we'll all be blown and buffeted and end up looking as though we've been storm-tossed at sea. On the other, cricket's congested calendar, top-heavy with Twenty20 and other assorted one-day jamborees, must squeeze in matches such as this one whenever it can.

As well as the glacial cold, rain or bad light are sure to act as prolonged punctuation marks during the next eight hours. But the visceral experience of the moment – to be at Lord's at the very beginning of the season – outweighs the discomforts. And enduring the foul bleakness of what Shakespeare euphemistically described as the 'uncertain glory of an April day' is yet another part of the ritual; a rite of passage into what will hopefully turn into a long hot summer. You have to be suffering from a gentle madness to want to be here in such wretched conditions. To miss it would still be the greater lunacy. I willingly pay my money. I take my purple ticket. I walk through the Grace Gates. I count a knot of twenty-eight others jostling beside me and calculate our average age as seventy-three; hardly older than the patriarchs of Genesis, but old enough in total years to suggest we've survived harsher mornings than this one.

The away dressing room at Lord's is small and sparse. The walls are apple-green and white. In one corner, there's a glass-fronted drinks cooler and a silver kettle with an assortment of cups and saucers. Cheap plastic coat hangers dangle from shiny gold pegs beneath the honours' board – black capital lettering on pale oak – which is like turning the pages of every *Wisden* ever published. There's S. J. (Sid) Pegler's 7-65 for South Africa two years before the Great War; Bob Massie's improbable 16 Ashes wickets in 1972; Gordon Greenidge's 214 in 1984; and centuries for Ganguly and Jayawardene, Mankad and Hardstaff. On the functional white board near the door, there are three points written in streaky blue ink:

10.25 a.m.: Toss
10.30 a.m.: Photo in Harris garden
11.00 p.m.: Scheduled start

The two captains, Rob Key of MCC and Durham's Will Smith, walk through the Long Room and trot down the pavilion steps punctually. In the Long Room, where Lord's alternates displays from its collection of 2,000 paintings, someone has mischievously hung Sir Donald Bradman's portrait directly beside Douglas Jardine's. When Jardine died, aged only fifty-seven, in June 1958, Bradman was asked to provide a few perfunctory sentences about him for posterity. With Bodyline still a sore on his flesh, Bradman gave a terse 'No comment'. Below them is the round, pink face of Pelham Warner, the MCC's manager on the tour, who betrayed the captain after it was over. With the second Ashes Test at Lord's only two and a half months away, I doubt politics and politeness will allow the Bradman–Jardine–Warner juxtaposition to survive until then.

The Long Room floor is well swept, and the sturdy wooden chairs stand in two immaculate rows, as if as regimentally as troops on parade. Alan Ross's poem 'Test Match at Lord's' immediately comes to my mind.

> Bailey bowling, McLean cuts him late for one
> I walk from the Long Room into the slanting sun
> Two ancients stop as Statham starts his run
> Then, elbows linked, but straight as sailors
> On a tilting deck, they move. One square shouldered as a tailor's
> Model, leans over, whispering in the other's ear:
> 'Go easy. Steps here. This end bowling'
> Turning, I watch Barnes guide Rhodes into fresher air
> As if to continue an innings, though Rhodes may only play by ear

Ross's poem is like a bridge arching back into the past, and the image it leaves on the eye lingers like a handprint on glass. Reading these nine lines summons Sydney Barnes and the sightless Wilfred Rhodes into the Long Room again. In my imagination I half expect Walter Hammond or Frank Woolley also to pass through in their pomp: fit and lithe and lean with their faces unlined, a bat tucked underneath the arm or a long-sleeved sweater draped across the shoulder. Appearing instead is Michael Vaughan. The build-up to the game has focused almost exclusively around him. The question is whether he can recover his England place four years after his captaincy wrestled the Ashes from Australia. The television cameras and photographers stare hard at Vaughan. The lenses of both trail him wherever he goes like a stage spotlight.

It is impossible not to think about his lachrymose but dignified farewell from the England captaincy in 2008; the way Vaughan slowly dissolved into soft sobs when telling a press conference what his father had said to him. 'You can walk away a proud lad because you've given it everything.' A week or so after his resignation I watched Vaughan in the County Championship at Scarborough, where he was awfully out of form and kilter. The devotion of his home crowd, like palliative care, dragged him through a difficult four days. The same level of devotion is palpable today. There is a choreographed approval for Vaughan; murmurs of good luck, handshakes and slaps on the back. Indeed, the crowd seems intent on treating him like a convalescent.

The previous afternoon Vaughan was in the Nursery End nets. He wore his black Yorkshire helmet and tracksuit top and strapped gleaming pads on to bare calves. With each ball, he came forward with a big, decisive stride; the sort of stride, in fact, that Geoffrey Boycott always maintains was the true sign of his own prime form. But Vaughan didn't middle every shot. He mistimed a drive off Sajid Mahmood, which ballooned in the direction of extra cover. He took an extravagant swish at a ball from Kabir Ali and got a faint but audible nick. The ball swished and bulged against the back of the net in front him. 'That'll do,' he said, moving into the next net, where Adil Rashid was bowling; Yorkshire master faced Yorkshire pupil. Rashid is just twenty-one; Vaughan is thirty-four. He came down the pitch and tried to lift the leg spinner towards the Indoor School. He was too early on the shot. The ball struck the bottom of the bat and squirted miserably along the ground. Rashid smiled and playfully wagged his finger at him. 'Nearly got you there,' he said.

Vaughan will have to wait to find out whether his coordination has returned properly. Key wins the toss and decides to bowl. He plants his right hand into the pocket of his MCC blazer – in the manner of the Duke of Edinburgh at an official function – and strides off, smart enough to have wandered out of one of the cigarette cards of the 1930s. Hard though it is to believe, the sky has become greyer and more swollen, and so low that I wait for it to descend like a heavy wool blanket across the impeccably mowed and rolled turf. Robertson-Glasgow wrote about the greenness of Lord's in comparison to the 'huge, glaring, yellowy arenas of Australia'. It is true. Even in this murky light, the ground is a brilliant emerald and as lush as crushed velvet. The Old Father Time weather-vane is already manically spinning, as if it might take off like Dorothy's house in *The Wizard of Oz*. It is a morning for coats, scarves and hats, a thermos of strong tea and a portable heater. But, as Key drops the new ball, as glossy as a conker, into Ali's hand, there is the celebratory pop of a cork. A young couple, sitting in the Grand Stand, hug one another and toast the new season with a bottle of Marks and Spencer champagne.

Sprinting in from the Pavilion End, Ali's first delivery is well up to the left-handed Michael Di Venuto, who unflappably pushes it straight back, as though already well set for run-making. The sound of ball on bat is like a pistol shot around the cavernous, empty ground. The echo of it vibrates for a long time afterwards. Ali's fourth delivery is much wider, shorter and looser, and Di Venuto darts at it eagerly. He squeezes a thickish outside edge past gulley, and Rashid gives pursuit, as urgently as a man chasing his hat in a gale. The ball easily beats him to the rope. Perhaps bowling at a pair of left handers – Mark Stoneman is Di Venuto's partner – disturbs Ali and Mahmood, both of whom don't properly exploit the bruised, overcast conditions. Rather than pitching deliveries up, and letting swing and seam occur naturally, the ball is frequently too short, and Di Venuto and Stoneman cut and pull and lean away to drive impressively off the back foot. The bowlers' spikes tear up the turf, revealing the black, wet earth beneath.

Key and Vaughan are positioned, like Donne's extended compass points, at mid-on and mid-off. Vaughan is swaddled in two sweaters, a shirt and his full-body Skins ICE, which he advertises – arms folded and gaze proud and intense – in the pages of cricket magazines in the manner of a modern-day Captain Webb resplendent on a box of matches. Even with all these layers, which includes the best contemporary science is capable of designing, he still looks perished, as if in need of a bowl of soup and a wood fire. He has incongruously wedged a wide-brimmed sunhat on his head. Key presses his hands beneath his armpits for warmth and lets his chin drop to his chest, like someone huddled in a doorway waiting for the last bus home. Neither has much to do. Apart from a balletic dive to stop a Di Venuto drive, Vaughan's main duty early on is to scoop up handfuls of sawdust and sprinkle them over the bowler's footholds.

A thin blowing of rain, which drifts like a dirty veil from the direction of the Tavern Stand, forces an interruption after just 53 minutes and 67 balls. Di Venuto and Stoneman are reluctant to leave, like poker players forced to give up a good hand of cards. Di Venuto has been especially solid. His runs have come with stylistic correctness. At 48 for no wicket, the electric scoreboard unhelpfully points out in vivid blue what we already know – rain has stopped play. Vaughan sits on the middle step in front of the pavilion gate and tilts his eyes skyward, like an inquisitive bird. He climbs up, nods in the direction of an MCC member and vanishes inside.

No day is without virtue at Lord's. That is because no sport is more conscious of preserving its relics, however eclectic, than cricket. If we are all truly reflected in the things we own, then the game has a well-stocked mind, an eccentric personality and an obsessive penchant for hoarding.

The museum behind the pavilion contains an idiosyncratic miscellany of curios and curiosities: ancient bats and china bowls, pictures and mounted cricket balls with silver bands, caps and gold medals and, of course, the inconspicuous Ashes Urn, which sits in a thick glass case like the Imperial State Crown in the Tower of the London. I twice pass it without a flicker of recognition; perhaps because the personal minutiae of the museum are more fascinating than the shiny, teak-stained perfume bottle, so frequently photographed that an actual sighting of it has no impact whatsoever. What leaves the deepest impression are the intimate, quotidian items of the famous: K. S. Ranjitsinhji's silver cigarette case, which he used most days of his life; W. G.'s snuff box and his enormous boots, which reveal his bulk's ample proportions; R. E. Foster's immaculately kept black bound diary of the 1903–04 tour of Australia, the handwriting shaped and flourished with upward swirls and downward curls, in which he details an innings of 287 not out; Len Hutton's silver hip flask; and the oddity of Denis Compton's kneecap, which lies in a case like an ageing and unsightly lump of wax.

On the first day of the season, and particularly when rain has interrupted it, the sensible thing is to act as a lazy browser or Parisian *flâneur*, ambling across Lord's 5½ acres without apparent purpose. In the 1830s, well after Thomas Lord's strategic threat to build houses on the land – a crude bargaining chip which brought him £5,000 after its eventual sale – Lord's was ridged and furrowed and surrounded by laurels and shrubbery. A sheep pen sat in the upper north-east corner; the sheep kept the grass short. Early paintings reveal a pitch of uneven parkland across which horses were ridden, leaving hoof marks in the soft grass. Today Lord's is a slick brand and carries a leaden gravity about it. It has a corporate and colour-coordinated feel. Almost everything is sugar white: the stylish lines of the Grand Stand, its fine metal like the threads of a spider's half-finished web; the Mound Stand, with its cone-like pediments; the bucket seating and the glass-fronted Media Centre. The pavilion remains the jewel: the red brickwork with its nooks and niches, the sculptured balconies and the symmetrical, semi-circular windows, which conceal the secret life of the place. Near the Grace Gates, and attached to the back of the Allen Stand, there are enormous photographs of contemporary Test captains, such as Daniel Vettori and Ramnaresh Sarwan. Accompanying them are exuberant testimonials, like the excitable puffs on film posters, which convey the privilege of playing at

Lord's, as if Lord's really needs to advertise itself, let alone so brazenly. The first photograph is Kevin Pietersen's. After his abrupt fall during the winter, the description of Pietersen as England captain has been clumsily obscured with strips of uneven white tape. Soon I suppose Pietersen's photograph will go too, and be quietly replaced in the dead of night; much in the same way that the Cold War Soviet Union once sent out portraits of its new leader and disposed of the old with subtle sleight of hand, as if nobody could tell the difference.

Somehow Lord's manages to be simultaneously intimate and intimidating. Sometimes it acts like a hostess, who professes that she's so pleased to see you while at the same time edging you out of the door and on to the pavement. There can be a snooty aloofness about the place, as if some of the more over-mannered stewards regard you as a nuisance and ripe for patronisation. I always expect to be ticked off, moved on or told I should sit up straight. When my geography goes awry, I turn by mistake into the lower tier of the Warner Stand, not noticing the sign which says 'Members and Friends'. Groucho Marx, on a visit to Lord's in 1954, registered the same sign and took his cigar out of his mouth long enough to say: 'That's the most ambiguous thing I've ever heard.' Ambiguous or not, Lord's still adheres to it; no one but members and friends are allowed to put their backside on Sir Pelham's seats. I've taken no more than a quarter pace towards doing so when a steward appears. 'I'm sorry, sir,' he says, immediately flattening his hands together and half bowing. 'This is for members and friends only.' There is a short pause before he adds with an edge of superb condescension: 'Why don't you come back when it's less busy?' Leaving aside the obvious contraction – for I'm unlikely to become a 'member' or a 'friend of a member' in the next six hours – I'm struck by the evidence of my own eyes. The Warner Stand has a capacity of 3,000. I count the number of members and friends presently occupying it. There is one person in the whole stand; a middle-aged man in a blue jacket sitting on the front row and jammed next to the pavilion. Everyone else is disguised as rows of empty seats. 'Thank you, sir,' the steward says as I slink off, suitably chastised. 'Enjoy your day.'

Like me, the rest of the unwashed and underprivileged mostly occupy the middle, covered tier of the Grand Stand. Lord's is sombre and silent, and rain slants in silvery sheets across the pavilion. When the rain becomes heavier, and the clouds are dragged across the sky behind it on a vigorous wind, the pavilion resembles a man o' war galleon cutting through the ocean with its flags aflutter. To add to the naval image, a seagull alights on the left-hand turret and turns in profile, as if posing like the figurehead on the prow. Looking at the pavilion, I find it difficult to believe that the Australian Albert Trott cleared it with a drive off Monty Noble in 1899. Trott's shot made him famous, and he often got himself out in vain and vainglorious attempts to repeat it; a case of the best possible intentions leading to the worst possible consequences. He only attempted it in the first place to keep warm. Trott was wearing a thin silk shirt on a day so bitter that his partner, Cyril Foley, promised he'd see snow for the first time. Those of us in the Grand Stand wouldn't be surprised to see snow now too. Around me lunch is already underway: thickly cut sandwiches emerge from Tupperware boxes, black coffee or tea the colour of riding boots is poured. In the roaring heat of mid-summer we'll remember this day at Lord's and tell everyone how much we deserve whatever sunshine we get as a reward for enduring it. In the meantime, we wait patiently and stoically for something to happen. We stare at the covers, as though we might remove them through sheer force of our own will.

In early afternoon the rain finally lifts and the light clears, and Di Venuto and Stoneman press on. Di Venuto square cuts Tim Bresnan and brings up his half-century in 103 minutes off 67 balls. Bresnan is only in the team because of someone else's misfortune: Middlesex's Steven Finn was a late withdrawal after turning an ankle. Bresnan is burly, bull-necked and slightly barrel-chested. If there's ever a remake of *The Go Between*, he'd be ideal casting in its cricket match as the village smithy, dashing in and cresting the brow of the hill before heaving his arm over. He is nonetheless the MCC's most savvy seamer. In 15 balls, he removes first Di Venuto – caught by Ian Bell at second slip – and then Stoneman, clipping his off bail. The other notable bowler is Chris Woakes. A year ago Woakes had made only one first-class appearance for Warwickshire. By the end of 2008 season, he'd taken 42 wickets at 20.57 to become, at nineteen, the county's youngest-ever leading Championship wicket taker. Until collecting his MCC kit the previous day, he'd never seen Lord's, let alone played here. When the pre-match photographs were taken in the Harris Garden, Woakes looked wide-eyed, slightly bewildered and overwhelmed, as though he was apart from the event rather than a part of it and half-expecting to be jabbed awake from this most unlikely of

Chris Woakes, who progressed from a wide-eyed and slightly bewildered on-looker to become one of the MCC's most impressive seamers.

sweet dreams. He could easily pass for sixteen rather than the twenty-year-old he became just five weeks earlier.

At first Woakes is so anxious and jittery that the wicketkeeper, James Foster, tumbles and lunges in pursuit of a series of wayward deliveries. But, as he shakes the nervousness of out his young system and realises that Lord's won't bite, he finds extravagant movement off the pitch. He is stringy and raw-boned, and burns energy like rocket fuel. Eventually he gets one to jag away from Gordon Muchall, and Foster is yelling his throaty appeal. Woakes is phosphorescent with joy. Next, Dale Benkenstein moves slowly and cumbersomely, as if wearing full body armour, in a tame effort to pull Mahmood. He gets the ball high on the bat instead and spoons a catch in front of square. He shakes his head, unable to believe his own rashness and hair-trigger judgement. As the match froths up, the plot of the play tilts unexpectedly towards the MCC. From 104 without loss,

Durham sink to 141 for four. Their first 100 came up in 154 balls. The 150 isn't reached for another 144. It is dour and dismal work until the fizzing spirit of Durham's new recruit from Somerset, Ian Blackwell, takes over. By now, the clouds have gone, the sky has turned from pewter to cobalt, and the temperature has risen to a level that makes only frostbite, rather than full-blown hypothermia, a possibility.

There has been a dull orthodoxy to Key's captaincy, which never comes vividly alive. He serves the staple but unimaginative diet of pace and seam, much to the vexation of the spin connoisseurs longing to watch Rashid use the ball decoratively with his flight and twirl. As each bowling change leaves Rashid redundant, frustrated grunts and muttered syllables are heard from the Grand Stand. After 62 overs, there are long, ironic hosannas and shouts of 'at bloody last' as Rashid marks out his short run from the Nursery End. The cold has infiltrated Rashid's joints. The ball repeatedly drops on the back of a length, and Blackwell savages it with pure, clean slices. His 50, including ten fours, takes a mere 44 deliveries. Rashid wears the glum expression of someone wasting his time. Occasionally he appeals, but these are more tender wails than shouts of conviction.

For a shilling on match days during the mid-nineteenth century, you could hire bat, ball and stumps and play on one of the Lord's pitches. If someone other than the ground-staff or a cricketer so much as sets a toe on the outfield in this game, the stewards fuss like over-protective, whining nannies. At long leg, Vaughan is asked to sign numerous books and photographs by teenage boys who lean over the fence. He solicitously beckons them towards him. The boys dash as a pack into the Warner Stand and some scale the low fence. A steward in the Grand Stand acts as though this is a wilful act of sacrilege. Immediately he starts barking into his walkie-talkie, which crackles back at him. The urgency and shard of panic in his voice is an extreme over-reaction, as if someone has toppled over and shattered an exhibit in the Victoria and Albert Museum. As he rushes closer, with the intention of restoring order and decorum with a hardline approach, a balding spectator, well upholstered around the girth, leans back in his seat and casually tells him that Vaughan is responsible. 'He asked the lads to come to him,' he explains. The steward shrivels, like a balloon abruptly deflated, and backs off. Robertson-Glasgow would have recognised the charmless streak and over-officiousness of the Lord's stewards, who even in his era saw the average spectator as a foe to be fought and dealt with him gratuitously. The proof is in the last paragraph of his 1951 account. 'Two attendants,' he wrote, 'persuaded some 50 spectators who had emerged on to vacant benches in the sun to return to the cold shade of the covered seats.' His final line implies incredulity at both the imperious nature of the stewards and the pacifism he witnessed in response to it. 'They would not have retired so obediently at Sydney,' he concluded.

At least the day's play ends at 7.01 p.m. in quiet serenity, and beneath the vaulted canopy of a Windsor blue sky, which was unimaginable in the morning. I am convinced already that Durham will retain the Championship and pocket the much-improved £500,000 winners' cheque this season.

On my way out I walk past the latest additions to Lord's – two floodlights, which poke from either flank of the pavilion like a pair of ugly jug ears. I imagine Robertson-Glasgow turning the corner at the top of Lisson Grove and shaking his head in sorrowful regret at the sight of them. I return to Dorset Square exactly the way I came, and dawdle because of his instance that 'life is too short to hurry'. Alas, life proved all too much – and far too short – for Robertson-Glasgow. He died, at sixty-four in 1965, by his own hand after swallowing a handful of pills. He was a good, unpretentious man who too often felt depression's darkness at noon and tried to combat it with bouts of extreme high spirits – the consequence of his bipolar condition. That he was also unfailingly modest is reflected in his autobiography, *46 Not Out.* He records his career-best bowling figures, as though dismissing them as strictly mundane, in no more than two factual sentences on page 142. 'In 1924,' he wrote, 'Somerset beat Middlesex at Lord's by 37 runs. In their first innings of 128, I had 9 for 38.'

Robertson-Glasgow was always more expressive about others. He memorably said of Donald Bradman that 'poetry and murder lived in him together'. He thought the task of trying to remove Jack Hobbs was 'like bowling to God on concrete'. He described Hampshire's Philip Mead as taking guard 'with the air of a guest who, having been offered a weekend by his host, obstinately decides to reside for six months'. The best thing ever written about him belongs to David Foot. He called Robertson-Glasgow 'sweet of nature, uplifting, funny, poetic, gently sagacious, a profound student of the human condition, scholarly without ever making it appear so, happy in every word . . . and ultimately tragic'. The tragedy was that Robertson-Glasgow was obliged to hide so much of himself from others and wear his joviality like a mask until, finally, it slipped off, and he slipped away. What, thankfully, he never hid was his love of Lord's. It drew me here today. It takes me slowly home again.

And I feel as if I'm walking in the footmarks Robertson-Glasgow left behind.

Umpires: N. L. Bainton, J. W. Lloyds
Toss: MCC

Durham first innings

D. M. Di Venuto	c Bell	b Bresnan	**53**
M. D. Stoneman		b Bresnan	**49**
W. R. Smith*	not out		**71**
G. J. Muchall	c Foster	b Woakes	**5**
D. M. Benkenstein	c Ali	b Mahmood	**12**
I. D. Blackwell	not out		**102**
Did not bat: P. Mustard†, G. Onions, L. E. Plunkett, M. E. Claydon, C. D. Thorp			
Extras	(2b, 12lb, 2nb, 3w)		**19**
Total	(4 wickets declared, 89 overs)		**311**

Fall of wickets: 1-104, 2-113, 3-128, 4-141

MCC bowling	O	M	R	W
Ali	20	2	69	0
Mahmood	18	3	68	1
Bresnan	25	6	56	2
Woakes	20	2	76	1
Rashid	6	0	28	0

MCC first innings

S. C. Moore	c Mustard	b Thorp	**45**
R. W. T. Key*	c Plunkett	b Thorp	**5**
M. P. Vaughan	c Mustard	b Claydon	**12**
I. R. Bell	c Mustard	b Thorp	**12**
T. Westley	not out		**18**
J. S. Foster	lbw	b Thorp	**4**
A. U. Rashid		b Plunkett	**20**
T. T. Bresnan	lbw	b Onions	**0**
K. Ali	not out		**0**
Did not bat: S. I. Mahmood, C. R. Woakes			
Extras	(3b, 4lb, 2nb, 1w)		**10**
Total	(7 wickets, 47 overs)		**126**

Fall of wickets: 1-18, 2-50, 3-76, 4-77, 5-81, 6-124, 7-125

Durham bowling	O	M	R	W
Onions	14	2	42	1
Thorp	13	5	15	4
Plunkett	12	2	41	1
Claydon	7	2	14	1
Benkenstein	1	0	7	0

Result: Match drawn

CHAPTER TWO

FOR THE ISLANDS,
HE SANG

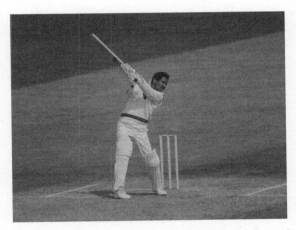

The savage grace of Garry Sobers – four cricketers in one and possessor of a dancer's feet, a regal bearing and an almost aristocratic entitlement to runs and wickets.

Grace Road: Tour Match:
Leicestershire v. West Indies, 20–22 April

On the way to Grace Road, the memory returns as vivid as lightning. It is a hot August afternoon at Lord's, and Bob Willis, his face as grimly set as an undertaker's, begins his jerky, angled run from the Nursery End. The batsman waiting for him is serenely composed. There is an impassive majesty about him: no nervous twitch in the shoulders, no frantic tapping of the bat against the boot or into the block hole. Willis grimaces as he bowls, as if in pain. A full ball lands on the line of off stump. Willis grimaces again as the batsman retreats just one quarter pace in his crease, his weight perfectly balanced, like a dancer's, and with scarcely any backlift drives square to the boundary. The execution of the stroke is sublime – an amalgam of impeccable timing and savage intent. The batsman thinks nothing of it. What constitutes high art to those watching it is no more than mechanical, familiar routine for him. It comes easily too; but then everything always came easily to Garry Sobers.

Sobers was responsible for igniting my true love for cricket, and specifically the West Indies, who came to represent its carnival soul for me. Not Australia – dour and steely by comparison. Not India – despite the trickery of their spin. Certainly not England – then manifestly more successful, but rarely capable of making the heart beat faster.

My conversion to the West Indian cause stemmed from a combination of circumstance and serendipity. I was brought up in Nottingham, where Sobers made his home for seven summers. I would catch the corporation bus to Trent Bridge and pay my shilling fare specifically to see him. There was one West Indian bus conductor on the route, and he came to know me and understand why I always got off at the stop almost directly opposite Trent Bridge. 'You're off to see Sir Garry again,' he'd say, long before the Queen, in her blue paisley dress and a white pair of gloves, dabbed each of Sobers' shoulders with the tip of a sword and made the title official. On the way home he'd ask: 'How many did Sir Garry get today, then?' I'd sit in the George Parr Stand, which was then still shadowed by the tall elm that Parr had peppered with sixes in the days when Victoria was on the throne and Palmerston was Prime Minister.

Sobers and the West Indies became an integral part of my growing up. Looking back on it, the West Indians in the crowd now remind me of

Moses in Samuel Selvon's trilogy of books, which began with *The Lonely Londoners*. They wore bright, light suits and pork pie hats, and white shirts with pencil-thin ties and gold clips. These were the men of generation *Windrush*, the boat which carried them from their own baked land to wolf-grey skies, shivering cold rain and signs that hung as warning insults on the doors and in the windows of boarding houses: 'NO IRISH, NO COLOUREDS, NO DOGS'. I'd overhear them talk in their Caribbean vernacular – the voices smooth as Navy rum and warm off the lips. They'd speak of names I'd never heard of before (Frank Worrell, Learie Constantine and George Headley) and places which seemed distant and unreachable to me (Bridgetown, Kingston and Port of Spain). I knew the geography of the West Indies only as shapes on the school globe. Each polished island was strung across a cerulean-coloured sea like pearls on a necklace. But I had no appreciation of the distance between the islands or the disparate and quite separate peoples who lived on them.

By the early 1970s the West Indians dominated the overseas contingent in the County Championship, an unprecedented arrival of starry talent that began in 1968. The counties – some reluctantly and one (Yorkshire) not at all – abandoned, after much nervous debating, the five-year registration period previously necessary for any player to qualify for the Championship. The regulations were changed to allow anyone paying income tax in Britain to be regarded as a resident; he could sign immediately for whoever would hire him. West Indians soon gleamed at the edges of my long summers. Among them were Rohan Kanhai at Warwickshire, Clive Lloyd at Lancashire, the all-rounder Bernard Julien at Kent and two quick bowlers, Vanburn Holder at Worcestershire and Keith Boyce at Essex. Whether individually or collectively, the West Indies embodied for me the exotic and cavalier way in which cricket ought to be played. I was entranced by their dash and daring, which transmitted itself like an electric charge from pitch to boundary. And Sobers was the most lyrical and irresistible expression of it. For the islands, he sang. He moved to Nottinghamshire, who with flagrant self-interest became the prime and most persistent movers behind the overhaul of the registration rules and gradually nudged – and also sharply elbowed whenever necessary – the other counties into accepting it as a way of reinvigorating the staid, flat domesticity of English cricket. Of course, Nottinghamshire did so knowing that Sobers – despite competition, most vigorously from

Lancashire – would sign for them. The price was high: £5,000 per summer. The rewards were high too: Nottinghamshire's membership doubled and the crowds came to gawk at Sobers.

Just as Oscar Wilde was incapable of creating a dull epigram, so Sobers was incapable of building a dull innings. Even if he was out early on, his walk to the wicket was worth the admission money. It was a grand piece of theatre. No one of that era walked out of the pavilion gate like Sobers. He came closest to matching the regal bearing and sense of aristocratic entitlement of Walter Hammond, who, J. M. Kilburn said, 'came like a King and was like a King in his coming'. With the upturned collar, the loose, billowing shirt buttoned at the cuffs, the fluid stride, as though his spikes were barely touching the turf, and the upturned gaze, there was swaggering grace about Sobers and a liquid, rippling movement to his limbs. I remember him as imperious and relaxed. If Sobers was ever nervous, he didn't betray it. He took his time, as though challenging someone to rush him. A great man has the prerogative to do what he likes in his own way, and no one ever had the temerity to hurry Sobers along. With a breezy swivel, like a weather-vane caught in a changing wind, he would glance around him at the set of the field and then at the bowler. He settled into a stance that was compact and solid – the bottom left hand an inch from the splice and half an inch apart from the right. When he played, with such supple strength, the bat itself seemed to me to be an extension of his physical being, and divine sparks flew from it. He cut and pulled, drove and hooked. He bowled whatever he liked: fast, seam or spin. And he fielded wherever the fancy took him. He was four cricketers in one – batsman, bowler, fieldsman, captain. Nothing was beyond his full compass.

Most of all I liked to watch him bat. There are batsmen who become the absolute masters of form to such an extent as to be slaves to 'correct' and proper technique. Every shot is analysed and fretted over to ensure it was played just as the coaching manual demands. Any slippage in standard, however minimal, is followed by anxious hand-wringing, the checking and rechecking of the shot, the placement of the feet and the adjustment of the hands. A suffocating orthodoxy overcomes them, the cricket equivalent of writer's block, and the runs come – if at all – with painstaking slowness. Sobers was never like this. Some batted out of duty; Sobers batted out of pleasure. For him there was no such thing as 'orthodox', and only thinking made it so. His definition of the word was entirely based on whatever came naturally to him. As almost everything did, it was justifiable for him to take a delivery which anyone else would have played on the on side, and lash it through the off. Sometimes it was seen as reckless insouciance or arrogance when, in fact, it was only Sobers being Sobers.

He borrowed a slice of philosophy from Donald Bradman and made it his own. His principal aim was always to pick out the gaps – irrespective of where the ball pitched. Like Bradman, he was perfectly still in advance of the stroke. Also like Bradman, he saw the ball in the micro-second it left the hand. I swear that his eyesight was so acute that he could count the stitches across the seam and instinctively calculate the number of full revolutions necessary for it to travel the short distance from bowler to bat. He was in position to play his shot – and often had already played it – well before the bowler came to the weary, wasted end of his follow-through. Sobers' coordination of brain, eye, feet and hands was so fast that the bowler saw only the aftermath of the ferocious onslaught and winced at the damage to his figures when he read them in the scorebook later on. To take Sobers on was to suffer hideous losses. Most bowlers didn't try; or tried at the start and then gave up.

By 1973, when he cracked Willis to the fence at Lord's, his knees were rusted hinges and the accumulated strain of almost thirty years of perpetual first-class cricket had made him bone-tired. He was the lion in the winter, and yet he still roared. His unbeaten 157 was his last Test hundred; both beautiful and sad for that reason.

Already suspecting what his answer would be, I once asked him whether he would countenance wearing the helmet and grille, and the bulky, stuffed padding that batsmen have regarded as indispensable almost from the moment of his own retirement more than three decades ago. Sobers, who thought even a thigh pad was unnecessary, squinted and gave a short, regretful shake of his head. 'No,' he said, 'it restricts movement too much and slows you down. I'd feel constrained and claustrophobic with a helmet. It would cut down my vision too. I wasn't afraid of being hit. I had no fear of the ball at all. My reflexes were quick enough to take me back, forward or across the crease to deal with anything and avoid trouble – even if Freddie Trueman was bowling. The great batsmen don't need a helmet. Look what Viv Richards achieved without one.' Given the choice, ordinary mortals wouldn't bat against pace without the insurance of enough armour plating to cover a desert tank. Judged in the round, Sobers' disdain for helmets makes rational sense only if you appreciate the depth of his talents. He could survive on his wits alone because the skill which accompanied them was rare and limitless. If Sobers had a fault, it was that he made no allowances for his own genius. Often he was unable to comprehend why others could not do what came automatically, and without conscious thought, to him.

Only he mattered to me. I still compare every West Indian against the achievements of Sobers. I know it is unfair and illogical, like comparing every painter to Picasso. But there it is. As Jonathan Swift wrote:

Who'er excels in what we prize
Appears a hero in our eyes

How true it is in my devotion to Sobers.

Were Sobers still playing, he'd now be otherwise engaged – like Chris Gayle, the West Indies captain, and the fast bowler Fidel Edwards – in the showbizzy hoopla of the Indian Premier League. The absence of Gayle in particular for the West Indies' opening tour match against Leicestershire encapsulates the fractured, dislocated nature of the season and the disturbing domination of Twenty20, which is spreading uncontrollably, like ivy, across the fixture list, where it obscures and threatens to choke all but the Test matches; and perhaps, eventually, the Test matches too. The fact that money now regularly soils, if not violates, the bond between player and country is quietly tolerated in this instance by the West Indies Board of Control. It can't be stubborn in refusing Gayle his bounty for batting for Kolkata Knight Riders. Indeed, it is compensating him for returning early from the IPL for the forthcoming Test series against England. So far, in his black tunic and glistening gold helmet, he's been swatting the bowling in South Africa as casually as a man with a rolled-up newspaper would swat a buzzing fly against a window. Edwards has been playing for Deccan Chargers. By a twist of irony, Gayle and Edwards faced one another on the day the West Indies arrived at Grace Road for net practice. And on the morning of the game, the IPL again devours the column inches given to cricket in the newspapers. The Chennai Super Kings versus the Bangalore Royal Challengers is winnowed down to the matter of personalities – the duel between Andrew Flintoff and Kevin

Pietersen, who are both pocketing $1.55m for the next few weeks' work. I find Flintoff worth appreciably less on Grace Road's second-hand bookstall in front of The Cricketers' pub. His 2005 autobiography is a knock-down £2. 'No one wants it,' says the bookseller, unperturbed. Whether from emerald-eyed envy or the genuine belief that the amount of money changing hands for 'mere sport' is obscene (especially in the current financial malaise) and might destabilise the long-term future of the four- and five-day game, there has been a lot of huffing and grumbling about the amounts paid to Flintoff and Pietersen. But Sobers in his pomp would have been worth far more to any IPL team than Flintoff and Pietersen combined. So much, in fact, that the size of his salary would have made their wages look like a bag of loose change.

Without Gayle, Edwards, plus Shivnarine Chanderpaul and Jerome Taylor, who will join the team at the end of the week after resting with minor injuries, it is a distinctly low-key start to the West Indies tour. A few days earlier the rest of the squad arrived so unobtrusively in England as to be almost in disguise. The players are wealthier, however, after another ratcheting-up of the pay scale. Civil wars are nearly always the bloodiest, and the battles lately between the West Indies Board of Control and its players over myriad factors – contracts, fees, sponsorships and standards of management – have gone beyond mere bickering. At the end of England's winter tour in March, there were threats of working to rule or even a strike. The language was reminiscent of 1970s-style industrial pugilism – and with the gloves off too. Nor is this new. As Alan Bennett wrote, history is just one bloody thing after another, and it seems intent on repeating itself in a depressing, fractious cycle as far as the West Indies are concerned. In 1978, when World Series Cricket was in its squealing infancy, Clive Lloyd resigned after a furious quarrel over the abrupt and pointless axing of Test players contracted to Kerry Packer. Lloyd was captain again within twelve months. In 1998, Brian Lara was sacked, and then rapidly reinstated, after a pay dispute. In 2005, following a spat over the consequences of one sponsor replacing another, the West Indies found themselves taking a weakened team into the First Test in South Africa. Later, in Sri Lanka, internal strife obliged the Board of Control to scratch around before fielding a team at all. And these are only the slim, edited highlights. Diving into a heap of yellowing, brittle newspaper cuttings, I find that the West Indies' propensity for arguments and squabbles among themselves has a long lineage. Under the headline 'Tour Terms No Better', two West Indians are described as 'rebels' after bemoaning the Board of Cricket's financial reward for a series in England. It is £800, plus £200 bonus and £7 per week 'out-of-pocket' expenses. The year is 1963, and the players are Wes Hall and Sobers. Nothing, it seems, changes. For the time being, though, peace has been restored. Normally the West Indies would expect to earn $250,000 to $300,000 for the series to come, which is an appetiser before the Ashes. The Board of Control has agreed to pay them $1.5m – roughly a 500 per cent increase.

If tourists' pay were dependent on the size of the gate at Grace Road, the West Indies would be taking home coppers, rather than silver. 'There's not many here,' says a dumbfounded man at the refreshment bar, reflecting on the stillness of this Monday morning. He is wearing a white flat cap and grey cardigan, and hitching up his trousers with his thumbs as he speaks. He is also standing beneath Leicestershire's symbol – a stuffed fox with a bloody chicken in its mouth, which is encased behind glass and hooked on to the wall. 'Well,' says an elderly woman beside him, her hair like a mop of wire wool, 'the dates got confused.' On every advance fixture list, including *Wisden*'s, this match isn't due to start until tomorrow. 'I bet people don't know it's even on,' she adds, staring around at tiers of unoccupied seats. 'Most of them will turn up tomorrow thinking it's the first day.' Even the local newspaper, the *Leicester Mercury*, wraps the game in the cloak of anonymity. Its preview, comprising one sentence, is an embarrassed whisper.

After the high-church majesty of Lord's, Grace Road is like a village Methodist Hall in comparison. It is Spartan and functional with almost nothing elaborate or decorative; a peculiar patchwork quilt of a place. The architecture spans at least three decades, from the flat-topped pavilion (1960s cum 1970s) to the contemporary and streamlined Bennett End. In one corner stands 'The Meet', a long, unattractive building with a curved roof, resembling a farm barn, which was previously an open stand at Aylestone Road, where Leicestershire played from 1901 until 1946. The seating is a jumble of colours too, as if tins of paint were bought piecemeal and when one colour ran out another simply replaced it: bright yellow, dull green and deep red. Grace Road's most strikingly visual feature is the neat, square scoreboard crowned with a cupola box clock and the weather-vane of a gilded fox. As there are only red-brick, two-storey Victorian homes around it, and because the ground is fringed with greening trees – sorbus, limes and silver birch – it nonetheless has a semi-pastoral atmosphere; a cloistered intimacy in which it is possible to believe that the nearest city is another county away rather than right on the doorstep. Unless you walk to the top of the pavilion, gaze across the urban sprawl and see the trains sliding in and out of Leicester station in the middle distance, you can pretend that you're anywhere.

It is a deep-blue day, almost Caribbean-like, and Grace Road is drenched in sun. There is no wind to take the edge off it either. The sky is a cobalt tent fading into milky white at the horizon, and the shadows are hard-lined and inky. It is ostensibly a perfect day for batting, which is what Leicestershire decide to do after winning the toss. Cricket's frequent, tiresome tendency to ape whatever football does brings the usual confusion. Number one on the scorecard, Matt Boyce, is wearing the number 11 on his shirt.

The West Indies start erratically, as though travel fatigue has disorientated them. Lionel Baker, who was hired as Leicestershire's overseas player for the summer before recruitment to the tour rearranged his season, begins from the Pavilion End with a wild wide, which his captain Denesh Ramdin takes in front of first slip. The fourth ball is worse. It scoots along the ground and beyond the wicketkeeper's reach. Extras are soon the dominant feature of the innings, and Ramdin is overworked and overstressed. In the next over Baker bowls a ball so wayward that not even the elastic Ramdin can reach it. It escapes his dive by two yards, and rattles against the wooden sightscreen like musket shot. Two balls later Baker does the same thing again. Ramdin looks intolerantly at him. Finally, though, Baker makes the breakthrough. In the thirteenth over he gets a ball to nip back at Boyce's partner, Tom New, which raps him above the roll of the front pad. After being given out, New looks down forlornly at the edge of his bat, as if searching for a mark that he can use as evidence to reverse this clear miscarriage of justice. He lingers, reluctant to leave after a fumbling innings. At the other end Boyce is spare and undemonstrative. He collects his runs solemnly, occasionally breaking free with a back foot shot square or a clip off his legs.

With the First Test against England only sixteen days away, and practice strictly rationed, the West Indies have to be grateful for whatever blessings this warm-up brings. Predominant among them is the contribution of the twenty-seven-year-old Sulieman Benn, who stands at gully as conspicuously as a steeple in a Fenland landscape. At 6 feet 7 inches tall Benn appears to be on stilts. His body is shaped like a bone-

*At 6 feet 7 inches tall, Sulieman Benn stands in the field as
conspicuously as a steeple in a Fenland landscape.*

handled knife: slightly stooped, long frame, long legs and long sensitive
fingers, which he wraps around the seam as tightly as twine. His spinning
finger is already callused, and the knuckles are as prominent as knurls on
a tree. The thumb of his right hand and the back of his left are wrapped
with pink sticking tape. He is capless and wears a pair of sunglasses as
tight as a visor. He doesn't so much bowl as gradually uncoil himself, like
a line of stiff rope, in the five sure steps he takes from mark to crease. He
holds the ball tight to his chest, his sharp elbows extended, as though
rocking a baby between his arms. It isn't easy for someone of Benn's
height to judge drift and flight. But he manages it with adept fingers,
subtle changes of pace, almost undetectable from his action, and his wily
use of the crease. He entices the batsmen forward like a beckoning finger.

Boyce and the new batsman, Josh Cobb, are travelling cautiously so
far, and are doing so at the pace of a state funeral. With the score on 77,

and lunch approaching, Cobb loses patience and falls for what appears to be an innocent delivery from Benn that he intends cross-batting above the head of mid-wicket. The ball dips, however, and he is abjectly deceived in the air. Cobb swipes, and Benn claims his middle stump. Early on in the afternoon session, Benn is sure he has Boyce caught behind too. Boyce stands perplexed, and the umpire ignores the decibel level of the appeal and Benn's pleading, outstretched left hand, which adds to the stagey impact of it. Half turning, Benn glares down the wicket at Boyce and gives him a stare of such penetrating directness that it requires no accompanying words. In frustration Benn begins to readjust his field with short-armed waves, as though pushing cobwebs away from his face. He doesn't have to wait long for revenge. With his half-century in sight, Boyce misjudges the speed of the ball out of the hand and mistimes his shot too, dragging the ball to mid-wicket. The Leicestershire batsmen are struggling to pick Benn.

Leicestershire have chosen to rest the experienced Paul Nixon, Hylton Ackerman and Claude Henderson and still await the arrival of New Zealander Iain O'Brien, which leaves the side with only one capped player: Boeta Dippenaar, the South African. After only 11 balls, he falls to Benn as well, caught in the slips by Devon Smith. Benn's fourth wicket – another edge and another catch for Smith – is Jim Allenby. At 129 for 6, Leicestershire are listing like a half-chopped tree. When Benn, after 15 straight overs, takes his short-sleeved sweater and sunglasses and ambles into the outfield, he's claimed four of the six top-order batsmen for only 31 runs. Hands casually on hips, he tilts his face to the bright sky and follows the flight of a blackbird as it turns and swoops, like one of his own deliveries, directly in front of him. He then watches Andrew Richardson take care of the tail with three wickets from 14 pacey overs. Leicestershire are all out for 182.

Those who didn't come specifically to see Benn bowl did so to see Ramnaresh Sarwan bat. Rather than bleeding bowlers dry, he grinds them down with a patient gathering of runs, which is lit with the occasional flare of a drive or flicked, soft touch. Even though he doesn't have the flamboyance or panache of the old masters, such as Sobers or Kanhai, Sarwan's 626 runs against England during February and early March – including 291 in Barbados – made him Man of the Series, which turns him into Man of the Moment as far as this meagre audience is concerned. At the fall of the first wicket – Dale Richards driving lazily to point in the eighth over – Sarwan appears. He comes to the middle slowly, as if letting his eyes adjust from the semi-darkness of the dressing room to the flood of early evening's light. He uses his bat, clutching it from toe to the top of its white handle, to perform upper-body callisthenics – stretching and twisting and loosening the tension in his back and spine. He takes the off bail and marks out his guard with it before punching gloves with the non-striker, Smith.

Sarwan is facing the eighteen-year-old Alex Wyatt, who has taken a gap year to play for Leicestershire. His one previous first-class appearance was against Loughborough UCCE. Wyatt, though still growing, is already the same height as Benn, but wider in the shoulders and not as sinewy. He has blond, curly hair and sticky-out ears. He runs in hard and hits the pitch hard too. When Sarwan leans into a drive and smartly sends an early Wyatt delivery gliding past wide mid-off to the white picket fence, it seems as though he's moved effortlessly from Test series to tour. As he waits for the next ball, his bat barely touches the turf. It hangs in the air, anywhere between the top of the pad and the knee roll. When he does eventually ground it, the bat is in front of the right boot. He steadies himself again, and this time Wyatt uses the new ball to give him an out-swinger. Sarwan is surprisingly hesitant, as if unsure about the line, and pushes forward half-heartedly. The bat is a fraction too far from his body and he gets an edge, which Allenby takes waist-high at first slip. If you're a teenager, striving to make an impression, you can hardly do better than to remove Sarwan, whose innings has lasted just 17 balls and 17 minutes. Wyatt wears a slightly dazed expression, as though unable to comprehend what he's achieved, as he watches Sarwan tuck his bat beneath his arm and march briskly to the pavilion. With the star turn gone, the small crowd retreats to the bars.

I am still thinking about Sobers. He was dazzling to the extent that he turned everyone around him into pale silhouettes. When I was a boy, he came to open the village fête and agreed to face whoever wanted to bowl at him. I assumed he would be wearing crisp whites and already be padded up. But he arrived in a suavely tailored silver suit, cream shirt and a dark tie. He didn't bother with the encumbrance of gloves or pads. He merely took the first bat that was handed to him and stood in front of the stumps. I lived in a mining community, and so most of the weekend cricketers were miners: muscled, hard-boned, broad and strong-backed.

By mid-afternoon on this July Saturday most of them had a pint or two swilling inside their bellies. The snaking queue to bowl to Sobers was dominated by these men, who were used to making club cricketers duck and sway and pray silently. The unpadded, ungloved Sobers was a target to them – a knight bereft of armour and exposed to the point of the lance. The bowlers thought about cracking him a fearful blow on the bare knuckles or on knees protected only by Savile Row cloth. The ball, after all, would also be coming at him out of the dark green shrubbery of the vicarage garden.

The next twenty minutes gave my impressionable eleven-year-old eyes an appreciation of his absolute genius. I felt like some watcher of the skies as a new planet swam into view. The harder the ball was bowled at him, the harder Sobers hit it. It was thumped so ferociously that at any moment it might disintegrate into a heap of cloudy red dust, still smouldering and hot after its incineration. He went through his full repertoire: drives and cuts, pulls and sweeps. To save the hurt feelings of the most desperate of the sweaty amateur bowlers, he graciously defended the occasional delivery, which in reality he could have dispatched into a tree of his choosing. As Sobers made each stroke, he extravagantly puffed out his cheeks, like Louis Armstrong reaching the top note with his trumpet.

In particular I remember one shot that I've never seen again – even in the improvised, switch-hitting, reverse-sweeping world of Twenty20. This specific ball was heading down the leg side. Sobers let his knees drop slightly and pushed his feet together. He brought the bat down behind his legs in a high, swift arc and drove the ball full on the face with such force that it took off like tracer fire across the outfield (the only a strip of netting was pitched behind Sobers). It missed my left ankle by six inches. The ball slipped through the iron railings of the fence and on to the main road. For all I know it's travelling still.

Umpires: M. J. D. Bodenham, A. Hicks
Toss: Leicestershire

Leicestershire first innings

M. A. G. Boyce	c Simmons	b Benn	45
T. J. New†	lbw	b Baker	4
J. J. Cobb		b Benn	11
J Allenby	c Smith	b Benn	28
J. W. A. Taylor	lbw	b Sammy	4
H. H. Dippenaar*	c Smith	b Benn	4
W. A. White	not out		37
C. D. Crowe		b Richardson	21
J. K. H. Nalk	c Sammy	b Richardson	0
H. F. Gurney		b Richardson	0
A. C. F. Wyatt	run out		3
Extras	(20b, 2lb, 3w)		25
Total	(all out, 62.3 overs)		182

Fall of wickets: 1-30, 2-77, 3-90, 4-95, 5-108, 6-129, 7-166, 8-166, 9-174, 10-182

West Indian bowling	O	M	R	W
Baker	9	2	11	1
Richardson	14.3	5	46	3
Nash	5	3	7	0
Sammy	14	2	51	1
Benn	15	5	31	4
Deonarine	5	2	14	0

West Indies first innings

D. S. Smith	lbw	b Nalk	24
D. M. Richards	c Taylor	b Wyatt	15
R. R. Sarwan	c Allenby	b Wyatt	4
L. M. P. Simmons	retired hurt		102
N. Deonarine	lbw	b Gurney	15
B. P. Nash	retired hurt		78
D. Ramdin*†	c Boyce	b Dippenaar	36
D. J. G. Sammy	c Dippenaar	b Wyatt	3
S. J. Benn	not out		23
Did not bat: L. S. Baker, A. P. Richardson			
Extras	(8b, 6lb, 1nb, 5pen)		20
Total	(6 wickets declared, 99.5 overs)		320

Fall of wickets: 1-16, 2-34, 3-56, 4-80, 5-266, 6-320

Leicestershire bowling	O	M	R	W
Gurney	22	6	58	1
Wyatt	21	7	42	3
Allenby	4.1	1	13	0
Nalk	16.5	6	33	1
Crowe	17	3	48	0
White	14	1	82	0
Cobb	4	0	19	0
Dippenaar	0.5	0	6	1

Leicestershire second innings

M. A. G. Boyce	c Richards	b Simmons	55
T. J. New†	c Sammy	b Richardson	0
J. J. Cobb	c Ramdin	b Benn	53
J. W. A. Taylor	c Simmons	b Benn	5
H. H. Dippenaar*	not out		40
W. A. White	c Ramdin	b Baker	18
C. D. Crowe		b Sammy	16
J. K. H. Nalk	not out		16
Did not bat: J. Allenby, H. F. Gurney, A. C. F. Wyatt			
Extras	(18b, 13lb, 3nb, 1w)		35
Total	(6 wickets, 91 overs)		**238**

Fall of wickets: 1-13, 2-117, 3-129, 4-134, 5-185, 6-214

West Indian bowling	O	M	R	W
Baker	21	7	62	1
Richardson	19	8	32	1
Sammy	17	7	36	1
Deonarine	1	0	2	0
Benn	25	5	53	2
Simmons	8	2	22	1

Result: Match drawn

CHAPTER THREE

TAKING TEA
WITH NEVILLE CARDUS

*Sir Neville Cardus, who regarded Trent Bridge as a lotus land
for batsmen and believed: 'A boy looks upon his heroes at
cricket with emotions terribly mixed'.*

Trent Bridge: LV County Championship Division One: Nottinghamshire v. Somerset, 6–9 May

I have a lifetime ambition, which I suppose will now go unfilled. I want to be at Trent Bridge at the precise moment when Neville Cardus's dreamy evocation of the place becomes truth. In my imagination, it is a warm, sticky afternoon – preferably in the pure white light of mid July when the sky is an upturned bowl of polished glass. I will be sitting in the top tier of the Radcliffe Road Stand. It will be 3.15 p.m. or thereabouts. I will glance across at the scoreboard, and I will find it is, as Cardus once promised, 360 for 2. And I will think of the slender, bespectacled writer in his grey double-breasted suit, his dark, thinning hair receding into a widow's peak, standing beside the pavilion with pipe in hand, and a contemplative expression across his face as he talks expressively about the cushion of marl that once made Trent Bridge a 'lotus land' for batsmen, and 'fit for heaven' itself.

As a hopeless romantic, Cardus adored Trent Bridge as much as his beloved Lancashire and Old Trafford. The affair began when he saw his boyhood idol, R. (Reggie) H. Spooner, wristly cut and drive his way to 247 there in 1903. Cardus was fifteen, and the image of Spooner never left him. He claimed Spooner made him love cricket the way Mozart made him love music. Cardus also once wrote: 'A boy looks upon his heroes at cricket with emotions terribly mixed.' Cardus believed these cricketers were gods, yet at the same time he had no real confidence in them. He thought 'they [were] going to get out nearly every ball'. He certainly felt this way about Spooner. 'I loved Spooner so much,' he said 'that I dare not watch him make a stroke. It is a curious thought – I probably never saw him at the moment at which he actually played a ball.' To Cardus's fatalistic mind, he alone was responsible for Spooner's good or bad fortune. The batsman's success was wholly dependent on Cardus adhering to superstitious rituals. He made sure not to tread on the cracks in the pavements on his way to Old Trafford. He would touch every lamp-post. If he missed one, or failed to touch it with enough thought, he would, like the neurotic, obsessively compulsive Dr Johnson, return to touch it again more emphatically. Cardus believed he was protecting Spooner from the miseries of failure and also protecting himself against witnessing them. 'No later crises of life – and I have known a few – have so sorely tried me,' he claimed. For Cardus, a corner of Trent Bridge's 'foreign field' was forever Spooner's. Whenever he returned there, he saw, irrespective of who was batting, Spooner as he had originally seen him through the fervour of youthful eyes.

Whenever I go back, I always see the ground as it used to be too – in the ghostly, faraway beauty of the late 1960s when I first walked into it. The concrete and glass office block has yet to be built there. The Fox Road Stand is open and uncovered rather than crowned with an aircraft-wing roof. The Radcliffe Road End has its long, wooden press box with narrow pillars and rough seating below it. Parr's elm is still standing. The doors to the Old Tavern are flung open, and I can smell the beery warmth from it. The glare of its neon bulbs breaks into the gentle darkness of mid-evening. Our emotional response to most things – books and places, sounds and scents – is grounded in the age at which we first experience them. That is why Trent Bridge for me is about so much more than merely cricket. It is about nostalgia and belonging. It is a yearning for yesterdays, like Housman's land of lost content, which I can't reclaim. Of course, I don't see Reggie Spooner here. I see my grandfather instead. He steps through the Dixon Gates with me. He is wearing his dark-brown suit and heavy black shoes. The sun glances off them. The peak of his grey, flat cap hoods his eyes. The barley-twist cord from his hearing aid hangs across the front of his waistcoat, the last button – as sartorial etiquette demands – is unbuttoned.

He is with me again today.

Brian Statham insisted that his preparation for a morning's bowling – whether for England or Lancashire – was minimal to the point of casual insouciance. According to Statham, it comprised 'a fag, a cough, a cup of coffee'. He wouldn't get away with it now. Statham would be compelled to limber up as vigorously as Ryan Sidebottom, who is proving his fitness again after a winter disrupted by Achilles surgery. More than an hour before Nottinghamshire's County Championship match against Somerset begins, the tracksuited Sidebottom is in the nets, which I calculate are pitched almost on the spot where my grandfather and I sat forty years ago. Even off a shortened run, Sidebottom puts the devil into his action, stretching the net after beating the bat. His curly, flopping head of hair still looks slightly out of fashion, as if he belongs to the 1970s. He's like a Cavalier in the age of the Roundhead. After his energetic bowling stint, he takes his turn at catching practice, positioning himself under skiers that twist awkwardly in the high, dragging wind. He takes every ball without a fumble. He also throws at a single red stump, and solidly clips the top of it, as if toppling a coconut on a fairground stall. Sidebottom lifts up his arms in mock celebration, as though waiting for his prize. Finally he goes through stretching and rolling exercises, turning his hips and upper body like a sideshow contortionist. All across the outfield pockets of players prepare in the same way. It's like watching a series of mini-plays performed on the same stage. By now Statham would be unwrapping his second packet of fags, and asking for a light. Sidebottom asks for another five minutes' preparation before jogging to the dressing room.

Anthony Trollope once wrote: 'Let no man boast himself that he has got through the perils of winter till at least of the seventh of May.' Although the calendar has another day to turn before reaching what the sceptical Trollope regarded as the first day of spring, the weather can't be faulted. In the morning sun Trent Bridge looks glorious. While everything around it has bowed to modernity – its new appearance achieved with care and sensitivity as well as £16 million – the tiled and gabled pavilion remains blessedly free from the spit and polish of reinvention. It's reassuring, like meeting an old friend again and finding him unchanged. This pavilion deserves to be preserved like one of England's grand country houses. To spruce up its façade with anything but coats of gloss paint would be to strip the character from Trent Bridge's face and leave it flat and blank-eyed. Its trim architecture and creaking wood represents Nottinghamshire's heritage, the silver and gold of the ground's past. Here, in 1921, Charlie Macartney hit 345 in less than four hours. In the scorebook, its faded cover partly water-damaged, Macartney's innings has spilled into the space that belongs to the batsman below him, Johnny Taylor. When the roaring twenties were about to make way for the Devil's Decade of the 1930s, Harold Larwood and Bill Voce petrified batsmen into submission. Voce would ostentatiously take a white handkerchief from his pocket, like a magician brandishing a trick, and raise it above his head to test the direction and strength of the wind. He'd then unselfishly tell his friend: 'Here, Lol. This end will suit you better – you'll get the breeze at your back.' And the batsman about to face Larwood would feel his stomach lurch. From the pavilion balcony in 1938 Donald Bradman saw Stan McCabe stroke 232 at the rate of one run per minute and beckoned the other Australians around him. 'Come and watch this,' he said 'you'll never see anything like it again.' Bradman became so over-wrought at the beauty of it – later describing McCabe's mastery as the greatest innings he had ever witnessed – that he wept at its conclusion. When McCabe came in after it, Bradman told him: 'If I could play an innings like that, I would be a proud man.' In 1950 Frank Worrell fell asleep on the dressing-room benches before batting an hour before lunch. At the close of play, he'd made 261. And through the pavilion's arched doorways, after passing through the short dark corridor, where three hanging pennants make it look like a medieval banqueting hall, came Ian Botham for his Test debut against the Australians in 1977. He bowled with the ferocity of a blasting wind and took 5 wickets.

I remember Trent Bridge in the days when the wicket was almost indistinguishable from the outfield – a bright sap green, as though the groundsman Ron Allsopp had painted rather than rolled or cut the grass. The conditions were bespoke for the seam, swing and speed of Clive Rice and Richard Hadlee. With his gaucho-like moustache and belligerent expression, Rice had a bare-knuckle toughness about him. He looked constantly intimidating, as if always on the verge of picking a fight. He seemed to me to approach each game as a raw, pugilistic exercise – round after sweaty round of bloodying punches, as if the 22 yards from wicket to wicket was a roped ring. And yet, as a captain, he had an air of unruffled authority about him. He controlled his team the way the falconer controls the falcon. The bare minimum of words or gestures was needed to make it do his bidding; and he spoke about what he did with the poised, tactical acumen of the strategist rather than the street-fighter.

Hadlee was suave and neat, always well pressed. His shirt never creased. The knees of his flannels were never grass-stained. The wide white sweat bands on both wrists were perfectly aligned. Small things mattered to him. The run from mark to crease – deliberately reduced from twenty-five strides to fifteen without losing a yard of pace – was as drilled and ordered as a military march. There was never a step out of place, and he bowled with the precision of a diamond cutter. Under Rice's leadership, and with Hadlee's capacious mind and meticulous pursuit of targets, Nottinghamshire won two Championships in 1981 and 1987, and Hadlee claimed the double of 100 wickets and 1,000 runs in 1984.

The two of them would find conditions different today. The new stands at Trent Bridge, wrapped tightly around the pitch, have created a micro-climate for swing. Nottinghamshire's bowling attack no longer requires the billiard-table top indispensable to Rice and Hadlee. It is, however, weakened by injuries and Test calls. Charlie Shreck, last season's leading wicket taker, hasn't recovered from a knee operation. Darren Pattinson has ankle trouble. Stuart Broad and the spinner Graeme Swann are at Lord's, where England face the West Indies in a preposterously early start to this summer's Tests. There have only been three previous May Tests. In 1909, it rained so hard on Edgbaston that the two captains – A. C. MacLaren and Monty Noble – weren't able to toss the coin until five o'clock. In 1965, according to *Wisden*, the weather was so insufferably 'cold and cheerless' that coffee was served during the drinks break. In 2000, Zimbabwe were bowled out for 83. This dawn chorus is necessary because the World Twenty20 Cup, which begins in June, disrupts the fixture list to such an extent that what is left – the Championship, the Friends' Provident Trophy and even the Ashes series – has to fit in around it. It does more than unbalance the season. It gloomily persuades those of us utterly devoted to County Cricket that Twenty20 might soon squeeze the last breath out of it.

However unfashionable, humdrum and anachronistic it seems, especially against the garishness of Twenty20, the Championship is well loved if sparsely attended. It has an irresistible, sentimental pull for me, a true addict cum hardcore anorak. Like classical music, it has dull or ponderous movements, but pleasure comes from its pre-established order. The connoisseur derives interest from the minor variations and craftily subtle confrontations that exist within it: a clever change in the field, the almost imperceptible variations in pace or angle or flight, the doughty defence against the difficult ball. Its evolutionary aspects are intriguing. It also offers the chance to see the travelling, disparate troupe of cricketers who come together in the Championship as if turning up for a tour of theatrical rep: the old pros, who have made a dozen or so laps around this treadmill course – often for two or three counties; the odd ex-Test batsman or bowler, who knows in his heart of hearts that the international call won't come again; the ubiquitous overseas 'guests', who drop in for a month or a few weeks before haring off at full pelt towards another hotel and another dot on the globe to keep lucrative appointments; and the Kolpak player who, controversially, isn't classed as overseas because of the small print in European employment law, the wrangles of which are on-going and complicated. He counts as a domestic signing only because his country has an 'associate' or trading agreement with the EU. There are two more categories, which Nottinghamshire v. Somerset coincidentally illustrates.

A Championship match always offers time to time to talk and listen and wander. Those who come regularly devour the statistical minutiae, studying the tables and bonus points, averages and scoreboards in the newspapers with a beady intensity. They know which batsman or bowler is in prime form and can recite, like a line of verse, performances and partnerships not just from the current or previous season, but also from summers of long ago. A copy of *Playfair*, its spine frayed and corners turned, is often dragged out of a holdall or jacket pocket to settle disputes. It happens in front of me when three friends sitting on the back row of the pavilion debate how many overs Sidebottom bowled for Nottinghamshire in 2008.

'I'm giving you the facts,' says the first, who looks like Frank Lloyd Wright minus the silver-topped cane. He has a hook nose and a wide-brimmed straw hat slightly askew on his head. 'Sidebottom didn't bowl 100 overs. He either wasn't here or he wasn't fit.' The man to his right with soft-looking, foxed skin disagrees. 'That's rubbish,' he insists, incredulously. 'I saw him, didn't I? He must have bowled 250.' This mild difference of opinion ping-pongs back and forth. The third friend shows quiet impartiality, his head swaying right and then left, like the steady click of a pendulum, as he absorbs the arguments before intervening with a flourish. He fishes into his rucksack, pulling out sun lotion, a radio and his packed lunch, before producing the current *Playfair*. On the cover is a photograph of Ricky Ponting and the words 'ASHES YEAR' in white capitals on a cricket-red background.

At first his companions take no notice of what he's doing. After cracking open its glued binding, and flicking to the appropriate page with the brashness of a bank teller counting out ten-pound notes, he holds up his hand. 'Hush,' he says. 'I have the definitive answer.' The competing voices are suddenly still. The two friends shuffle on to the edge of their bucket seats, and each attempts to peer over his shoulder to catch sight of the single fact that will settle such a trivial matter of pride. The *Playfair* owner draws the book to his chest, as though shielding the page against prying eyes. 'Come on, hurry up,' he's told. He stands up and faces them. 'Eighty-seven,' he says slowly and flatly. The page contains Sidebottom's average too: 10 wickets at 20.80.

'Bloody knew I was right,' says the first friend.

'Are you sure it's not wrong?' replies the second with a bracing grumpiness, reluctant to accept defeat. 'Might be a misprint.'

He folds his arms and looks away, pretending not to care. 'He's not the player he was anyway,' he says, as if blaming Sidebottom for his own malfunctioning memory. His sulk passes like a rain shower.

Shortly before eleven o'clock, after Somerset have won the toss and decided to bat, Sidebottom, unaware of the minor rumpus he's caused, is pacing out his run from the Pavilion End and stamping his white marker disc into the turf like a man trampling a beetle underfoot. He fits into one of the two other Championship categories: Man on a central contract. There are twelve of them, earning £250,000 per year, and their appearances outside the rarefied atmosphere of Tests or one-day internationals are nearly as rare as comma butterflies in February. If he didn't have to confirm his fitness, Sidebottom would be at Lord's rather than Trent Bridge. So would Geoff Miller, National Selector, who has arrived to check on him with the furrowed brow of a GP making a stressful house-call. Sidebottom is bowling to Marcus Trescothick – left-hander to left-hander, the bowler desperate to reclaim his England place against the batsman who has, for reasons documented so explicitly in his autobiography *Coming Back to Me*, voluntarily abandoned Test cricket. The most searing description of Trescothick's depressive illness is on the first page. He describes being 'hunched up, sobbing, distraught, slumped in a corner of Dixon's electrical store at Heathrow's Terminal 3'. He can't face boarding an aeroplane for a pre-season tour of Dubai. At Trent Bridge, his bearing is so imposing and militaristic, like a guardsman, that it is impossible to imagine him coiled and shrivelled. Trescothick initially survives – albeit narrowly – what Sidebottom offers up to him. He lunges and misses at six of Sidebottom's nine balls, and uppishly steers the tenth off his pads to square leg for four. He uses a bat with enough wood in it to build a log cabin. The edges are thicker than a giant's thumb. Mounted on the wall in Trent Bridge's pavilion are bats from the late nineteenth and early twentieth centuries, with slender handles and blades as thin as credit cards. But, however good the bat, and however light the pick-up, it requires the skill of Trescothick to make plundering use of it. His most forceful shot is pushed through the covers, the bat descending on an overpitched ball with a powerful, heavy swat.

Sidebottom's new-ball partner is twenty-year-old Luke Fletcher, who falls into the County Championship's final category: unknown but promising. He is 6 feet 6 inches tall and so broad that Bill Voce's

Ryan Sidebottom, who resembles a Cavalier in the age of the Roundhead in the flowing way he approaches the stumps.

handsome England blazer, hanging behind glass in the pavilion, would be too tight for him across the shoulders and chest. This is only his second Championship appearance. He runs in to bowl from the Radcliffe Road End with his arms raised, but his hands tight against his upper ribs, and almost instantly claims Trescothick's fellow opener, Arul Suppiah, who meekly edges Fletcher's fifth ball to the wicketkeeper, Chris Read, who takes it low to his right. The breeze is travelling across Fletcher, enabling him to move the ball away, which is how Trescothick becomes scalp number two. Trescothick complacently tries to steer the ball through the slips and gives Andre Adams catching practice instead. In Nottinghamshire's *Yearbook*, Fletcher is described as 'fast-medium'. Read, however, regularly takes the ball with his fingers pointed upward. With Trescothick gone, Somerset embark on a roll call of near and actual calamity. James Hildreth is unable to get either his footwork or his timing right. Fletcher quickly puts him out of his misery with a ball that knocks over two stumps. After an hour Somerset are 19 for 3 and Justin Langer, the captain, and Zander de Bruyn are tasked with urgent repairs. Langer will be thirty-nine later this year, and his career has been long and sufficiently eventful enough to fill nearly three pages of *The Cricketers' Who's Who*. There is a compressed elegance about him. His shots are straight, clean, effortless. He has one peculiar twitch. After letting the ball go past off stump, he moves the bat in a rapid, circular motion across the front of his body, as if sweeping a harvest scythe across a wheat field. Often, if the ball beats him, he demonstrates the shot he would prefer to have played to it.

One of the dominant motifs of a Langer innings is the pull. But everything in this session is pitched up, and bowled to a tight line, which tethers him. After Adams replaces Sidebottom, and settles into his bowling groove, he gets a ball to rise. Langer squirts it to Mark Ealham at backward point. He's taken 58 balls to score 11. Worse follows for Somerset. The usually effervescent Craig Kieswetter misses a straight one from Adams and is lbw. The middle-order batsmen return to the pavilion looking like sea-sick travellers tumbling, dazed and reeling, out of a small boat. At lunch Somerset are 57 for 5. 'Just the five wickets to fall,' says the tannoy announcer drolly, as though the bowling performance was routine and unexceptional.

Fletcher leads Nottinghamshire through the gate, cap folded in his right hand. He accepts the honour for his three wickets self-consciously, looking around to make sure he hasn't misread the invitation. In Harold Larwood's era, when the county was an underground latticework of mines in which men lived like moles, seldom emerging for weeks on end from the blackness into bright light, Nottinghamshire hollered down a pit shaft to draw up a queue of brawny fast bowlers. Fletcher merely had to trot over from a far corner of Trent Bridge. At the end of the 2007 season he took a winter job as a car-park attendant so he could stroll straight into the gym for fitness training after his shift. He was overweight and ordered to 'shed a few pounds'. Last winter he shed a few more at Darren Lehmann's Cricket Academy in Adelaide. His favourite player is Andrew Flintoff; and there is certainly something Flintoff-like about him – the build, the slope of the shoulders, the head slightly bowed in contemplation as he stomps back to his mark and the close-cropped blond hair, shaved in a number one on the back and sides.

His hands, with fleshy palms, are enormous, and his wide, sturdy fingers look strong enough to crush coal, let alone hack it out of the earth as Larwood once did.

Nottinghamshire continue to be too strong for Somerset. Fletcher makes them, and specifically de Bruyn, look uncomfortable. One over is especially troubling for the harassed batsman. When Fletcher tries a yorker, de Bruyn digs it out at the root. When he bowls a slower delivery, de Bruyn picks it early but cannot force it in front of square. When he tries a quicker, shorter retort, de Bruyn is flummoxed, and the ball flies off the shoulder of the bat and shoots through the slips for four. And when Fletcher increases his speed, and slightly alters the angle of his attack, de Bruyn makes another false, but fortuitous, stroke. The ball slithers through the slips again and runs unchallenged to the rope. Yeats believed that we must labour to be beautiful. De Bruyn is labouring; but his strokes are not beautiful. The moral victory rests with Fletcher, and those of us still watching recognise it unequivocally. To his credit de Bruyn perseveres, however, and his half-century comes from another edged four. If he'd been facing Fred Trueman, rather than the novice Fletcher, he'd have been stared out and then given F. S. T.'s hoary rebuke about using a bat with 'more edges than a broken piss pot'.

As the play wears on, Sidebottom becomes understandably frustrated. He's made one batsman after another play and miss without a sliver of luck. The foil for de Bruyn is Omari Banks, who drives a ball of decent length to the extra-cover boundary. It is the last straw for Sidebottom, who makes him pay for it with another delivery that cuts back and rams painfully against his box; hitting the spot which Cardus delicately called 'between water and wind'. Banks drops to the floor, slowly at first like a factory chimney collapsing from the top down, and is soon splayed near his stumps. Sidebottom turns his back on the scene, ignoring Banks's discomfort, and prepares to deliver the next ball. When, after a short delay, he bowls it, Banks wafts and gets an inside edge, scattering his own stumps. The long-awaited wicket refreshes Sidebottom, who gets another two before Fletcher's fourth ends the Somerset innings on an embarrassing 138.

I cast a baleful eye across Trent Bridge. Like the children's game of guessing the number of sweets in a jar, I try to make a head count. I estimate no more than 700 people are in the ground. Well over half will be members, which means Nottinghamshire's takings at the gate today wouldn't fill a collection bucket to the brim. The County Championship always seems to be wobbling on the financial precipice. Before the Second World War, when J. M. Kilburn was writing his reports on Yorkshire in an elegant, looping hand and with a gold-tipped fountain pen, 8,000–10,000 squashed into Headingley. With the exception of the period of postwar austerity, the Championship has been in decline ever since. In 1950, it had two million paying customers. By 1966, a summer dominated by England's 'They think it's all over' World Cup, the figure fell to 500,000. Early in 2009 the English Cricket Board claimed, with bells, whistles and much hallelujah fanfare, that crowds from 288 County Championship matches in 2008 had gone beyond the half a million mark for the first time since 2003. Not true. Glamorgan added tickets sold to total membership, including games washed away by Noah-like rain, which exaggerated the numbers and distorted the averages. The final figure was 490,000-plus, which leaves attendances almost unchanged since the mid-1960s.

I am always torn. I want to yell about the charm of the Championship, but, like the devoted rambler who talks of beautiful country walks and scenery, and then frets about turning footpaths into litter-strewn dust through overuse, I selfishly don't want to change the tone or atmosphere of the Championship either.

I head into the pavilion to pay belated respects to William Clarke. In the early 1800s he cast a lover's glance towards a widow called Mary Chapman and achieved most men's dream. He married an attractive woman who ran a pub. The future Mrs Clarke was in charge of the Trent Bridge Inn. It is a moot point whether Clarke was smitten most by her dainty beauty, the hoppy scent of ale or the vast, open fields at the back of the TBI. The business part of his brain whirled and clicked. After saying 'I do' in 1837, he laid out and fenced in those fields. By 1846 he'd created his own travelling team called the All England XI, for whom he specialised in leg-breaks bowled from hip height. He concentrated on slow, high deliveries which fooled the batsmen into early shots. Only the long reach of Fuller Pilch was capable of dealing with him expertly. Clarke's portrait is on the wall near the side entrance to the pavilion. He is top-hatted and wears a black silk bow tie. His eyes (he was blind in one of them) are half closed, and his eyebrows oddly narrow, as though he plucked them. His sideburns are as thick as a privet hedge and stretch to the generous curve of his chin. Clarke would be aghast at the dilapidated state of the gold sign on the back of his venerated TBI, which hangs above its mullioned square windows and reads:

THE WORLD ENOW ED TRE T BRIDGE INN

The dropped-off letters are conspicuous, like missing teeth in a smile. But Clarke would feel better if he could read the verdict Cardus once passed on Trent Bridge: 'I could be happy there even in hours of defeat for Lancashire and England,' he said. I recognise the sense of peace Cardus always felt here. In late afternoon I sit in the middle deck of the Radcliffe Road Stand (row G, seat 81) in the company of strangers. We move from silence into silence with the occasional brief stir in between. There is a short discussion about the contrasting styles of Sidebottom and Fletcher, a conversation which leaps improbably into the question of how sorely Australia might miss Langer during the Ashes series. We talk about the new pavilion at Worcestershire. We swap suspicions about Twenty20 and how it could conceivably make these languid Championship days rare five or ten years from now. Probably, I say with a degree of breezy optimism that I don't honestly possess, we're worrying ourselves unduly. The clock ticks on. We sit and watch the cricket unfold and say nothing more; just glad to be here and sharing the sun and the companionable silence. Instead of Cardus's fabled 360 for 2 – his *Et in Arcadia Ego* – Nottinghamshire are 40-odd for 3, a vapid and sloppy reply in the circumstances. But it doesn't really matter.

Returning to England from Spain and the roar and glare of bombs, George Orwell took solace in the 'railway-cuttings smothered in wild flowers' and the 'larkspurs in cottage gardens' which he saw from the window of his railway carriage and which created the illusion of everything being well and normal. I take solace in the collage of the countryside spread around me. To the south, there is a field of oil seed rape on the crown of a hill – a rich, Van Gogh yellow that catches the sun like flame. To the north, there are the scattered roofs of the city and Nottingham Castle on its pale stump of sandstone rock. To the east, visible in the far distance, are the tips of a power station's four cooling towers beside the M1. Smudges of steam leak slowly out of them, as though the Mallard or the Flying Scotsman is pulling into a station platform. To the west are the fields that eventually flatten out into the saucer land of Lincolnshire. And below me – in what I cherish as the best view in English County Cricket – Somerset's Charl Willoughby is running in to bowl. In the rows of seats beside me the final squares of *The Times* crossword are being completed; someone else turns one page of a detective novel, yawns as if just waking and starts reading; boiling tea is poured into a thick-rimmed white mug. These oddly comforting and quietly civil, quotidian acts are integral to the soft beat of a County Championship match. It's possible to believe – if only for a minute – that nothing of consequence is happening elsewhere: no recession and no job losses and no faraway wars hidden from us by the curvature of the earth. 'There can be no summer in this land without cricket,' said Cardus. The sentence would be truer still if he'd tagged three words to the end of it: 'at Trent Bridge'.

Umpires: M. J. D. Bodenham, T. E. Jesty
Toss: Somerset

Somerset first innings

M. E. Trescothick	c Adams	b Fletcher	13
A. V. Suppiah	c Read	b Fletcher	0
J. L. Langer*	c Ealham	b Adams	11
J. C. Hilldreth		b Fletcher	2
Z. de Bruyn	c Read	b Sidebottom	64
C. Kieswetter†	lbw	b Adams	5
P. D. Trego	c Read	b Adams	4
O. A. C. Banks		b Sidebottom	28
B. J. Philips	lbw	b Sidebottom	0
D A Stiff	c Adams	b Fletcher	9
C. M. Willoughby	not out		0
Extras	(2lb)		2
Total	(all out, 59.4 overs)		**138**

Fall of wickets: 1-0, 2-13, 3-17, 4-43, 5-53, 6-61, 7-129, 8-129, 9-130, 10-138

Nottinghamshire bowling	O	M	R	W
Sidebottom	19	7	32	3
Fletcher	16.4	8	38	4
Ealham	13	4	36	0
Adams	11	3	30	3

Nottinghamshire first innings

B. M. Shafayat	c Kieswetter	b Willoughby	19
A. D. Hales	lbw	b Willoughby	0
M. A. Waugh	c Hildreth	b Phillips	10
S. R. Patel	lbw	b Willoughby	11
A. C. Voges	lbw	b Willoughby	63
A. D. Brown	c Hildreth	b Trego	63
C. M. W. Read*†	c Phillips	b Willoughby	41
M. A. Ealham	c Langer	b Trego	5
A. R. Adams		b Trego	24
R. J. Sidebottom	c Hildreth	b Stiff	13
L. J. Fletcher	not out		0
Extras	(2lb, 2nb, 8w)		12
Total	(all out, 82.5 overs)		**261**

Fall of wickets: 1-1, 2-20, 3-37, 4-46, 5-175, 6-183, 7-189, 8-231, 9-261, 10-261

Somerset bowling	O	M	R	W
Willoughby	28.5	7	81	5
Phillips	15	6	30	1
Stiff	20	3	63	1
Trego	12	3	53	3
de Bruyn	2	0	13	0
Banks	3	0	13	0
Suppiah	2	0	6	0

Somerset second innings

M. E. Trescothick	c Shafayat	b Fletcher	98
A. V. Suppiah	c Read	b Adams	14
O. A. C. Banks	lbw	b Sidebottom	4
J. C. Hilldreth		b Ealham	18
J. L. Langer*	c Read	b Ealham	35
Z. de Bruyn		b Fletcher	54
C. Kieswetter†	c Read	b Ealham	52
P. D. Trego		b Fletcher	23
B. J. Philips	c Shafayat	b Adams	39
D. A. Stiff	st Read	b Patel	21
C. M. Willoughby	not out		0
Extras	(23lb, 2w)		25
Total	(all out 99 overs)		**383**

Fall of wickets: 1-50, 2-59, 3-92, 4-153, 5-193, 6-287, 7-304, 8-325, 9-373, 10-383

Nottinghamshire bowling	O	M	R	W
Sidebottom	21	6	38	1
Fletcher	22	2	71	3
Adams	23	2	70	2
Ealham	21	4	74	3
Patel	12	1	59	1

Nottinghamshire second innings

B. M. Shafayat	c Kieswetter	b Stiff	32
A. D. Hales	c Langer	b Stiff	28
M. A. Waugh	lbw	b Willoughby	14
S. R. Patel	lbw	b Willoughby	35
A. C. Voges	not out		73
A. D. Brown	not out		63
Extras	(6b, 4lb, 6w)		16
Total	(4 wickets, 71.1 overs)		**261**

Fall of wickets: 1-51, 2-78, 3-79, 4-137

Somerset bowling	O	M	R	W
Willoughby	24	5	89	2
Stiff	19	7	57	2
Phillips	10	1	40	0
Banks	6.1	1	22	0
Trego	4	0	21	0
de Bruyn	8	3	22	0

Result: Nottinghamshire won by 6 wickets

CHAPTER FOUR

SEE THE CONQUERING HERO COMES

The elegance of Learie Constantine was evident in everything he ever did –
batting, bowling or fielding – and his legacy lives on in the Lancashire League.

Acre Bottom: Thwaites Lancashire League:
Ramsbottom v. Accrington, 23 May

On the pavilion steps, the portly gent in a beige felt cap, tight chequered braces and a pair of gold-rimmed spectacles is demonstrating the textbook forward defensive stroke with a rolled-up copy of the *Rossendale Free Press*. 'It'll be slow and low at first,' he predicts. 'The batsmen need to smother the ball.' He angles his newspaper and drops into the perfect sideways pose of the coaching manual: long stride forward with his left leg, a jutting elbow, knife sharp, and straight left arm. His gaze is low, and his glasses begin to slide loosely down his nose. 'Beware the variable bounce,' he says, as though warning his son against the Jabberwocky and using the *Free Press* as his own Vorpel sword. 'The odd one will scoot and belt someone on the toes,' he goes on, warming to his didactic theme. He readjusts his glasses. 'Or else it'll stick a bit and force the batsman into a false shot.' There's an element of the bombastic 'I've-seen-it-all-before-you-know' about this forecast.

The pitch at Acre Bottom sits at the smooth foot of the River Irwell Valley. After several days of hard rain the going is soft. There is moisture in the air, and ribbed layers of cloud too. The outfield is lush and spongy, and sun is guaranteed at the end of the afternoon, which ought to improve the chance of making runs later on a drying, hardening pitch. The conditions mean one thing: bowl first and make maximum use of the patches of damp dotted across the wicket. Every captain, from Pelham Warner to Richie Benaud, wouldn't hesitate to do so. So those of us at Acre Bottom struggle to understand the motives of Ramsbottom's captain, Keith Webb, who chooses to bat after winning the toss. 'Hard to believe, isn't it?' says the man in the felt cap with a reproachful, weary sigh. He throws his dog-eared newspaper on to his seat like a gambler tossing away a losing stub at the race track. 'Won't make 150.' He sits down, pushes his thumbs between the top of his braces and then rocks back, determined to watch the game anyway, just to be proved right. This is, after all, the Lancashire League, where those who follow it demonstrably take these things to heart.

For its twelve clubs, scrapping one another for more than 100 years, bragging rights and pride are paramount. The League is strong drink to them – heady and intensely competitive. The tight geography – the clubs are clustered within a 30-mile radius and linked by birth and blood as much as landscape – turns each weekend into tribal conflict, like a mini-blast of civil war. The League adheres to the phrase originally minted across the Pennines, belonging to the White Rose rather than to the Red, and attributed to both Wilfred Rhodes and Len Hutton: 'We don't play it for fun.' There'll certainly be no fun today because Ramsbottom are locked together with Accrington on 48 points at the top of the table. Accrington were last season's champions; Ramsbottom are pushing for their first title since the League's centenary in 1992. While there will be a razor edge to it as a consequence, the match also encapsulates – at least to a naive outsider like me – the difficulties the League is facing in maintaining its traditions. The pressing issue is the long-term future of hired professionals. The League's pedigree and status is rooted in its heritage. There are pros who have starred Lancastrian grass with their presence. These are the names who light up the densely typed record pages of *Wisden*: almost anybody who was somebody once carried their bag through a League season and across towns which sound unmistakably northern off the tongue, such as Rawtenstall, Bacup, Rishton, Nelson, Todmorden. A short roll call of the grand and the good who played in it emphasises the influence of the League, and the money it was once able to pay: West Indians such as Learie Constantine, George Headley, the three W's – Frank Worrell, Clyde Walcott and Everton Weekes – and then Clive Lloyd, Michael Holding and Viv Richards; the Australian pace bowlers Ray Lindwall and Dennis Lillee, and captains Bobby Simpson, Allan Border, Ian Chappell and Steve Waugh; Hedley Verity used the League to change from left-arm swing to spin and became a genius at it; Frank Tyson closed the English leg of his career in it before emigrating to Australia.

Originally the pros were Victorian artisans rather than artists, signed as much for muscular labour as cricketing skill. The pro rolled, cut and prepared a good pitch. He put up the nets. He made certain the pavilion was kept in decent repair. He coached emerging talent. In return, he was fêted and fussed over and treated as deity each Saturday. As the League, formed in 1892, gained credence, so figures such as the taciturn and 'humorously cynical' Sydney Barnes preferred it to the physical slog of the County Championship because it was physically less taxing and financially more profitable. It was said that Barnes treated the League as he treated life – with deadly seriousness. His character, which eschewed showmanship or gimmicks, obliged him to 'accept praise and criticism with equal disdain'. Like a tale from *Ripping Yarns*, A. C. MacLaren took Barnes, then of Burnley, on the 1901–02 tour to Australia on the basis of one net practice at Old Trafford. He twice struck MacLaren, thumping him on the thigh and rapping his gloves off a length. 'He actually said "Sorry Sir",' according to MacLaren, who replied, 'You shouldn't be sorry. You're coming to Australia with me, Barnes'. He took 19 wickets in the first two Tests before breaking down in the third with a leg strain. For his efforts in the League, he was never paid more than £10 a week – though always in gold sovereigns.

The League's pomp, however, arrived in the era when it was synonymous with, and inseparable from, the clichéd image of Lowry's Lancashire – cobbles, whippet-thin men in mufflers and scarves (even in early to mid-June) and sooty mill chimneys. It attracted the most patrician West Indians, who shivered through its early months on slow, low, damp pitches before gradually emerging, like butterflies, into full beauty. Nelson's signing of Constantine in 1929 was the equivalent of lifting Douglas Fairbanks out of Hollywood for a summer's 'turn' at the town's fleapit theatre. There was an inescapable novelty about Constantine too. No one in Nelson had seen a black-skinned man in the flesh before. 'A little afraid at first,' said Constantine, explaining the reaction he found on its streets. Constantine soon assuaged that fear in all but the opposition, who stared at him with trepidation not because of his colour, but because of the damage he was about to inflict on them. There is a sumptuous photograph of him in the nets at Nelson. The crowd is jammed against the dark picket fence behind him, and the camera freezes Constantine at the end of his follow-through after a swashbuckling cover drive. His back leg is flat along the turf. The front leg is well down the pitch. His hands are fixed at the top of the handle. His eyes are fixed on the ball. Constantine holds the shot, as though posing for a sculptor who is about to strike his chisel against a huge fresh block of stone and free the shape concealed within it.

Worship for Constantine was unconditional. He inspired true love – in a period when such love was expressed hesitantly and shyly; often without words. He earned £500 per year, plus a return ticket to Trinidad and 'third-class rail travel and tea' for away matches. His lordly package, worth £90,000 in today's money, proved justified; a blue chip investment, in fact. Gate receipts wherever Constantine went averaged a '1930s fortune' – £150. Some came just to see the spontaneity of his fielding.

Like a practised party-trick, in which a coin vanishes after being skilfully palmed, Constantine would stretch to take a slip catch and drop the ball imperceptibly into his hip pocket while simultaneously turning his head towards the boundary to pretend the edge had escaped his dive. He knew the value of being a showman – both for himself and the League. In 1931 he squared up to Barnes, who was then fifty-nine years old, and subsequently rated the 96 he scored against his bowling as his best ever innings. Barnes still finished with figures of 7 for 68. Constantine lived in Nelson for twenty years, played there for nine and won seven League titles. Scoring nearly 6,500 runs and taking 776 wickets, including all ten against Accrington, who were bowled out for 12, he transformed the League the way the first goldrush pioneers transformed the dusty American West. The League became what Constantine made it.

Now it is suffering because of circumstances beyond its control and compass. The conjunction of the game's choked fixture list and the rise of the specialised, itinerant pro, flitting from one continent to another to satisfy both bank balance and the constant demands of the calendar, paralyse the League's hand. Even if any club was able to scrape together bags of Barnes-like gold sovereigns to hire a stellar figure, his feet wouldn't touch Lancashire soil long enough to turn a worthwhile profit. Soon he'd be off to Tests, Twenty20 or the assorted one-day international tournaments, which briefly flicker and are soon gone and forgotten, but still satisfy the cravings of television companies, sponsors and advertisers; and also reward the pro. The stock of experienced pros is further diminished because moneyed counties parachute in Test batsmen or bowlers for specific competitions, or for the business end of the Championship season. The League can't compete. If there is almost as much – or more – hard cash to be made from just a week or two's work, then why spend an entire summer toiling in the League?

Tighter controls and the complicated bow of red tape meant eight of the League clubs began this season waiting for their pro to arrive anyway. Form-filling and the tedious checking process, which used to take up to five days, can drag on a month or more because of the new regulations. The Sports Visitor application – code VAF1J – includes the question: 'Have you ever been involved in . . . war crimes, crimes against humanity or genocide?' The applicant 'may' have to provide a record of fingerprints and biometric data too. All this to bowl or bat. The pros are no longer in the Constantine mould, but instead are fished out of a shallow pool of burgeoning talent or are recruited from the group of players whose international careers have all but glimmered out. The League's 'main draw' this season is Brendan Nash, who will join East Lancashire at the end of the West Indies' current tour.

The clubs survive on pinched finances. Watching Accrington just two summers ago was like visiting the sick. The club had a ghastly pallor and a faint pulse. Recovery began with an Extraordinary General Meeting, a business plan and the exuberance of David Lloyd, of Accrington, Lancashire, England and Sky Sports. When Lloyd made his debut for Accrington as a sixteen-year-old, the swinging sixties still hadn't got into their psychedelic gallop. It was the year in which Philip Larkin insisted that sexual intercourse began. With an appropriate piece of symmetry, Lloyd's age had flipped when he turned out for them in an improbable cameo in 2008. Borrowing Nasser Hussain's bat, James Anderson's gloves and pads, and ignoring sarcastic text messages questioning his sanity from Mike Atherton, Lloyd put his sixty-one-year-old body through 100 overs. His son Graham returned to the club too. Also ex-Lancashire and ex-England, he proved pivotal, making 849 runs and averaging 53. Adversity bound Accrington together and remade them afresh. After finishing bottom in eight of the previous fourteen seasons, it won the title (17 points separated them from Rawtenstall) and the Worsley Cup – a double for the first time in the club's 165-year-history. But like everyone else in the League, Accrington's financial health is delicate.

The news is bleaker still for Ramsbottom. Recession has forced the packaging company, whose factory walls border one end of Acre Bottom, to withdraw sponsorship for next season. In the twenty-four-page match programme, the 'honours list' of match sponsors, match ball sponsors and player sponsors contains a disturbing amount of white space. It's why there are tentative mutterings about scrapping the pro system, or introducing a moratorium for one season to 'see how it goes' without them. The mythology of the League, acutely aware of the heft of its past, grew directly out of the achievements of its professionals. But the ever-widening disparity between expense and income makes it difficult to sustain them. This is Hobson's choice. Without pros, the League risks losing its lustre and becoming dully parochial. With them, it leaves each club to raise a minimum of £25,000 to £30,000 – the norm for a season's contract – before a ball is bowled. And Ramsbottom charge only £38 to be a full member or £4.50 on the gate. Social events at Acre Bottom – such as wedding receptions and wakes – ensure their solvency. So does the volunteer spirit. Rod Hamer, the club's chairman, is tanned and silver-haired with a sharp peak of a nose. In short-sleeved checked shirt and pale khaki shorts, he buzzes from one corner of Acre Bottom to another like a wasp in an upturned jar. One moment he's announcing the scorecard changes from the secretary's office, the next, he's dealing with a complaint in the bar about cold pie and chips and lumps in the gravy.

He remembers watching Wes Hall bowl for Accrington against Ramsbottom in the early 1960s. When Accrington signed Hall, it was akin to acquiring a nuclear warhead. 'He bowls in Lancashire,' said one report in the *Manchester Guardian*, 'but begins his run in Yorkshire.' With his shirt unbuttoned almost to the navel, and his crucifix glinting as it made its pendulum swing from a long gold chain around his lean neck, Hall merely had to lean into the crease to convert most batsmen to pacifism. The only way to protect yourself from a pounding was to sandbank the batting crease, as if it were a trench. Rod explains that he worked with one Ramsbottom batsman who arrived in the office on the Monday after facing Hall and removed his shirt to reveal bottle-blue and chrome yellow bruising over his ribs. 'The batsmen today,' he points out, staring across the outfield, 'wouldn't survive if Hall was bowling at them

A scene fit for a gilt frame. Ramsbottom's Acre Bottom with its cream and green striped pavilion beneath Peel Tower.

– even with helmets and wads of padding. He pauses, thinking about the tender grace of dead days before concluding. 'It's not like the old times, I'm afraid.'

In a literal sense, for a day, he is wrong. It is like the old times. In the heart of the town, just a spit and a stride away from the ground, it is summer 1941. The High Street is decked in Union Jack bunting. Women in dark seamed stockings, long fur stoles, floral, swirling dresses and box hats with coloured veils stroll with wide wicker baskets looped over one arm and a uniform-wearing Tommy draped across the other. There is the odd, black-suited spiv in spats and a trilby, jauntily tilted on his head, and a stuck-on toothbrush moustache. Everyone carries a gas mask in a fawn cardboard box. In shop windows the *News Chronicle* darkly records the torpedoing of ships with all hands lost. *John Bull* patriotically parades Churchill on its cover in tinted, touched-up colour. *Woman's Weekly* advises on 'ration book recipes' for the kitchen. Posters urge the nation to 'Dig for Victory' and caution against 'Careless Talk'. The swing of big band music leaks under pub doorways. Ramsbottom's annual 1940s War Weekend is surreal. I feel I've taken a wrong turning in the present, landed in the past and have arrived improperly dressed for it. The spell is only broken when a gangling man in the tailored grey of a Nazi uniform takes a call on his mobile phone and promises to be home before five o'clock. The war, it appears, will be over well before tea. Turning into Acre Bottom I half-expect to find time out of joint there as well. I look for Constantine padding up, Verity tweaking the ball with his slender fingers and Lindwall marking out his long run.

When C. L. R. James first arrived in the north-west, he did so with a pre-conceived idea of what he would find here too. 'I had imagined a small piece of grass, fighting for its life against the gradual encroaching of cotton factories, menacing with black smoke, machine shops and tenement houses,' he said. James was writing specifically about Nelson, where he'd gone in the 1930s to lodge with Constantine and, eventually, to ghost his book *Cricket and I*. Even though the woollen industry and the mills have long gone, the stereotypical image of the League still lingers; especially, it has to be said, in the south. Ramsbottom disproves it.

The view beyond the far boundary is classical; romantic enough to be gilt-framed. Low to my left are the four finely carved, dark finials of one church, St Andrew's. High to my right is the steeple of another, Holcombe

Emmanuel. Far above, crowning the steep rise of Harcles Hill, is Peel Tower, the 128-foot monument to Sir Robert Peel. The hill is thick with woodland, which hides all but a few poking roofs and windows and the sturdy square blocks of homes. The tracks of the East Lancashire railway run parallel to the ground. Steam trains chug along and punctuate the afternoon's cricket with long, shrill whistles and short, low blasts of a hooter, which sounds like bottled thunder. The single-storey pavilion is striped cream and olive-green, like a deckchair. Bushy, wide trees – gold-tinted green – swaddle the ground. The pattern of mottled greens is broken only once. A red maple stands at the Scoreboard End, glowing like embers in a grate

It is poignant to be here during War Weekend. The League was in its roaring heyday immediately before Hitler rearranged the fixture list and immediately after his defeat. Crowds were counted in the high thousands rather than today's low hundreds. Success in the League fashioned a town's reputation and identity. The class of the pro it enticed was a reflection of its pull and prosperity and also dictated the size of the gate. No longer. With Lancashire facing Essex at Old Trafford in the quarter-final of the Friends Provident Trophy this afternoon, and live cricket and football on satellite TV, there are no more than 200 of us dotted on the wooden benches around Acre Bottom.

Hanging on the walls of the pavilion are framed photographs of the club's pros: from Tony Lock to Michael Clarke and from Keith Stackpole to Wasim Raja. There are wistful reminiscences of Murali Kartik, the Indian left-arm spinner, who took 9-30 in only his second appearance in 2004. 'The best spinner the League's seen since Johnny Wardle,' I hear on three separate occasions. Much still depends on the pro; and much is expected of him too. He must be stoic and humble enough not to bark patronisingly at the amateurs, and be prepared for the furnace heat of criticism from members if he fails. A pro who is perceived as poor value for money is soon replaced. Sometimes too rashly. Accrington decided not to re-engage a leg spinner for the 1992 season. The player – an Australian with wheat-coloured hair – took 73 wickets at 15.4, but didn't blunt the scorer's pencil with his number of runs: 330 at 15. He became dispensable. Indeed, in what turned out to be his farewell appearance for them, his figures were a miserable 1-72. So it was that Accrington decided Shane Warne's leg spin alone was an insufficient reason to retain him. In his autobiography Warne devotes only half a sentence to Accrington (though he does include a black-and-white photograph of himself in the club's sweater): 'and in 1991 I returned to play for Accrington in the Lancashire League,' he says factually and without elaboration. We think of Warne as boisterous and brazen – dancing a hip-swivelling jig with a stump in his outstretched hands on the dressing-room balcony at Trent Bridge in 1997 after retaining the Ashes; the celebratory whoop from sun-screen-smeared lips after taking a wicket; embroiled in a slew of off-the-field transgressions, which the tabloids, in pursuit of prurient, juicy copy, documented in detail. The twenty-one-year-old Warne of Accrington was different: exuberant without being cocky, confident in himself without being overly brash, socially gregarious without letting that streak of laddish bonhomie spill into self-indulgence or over-extravagance. He was dedicated too. Warne arranged practice nets – which no other pro had done before him – and became fastidious in his own preparations. 'He worked incredibly hard almost all the time,' I am told. Less than two years after Accrington casually let him go – and within county boundaries too – Warne gave the ball a flick, spun it as wide as the Manchester Ship Canal and clipped the top of Mike Gatting's off stump. By 1994, he was International Cricketer of the Year. In 2000, *Wisden* named him as one of its five Cricketers of the Century.

Today Accrington has the twenty-nine-year-old Roy Silva, a Sri Lankan, and he bowls the opening over with an ever so slightly shuffling, but deceptively brisk, run. Pensive and brooding, Ramsbottom's members are still muttering – and struggling to comprehend – the captain's choice of bat over ball.

The mistake he's made is soon apparent. Roy clean-bowls Alex Bell with a delivery which dips abruptly after landing on one of the damp patches and hits only a third of the way up the middle and off stumps. Enter Ramsbottom's counter to Silva – the Jamaican Brenton Parchment. His CV includes two Test appearances (against South Africa and Australia) and seven one-day internationals. On the cusp of his twenty-seventh birthday, Parchment is lean and straight-backed and he strides with purpose from the pavilion. He is quickly striding back into it again, head sheepishly bowed, bat dangling limply from his right hand. Whether from the need to establish authority early on, or just because of a momentary, Niagara Falls rush of blood to the head, Parchment decides to take a swing at a full-ish ball from the medium pacer David Ormerod.

He doesn't account for the slowness of the surface. The ball sticks on him, coming off with such a lack of pace that I think it might defy the laws of motion and start to seam backwards. Parchment is through the shot too early and scoops his drive in a whirl of his flaying arms towards mid-off. Like a kite taking off in a gentle gust, the ball rises steeply and gradually from the thickish edge of the bat. The fielder, Stuart Crabtree, has to wait more than five seconds – agonisingly difficult when standing beneath a spinning catch – before the ball descends, like a dropped stone, towards him and deviates in flight in the second half of its fall. Crabtree dives half a length to his left and clings on to the ball despite a jarring fall that could easily have shaken it free. Ramsbottom's more vocal members bristle. 'Rubbish, that,' says one man in a blue cardigan and corduroys. 'Useless. Our lass could have played it,' joins in another, stuffing his hands into his pockets in a huff and turning his back on the retreating pro. 'You'd expect a professional to be able to read a pitch,' says a stout-calved woman, who puts down her *People's Friend* and offers analytical observation rather than plain gut reaction. 'He didn't wait and let it come to him,' she says. 'Too impetuous by half.' Were there a guillotine on the boundary, there's no doubt Parchment's head would by now be spilling sideways into its basket. He shouldn't take it too personally. Lindwall, bowling on his debut for Nelson in 1952, was barracked by an old-time member, who regarded the Australian as arrogant and petulant for glaring at the amateurs who dropped slip catches. 'It serves thee reet,' he yelled at Lindwall. 'Tha should bowl at the bloody wickets.' Parchment gets away with a few indistinct muttered oaths before the church-like silence of reproach.

The Indian Premier League Twenty20 commentators tend to talk to the viewer as though he is incapable of both logical thought and understanding, and unable to see the ball that has just been bowled. This might be excused as benevolent didacticism – but only if you wanted to be charitable. The truth is that, whether through ignorance, arrogance or inarticulacy, the IPL commentator generally re-enacts with words what your eye has already registered and what your brain has already absorbed a full second before he spoke. The art of TV commentary is to supplement, rather than replicate, what is on the screen, which is why Richie Benaud and Mike Atherton are so good at it. The technical observations about Parchment and Lindwall are germane to this argument because they emphasise two things: that criticism in these parts can be concisely barbed to the point of bluntness (there's nothing wishy-washy here); and that the Lancashire League regular doesn't need the bloody obvious explained to him because he is already schooled in the finer points, as well as the fundamentals, of what's in front of him. The IPL commentators ought to learn from it.

In keeping with every other game I've seen so far this summer, the ball dominates the bat. Ramsbottom disintegrate to 39 for 6 and then 52 for 7. The swiftness of the collapse overworks the wiring in Acre Bottom's new electronic scoreboard. For each batsman Accrington claim, the scoreboard lops a wicket off instead of adding it on. A case of wishful thinking.

There is no sustained rigour down the order. But just when it seems Ramsbottom won't make it beyond an embarrassingly modest 75, Accrington change tack, as if out of pity for them. Instead of crowding the bat, the fielders are pushed back, and Ramsbottom – chiefly through wicketkeeper-batsman Richard Hevingham's alertness – manage to filch singles and the odd two. Each of Hevingham's 29 runs is painstakingly compiled. The highlight of this wagging tail, though, is the dismissal of number nine Nick Murphy. Left-arm spinner Damian Clarke bowls him the slowest of slow deliveries; so slow, in fact, that it seems to stop in the air. Murphy takes what I count (with only slight exaggeration) as half a dozen cross-batted swipes at it, like an apprentice Zorro, before the ball finally plops on to the turf, dribbles under his final swish and strikes the bottom of middle stump. Ramsbottom get to three figures almost in spite of themselves. The forty-year-old Ormerod, who the previous season passed 1,000 League wickets, nags away, applying straightforward principles of length, line and accuracy. He's the archetypal League pro – nowt fancy, but effective – and finishes with 4 for 31.

By tea, the clouds have skedaddled across the sky, as if in some strange meteorological race, and the sun has burned away the last wisps of them. Acre Bottom is a beautiful hollow of white light. I can't think of a grander place to be; not even Worcester or Trent Bridge. While the rest of us potter around the boundary or queue for tea and lemon cake, the indefatigable Rod Hamer is out on the square with the hand roller, which he shoves with his whole body. As soon as that job is done, he begins another. He tours the boundary with one-pound raffle tickets, afraid that Accrington might knock off the necessary 107 runs before he has time to sell them, let alone announce the winning numbers. He needn't have rushed. What ought to be straightforward for Accrington is suddenly complicated with a ridiculous run out. Jimmy Hayhurst resembles Stuart Broad when he bowls. With pads on – as a very correct batsman – he sets off at a fair clip in pursuit of the runs, as if he has an early-evening appointment and can't possibly be late. His aggressive intent peters out only after his partner, the rotund Paul Carroll, doesn't respond to a legitimate call for a single. Hayhurst, dashing to the danger end, has to retreat and is a yard short of his crease when he hears the awful click and clatter of the stumps being broken. Carroll doesn't last long either. He is caught behind for a scratchy five. When Graeme Sneddon goes too, trapped lbw to a ball which barely rises above his laces, Accrington are 18 for 3 and grateful that their earlier good work has kept the rate low. Even at 54 for 4, after a compact 19 from Silva, the advantage always lies with them.

Parchment, as though straining to atone for his abject batting, bowls seam rather than his preferred spin from the Scoreboard End. Frustrated and tetchy, he barks out unsuccessful appeals at Silva, Crabtree and Lloyd, as if decibel level alone might dislodge them. 'Get away with it. No chance,' says an exasperated, blazer-wearing Ramsbottom member, who gathers up his bag, his folding chair, his dog and, lastly, his wife and departs without a backward glance well before Accrington canter to a 6-wicket win with more than 21 overs to spare. The pavilion clock has just turned 6.35 p.m. The end has come very early by Lancashire League standards. The not-out batmen, Lloyd and Crabtree, punch gloves to signal the simultaneous feat of bringing up the half-century partnership and accomplishing the overall mission.

The victorious Nelson team of the 1920s was serenaded by the town's Old Prize Band. Waiting in its gold-braided livery, the band escorted the club's charabanc through the streets to the tune of 'See the Conquering Hero Comes'. Lloyd and Crabtree are given polite applause from the straggling band of Ramsbottom members who have seen the last rites and now gaze across the shadowed pitch before heading off to complain in the pubs or beside the fire tonight.

Rod Harmer is busy again. Already he's tidying up, removing the chalk board in front of the social club and rearranging benches. 'Can't believe it,' he says, slightly tilting his head to one side, like a quizzical owl. 'Why did we bat first?' He thinks about his own question before answering it with a head-shake. 'He's a new captain,' he explains. 'Perhaps he just wants to go against the grain. No accounting for it, though. Daft, really.'

The steam trains have stopped running, the Second World War is over for another year, and stillness has descended across Acre Bottom. That copy of the *Rossendale Free Press*, used to demonstrate the forward defensive shot at the start of the afternoon, lies on the bench where its owner left it, no doubt angrily. Its pages flap in the thin breeze like the wings of a snared bird.

Umpires: J. C. Ashworth, P. Hargreaves
Toss: Ramsbottom

Ramsbottom innings

A. I. Holt	c & b D. N. Ormerod		5
A. W. Bell	b Silva		2
B. A. Parchment	c Crabtree	b D. N. Ormerod	0
D. M. Bell	c J. M. Ormerod	b D. N. Ormerod	12
K. T. Webb*	c Lloyd	b D. N. Ormerod	14
M. J. Dentith	c Hanson	b Hayhurst	0
R. L. E. Brown	c Crabtree	b Hayhurst	3
R. D. Hevingham†	b Silva		29
N. Murphy	b Clarke		11
J. Walmsley	not out		15
M. G. Haslam	b Carroll		2
Extras	(4b, 1lb, 1nb, 7w)		13
Total	(all out, 49.4 overs)		**106**

Fall of wickets: 1-10, 2-11, 3-11, 4-38, 5-38, 6-39, 7-52, 8-75, 9-103, 10-106

Accrington bowling	O	M	R	W
Silva	10	3	25	2
D. N. Ormerod	19	7	31	4
Hayhurst	10	2	16	2
Clarke	5	0	14	1
Carroll	5.4	0	15	1

Accrington innings

P. D. Carroll	c Hevingham	b Haslam	5
J. E. Hayhurst	run out		5
S. P. S. Crabtree	not out		29
G. L. Sneddon	lbw	b Walmsley	3
K. R. P. Silva	c Murphy	b Parchment	19
G. D. Lloyd	not out		30

Did not bat: S. J. Hanson, J. M. Ormerod†, T. Hussain, D. N. Ormerod*, D. W. Clarke

Extras	(1b, 2lb, 4nb, 9w)		16
Total	(4 wickets, 28.4 overs)		**107**

Fall of wickets: 1-7, 2-11, 3-18, 4-54

Ramsbottom bowling	O	M	R	W
Haslam	8	3	23	1
Walmsley	6	0	21	1
Parchment	7	0	30	1
Brown	6.4	2	27	0
Murphy	1	0	3	0

Result: Accrington won by 6 wickets

CHAPTER FIVE

AND STILL
THE GAS-WORKS . . .

Just as the poet John Masefield once saw it – minus the dancing girls.
The Oval's most distinguishing landmark looms over the
hoopla of the Twenty20 Cup.

The Brit Oval: Twenty20 Cup:
Surrey Brown Caps v. Sussex Sharks, 26 May

Terence Rattigan used his screenplay *The Final Test* – a 1953 black-and-white film about an ageing batsman's emotional farewell innings against Australia – to explain why cricket was so important to him. Appropriately, he feeds his feelings about it into the mouth of a poshly pompous, over-fed, obstreperous poet-cum-playwright, who is played by Robert Morley. In one of the crucial scenes Morley is motoring helter-skelter, jagging his open-topped car around traffic, as if on a fairground ride, towards the Oval. Beside him is the son of the player Morley longs to see again before the swish of the curtain draws his career to close. The son is estranged from his father; quite separate in temperament and culture. He doesn't understand him and consequently dismisses as irrelevant and inferior his lifetime achievements. On the way to the Oval, he confesses that he doesn't much care for cricket either. It is too dull for his taste. Morley is incredulous.

'Of course, it's frightfully dull,' he spits irritably at the son. 'That's the whole point. Any game can be exciting . . . the measure of the vast superiority of cricket over any other game is that it steadfastly refuses to cater for this boring craving for excitement.' Morley-Rattigan hasn't finished. He's on his high horse now, galloping fast. 'To go to cricket to be thrilled is as stupid as to go a Chekhov play in search of melodrama,' he says.

Rattigan wrote *The Final Test* during a decade in which the Lord Chamberlain was still in his censorious prime and wielding his blue pencil as regularly as Len Hutton wielded his bat. Hutton, along with Denis Compton, Jim Laker and Godfrey Evans, took a cameo role in the film. Even as himself, Hutton was slightly miscast. The central figure of Sam Palmer was given to Jack Warner two years before Dixon of Dock Green strolled, hands behind his back, under the blue lamp and said 'Evenin' all' on the BBC. Warner was nearly sixty – visibly older than Wilfred Rhodes when an ancient pair of knees carried him into his own last Test in 1930. Rattigan's sentimentally loaded script impeccably captures England at the start of the second Elizabethan age: stiff-lipped, strait-laced, emotionally rigid, over-concerned with preserving middle-class respectability and keeping the net curtains clean. But cricket rarely transfers from page to screen fundamentally because it is a game of Empire and also because

American audiences are able to grasp the broad outlines of the play, but not its intricacies, which are unfathomably complicated to them. Shortly after *Chariots of Fire* won the Oscar for Best Picture in 1981, its producer David Puttnam planned to turn the 1932–33 Bodyline series into a similarly character-driven drama. The script didn't include a solitary lbw decision. Now Lord Puttnam of Queensgate, he remembers: 'The Americans couldn't understand the leg-before law, so we left it out. Sadly, in the end, we couldn't make the picture either.' This scarcity of cricket movies makes the *The Final Test* precious. Rattigan essentially uses it to make a statement about filial relationships. In doing so, he makes more valid points about the inherent decency of cricket, the poetry within it and how much it means to the English. The Morley-Rattigan character goes further in his lofty comparison of a match to a Chekhov play, claiming it has the same sense of 'shape, pattern, form and design'. It is an 'art that conceals an art' . . . and 'is beautifully inconclusive'.

Walking around the Oval, before the start of Surrey's opening Twenty20 Cup game of the season, I imagine Rattigan sitting among the crowd; probably on the top tier of the Vauxhall End Stand and at the apex of the impressively smooth curve of its white metal roof. Rattigan was so highbrow and snooty – Rolls-Royce with personalised number plate, Belgravia town house and silver cigarette holder – that he refused to speak to his own butler. So I guess he'd dismiss the Twenty20 Cup with a sardonic curl of his lip and think it an insult to eye and brain, like watching a street brawl. He would regard even three hours of the Twenty20 Cup the way Dr Johnson regarded reading *Paradise Lost*. 'None,' said Johnson, 'ever wished it longer.' I relate to Rattigan's view. To describe yourself as a 'cricket purist' nowadays risks derision. You're dismissed as ultra-conservative, unprogressive and as fogeyish as a pocket watch and chain. I am that cricket purist. The contemplative aspects of cricket attracted me – the pauses, the silences, the gradual unfolding of its strategies. So let me count the ways in which I am ambivalent towards the Twenty20 Cup. I dislike the razzmatazz: the show-off announcers who yell about what has just happened, or what is to come. I dislike the acts of forced jollity, like someone at a party constantly blowing a streamer in your face and telling you to enjoy yourself. I dislike the coloured clothing and the white ball, which always ends up looking grubby. I dislike the asinine suffix monikers attached to each county– the Sharks, the Outlaws, the Hawks. I hear almost no one – apart from the TV commentators or marketing men – use them in ordinary conversation. Most of all I loathe – and always will – the weary, tedious soundtrack accompanying every boundary or wicket: a melody from the era of flares and the feather cut, and now so tiresomely familiar that it does nothing but either numb or grate.

The problem of building a game on gimmicks is what to do when those gimmicks become familiar; when they are no longer fresh, and the newfangledness fades. There is nothing for it except to create another set of gimmicks . . . and then, of course, another still. The difficulty of persuading the viewer that he hasn't seen it all before – and with such awful regularity too – became conspicuous during the Indian Premier League. The tournament is one of the most vapid and tedious sporting events on earth because it is a prefabricated structure constructed solely around the irresistible craving for the dollar and the pound. The evidence so far points to the IPL writing off the cricket watcher as gullible enough to believe its competition carries genuine significance or meaning; beyond, of course, peddaling a sponsor's product or stuffing someone's wallet. It's as if, dazzled by a constant, high beam of hype, the IPL think we'll just blink in admiration and be blinded to the baseness of the show. But everything about it is transparently formulaic and manufactured – starting with the teams and their rivalries.

The armchair viewer is treated as an imbecile. It is almost impossible to watch the matches without the volume muted or off entirely. The scripted name checks for sponsors have the same effect as water torture. There is a perpetual, steady and echoing drip of promotional banalities that make you want to tear the television plug out of the wall. The 'time-outs' are more patronising still. These are passed off as short periods of profound tactical discussion. But in keeping with the gerrymandering and artificialness of the IPL, the breaks are actually its way of jamming in extra commercial breaks. Worse – far worse, in fact – is the commentary.

Language becomes a dud currency when it is used for effect rather than purpose. Someone ought to warn the commentators that a sprint through the synonym dictionary – creating a tailback of worthless superlatives on the way – can never camouflage the ordinariness of what is on the screen. It's as fatuous as thinking that darkness destroys what it conceals. To compound things the commentators use the microphone like a megaphone. They don't so much speak into it as bawl down it, as if competing to be heard above a nuclear detonation. A routine flick off the pad is yelled to long leg as though Bradman had just reached 300; a dab to third man met with rowdy acclamation, as if the sublime grace of a Frank Woolley cover drive was contained within it; the clip of the bails saluted with a scream so loud that you'd think Verity had taken another 10 for 10. It makes you long for someone to pin Oscar Wilde's quotation to the inside of the commentary box: *He that praises everyone praises no one.* It also means there is nowhere for the commentators to go on the vocal register when the ball vanishes into 'the confectionery stand' and comes out again.

This was the IPL – plastic cricket, pre-packaged and oversold. Not worth seeing, and the embodiment of the rule that no one ever went broke underestimating public taste.

At its end – amid the rush and blur – it was impossible for me to distinguish between the Chennai Super Kings and the Kolkata Knight Riders, the Rajasthan Royals or Kings XI, Punjab. The final took place less than forty-eight hours before I set off for the Oval. For the purposes of this book, I watched every ball of it. Now I can't remember a solitary moment of it. I can't even remember who won. I don't care. The promise of 'Turbo-Charged' cricket, the slogan which adorns posters around the Oval and the front of the Twenty20 Cup 'Event Guide', means there is a queue outside the Hobbs Gate more than two hours before the start. The gate is exactly as Jack Hobbs, the most self-effacing of men, would have wanted it: unprepossessing to the point of understatement. The words, forged in black wrought iron, do their job without being flashy about it:

IN HONOUR OF A GREAT SURREY AND ENGLAND
CRICKETER

Hobbs once claimed there was too much money in cricket. At the time he said it, the match-fee for Tests was £60. He would blanch at the amount of cash available to the most skilful exponents of Twenty20. But he would be more concerned about the way in which those rewards have persuaded some players to mould their game primarily around it. An actor who only aspires to a part in a soap opera, and entirely styles his career towards achieving it, will never act beyond its range. A cricketer who concentrates wholly on Twenty20, and ignores the other disciplines of his craft, will always lack the breadth of technical ability needed to bowl a long spell or vary his bowling, bat for hours or adapt successfully to different types of pitches and conditions. This would have been more alien to Hobbs than coloured clothing.

The turnstiles, which are supposed to open at 4.30 p.m., stay stubbornly shut. The harassed, puzzled stewards in their fluorescent jackets meet every question about the delay with the pat answer 'Another ten minutes' – even though more than a quarter of an hour has passed since it was originally offered. Without apology or explanation, we're allowed in at 4.52 p.m. The Oval was once called an urban playground in an unlovely and industrial setting. At first glance there is nothing even faintly Arcadian about it in either landscape or mood. The skeletal architecture of the gasometer, rising and falling like a concertina, takes the eye first. There is an ugly block of flats in the distance; sore thumbs, indeed. Next to the pavilion, with its terraces and red brick, are glass-fronted hospitality boxes resembling seaside apartments. Only from its upper tiers are the summit peaks of London's panorama visible: the head and neck of the British Telecom Tower and St Stephen's Tower at the Palace of Westminster.

Already, despite the English Cricket Board's lavishing of £300,000 on advertising cut-price tickets, there is concern about Twenty20 overkill. Evidence of the ECB's guilt in trying to burn the candle at both ends is, however, far from conclusive, and the judgements made on the basis of it sound premature. Surrey, inaugural winners in 2003, began the campaign against champions Middlesex last night at Lord's. When the teams met there in 2004, the attendance was 27,509. Last year it was 16,378. Just 10,000 saw Surrey win at a canter this time, courtesy of Usman Afzaal's 98 and 61 from Mark Ramprakash. There could be mitigating factors. The competition began two weeks earlier than it did last summer – ironically to avoid clashing with another Twenty20 tournament, the World Cup. The group stages run until 4 June, resume on 22 June – a day after the World Cup final – and the quarter-finals aren't held until late July. The occasional cricket watcher, drawn to Twenty20 primarily because of the beer and the crash, bang, wallop, probably isn't attuned to this tweak of the calendar. The Oval – capacity 23,500 – is scantily dressed tonight; fewer than 8,000 people are here.

Sussex win the toss, and the familiar pattern of Twenty20 takes shape. In a typically bullish start, which ought to persuade late-comers not to be so dilatory through the turnstiles in future, Chris Nash swats Andre Nel for six to the furthest outpost on the ground – the square-leg boundary from the Pavilion End – despite a rolling effort from Stewart Walters, who dashes the ball out of the air after his foot has crossed the rope. The pace never slackens. Nash cracks his next six off Nel beyond deep mid-on. After only 4 overs of heaving and cutting, Sussex are 53 without loss, and Surrey are in disarray, always scattering fielders towards the spot where the last delivery landed. Even after Nash's partner, Ed Joyce, falls for 15, Sussex continue to roar along from the 2 pound 9 ounce bat of Luke Wright. After Nash hits 40 off 16 balls, an innings which ends when Collins yorks him in the 6th over, Wright takes it as a signal to assume control, which he does with belligerence and good fortune. Fate roots for Wright from his first ball. He paddles a delivery from Nel around the corner and over Collins' head at short fine leg. Collins runs back, fingers grasping for the catch, like a falling man reaching for a line of rope. He juggles with the ball twice before it spills free at his third attempt.

Mark Ramprakash, who makes the hard work of batting look effortless and plays almost every shot with the sweet luxury of time.

Wright is dropped again on 22. Ramprakash watches the ball spear towards him at deep long on and sets his stance to take it at rib-height. He misjudges it. The shot thumps against the hard base of his palm and bounces away. He fumbles for the ball on the floor, as if trying to pick up the loose pieces of a smashed plate. With two missed leg-side stumpings

– the ball either keeping low or ricocheting off Gary Wilson's brown pads below the roll – Wright's life is charmed. To rub it in he comes out of his crease and dispatches Afzaal's slower delivery into the Bedser Stand. The ball flies in a glorious arc and rattles along a row of empty seats, half tipping them forward like invisible fingers depressing the keys of a piano. Wright's half-century arrives in 39 balls. More than once he's scattered the feeding pigeons, which cluster together, like a heap of dirty laundry, on one of the old cut pitches

Surrey constantly rotate the bowling and switch the field without success. By the time Wright is finally out – clean bowled by Chris Schofield after an inelegant lunge – Sussex are already well past 160 with 12 balls of the innings left. Another 20 valuable runs come before Surrey, looking ragged and left to pursue 185, are able to regroup and reply. The contributions of Nash and Wright emphasise the high entertainment level of Twenty20, which makes it churlish to ask whether this is 'real cricket' or not. As George Bernard Shaw said, deliberately accentuating the positive after another of Ellen Terry's overwrought stage performances: 'It must be accepted for what it is and not for what it isn't.'

Of course, village and club cricketers have been playing this cut-down, frenetic version of the game for years, albeit in 16 eight-ball overs designed to combat fading light and maximise pub opening hours. The coarseness of this weekly thrashing exercise was never taken too seriously, and didn't impinge overmuch on the character of the Saturday Leagues. Improvisation, borne out of circumstance in Twenty20 and executed like wild riffs of jazz, has been carried into the County Championship and into Tests. More importantly, Twenty20 has changed attitudes; specifically in determining how many runs can feasibly be scored in a day, a session or an hour in pursuit of a target. But – and it's a substantial one – Twenty20 continues to feel the need for embellishment and the slavish devotion to blaring music, scoreboard displays of the figures 4 or 6 whenever either is scored or the word OUT as soon as a wicket falls. Shakespeare's Globe would never countenance putting LOVE or DEATH in hot flashing neon over the closing acts of *Romeo and Juliet* for an audience unable to the follow the basic plot. Twenty20 has no need for such hokey either. It's as though the cricket itself, however compelling, lacks confidence in itself and feels it can't possibly be sufficient to hold the gaze on its own merits. Every crowded minute has to be filled with noise and dumbed-down distractions – even if the lyrics of 'Howzat', 'Another

One Bites the Dust' or 'Celebrate Good Times' have been played and replayed on a moronic loop until the CD containing them is worn thinner than a communion wafer.

Freud was right when he wrote that our desire is always in excess of the object's capacity to satisfy it, which explains why the ECB is already talking abut expanding next season's Twenty20. Pity the County Championship. Pity the player whose game isn't naturally suited, or can't be squeezed into the tight corset of twenty panicky overs. Cricket's administrators are so enamoured with Twenty20 that the sole purpose seems to be to propagate it everywhere, irrespective of whether any other form of the game wilts in its shadow. But then Freud did add a coda to his thesis on desire: 'Consumption will almost always override common sense.'

The start of the Surrey innings is stagnant water; nothing moves. It takes them 13 balls to get off the mark and 21 to register a boundary. In Twenty20, a maiden over is a collector's item; two in a row is as rare as a Penny Black on an old postcard. It brings a Coliseum-like intolerance to the Oval. In a restless response to timid batting there is loud jeering and the sight of turned-down thumbs. Eventually Newman gets Surrey off the mark, pushing Wright to mid-off for a paltry single. It only brings more jeering. John Arlott used to claim that the cricket played reflected society. What does Twenty20 – and the crowd's disillusionment with Surrey – say about the way we live now? That we demand instant gratification; that we are impatient; that our attention span hovers close to zero; and that we are more aggressive about expressing it.

Whoever wins the final at Edgbaston in August will collect two separate cheques of £40,000 – one for the club, the other for the players – and qualify for the Champions League tournament in India in October. Surrey don't remotely look contenders – even against a side who won just two of twelve matches in the competition last summer. But, after Afzaal is caught at third man off a thick edge, Mark Ramprakash climbs out of the glass hutch beside the advertising boards.

I have been waiting for him all night . . .

In 2006 I saw Ramprakash make his landmark 196 at Worcester – his fifth consecutive 150, an unprecedented feat. It took him to 2,000 runs for the season after only 20 innings, faster than anyone else in history; even Bradman. At thirty-six years old, he finished the summer with 2,211 runs at 105.28, the highest average by an Englishman since Geoffrey Boycott's 102.53 in 1979 and the sixth-highest by anyone since the Championship began. The following season he made 2,026 runs at 101.30. On his behalf in 2008 I experienced what I call 'My J. M. Kilburn moment'. Kilburn once wrote that he felt more anxious for the players, such as Hobbs or Woolley, than he supposed the players felt for themselves. 'Early dismissal could not lessen them in esteem in my eyes,' he wrote, 'but until they were established at the crease I was fearful lest some accident of cricket should deprive me of the thrill of their splendour, of a basking in their authority.' On the first Saturday in August – and at Headingley too – I knew exactly what Kilburn meant. Ramprakash was on ninety-nine first-class hundreds, close enough to reach out and touch his century of centuries on the ground where he'd scored his first nineteen years earlier. I felt nervous for Ramprakash. I also felt nervous for myself. I wanted the kudos of saying 'I was there.'

I expected to be jostling for a space after lunch on the final day. The cloud was high, the sun barging through it, and there was just a mild breeze, which scarcely ruffled the outfield. A near-perfect afternoon. I arrived at Headingley and easily found a prime seat in the upper tier of the rickety Football Stand. There were barely 1,200 of us there, a tight, exclusive band who appreciated the significance of what Ramprakash was about to do. Whenever I'd seen him – especially at Worcester – Ramprakash had been princely. It is hard work to make batting look effortless, but he managed it by following, consciously or not, Ranji's three simple precepts of batting: 'Find out where the ball is. Go there. Hit it.' Every stroke was quick with life and struck with the sweet luxury of time. The strokes themselves were expressive in a wristily fluid way, the backlift looping and lengthening. It was as though Ramprakash was weightless when he reached the ball. There is pleasure even in something as mundane and ostensibly routine as his forward defence – a model of assurance and orthodoxy, the bat brought alongside the pad with such exquisite timing that it strikes the middle as assuredly as a clock strikes noon. There is always just a thin crack of light between pad and bat, and the delivery is always pushed straight down the pitch.

At Headingley, Ramprakash was circumspect, aware not only of his own destiny and his recent indifferent form – ten innings without a fifty – but also the balance of the match. Surrey were close to defeat – 210 behind – and he came out of the pavilion after only the seventh ball of the morning. Ramprakash is particular about his bats, always fussing over the grip and string on the handle, the shape of the toe, the pick up. After cracking his favourite, a gift from Shane Warne which he'd used during the previous, prolific two summers, he'd discarded four more before settling on a fifth, filched from Scott Newman. Early on Ramprakash used it to gather his runs almost by stealth, surreptitiously nudging ones and twos, before becoming freer and less inhibited. The scoreboard moved on. He went past 50 and into the 60s, 70s and eventually the 90s until only one scoring shot separated him from being yoked for ever to Grace and Hobbs, Boycott and Bradman. At 4.12 p.m. the sky was clear, as though wanting to canopy him in vivid blue for the occasion. Ramprakash, who had waited and waited again for the wayward delivery, eventually got one from the Kirkstall Lane End. The spinner, David Wainwright, tried too hard to push the ball through and instead dropped it short and wide of off stump. Like every master batsman, Ramprakash was able to judge where it would land in the very moment it slipped from Wainwright's fingers. For he was already smoothly rocking back and preparing to cut the ball past point well before it pitched. As soon as it left the bat, the relief around the ground was tangible – as though a long-held breath had been let out. Wainwright turned his back and kicked the turf, sending up an ankle-high puff of dust. Ramprakash swivelled too, tearing off his helmet and facing the dressing rooms with his arms aloft. Fittingly, his partner was Newman, who had seen his borrowed bat make history in Ramprakash's hands. No one is ever likely to follow him. He became the twenty-fifth batsman – and probably the last – to reach 100 hundreds. With central contracts, and first-class innings limited to the mid-twenties at most, someone Bradmanesque will have to appear to defy the daunting mathematics. It is hardly likely.

Ramprakash arrives at beginning of the 4th over, and Surrey are already impossibly behind the rate. He manages to work the ball away and finds the boundary once. Everything about him looks classy and convincing: the comfortable stance, the way he lets the ball come to him and the execution of the shot. With Newman, he picks 22 off an over from Robin Martin-Jenkins. But Surrey's earlier batting was chained down for too long, and it has left them too much catching up to do. Ramprakash does what he can – each shot carefully thought out – until he throws his bat in desperation at a half-tracker from Michael Yardy, who bowls him. He has made 23 off 13 balls. Two deliveries later Newman, on 38, spoons a catch to Wright off Yardy too. The innings never finds momentum after their partnership of 63 in 5 overs is split. Surrey bank on one profitable over to get them near Sussex's total. It never arrives. In fact, it is a race to see whether Surrey or the sun, gradually sinking in a blaze of red behind the Vauxhall End, vanishes first. Even Walters' 34 off 20 balls can't prevent them running out of energy on 163. From the tannoy blares a final chorus of 'Another One Bites the Dust', and I file home with its lyrics buzzing in my head.

Rattigan would be forced to concede that Twenty20 fulfils one of Chekhov's fundamental rules about staging drama. If the audience sees a gun loaded in the first act, said Chekhov, then it has to be fired by the close of the third. The Twenty20 Cup unquestionably fires its gun. There is no false promise of action. Nothing blurred about its end. It rips along, compact and frenetic; as far removed as it is possible to get from Rattigan's definition of cricket. I doubt he'd approve of the Oval's £2.5 million floodlights either. These are switched on for the first time, like a new, battery-powered toy just taken out of its box. The night sky becomes inky, dissolving the flats, the Telecom Tower and St Stephen's Tower from distinct, hard-edged shapes into faint outlines. In contrast, the intricate geometry of the gasometer – with its crisscross web of slide-rule squares and rectangles and diamonds – becomes sharper, as though the gloom draws it closer to the ground. A curious trick of the eye in half-light, it seems taller and wider, as if freed from constraints of scale. I never thought I'd describe the gasometer as handsome. But I think of it that way now – a beautiful piece of engineering. Near the end of his life, the Poet Laureate John Masefield wrote 'Eighty-Five to Win' about an event which took place six years before he was born: the 1882 Test between England and Australia at the Oval. These are its opening lines:

> We have the game, we have The Oval
> And still the gas-works mark the gas-works end

So it did, and does; and may it always. Surely even Rattigan would agree about that.

Umpires: N. L. Bainton, N. G. B. Cooks
Toss: Sussex

Sussex innings

C. D. Nash	b Collins		40
E. C. Joyce	c Schofield	b Elliott	15
L. J. Wright	b Schofield		58
D. R. Smith	c Elliott	b Collins	0
M. H. Yardy*	c Spriegel	b Schofield	15
R. J. Hamilton-Brown	c Elliott	b Spriegel	11
Yasir Arafat	run out		6
B. C. Brown†	lbw	b Nel	7
R. S. C. Martin-Jenkins	run out		0
W. A. T. Beer	not out		16
R. J. Kirtley	not out		2
Extras	(2lb, 8nb, 4w)		14
Total	(9 wickets, 20 overs)		**184**

Fall of wickets: 1-53, 2-66, 3-66, 4-108, 5-139, 6-148, 7-164, 8-164, 9-168

Surrey bowling	O	M	R	W
Collins	4	0	45	2
Nel	4	0	35	1
Elliott	4	0	35	1
Schofield	4	0	32	2
Spriegel	3	0	22	1
Afzaal	1	0	13	0

Surrey innings

S. A. Newman	c Wright	b Yardy	38
U. Afzaal*	c Martin-Jenkins	b Kirtley	2
M. R. Ramprakash	b Yardy		23
J. G. E. Benning	b Beer		6
S. J. Walters	b Smith		34
M. N. W. Spriegel	b Yardy		3
C. P. Schofield	c Yardy	b Yasir Arafat	13
G. D. Elliott	c Yardy	b Wright	15
G. C. Wilson†	not out		8
A. Nel	c Hamilton-Brown	b Yasir Arafat	7
Did not bat: P. T. Collins			
Extras	(1b, 3lb, 10w)		14
Total	(9 wickets)		**163**

Fall of wickets: 1-8, 2-71, 3-72, 4-81, 5-108, 6-125, 7-147, 8-149, 9-163

Sussex bowling	O	M	R	W
Wright	4	1	18	1
Yasir Arafat	4	1	26	2
Kirtley	2	0	26	1
Martin-Jenkins	2	0	29	0
Yardy	4	0	21	3
Beer	1	0	8	1
Hamilton-Brown	1	0	15	0
Smith	2	0	16	1

Result: Sussex won by 21 runs

Man of the match: L. J. Wright

CHAPTER SIX

THE UNBELIEVABLE
LIGHTNESS OF FIELDING

W. G. Grace's Last Test, and the team – and umpires – with whom he shared the moment. Back row, from left: R. G. Barlow (umpire), T. W. Hayward, G. H. Hirst, W. Gunn, J. T. Hearne (12th man), W. Storer, W. Brockwell, V. A. Titchmarsh (umpire). Front row, from left: C. B. Fry, K. S. Ranjitsinhji, W. G. Grace, F. S. Jackson. Seated on floor: W. Rhodes, J. T. Tyldesley.

Trent Bridge: World Cup Twenty20: Sri Lanka v. West Indies, 10 June

He sits in the centre of the photograph in a striped dark blazer and a hooped MCC cap. A white handkerchief, folded into an imperfect point, is tucked into the blazer pocket. His legs are crossed at the ankles, and his loosely clenched left hand rests on his thigh. The eye is immediately drawn to his bulk, and the jagged edge of his long, square-cut beard, which hangs like a grey waterfall over his plump belly. It's an informal looking picture, which seems haphazardly arranged and impatiently taken, like a souvenir snap at a birthday party. It's as though the thirteen men clustered around the dominant, central figure were just told to slip into whichever pose felt most comfortable to them. If the photographer had known he was recording a piece of cricket's history, he would surely have given more thought and care to his composition, rather like a court artist arranging his blue-blooded sitters. But he's placed this Victorian team in shadow, and framed them against an untidy, distracting background – a curve of pillars and low pitched roofs – as though the job was a chore which he wanted to finish quickly.

What the camera captures is W. G. Grace before his final Test against Australia. The photograph is dated 1899. It was taken 110 years ago. The caption, embossed in bold capital italics, reads simply: 'The England XI at Nottingham'. Grace and his players were planted in front of the Hound Road Stand beside the Trent Bridge pavilion. Today, from its top tier, I peer over the rail at the exact spot where Grace sat between K. S. Ranjitsinhji, arms folded and a smile tracing his thin lips, and F. S. Jackson, with his cap slightly askew. A callow Wilfred Rhodes appropriately sits at Grace's feet. Rhodes, already baggy eyed, has a narrow-jawed face with a long blade of a nose and pointy chin. He is twenty-one and about to make his debut. He'll play his last match for England thirty-one years later in the West Indies – the only player older than Grace to appear in a Test.

No one anticipated that Trent Bridge would be Grace's farewell, or dared suggest it too strenuously in advance. He made 28 runs in the first innings and 1 in the second. He didn't take a wicket from 22 overs. In Australia's second innings he failed to bend his broad, belted back supply enough to take a low catch at point to dismiss Clem Hill, who went on to make 80. The Trent Bridge crowd began barracking him. Not even, according to *Wisden*, a 'brilliant' catch to eventually get rid of Hill – almost identical to the chance he missed – entirely pacified the critics, who wrote him off as hideously overweight and in decline. In the field Grace was as stiff as a walking stick. If the ball went past him, he was unable to run after it. He moved in the slow, laborious turning circle of a state liner. England were only saved from defeat against Australia by Ranjitsinhji's composed 93 not out, an innings based around his silky driving. Afterwards Grace was forlorn about the inadequacy of his performance. Ailing and achy, he could no longer disguise, or deny to himself, the fact he was a decade (and in some cases two decades) older than the rest of the team. With him, its average age was nearly thirty-four. Without him, it fell to twenty-eight. Travelling home on the train with Jackson, Grace said sorrowfully: 'It's all over, Jacker; I shan't play again.' When he made the confession, he was fifty years and 320 days old. It was still self-sacrifice, rather than a polite tap on the shoulder, that ended Grace's Test career. At the next selection meeting he had to force his withdrawal on Lord Hawke and C. B. Fry, who believed Grace's blunt question to him – 'Do you think that Archie MacLaren ought to play in the next Test match?' – meant his own axing was being proposed instead. Grace had made 22 Test appearances, scored 1,098 runs and taken 9 wickets. As captain in 18 of those Tests, he'd won 11, lost 4 and drawn 3. The more important factor is what he represented. Grace was so established in the England team that no one – and especially those who played with him – ever conceived the possibility of starting a Test without him. If Grace hadn't decided to drop himself – appalling Lord Hawke in the process – he could almost have carried on until his bones became brittle and snapped. In tribute, Ranjitsinhji thought Grace turned cricket from 'an accomplishment into a science'. But time's devouring hand always does its work, and Grace accepted it and decided to walk (something he never did when getting a thin edge) before being shoved or stabbed in the back. He was like an abdicating king.

These melancholic thoughts of Grace and his Trent Bridge goodbye start rolling through my mind because it offers proof of the impermanence of everything. Those who were used to seeing Grace's name on the England scorecard soon became used to not seeing it. Where Grace once walked others walked instead. And – just as every turn of extreme change is in the end absorbed and blithely accepted – England and the game got along fine without him. An hour before the start of Match 11 in the

Twenty20 World Cup I'm thinking about Grace because I'm also thinking about the future of Tests. And I'm specifically thinking about whether we'll eventually be talking about them in the past tense in the way that the late Victorians and early Edwardians spoke about Grace. Might we have to accept that Tests will one day slip away with a similarly brief and regretful 'It's all over'?

The question became relevant again after the West Indies captain Chris Gayle claimed it 'wouldn't be so sad' if Test cricket died and was quietly buried. He much preferred Twenty20, he added, and didn't 'see' himself in Tests 'much longer'. As soon as his thoughts were in cold type Gayle was castigated for his candour; odd, bearing in mind journalists frequently complain that sportsmen, so finely tutored in the anodyne art of PR, say absolutely nothing worth writing down, let alone preserving, during interviews. Asked for his opinion, Gayle gave it – treating the question the way he'd treat a long-hop. Afterwards, as the small earthquake he caused began to settle, he relied on the unoriginal defence of misquotation and misrepresentation, which no one believed. Gayle merely articulated in public what a lot of his contemporaries think in private. His view carried the sting of sounding like a prophesy because he shared it before the opening day of the First Test at Durham, which barely 5,000 turned up to see – the lowest crowd in the modern era. Stewards chattered amongst themselves. Scorecard and programme sellers were all but redundant. This had more to do with circumstance than apathy. The ticket touts were never going to make a killing during dark, showery, chilly early May at England's most northerly ground. The ECB arranged the series for financial reasons. And for financial reasons the customer stayed away.

It is Tests such as England v. West Indies in Durham which give credence and momentum to Gayle's argument. Gayle nonetheless worked himself into a corner in expressing it. No matter where he goes now his words are going to rattle behind him, like a tin can tied to a dog's tail. No one will ever let him forget them. A twenty-first-century Grace would have looked at Gayle's predicament sympathetically but handled things more astutely. He was clever in business, raking in £100 per match (nearly £5,000 at today's rates) to take his United South XI on tour in the late 1800s. Appreciating his value at the gate, he negotiated personal 'appearance fees' for other matches. He also charged his expenses at the first-class rate; no roughing it for him in second-class carriages or second-class hotels. He knew his worth and made a comfortable, though not extravagant, living from the game. He was a showman and a sham-amateur, and a peripatetic mercenary when it suited him to be so. As a bat for hire, he would have been off to the Indian Premier League at the drop of a white five-pound note. If asked, though, Grace would have pretended that Tests were the primary form of the game and inviolate. To suggest otherwise was fatuous, he'd no doubt have said, like questioning whether a church ought to be the primary place of worship. And then he'd have gone off for lunch with his agent and his accountant. Gayle could learn something from him.

Already Twenty20 is barging in on every summer like an exasperating holiday guest; not only demanding the best room in the house, but also insisting that everything is run to fit around its whims and for its benefit alone. To accommodate the domestic Twenty20, the County Championship came to a juddering halt, like a conversation interrupted in mid-sentence. Even though the Championship is back now, the season's focus is entirely on the World Cup. There is no escaping it. Nor is there any escaping, either, the success of the tournament. The steely sustained combat of Tests generates a visceral, wrenching tension. But this World Cup creates something markedly different and appealing. There is ebullience about it – on every face, from every tongue, in every pair of gesticulating hands. At Tests there are flags and banners, horns and shrill whistles, and fancy dress too. But the presence of them during the World Cup is celebratory, like the preparation for a fiesta. The need is for pure entertainment rather than to witness a hard, meaningful contest. It is noticeable how quickly Twenty20 crowds shuffle and become impatient if a few balls, let alone an entire over, go by without the adrenalin shot of a boundary or a wicket to stoke up and constantly hold the attention. For there is a devotion only to self-enjoyment; and the occasion is nearly always more important than the game itself. It is evident on the green double-decker bus, with its illuminated 'Cricket' sign, which sways like a rocking boat past the Gothic red brick of Nottingham's railway station and over the brown Trent, which sits low on the embankment steps. Some passengers wear jester's hats with bells. Others wrap a flag around them like a cape or are dressed in replica shirts. One West Indian is conspicuous, as though he's a figure from a different era. He is in his late sixties and immaculate in a grey suit, checked shirt and striped tie. His brogues are highly polished. He has a pale-blue peaked ruff cap and black overcoat that trails below the knee. He is carrying both a rolled-up umbrella with an ivory handle and a cane in a bright paisley pattern. On the second, middle and little fingers of his right hand are thick, glittering silver rings. He has a greying Elizabethan beard and puts an unlit, heavy-bowled pipe in his mouth. 'Comin' to see Gayle bat,' he says. 'How many sixes for him today?' His remark underscores both the appeal of Twenty20 and the perception of Gayle as its chief representative. Those with tickets not only demand, but also expect – almost as a base entitlement of the condition of sale – that the white ball will shrink into a dot as it is clouted into the clouds. Gayle is seen as the batsman most likely to do it. Against Australia at the Oval four days ago he eviscerated the bowling on his way to 88 off 50 balls, which included six fours and six sixes.

The question about the number of boundaries he'll hit today is answered at the toss. Gayle isn't playing. He is resting a bruised leg. Wearing an over-large pair of sunglasses with daffodil-yellow frames, which are actually designer chic but look tacky enough to have been bought cheaply in a seaside arcade, Gayle slouches in the dug-out with his arms folded. His vice captain, Denesh Ramdin, calls correctly and decides to chase a target rather than set one.

Sri Lanka's openers Sanath Jayasuriya and Tillakaratne Dilshan offer ample compensation for Gayle's absence. Jayasuriya will be forty at the end of the month. His international career began in the 1980s. So he is an old dog – with fourteen Test hundreds – who has learned the new tricks of Twenty20. To counter the 'nip' of the quicker bowlers – Dwayne Bravo, Fidel Edwards and Jerome Taylor – Jayasuriya takes guard inside the crease to give himself a millisecond longer to judge the length and pace of the ball. He attacks it with a combination of barbarity and grace. The left-hander goes through the full gamut of shots – the drive through cover and extra cover, the nudge off his legs, the venomous pull and cross-batted crack to the far corners of Trent Bridge. There is one delicate late cut that Denis Compton would have been proud to play in 1947. Soon the West Indies are under pressure and miserably ragged. The ball slips through nervous fingers. Even returns to Ramdin are waywardly sloppy. What follows is panic. The West Indies race around, as though carrying buckets of water in a futile attempt to put out a fire. Sri Lanka are 66 without loss after 6 overs, and 105 by the tenth. Jayasuriya hits the ninetieth and ninety-first sixes of the World Cup off Edwards, who is swiped to the deep-square-leg boundary in an ill-disciplined over that costs 17 runs. Jayasuriya is bearing down on a century when he tries to be too extravagant against the medium pacer Lendl Simmons. He misses a delivery which has nothing going for it apart from middle-stump accuracy and is leg before for 81 off only 47 balls.

Dilshan, who has been unselfishly subservient, begins to move the score along. He incorporates his signature shot of the paddle scoop into his expanding repertoire. When Kieron Pollard drops the ball short, and two feet outside off stump, Dilshan strides sideways, tucks himself up and turns away before lifting the delivery high over himself and Ramdin to the boundary with the full face of the blade. Requiring bravery as much as impeccable timing – for minor misjudgements risk Dilshan deflecting the ball into his own face – the shot has become known as 'the starfish' on the basis that any batsman needs to be almost brainless to attempt it. Dilshan's 50 comes off 36 balls. He makes 74 before, like Jayasuriya, he overstretches himself and is caught at long leg.

When it began no one really knew how to play Twenty20. The tactics were rudimentary. What constituted a decent score? Where should the field be set? At first captains arranged fielders with apparent randomness. Initial strategies were based on seam, assuming spinners would be gorged. This went on until someone realised one of the basic principles of physics – taking pace off the ball reduces the odds of being able to return it with pace. Even the fast bowlers have more profitably used the slow bouncer, the scrambled seam and the low full toss, which makes it difficult to get under the delivery. In return the batsmen have improvised and each new shot has looked idiosyncratic and slightly idiotic until overuse has made them familiar. Think of the reverse sweep – that vertical inside-out swing. Think of the 'baseball shot' – the wide-chested bash to the leg side. Think of Dilshan's 'starfish' in which, legs aside, like someone trying to block a pig in a passage, he lets the bottom hand slip to the base of the handle and top of the splice.

A combination of all these strokes and more take Sri Lanka to a formidable 192-5.

Without Gayle, the responsibility for competing with Sri Lanka's total is shared between the top order of Simmons, Andre Fletcher, Xavier Marshall, Shivnarine Chanderpaul and Ramnaresh Sarwan. Simmons sets off at a decent pelt; Fletcher isn't far behind him. When Lasith Malinga, bowling from the Radcliffe Road End, gives him sufficient arm room to swing properly, Fletcher dispatches him into the William Clarke Stand. Malinga brushes his hand through his curly, blond-dyed hair and stomps off to calculate his revenge. Even without the provocation of being belted for six, Malinga is mean-looking: heavy stubble, lips smeared with sun block, like war paint, and a wide nose spread across a flattish face, as if peering at you while pressing his features against a sheet of glass. He has heavy brows and a gold piercing over the corner of his left eye. His slingy, catapult action, which is difficult to pick, seems to be getting lower; so low as to be almost round-arm. When he hurls himself into it, you feel he might rip and shred his shoulder muscles with the effort. His deliveries are not just outstandingly fast, they also have a habit of vanishing against the camouflage of the umpire's coat pocket before reappearing a second before a stroke is needed to prevent either the stumps being flattened or

Lasith Malinga – lips smeared with sunblock, which he wears like war paint, proves too destructive and too wily for the West Indies.

the flesh being struck. He also slips easily through gear changes. So far in this over he's bowled at speeds of 89.5 mph, 85.6 mph and 91.7 mph. The ball to remove Fletcher is different. Malinga disguises it the way a card sharp hides the Queen in Find the Lady. It is slow enough – 74.5 mph – to persuade Fletcher to play through the shot before the ball has even reached him. The delivery almost floats past the glassy-eyed opener before tearing out his leg stump. Malinga celebrates as though he's just taken Fletcher's head as a mounted trophy.

Malinga is a rarity. There is a plain orthodoxy about most of today's bowling actions. One is almost indistinguishable from the other. Every bowler seems to deliver the ball in exactly same way, as if there's a computer programme that is downloaded into the brain to guide leg and arm in a single, uniform style. It's another sign of over-coaching. Any twitch or tic, which deviates from the gospel of the coach's manual, is soon worn off, stripped down or smoothed away. Nothing even mildly eccentric survives for long. It wasn't always like this. I remember Middlesex's John Price, who approached the crease from a curved run often so pronounced that its arc began at cover point (I exaggerate only slightly). Or Geoff Arnold, who took short, trotting steps like a gymkhana pony. Or Mike Procter, who bowled off the wrong foot. Or Tony Greig, who came in with short, jerky arm movements that resembled a robotic dance. Or Derek Underwood, who drew his arm back in fluent stages, like the bolting and cocking of a rifle. For me, the most striking of all was a yeoman bowler called Barry Stead, whom I watched on this very ground. He ran in with manic energy and hurled himself beside the stumps, as if he might actually catch the ball after releasing it. Like Malinga, he stood out by being different.

No one began going to Twenty20 matches for the pleasure of seeing someone bowl. Malinga, and Sri Lanka's spinners, Ajantha Mendis and Muttiah Muralitharan, are exceptions. With his three gold chains – the most prominent is a crucifix, which sways outside his shirt – and his right hand taped across the knuckles, the lanky Mendis 'flicks' the ball, holding it between thumb, forefinger and middle finger in the style of Jack Iverson, the original 'Mystery Spinner' of the 1950s. Mendis bowls the 'Carrom Ball', so titled because the propulsion required to deliver it resembles the flicking action of the Asian tabletop game Carrom. What was once said of Iverson applies equally to Mendis. 'What Jack had conceived was a delivery so unusual that it was not even clear what to call it,' wrote Iverson's biographer, Gideon Haigh. 'But even if you resolved what to call it, there was still the matter of playing it . . .' Like Iverson, Mendis is able to disguise the spin because the flick can be achieved almost imperceptibly. In one example, Xavier Marshall is confused after what he reads as an off spinner turns briskly away from leg. Already committed to the shot, he goes right as the ball travels left. He looks like a dancer who's taken the wrong step and found himself at the opposite end of the ballroom from his partner. And when Mendis, bowling tight to the stumps, isn't bewitching the West Indians, he leaves the job to Muralitharan and the doosra.

Malinga blows on the ball, as if giving an air kiss. Mendis crosses himself before each delivery. As he embarks on his run of ten short strides, Muralitharan licks his fingers, as if he's about to try to turn the stuck-down pages of a book. From around the wicket, the ball buzzes and cuts across the right-handers like a circular saw. He has Simmons, who makes 29, caught at first slip by Jayawardene and leaks only 21 runs from 4 masterful overs at the Pavilion End. Frankly, I'd pay to watch Mendis and Muralitharan bowl against a dustbin in the car park.

The forecast in the morning was dire. 'And you'll be fortunate to see any cricket at Trent Bridge today,' said the weather man in a pink shirt and matching swirled tie. He stood in front of a map dotted with Bible-black clouds; and one of them seemed to be directly above Trent Bridge. So, of course, the sun burns for the first three hours. Umbrellas are tucked under seats and raincoats folded into bulbous rucksacks. Only right at the end does the cloud on the weather man's map match the cloud in the sky and bring squally rain drifting in from behind the pavilion. West Indies can scarcely use it as an excuse. Sri Lanka find the conditions more irksome – forever drying the wet ball with blue hand towels – and yet never let the game off the leash. The rate climbs from 9.65 to 11.2 and finally on to an unattainable 14.4. The match bucks away from the West Indies. Their innings is an Escher-like staircase; it leads nowhere.

Chanderpaul arrives with his chest-on stance, which makes nonsense of Pelham Warner's prewar coaching claim that cricket would always be a 'sideways' game. Never at ease, he gets a thin inside edge on an ugly chop against Mendis and is bowled for only a single. Marshall falls to Mendis too. At 73 for four, the West Indies are surrendering meekly. Even though Sri Lanka's radar sometimes goes awry – their attack generously gifts the West Indies 17 wides – only Dwayne Bravo ever looks capable of giving them a fright. On this form, he ought to be batting ahead of the more circumspect Chanderpaul and the less flashy Sarwan. He belts a half-century off 38 balls before holing out at deep mid-off. The fight is already lost anyway. West Indies lose by 15 runs. A fan in front of me, who is wearing a pair of Elvis sunglasses and false Elvis sideburns, waves a Sri Lankan flag as huge as a bedspread.

A week before going to Trent Bridge I caught some film of Tests from the 1950s and early 1960s. Fred Trueman was bowling. Whenever I think of Trueman, I always see him in black-and-white because he is integral to TV's monochrome sporting era. There's the inky flop of hair, which he pushes away from his brow with his right hand before swapping the ball into it from his left. And there's the streak of bleached light, like a stab of lightning, as the agile turn of his body points him smoothly towards the crease at the end of his long run. Trueman used to half-joke that he always 'looked slower in black and white'. The Test I saw on an old strip of film looked a lot slower. In particular the fielders moved heavily – even between overs – as if trying to walk underwater. There was no dervish movement. Len Hutton used to say that in his day fielding practice consisted of someone throwing the ball in the air to see if anyone caught it. It was acceptable for the fielder to merely push out a hand – as casually as flagging down a lift – as the ball darted past him. Indeed, it was taken for granted that bones and joints wouldn't withstand the jarring of elaborate gymnastics and the sinews wouldn't stretch far enough to reach a wide ball. A so-called 'chase' to the boundary in the era of Hutton and Trueman was rather like watching a tortoise on a lettuce hunt.

Fielding athleticism was already high in the modern game without the impetus of Twenty20. With it, nonetheless, the acrobatics are sharper still and the superlatives about catches and lunging stops are nearly all spent. Already this season, in the domestic competition, Lancashire's Steven Croft has taken a catch in front of the rope at Old Trafford, which struck Michael Vaughan dumb in its audacity. Vaughan middled a cross-batted shot that travelled with the force of a military shell towards the pavilion. Croft dived upwards and to his left to take a catch with his right hand as he landed on his back. Vaughan's mouth fell into an oval of stupefaction at what he'd witnessed. He tucked his bat underneath his arm and walked off wearing the expression of someone who's just been flimflammed. If these moments were rare, like a comet burning itself out, each one could be regarded as a glorious fluke. But fielding is so intense and athletic now that no shot is ever out of range unless it goes straight from the sweet spot of the bat and into Row Z. The proof of it arrived during the West Indies innings.

An over or two can make a reputation in Twenty20. But only one delivery is needed to lock Angelo Mathews into the minds of everyone who saw what he did at Trent Bridge. For me, it was the defining moment, overshadowing Jayasuriya and Dilshan, Mendis, Muralitharan and Malinga. I doubt if I'll witness a more extraordinary act this summer or the next; or perhaps ever again.

It happened – in the 17th over – like this.

Usually the most classical of batsmen, Sarwan launches himself in desperation – with bat and slender body – at a ball from Mendis pitching near his leg stump. It flies off the bat, and every pair of eyes in the ground follows its steeply arching trajectory. The ball is heading towards long on. Bells are ready to be rung, and whistles furiously blown; flags and cardboard signs signalling six are about to be waved. Standing beneath Sarwan's shot on the boundary is the twenty-two-year-old Mathews. You can judge the likelihood of a fielder taking a high catch like this one purely from the set of his body and the look on his face. Some fielders, already mentally resigned to dropping the chance, squirm and half look away from it, as if the ball is a falling piano. Others never let it out of their sight. Their feet are solidly planted; their shoulders are slightly hunched; their hands are together. From the moment Sarwan makes the stroke – and Mathews realises it his heading his way – the fielder is in control. He leaps into the air to intercept the ball. The bullet-speed of the shot pushes him backwards. Falling over, Mathews loses his grip on it but somehow – through quick thought and dextrous, fast hands – he manages to throw the ball up and behind him. It is about to drop from the air and land two yards behind the rope. Mathews leaps back and across, his gaze fixed rigidly on the spinning, falling ball. He dives to his right, and his cap tumbles off his head. This dive is forceful enough for self-propelled flight. He takes off horizontally. He's three feet into the air and at full stretch. It's like watching a cat; Macavity breaking gravity and defying Newton's Law. Mathews is able to momentarily hang, as if suspended from a huge invisible web. From this impossible position, he gets the right hand to the ball and palms it back over the boundary. The umpires give Sarwan three instead of six – all run. Mathews hits the ground and, exactly like a cat again, immediately bounces off it, as though the turf were a sprung mattress.

The consequence of what Mathews has done – in terms of the runs he's saved – is immediately less important than the circus trick he's just performed. There's a silence, as if we've seen the first public demonstration of human levitation. Mathews has done it, too, less than twenty feet from the place where W. G. Grace posed for his last photograph in an England team and almost directly below where I'm sitting.

I think about a prize-giver who once in a speech consoled all those who finished second to Grace in the heyday of his youth. 'Never mind,' he said, 'he'll grow old and stiff someday.' And inevitably he did, which is why he missed his first chance to catch Clem Hill.

But Mathews?

To those, like me, who saw him at Trent Bridge, he'll never grow old and stiff. He'll be the man with wings who once demonstrated the unbelievable lightness of fielding and left us speechless because of it.

Umpires: B. F. Bowden, S. J. A. Taufel
Toss: West Indies

Sri Lanka innings

T. M. Dilshan	c Benn	b Simmons	74
S. T. Jayasuriya	lbw	b Simmons	81
K. C. Sangakkara*†	c Fletcher	b Simmons	5
D. P. M. D. Jayawardene	c Ramdin	b Simmons	4
J. Murbarak	not out		8
L. P. C. Silva	c Ramdin	b Taylor	7
A. D. Mathews	not out		3
Did not bat: B. A. W. Mendis, I. Udana, M. Muralitharan, S. L. Malinga			
Extras	(5lb, 1nb, 4w)		10
Total	(5 wickets)		**192**

Fall of wickets: 1-124, 2-147, 3-168, 4-172

West Indies bowling	O	M	R	W
Taylor	4	0	32	1
Edwards	2	0	37	0
Bravo	4	0	29	0
Benn	4	0	25	0
Pollard	3	0	45	0
Simmons	3	0	19	4

West Indies innings

L. M. P. Simmons	c Jayawardene	b Muralitharan	29
A. D. S. Fletcher	b Malinga		13
X. M. Marshall	c Silva	b Mendis	14
S. Chanderpaul	b Mendis		1
R. R. Sarwan	not out		28
D. J. Bravo	c Mubarak	b Malinga	51
K. A. Pollard	not out		19
Did not bat: D. Ramdin*†, J. E. Taylor, S. J. Benn, F. H. Edwards			
Extras	(4lb, 1nb, 17w)		22
Total	(5 wickets)		**177**

Fall of wickets: 1-38, 2-70, 3-71, 4-73, 5-150

Sri Lanka bowling	O	M	R	W
Jayasuriya	3	0	34	0
Malinga	4	0	45	2
Udana	4	0	36	0
Mendis	4	0	25	2
Muralitharan	4	0	21	1
Mathews	1	0	12	0

Result: Sri Lanka won by 15 runs

Man of the match: S. T. Jayasuriya

CHAPTER SEVEN

YES, I'LL REMEMBER AIGBURTH

Like a star glimmering out – but splendid in its dying –
Andrew Flintoff's innings for Lancashire against Hampshire ends all too soon.

Liverpool: LV County Championship:
Lancashire v. Hampshire, 17–20 June

For the past two and a half months one face has adorned the billboards and the newspaper advertising ahead of the Ashes series. Turn a corner, and it stares at you from the roadside. Turn a page, and it stares at you from the very foot of it in a strip of anchored photographs. Andrew Flintoff is always exultant – head tilted back and face contorted into the bellicose scream of an appeal. There are several variations on the same theme. In celebration, Flintoff's arms are aloft or outstretched with fists clenched or fingers spread, as if he's waiting to be embraced. His blond hair is shaved, which accentuates the roundness of his face and the narrowness of the eyes. His shirt is short-sleeved, which emphasises the muscular circumference of his biceps and forearms. And his pose is confident and conquering, which stresses his overall size and the strength of him. The only thing missing to identify Flintoff as England's saviour is a halo of natural light.

In these pictures the most striking thing of all about Flintoff is his hands: wide hard palms, square as a labourer's, rather than fluted, across the wrist. His fingers are thick enough to knock you off balance with a short prod in the chest. The ball almost vanishes into these cupped hands, as if it's been dropped down a well. In these enormous hands, too, the rubber-gripped handle of the bat becomes the size of a 2B pencil. Each image is from 2005: Flintoff's summer and Flintoff's Ashes. It's as if no one else mattered back then, or even had a photograph taken of them. Apart from the mild charge that it lacks original thought, there's nothing wrong with such base marketing: the emotional and nostalgic tug of one series – and its seminal, poster figure – used to promote the next. But there is something deeper attached to this concentration on Flintoff. It stems from the genuine fondness he generates off the field as well as on it. Even those who have never seen him play are well aware of what he does, and there is a live connection between them. The public relates to his blokey charm more naturally than it engages, for example, with the steely core and precocity of England's other alpha male, Kevin Pietersen. In the era of Victorian cricket, the signs on the gate used to read: 'Admission 3d. If Dr W. G. Grace plays, admission 6d'. Among England's players only Pietersen could legitimately inspire the same move today and expect the increase to be willingly paid. But, through manner and mannerisms, he seems more distant and detached than Flintoff; more clinical in what he does, and coldly imperious about it too. He is hard to love for himself alone. Self-belief and the fearsome pursuit of perfection is the rocket fuel propelling Pietersen on. But because of it he often comes across as cocky and bristly aloof. Even in Tests Pietersen gives the impression that he's already overgrown the space he is standing in – like Alice filling the room in John Tenniel's drawing of her – and can't wait to escape its suffocating confinement. There's also the *High Noon* swagger, the icy glare and the slight curl of the top lip, which reveals the upper teeth. Say a wrong word to Pietersen, and I've often thought the result would be like striking a match next to leaking gas. There's the inescapable sense, too, that he's perpetually checking himself in a mirror.

Flintoff doesn't seem to care much about appearances purely for appearance's sake, which is where a lot of his appeal lies. The rest comes from an ostensibly folksy ordinariness and an uncomplicated, open charm, such as the aw' shucks grin and the matey slap on the back. He doesn't act as though he's the cat's miaow, and everyone has to know and accept it. There's consequently empathy between Flintoff and those who admire and follow him – even only tangentially. They are also brightly appreciative of what he does; even though he hasn't done much recently. To them, he's Freddie or Fred, as if either he's a good friend or a filial bond exists. It's a cliché, but an apt one, that Flintoff passes the pub test. You want to buy him a drink and share his company. You know he'd stand his round too.

Wisden has tapped into Flintoff too this summer. He is on its comforting yellow dustcover again as an emblem of what's to come against Australia. He is caught at the impressively smooth mid-point of his bowling follow-through. The right boot is about to land and shake the ground beneath it. There is just one problem. By the time the Almanac went to the printer's and was then dropped by the tonne into bookstores, Flintoff wasn't actually bowling at all. Medical bulletins, rather than bowling figures, have lately filled out his newspaper cuttings file: from hernia operations to side strains, from a pulled groin to a broken foot, from a hip injury to back and shoulder trouble. The surgeons have come to know his body the way a cartographer knows the terrain he is mapping out. Flintoff has spent a good deal of his time walking on crutches. His whole career has been played out in brief instalments. You can only wonder at the mauled condition of his 18 stone, thirty-one-year-old body by now. Every muscle twitch of Flintoff's rehabilitation from this latest injury – the torn cartilage in his right knee, which prematurely yanked him out of the Indian Premier League and back on to the operating table less than two months ago – has been studied with nervous intensity. As far as England are concerned, there's an awful lot riding on Flintoff's fitness. It's as though, without Punch, there'll be no show this summer. It's why the television crews and the photographers have come to the relative outpost of Liverpool's Aigburth ground in rainy mid-June. The start of the Ashes series in Cardiff is only twenty-one days away, and Flintoff has still to conclusively prove his good health. Second stop for him is Lancashire's County Championship game against Hampshire. It ought to have boiled down to Flintoff versus Pietersen – a duel within a duel. But, while Flintoff needs match practice to regain his sharpness and make certain that his wobbly knee can survive a Test series, Pietersen requires rest to overcome an Achilles strain. Cortisone injections in the base of his spine have had only a palliative effect.

Flintoff is straining for form, let alone consistency. Since the end of the 2005 season, he's played in just ten Championship matches. He's taken 29 wickets and scored only 237 runs. His batting is the primary cause for concern. He hasn't made a century since the Fourth Test at Trent Bridge in 2005. In 65 innings since, he's mustered 1,521 runs at an average of 26. Rather than the authentic all-rounder he used to be, he has become a bowler who occasionally bats, which hardly qualifies him to come in at number six for England.

Flintoff began his comeback a week ago at Durham, where he took a wicket with his second ball. Michael Di Venuto pushed half forward and snicked a catch to Lancashire's wicketkeeper, Luke Sutton – a chance so straightforward that Sutton could have taken it with his bare hands. Cue the familiar Flintoff salute – feet wide apart, arms high above his head. If his bowling was hostile, his batting at the Riverside was hollow. He made 3 in the first innings and 0 in the second. On the face of it, Aigburth is the ideal place to get runs. It is a tight, comely ground with a chocolate-box pavilion: high gables and green and cream woodwork in Tudor style. It has a tradition of high scoring too. Johnny Tyldesley made 248 here, albeit in 1903. Walter Hammond once stroked 264. Gordon Greenidge ravaged 104 and 100 not out in a Championship game for Hampshire and then, as though Aigburth had been no more than a routine net for him, moved on to Old Trafford, where he got 164 in the Sunday

League for an aggregate of 366 over four days. Flintoff would be content to hear the reassuring sound of the ball regularly hitting the middle of the bat. He needs to occupy the crease.

What he occupies on the first day is the dressing room. By 9 a.m. rain is sweeping across the Mersey and it stays until early afternoon. At 2 p.m., with the weather clearing, Flintoff comes out of the red-bricked and tiled pavilion to inspect the pitch and outfield. He wears a dark-blue tracksuit top, the sleeves of which he pulls over his hands, a pair of matching shorts and sky-blue socks. He signs autographs and willingly poses for photographs and wraps his arms in a bear-hug around a friend, who arrives unexpectedly. 'I've come to see you bowl,' says a teenage boy to Flintoff, handing him a piece of paper on which he scribbles his name yet again. 'I've come to bowl,' he replies sympathetically, glancing up at the low, bruised-looking clouds. 'Not sure it'll happen, though,' he adds. The umpires inspect the wicket at 3 p.m. and decide to look again an hour later. The announcement is made just as I return to the pavilion after walking around the boundary, treading surface water wherever I put my canvas shoes. The shoes are soaked. There are plans for a 4.30 p.m. start. At 3.45 p.m., the rain returns. The defiant, optimistic knot of us who have stayed on – numbering no more than 40 – huddle in the bar on the second floor of the pavilion. The rain thumps against its windows and bounces like iron bolts off the balcony. The wind cracks its cheeks and sends the hanging baskets swaying on rusty hooks. The wood of the pavilion creaks, like the hull of a great ancient ship. Staring out of the rain-smeared, misty windows, it's briefly possible to believe you're at sea in the middle of a storm. Only looking directly down do you see land. The budding rose bushes in front of the pavilion are left bare, like crooked short sticks. The pegs tethering the hospitality marquees to the sodden grass are straining against the pull and gust of the canvas, which billows like sails. There are few more desolate and downcast places than a cricket ground in the rain. It's like visiting a seaside resort in mid-winter; everything bleakly barren and bolted, as though in hibernation, and grim-looking too. When play seemed possible, the ground-staff removed the covers and peeled off the outer sheeting. The outfield was mopped and rolled in preparation. Now there are pools of standing water strewn across it again. 'Not sure we'll even get any play tomorrow,' says a man in a thin grey windcheater, who has travelled from London specifically to see

Flintoff in the flesh. He set off at dawn and won't be home until midnight. 'At least I've seen the ground,' he says, waiting for the rain to clear before returning to the railway station nearby.

The man's pessimism about the weather is misplaced. The following morning is overcast, but dust dry. There are no visible signs of the previous afternoon's deluge. Flintoff is soon in the nets with his coach, Peter Moores, who is throwing balls at him from halfway down the pitch. Flintoff tucks these off his legs and pulls and cuts others. He only occasionally bothers to block the ball. It's as though he wants to feel the power of the bat in his hands again as the ball springs off the sweet spot. Whoever wins the toss is likely to bat, irrespective of the cloudy conditions. If the pitch breaks up, no one will want to chase on it in the fourth innings. And so it turns out. Lancashire's Glen Chapple signals his success to the dressing room as he walks away from the square. A short-arm jab with his left hand relays the message to his openers to pad up. Flintoff is number six on the scorecard. But, after Mal Loye misses a straight delivery from Dominic Cork, Flintoff is picking his way down the seventeen steps from the pavilion, side-stepping the slatted sightscreen and striding towards the wicket, head up and eyes blinking to accustom himself to the morning's dim light. Far sooner than anticipated, we're about to see whether Flintoff's fine tuning in the nets has worked. Even in the tight fit of his grilled helmet, and well before anyone registers the bright-red lettering of his name ironed on the back of his shirt, Flintoff is recognisable from his bulk and bearing alone. There's something of the confident warrior about him. He's greeted with silence, the respectful hush and rapt attention you get in the theatre just as the curtain swishes open. There is a collective will for him to get his lines right too. The air shudders with expectation.

Lancashire are 47 for 1. Flintoff takes guard briskly and gazes around with a snappish nod at every fielder, as though scanning each placement through his mind and locking them into a mental map: three slips, backward point, extra cover, mid-on and short mid-off, mid-wicket and long leg. In his over-eagerness to remove him immediately, Cork, who left Old Trafford in the winter with an acrimonious backward glance, strains for effect and bowls two innocently short and fairly wide balls from the Mersey End. Flintoff lets them hurry past him without offering – or needing to offer – a shot. The sun appears briefly, as if wanting to see for itself whether Flintoff is fit. He is off the mark in the next over against

Dimitri Mascarenhas, nudging the bowler watchfully off his hip to long leg for two. The applause, which stems partly from relief, is loud enough to suggest Flintoff has just reached his century. Shortly afterwards, he goes on to the points of his toes and clips Mascarenhas along the grass to the mid-wicket boundary. Purely for the purpose of giving himself something to do, rather than because the pitch needs it, he wanders out of his crease and begins brushing away scraps of loose dirt with the base of his bat. He looks like a 1950s housewife sweeping the front step. This, and a steady round of displacement fidgeting – constant gardening, raking his short spikes along the line of the batting crease, fiddling with his cuffs and the Velcro fastening on his gloves and tugging at the baggy sleeves of his shirt – are physical signs of the nerves that Flintoff is otherwise concealing; an indication, too, of how important it has become to make a decent score and how burdensome it is not to already have one.

Cork, bowling the odd fairly pointless bouncer, opens his lungs to half-scream and half-screech an appeal against him. The back-draft must have caught the ships on the Mersey. The umpire, Peter Willey, slightly lowers his head so the wide brim of his straw, black-banded hat partly hoods his dismissive response. Cork mouths a few grunts and muffled syllables to no one but himself. Flintoff has never relied over-much on forward defence. He doesn't like to be tethered like a dog to a post; his natural inclination is always to break the leash. Even after ten minutes he seems impatient, as if wanting to dash through the preliminaries and reach 10, 20 and then 30 so he can encroach into the high numbers as soon as possible. When Mascarenhas strays outside off stump, Flintoff devours the delivery in a single bite. He launches himself at it with a swing that comes straight from those brawny shoulders. Aigburth is blessed with low tree and roof lines around it. The Mersey End, which is where Flintoff is batting, has nothing more than a cluster of tennis courts and a row of houses behind it. The ball is visible against the pearl-coloured sky almost as soon as it leaves Flintoff's bat. It rises and then falls with a clatter against the bottom of the pavilion steps. The force of the impact scuffs the leather and flattens the seam. The crowd is certain this will be Flintoff's day. So, I guess, is Flintoff himself. It and he are wrong. Mascarenhas's next ball leaves him only slightly. Flintoff plays at it too firmly instead of letting the delivery drift by. It takes the edge and flies to Chris Benham at third slip. He takes it at stomach height. At the point of departure Flintoff looks at Benham, the pitch and the almost unblemished face of his bat, as though all three are somehow to blame for his own misjudgement. Reluctantly he walks back to the dressing room, irritably pulling off his gloves. His head is bowed. He's like a star that has suddenly glimmered out; splendid in its dying. The hand-clapping he gets is lukewarm consolation. Those providing it are also trying to console themselves after his early departure. With hindsight, Flintoff ought to have spent his net session polishing up on his forward defensive technique.

Aigburth's small electronic scoreboard doesn't identify batsmen by name. For the next half hour, the late-comers arrive with scorecards and assume Flintoff has still to bat. 'What do you mean, I've already missed him?' asks a spry but glum-faced man in a double-breasted blazer and a tie crested with Lancashire's red rose. 'I'd heard we were batting, so I thought I'd come down and watch Flintoff,' announces someone else, slipping into a brown leather tub seat in the pavilion bar and unzipping his black jacket. 'Then you've bloody mistimed your entrance,' says his friend, who offers to buy him a pint to assuage the crushing disappointment. Even well past two o'clock, as Lancashire stumble from 47 without loss to 127 for 7, one of the members turns to ask quietly: 'So when is Flintoff coming in?'

A week earlier I'd seen Flintoff in quite different surroundings. He'd chosen Nottingham to hold what was called *Flintoff's Ashes Preview.* The city's Arena was coincidentally covered in advance posters for *War of the Worlds.* These seemed very appropriate for England versus Australia, but were more prosaically drumming up the stage adaptation of H. G. Wells' novel. Flintoff arranged the evening to raise money for his own charitable foundation. The stage and its surrounds were draped in black curtains, like the sightscreens at a Twenty20 game. There was a soft purple light. I felt as though I'd walked into a cheap nightclub. Beside the stage was a big screen which displayed a photograph of Flintoff in Roman-like profile. Spread across the floor, in front of tiered seating, were twenty-seven tables of dinners (£1,250 for a table of ten), who had been eating and drinking long before the doors opened to let in the hoi polloi – who paid £15 – at 8 p.m.

Those of us who came to listen to Flintoff talk about the summer and the state of his own fitness had a long wait. We sat through a comedian, whose jokes were almost exclusively about male masturbation, and the predictable auction of signed shirts and bats and various 'champagne days out'. The auction dragged interminably, and didn't involve what I calculated as more than sixty per cent of the audience. Eventually the man sitting beside me left his seat and headed to the bar. 'Text me when he's coming on,' he said irritably to his friends. After a twenty-minute break, which is greeted with frustrated groaning, Flintoff climbed on to the stage. It was 9.21 p.m. He was wearing a pale suit and a pink washed tie. The stool on which he perched, pressing forward, seemed too squat for his long legs, which he sprawled across the stage. There were three vacant seats beside Flintoff's, and he introduced his guests: Graeme Swann, Stuart Broad and Rob Key, who, he said, would ask him questions from the loose sheets of paper he carried in his right hand.

The first one was obvious. When would Flintoff be fit? Flintoff took a long breath before rolling out the same answer he'd been giving for the past fortnight. He said he'd 'definitely' play for Lancashire 'in the next week or two' and then at Cardiff in the First Test. The second half of the sentence had hardly left his lips before he hastily added the perfunctory rider: 'if picked'. 'Don't know why it's Cardiff, though,' said Flintoff, pushing his tongue firmly into his cheek. 'You'll have the Aussies abusing you – and the Welsh too.' The rest of the conversation was conducted in the same harmlessly blithe spirit, designed to entertain rather than elucidate. There was no tactical insight about fending off a Brett Lee bouncer that threatens to punch your Adam's apple through your windpipe, or how to cope with a late in-swinging yorker from Mitchell Johnson. There was no scholarly thesis on Ricky Ponting's captaincy either. And no deep dissection of how England might regain the Ashes, which were lost 5–0 in 2006–07, when Flintoff was unwisely chosen as captain. Swann volunteered the opinion that Cardiff was sure to be 'a Bunsen burner'. Like Broad, he felt Chris Read was England's best wicketkeeper; Flintoff voted, perhaps diplomatically, for Matt Prior. Flintoff said that he thought Andrew Symonds, sent home from Australia's Twenty20 squad after breaching its disciplinary code, must be 'pissing himself' at the thought of everyone else spending two weeks in Leicester after their unexpected exit from the competition. 'Two weeks in Leicester,' said Flintoff loudly, as if adding his own italicised exclamation mark to the statement. It was hardly a code in need of breaking. Everyone recognised the tacit wink contained within those four words: that Leicester was the epitome of provincial grimness. The line went down well in Nottingham, which loftily regards itself as more sophisticated and brighter than its near neighbour.

Key asked Flintoff about his own indiscretions in the West Indies during the World Cup just over two years earlier. After late-night drinking, Flintoff fell off his hired pedalo and was half-rescued from the water. He was sacked as vice captain and banned for one match. 'I had a few bevies,' said Flintoff bluntly before the practised pause arrives. 'In my defence, you don't know how much they put into them rum punches, do you?' He awoke the following morning, he said, 'fully clothed, with sand between my toes and my jeans wet around the bottoms of the legs'. There was a knock at the door. 'I told them I didn't want the room cleaning . . . but it was Duncan Fletcher. He said he'd like to have a word with me. . . ' Flintoff described his bill on checking out. 'I ran down the list,' he said 'it read beer, beer, beer, pizza and a pedalo. They charged me £1,000 for the pedalo.'

Key moved on to the open-topped bus ride that followed England winning the Ashes at the Oval in 2005. Flintoff was 'tired and emotional', his eyes red and the pupils dilated to the size of dots on a dice. 'Ah,' said Flintoff, as if confessing to a prank, 'we had a few drinks that night . . . and then a few more drinks and suddenly it was eight-thirty in the morning. It was like being at school. My wife Rachael bathed me and dressed me and then put me on a bus. I thought to myself, "There's a lot of people in London today . . . is there a sale on at Selfridges's or something?"' He'd taken 24 wickets and scored 420 runs. No one cared then about Flintoff's tender or dishevelled state. As Flintoff was speaking, I tried to imagine a similar event being held before previous Ashes series; Denis Compton airily discussing his nightclub jaunts with Keith Miller; Harold Larwood and Bill Voce – who took wickets the way Bonnie and Clyde robbed banks – talking about their beery benders during the Bodyline tour, which Douglas Jardine conveniently ignored; Freddie Trueman confessing to one pint too many with Brian Statham. Decorum and good taste would have made it impossible for any of them to have admitted as much on stage. The past really is another country.

Asked if he'd ever want the captaincy again, Flintoff shook his head. 'Great honour to have done it,' he said, 'but I wouldn't want it again.' There was something tortured in his voice – the sharp bite of remembering – during the second half of his answer. He clearly wasn't built for the cerebral or emotional demands of leadership.

During lunch Aigburth benevolently allows the anoraks among us to inspect the pitch from behind a thin blue rope. It's a small, but kindly courtesy and common on out-grounds (try doing it at Lord's or Headingley). I stand within three feet of the spot where Flintoff struck Mascarenhas for six and I see what he saw: the pediments of the pavilion, the clock with its thin black hands and snow-white face, the banks of temporary seating in red and dark-green. I let my eyes follow the trail of spidery cracks and footmarks. The only tinge of green on the pitch is on its outer edges. Each of us nods in agreement when someone (perhaps it was me) insists it is a better batting pitch than the score suggests. The Lancashire batsmen toil nonetheless. For artistic merit, the highest marks belong to V. V. S. Laxman, whose use of his initials is redolent of the era of amateurs and professionals and whose use of his bat is redolent of Ranjitsinhji. He drives the ball sublimely through an arc between cover and backward point before pulling Chris Tremlett too early and top edging the ball, which takes flight and forces Nick Pothas to hurtle 10 yards to his left and wait for it to drop into his huge gloves. Lancashire are bowled out for 208 in only 60.5 overs. An unlikely 30 not out from Sajid Mahmood gives the total a modicum of respectability and brings Lancashire a batting point. Twenty minutes later Flintoff rolls out of the pavilion for the second time.

A sour breeze cuts across the pitch, and there is a spit of rain in the air. Flintoff, who will be second change, stands at second slip. He has a different technique to the slips either side of him: Laxman to his right and Paul Horton to his left. Laxman and Horton crouch and pull their hands together in preparation for the edge. In the manner of an Australian, Flintoff rests his palms flatly and more casually on the knees of his trunk-like legs. In between deliveries he rubs his hands together like a Boy Scout trying to make a fire with sticks. When the ball is tossed to him, he slips the first two fingers of his right hand over and then across the raised, stitched seam as a rehearsal for what's to come. He scratches his thin beard – no more than designer stubble – and begins his warm up exercises, turning his upper body like a wheel and bowling the ball out to cover point rather than lobbing it gently across to the fielder.

Hampshire are 50 for 1, and there are 23 overs left in the day when Flintoff unpeels his sweater and marks out his run from the Mersey End. Chapple walks across to him, more to offer moral and vocal support than constructive advice. Flintoff sets his own field. There's no question that he was leaner and fitter four years ago. There are more lines on his face. He is slightly more lumbering in his approach; not through age, it has to

The blasting impact of Andrew Flintoff, who strives to make a point about his speed and muscle to Australians as well as to Hampshire during the Championship match at Liverpool.

be said, but because each separate injury has left him wary about exactly how far his damaged joints and limbs can be pushed.

The abundant energy and aggression still remains, however. Flintoff's first ball to Michael Carberry is a typical loosener, but he deliberately follows it three-quarters of the way down the pitch, as though to announce his intimidating presence. Half turning, he glares at Carberry from over his shoulder through eyes that have become slits. The Hampshire opener doesn't return the stare delivered at a moment of emphasis. At 5 p.m. the light is the clearest and brightest of the day. And Flintoff is menacing now. He is ox-strong and mean with it. He's knuckled down too. Carberry and those who follow him – Michael Lumb, James Vince and Benham – find themselves fending off or swaying out of the way of short balls that threaten to decapitate them. There is no speed gun at Aigburth – there isn't even a tannoy to announce the bowling changes – but Flintoff is genuinely fast and hostile. Sitting 40 yards away, I instinctively dart my head to one side as Flintoff gives Vince, barely eighteen, a close encounter with the brutal realities of the Championship.

If Flintoff hits him, I worry that Vince won't see his nineteenth birthday next March. Sutton is standing 25 yards back for Flintoff and yet taking the ball at head height and with upturned fingers. Vince remains impressively composed and reaches 34 not out at the close. He clearly has a head much older than his body. The way he plays his shots in a tall and straight manner – especially the cover drive – is reminiscent of Michael Vaughan. Benham, however, suffers the physical pain and blasting impact of Flintoff's striving to make his point. He takes a blow on the wrist, which he involuntarily shakes as if the action alone will rid him of the pain. Flintoff's 7 overs don't bring him a wicket. But he concedes only 16 runs, which include 4 overthrows. England will be impressed; Australia will be apprehensive in case he has the hex on them again.

Yes, I'll remember Flintoff at Aigburth. The more I look at him, the more I think he fulfils Mark Twain's description of someone who is 'no more and no less than himself' but mightily significant all the same. Popularity ought never to be confused with greatness; and the basic facts and figures frankly don't illuminate Flintoff as statistically great. He can't be bracketed with Garry Sobers or Imran Khan or Ian Botham. And he still has to step out of 2005 and prove the series wasn't the early culmination of his achievements. But there was something other-worldly about him here, nonetheless. The feeling persists that, if only briefly, he'll accomplish the unexpected – reaching a catch no one else can lay a finger on, striking the ball so hard that it tears into the topmost branches of the spreading trees or taking wickets with some rapid-fire, rat-a-tat bowling that would make even Bradman hop and jump. He's responsible, too, for drawing thousands of youngsters towards cricket – faces he doesn't recognise and names he'll never know, but lives he has touched all the same. That's why we are still looking for another Flintoff in the way we once looked for another Botham.

Umpires: T. E. Jesty, P. Willey
Toss: Lancashire

Lancashire first innings

P. J. Horton	lbw	b Mascarenhas	37
M. B. Loye	lbw	b Cork	18
A. Flintoff	c Benham	b Mascarenhas	12
V. V. S. Laxman	c Pothas	b Tremlett	21
F. du Plessis	c Benham	b Tremlett	6
S. J. Croft	c Pothas	b Tremlett	7
L. D. Sutton†	lbw	b Cork	25
K. W. Hogg	lbw	b Tremlett	9
G. Chapple*	lbw	b Cork	27
S. I. Mahmood	not out		30
G. Keedy	lbw	b Tomlinson	2
Extras	(2lb, 10nb, 2w)		14
Total	(all out, 60.5 overs)		**208**

Fall of wickets: 1-47, 2-70. 3-75, 4-101, 5-101, 6-113, 7-127, 8-168, 9-181, 10-208

Hampshire bowling	O	M	R	W
Tremlett	13	3	49	4
Tomlinson	9.5	0	54	1
Cork	16	4	43	3
Mascarenhas	15	4	46	2
Imran Tahir	7	2	14	0

Hampshire first innings

M. A. Carberry	c Croft	b Keedy	25
J. H. K. Adams	c Sutton	b Chapple	9
M. J. Lumb	lbw	b Hogg	16
J. M. Vince	c Sutton	b Chapple	46
C. C. Benham	c Sutton	b Keedy	1
N. Pothas†	b Hogg		86
A. D. Mascarenhas*	c Sutton	b Mahmood	108
D. G. Cork	c Horton	b Flintoff	5
C. T. Tremlett	c Croft	b Flintoff	0
J. A. Tomlinson	c Sutton	b Chapple	6
Imran Tahir	not out		24
Extras	(1b, 2lb, 14nb, 2w)		19
Total	(all out, 86.1 overs)		**345**

Fall of wickets: 1-13, 2-50, 3-65, 4-71, 5-157, 6-212, 7-235, 8-235, 9-313, 10-345

Lancashire bowling	O	M	R	W
Chapple	23	6	77	3
Mahmood	18.1	0	98	1
Hogg	9	0	48	2
Flintoff	17	2	60	2
Keedy	19	5	59	2

Lancashire second innings

P. J. Horton	lbw	b Imran Tahir	55
M. B. Loye	lbw	b Tremlett	39
A. Flintoff	c Lumb	b Mascarenhas	54
K. W. Hogg	c Cork	b Imran Tahir	16
V. V. S. Laxman	run out		1
F. du Plessis	c Adams	b Imran Tahir	15
S. J. Croft	c Adams	b Imran Tahir	0
L. D. Sutton†	c Benham	b Tremlett	17
G. Chapple*	not out		34
S. I. Mahmood	c Pothas	b Imran Tahir	0
G. Keedy	c Cork	b Imran Tahir	0
Extras	(8b, 1lb, 4w)		23
Total	(all out, 79.5 overs)		**254**

Fall of wickets: 1-83, 2-128, 3-176, 4-177, 5-181, 6-187, 7-204, 8-237, 9-238, 10-254

Hampshire bowling	O	M	R	W
Tremlett	11	3	35	2
Mascarenhas	16	2	43	1
Cork	8	1	17	0
Imran Tahir	32.5	4	108	6
Tomlinson	9	2	32	0
Carberry	3	1	10	0

Hampshire second innings

M. A. Carberry	not out		62
J. H. K. Adams	not out		46
Extras	(10b)		10
Total	(0 wickets)		**118**

Lancashire bowling	O	M	R	W
Chapple	5	1	19	0
Flintoff	3	1	12	0
Keedy	10	1	52	0
Mahmood	1	0	7	0
du Plessis	4.1	0	18	0

Result: Hampshire won by 10 wickets

CHAPTER EIGHT

HE THAT PLAYS THE KING

Every Australian cricketer walks in the shadow of Donald Bradman at New Road – a ground he made his own with typically sublime batting.

Worcester: Tour match: England Lions v. Australia, 1–4 July

The clock is nudging towards eleven. Heat haze shimmers in the sultry air, distorting the horizon like a fairground mirror, and the milky-white cloud is broken with vivid blue veins of sky. The early summer's light is ravishing enough to pick out fine detail in the stonework of the 172-foot cathedral tower, which Pevsner described as 'the noblest of its kind'. The points of the finials and dark niches, the balustrade and the slats of slender arched windows, as well as the outline of the intricate saw tooth and beak head carving above them, stand out, as though the cutter has only recently finished his work. The trees, which divide New Road from the Severn, are swollen and dark with foliage. Inside the ground flower baskets hang in full bloom like shots of colour.

Waiting at the top of his run the bowler unconsciously wipes his right hand across the stitched emblem on his shirt. He takes the new ball and examines the shiny gold stamp that proclaims its maker's name, as if searching for a minor chip or imperfection. The opener fidgets at the crease, readjusting his gloves and his pads. He scratches out his guard, like a nervous hen in a coop, before settling down and jutting his chin towards the bowler, as though challenging him to hit it. The fielders glide into position. And, at that very moment, the cathedral's twelve bells begin to peel, as if Elgar himself is pulling the ropes and orchestrating the hour.

I see and hear all this from the squat, double-gabled ladies' pavilion, with its park-bench seating and the faded yellow spines of *Wisden*, which fill and furnish a glass-fronted bookcase inside the door. I know – after this season is long gone and the minutiae of it exists only on scorecards and ceases to matter – that this image and the chime of cathedral bells will remain still and absolutely perfect in my mind. The tableau will be real and solid enough to step straight back into again, as though entering a painting through the frame. On a morning like this I could be persuaded that New Road was created first; and that the cathedral and St Andrew's spire were built in response to it. In his poem 'Cricket at Worcester 1938' John Arlott almost suggested so. He thought of the cathedral tower as 'grey stone, majestic over green' and wrote:

> The back-cloth, setting off the setting,
> Peter's cathedral soared
> Rich of shade and fine of fretting
> Like cut and painted board

Whenever I think of Worcester, I always think of Donald Bradman, who belonged here and made it his own. Whether it is consciously acknowledged or not, every Australian touring team plays in the long shadow he cast. Even though sixty-one years have slipped by since he last faced a ball with Arlott's back-cloth of tower and spire as decoration, the ground still resonates with the clean sound of his stroke-making. He made New Road hallowed earth, and he lingers across it for that reason. Worcester always used to offer the first – or one of the first – gleaming glimpses of the faraway tourists. Bradman's double centuries – 236 in 1930, 206 in 1934, 258 in 1938 – all came before May was half a week old and its darling buds were still coiled and shut. While the mist from the Severn and the dampish air made the outfield dark and dewy, the pitch itself was wheat-coloured and bland for batting; especially with an eye like Bradman's and a bat made without edges. Everything was middled – and, according to Jack Fingleton, he 'pounded the Devil' out of the ball. Were Bradman batting now, digitised graphics would reveal where he scored most of his runs and where each ball was pitched to him. Australia's 1930 scorebook has an artist's touch about it instead. A line drawing of the Worcester pavilion sits in the left-hand corner, replete with low picket fence and the round-faced clock at its crown. The handwriting is curled and looped. Each name is written with the flourish of an autograph. It reveals that Bradman began with the simple building blocks of ten straight singles, two twos and then another single before his opening boundary became the spring which released the imaginative flow of strokes that followed. The regal procession of his 236 runs spills into the horizontal column of the next batsman, Stan McCabe.

Bradman stripped bare the over-fussy complexities which often gum up a batsman's style and was constrained by nothing but the size of his appetite for runs. There are only snatches of film of him in the 1930s, which adds to his mystique for those of us born too late to see the blade of his bat cut the bowling. The contemporaneous reports mention, of course, his quick hands and rapid footwork, which make him sound like a boxer expert in ring craft. There's McCabe's belief, too, that Bradman 'saw' the ball earlier than anyone and knew, almost before the bowler himself, where it would land. The film which does exist is in sepia or black and white, and shakily taken with a pedestal camera that weighed almost as much as a telephone box. Bradman is shown working with the ball rather than against it. Sometimes he sets out to trap it, like a lepidopterist with a net trapping a butterfly. Mostly, he lets it come to him. He is waiting for it – body and bat in perfect position to push the delivery wherever he wants. In this way Bradman dragged the field around. The opposing captain felt like a novice chess player. For Bradman would almost always place his shot into the very square of grass that had just been vacated. 'I seldom saw him hit the ball directly at a fielder,' said Len Hutton. 'It was as if he'd be wasting his time.'

So it was murder in front of the cathedral, and Bradman lightly stepped over the bloody corpse of the bowlers with his small, nimble feet on which everything blissful ran. He never had to talk up what he'd achieved for the sake of cheap applause. His high numbers demanded neither elaboration nor explanation – both of which were superfluous – but only awed admiration. In 1938 the Royal Worcester Company gave him a painted porcelain vase to commemorate his third successive double hundred at New Road. The vase, which depicts Bradman batting, is behind heavy glass in Adelaide, the city which became his home. Like his reputation, it has lost none of its colour or impact. In 1948, when the men who came to watch him were still in demob suits, Bradman's tendency for understatement, often verging on extreme drollery, became clear when he said, during his valedictory tour with the Invincibles, that he 'enjoyed Worcester'. But the Worcester crowds used to hold their breath for Bradman and only breathed out again when his innings was over.

It's because of Bradman that Australia at Worcester, whatever the circumstances, has a particular frisson about it. It is interlaced with history, spectacle and tradition, and never shorn of significance. The importance of this game is magnified by the calendar. The First Ashes Test at Cardiff is only a week away. The structure of this summer's fixture list means Australia's four-day preparation for it is minimal: a solitary match, against Sussex at Hove, immediately before this one. Bradman's Invincibles played twelve games before their opening Test. In 1972 – the first Ashes series I am old enough to remember in its entirety – Ian Chappell's Australia began with cocktails and canapés against the Duke of Norfolk's XI at Arundel, came to Worcester in April and then had another dozen matches before facing England at Old Trafford. Questions about the composition of Chappell's side were resolved well before the Australians headed to rainy Manchester. Questions about the current team – blanks to be filled in like squares of a crossword – will only be definitively answered here. The old gang has gone. Shorn of Shane Warne, and without Glenn McGrath, Justin Langer, Matthew Hayden and Adam Gilchrist from 2005, the optimistic view, albeit only whispered, is that Australia can be picked off this time. But, along with Ricky Ponting and Brett Lee, the tourists have the strokes of Michael Clarke, the potentially devastating left arm of Mitchell Johnson, the mid-order stability of Mike Hussey and the relatively unknown Peter Siddle, who is being held back for Cardiff.

The crowd, about 3,000-strong, have come here to study the form and try to make intelligent sense of what England will have to beat to regain the Ashes from Ponting.

The bowler examining the seam, as if the maker's name might contain a misprint, is Graham Onions. The opener waiting for him is Phillip Hughes. The previous day soft, warm rain swept across New Road and gave everything a glistening sheen, like a thick coat of polish. The rain became so heavy that a family of ducks took a bath in one of the puddles on the plastic sheeting protecting the outfield. So, after Ponting wins the toss, there is at least lingering moisture in the pitch to encourage England's frontline bowlers, Onions and Harmison. An awful lot is expected of the twenty-year-old facing them, who comes laden – and burdened – with wreaths of praise. Hughes scored 882 runs in 13 innings for Middlesex, including 118 on his Championship debut against Glamorgan at Lord's. His career average is already 69.37. He is a tough product of a tough environment, embodying Len Hutton's succinct characterisation of a tour of Australia itself – 'the pitches are hard, the ball is hard and the men are hard. You have to be harder to beat them.' Hughes is original in his approach. He stands outside leg with his stumps visible. If, in this opening over, Onions strays, Hughes has the skill to cut and drive him savagely. If he pitches the ball up, Hughes will back away to deal with it. His front foot is planted slightly askew on leg stump to give him more room to fire deliveries through the offside. His strategy is to buttonhole the bowling and command it from the start. When he bats well, no one goes for an early lunch; it lies cold on the plate instead. His partner, Simon Katich, has been moved up from the middle order, where he accumulates rather than blazes his runs. He steps across his stumps and covers them, like a bulldog guarding a gate.

There is not a breath of wind around Worcester as Onions comes in and, as early as his third delivery, is appealing for lbw against Hughes, oblivious to the fact the ball has pitched two inches outside leg. Onions' jaw hasn't felt the blade of a razor for at least three days. If the dark stubble is there as a prop, designed to give him a rough edge and the aura of menace, it isn't entirely working. Onions bowls tightly to the stumps, which gives him added accuracy. But he's a thin, slightly gangling figure and still has the face of an estate agent on his morning off. The juice in the pitch is more of a spur to Harmison, who immediately peppers Hughes and Katich from the Diglis End with short balls to a field of three slips, a leg slip, a gulley and a short leg. Hughes looks cramped and ill-at-ease against him, as though he's been cornered by the school bully. Harmison welcomes him to Worcester with a ball that lands on middle and leg before it rises to crack him on the helmet. Hughes is trapped, unable to get out of the way because of the tight limitation his own footwork places on his movement. He reels backwards. His spikes dig in and save him from falling. He has no clue about where the ball has gone, or how he might have avoided it in the first place. With wanton theatricality, Harmison ignores Hughes's distress in the same off-hand manner that Harold Larwood once ignored Bill Woodfull after belting him under the heart at Adelaide during the Bodyline series of 1932–33. Harmison turns his back and returns to his mark, like someone who's shot a bird and expects the gamekeeper to fetch it for him.

This is the mean, sour, lethal Harmison of the 2005 series – during which he cut and bloodied Ponting's cheek at Lord's after trying to rearrange his facial bone structure – rather than the unconfident and homesick Harmison of 2006–07, where he began at Brisbane with a delivery wayward enough to have finished in the Northern Territories. So erratic was Harmison's form in Australia, and so negative his conception of himself throughout the tour, it became difficult to recognise his downtrodden, huddled figure. Home thoughts from abroad shredded both his equilibrium and concentration. Neither his heart nor his mind was in it. He is different today: straight-backed and sinister-eyed and bowling close to 90 mph. He couldn't be more threatening to Hughes unless he brandished a Bowie knife at him. In the 8th over he gets his reward. Hughes has made a nervy 7 runs – never suggesting a long occupation – when he's skewed back on to his stumps by a ball off a length. His elbows are raised like a pair of sharp wings.

Hughes doesn't get into line and gloves a catch to Joe Denly at gulley. Australia are 19 for 1.

Ponting arrives, swishing his bat either side of his body, as if he's aggressively paddling a small boat to the crease. He looks as out of sorts as Hughes. His first shot against Harmison is tentative; a half-stab, half-withdrawal that raps the bottom of the bat and nearly rebounds on to his stumps. This is Ponting's fourth Ashes tour, a distinction he shares in the modern era with Warne, Steve Waugh, Allan Border, Neil Harvey, Doug Walters and Rod Marsh. He knows Worcester as well as Bradman, who also made four tours. Ponting has still to captain Australia to the Ashes in England. It is the conspicuous gap in his CV – as large as a hole in a Henry Moore sculpture. England tend not to mention the 5–0 defeat Ponting's Australia piled up against them two years ago. That series is treated with collective and voluntary amnesia. Another way of not talking about it is to talk about something else instead, such as the two critical and calamitous miscalculations Ponting made during 2005. The first betrayed arrogance: a decision to bowl first after McGrath trod on the ball and damaged his ankle at Edgbaston in the Second Test, which presupposed that England could be blown out, as easily as a candle flame, whoever Australia bowled. The second betrayed insecurity: his angry, snarling strop after being run out in the Fourth Test at Trent Bridge by the substitute fielder, Gary Pratt. Ponting's wild over-reaction, flinging his arms towards the England dressing-room balcony, surrendered the psychological high ground. It was as though the possibility of England actually winning the series had only just struck him. It is a captain's job to propagandise on behalf of his team, and Ponting often does it skilfully, wrapping several shades of meaning around what he says in the stern voice of duty. His character is ready-salted. Ponting doesn't go in for smarmy genuflection and he plays his cricket in the same way he approaches life: with a pugnacious toughness and a natural, imposing gravity. Already, he's tried to needle – in no particular order – Andrew Strauss, Kevin Pietersen and Andrew Flintoff. Still, there's something of Captain Ahab about Ponting – a constant edge of desperation in pursuit of the whale.

Early on he looks as though he's a complete stranger to New Road. He's too eager to lay bat on ball, the sure sign of someone who isn't in good touch and needs to spend five hours in the middle. The pitch, slower than he imagines, fools him into going through his shots before the ball has reached him. Afterwards he's statuesque, like a model holding a pose before the photographer is ready to press the shutter. Ponting makes only a single – and faces seven deliveries – before Onions digs the eighth in. Ponting goes at it with hard hands, a big backlift and an angled bat, which suggests he's undecided about how to play it. Vikram Solanki grips the catch at chin height at first slip. Ponting is mortified.

Myths linger long after being disproved. So it is with the rancorous loathing Australians are supposed to have for effete Poms; and the distaste Poms are supposed to nurture for uncouth Australians. Even in murderous rivalry we like and respect one another more than either country ever lets on. Arlott asked: 'Why is a Test match against Australia different from a Test match against any other country? And why do we *feel* it is different?' Because, beneath the thick crust of cynicism, England and Australia are like the two old men in Somerset Maugham's short story 'The Sanatorium', who squabble and feud, complain about and provoke one another – mostly over trivialities. The fractious relationship gives meaning and purpose and identity and definition to both their lives. When one of the old men dies, the survivor loses the will to live also. That's England and Australia too. We have more in common than we prefer to acknowledge; and cricket binds rather than separates us, which makes the contests important well beyond the narrow confines of pure sport. To point all this out risks being dismissed as 'soft'. So we remain one-eyed, jingoistic patriots for the duration of the Ashes. But, typically at New Road, admiration for Australia cannot be concealed or contained for long. There's a generous and genuine appreciation for Katich and his new partner, Hussey, the third of four left-handers in the top six.

Katich is an innings-builder. He grafts out his runs, picking off deliveries with stabbing or short-arm jabs between backward point and extra cover. The cloud cover has all but gone now, and the noon sun is baking the pitch a biscuit yellow. The bowlers – Tim Bresnan replacing Harmison and Sajid Mahmood taking over from Onions – have to sweat hard. Katich and Hussey employ basic tactics. If there is a bowling lapse, the batsmen latch on to the mistake and keep the scoreboard turning. If facing reliable length and line, the ball is met with the bat's broad face or left alone. Hussey's technique is uncluttered and straightforward. He drives whatever comes to him on the full. He cuts whatever is short. A stick of gelignite might be the best way of getting rid of him today.

Half an hour before lunch, Adil Rashid rolls the ball across each palm and twirls it between his fingers before starting his run from the Diglis End. Expectation is already flying at a high altitude for Rashid. In his first Championship season, during 2006, I watched him from the upper tier of the Rugby Stand at Headingley. He was a beguiling, instinctive figure, each delivery like a tin full of bait presented to the batsman. I studied him through binoculars, following the sharp flick of the wrist, the flight of the ball and rotation of the seam in the air, the subtle changes of his hand position. He used the width of the crease well to alter his angle of attack. The ball buzzed from the hand like an angry wasp, and a succession of batsmen strained to read him. Rashid is constantly learning, adding variations to his stock deliveries and intricately plotting new ones. The action is smooth and poetic, as if aesthetics matter to him. But he bowls as much with his brain as his alert body, which is how the best have always done it. He still looks younger than his twenty-one years, and is bird-like in a Clarrie Grimmett sort of way. Life hasn't yet taught him any stern lessons, or given him any sleepless nights, or blemished his face with creases and crevices. No doubt these will come, but Rashid looks phlegmatic enough to absorb them and move on, adjust and fulfil his starry promise. Bill O'Reilly described Grimmett as a 'wiry little leg-spinner' and 'the best and most constantly active cricket thinker I ever met'. Rashid tosses the ball higher than Grimmett and is much more likely to beat a batsman by spin alone (Grimmett, added O'Reilly, was mostly about 'unerring length and tantalising direction'). Katich and Hussey give him the respect his potential warrants. The Australians are watchful, as though Rashid might suddenly pull the pin on a ball and detonate it in front of them. He can't, however, dislodge either of them. The pitch is a yard too slow for him. Katich reaches his half century, off 87 balls, in the last over before lunch. Straight-driving Mahmood to the long off boundary, he also carries Australia into the respectable territory of three figures. The lunchtime talk in the pavilion is all about Harmison, who has figures of 6-1-6-1. On paper it looks like a straight-sets win for one of the Williams sisters at Wimbledon.

John Arlott began 'Cricket at Worcester, 1938' with the lines 'Dozing in a deck-chair's gentle curve / Through half-closed eyes I watched the cricket'. Most of the deckchairs have gone and been replaced with tubular steel stands and tip-up seats. And no one is dozing in them. For Katich is more carefree in the afternoon. He begins to dominate to such a degree that Hussey selflessly feeds him the strike. Katich regularly scores around the vacant third-man area, slapping the ball against the board that is advertising the hotel where the Australians are staying. After an hour, and only 13 runs shy of a 150 partnership, Katich strokes Harmison through extra cover for four to take his score to 95. Perhaps the shot releases too many endorphins into his system, pumping and puffing him up and making him feel momentarily infallible. Or perhaps, well out of character, he just wants to showboat by bringing up his century with the lavish indulgence of a six. Whatever the reason, he turns gambler. As Harmison drifts the ball on to leg side, Katich doesn't get inside it sufficiently to connect with full force. He shovels it away with a nonchalant heave over his shoulder. The ball dies in the air on the way to long leg, and Onions takes the catch near his boot laces. Given the circumstances and the conditions – bland pitch, the hot afternoon and the bowlers beginning to wilt – Katich could easily have made the first double century by an Australian tourist at Worcester since Keith Miller's 220 in 1952. He climbs the pavilion steps apologetically, as if aware of it and privately admonishing himself for the chance he's squandered. It is evident in his eyes, the drawn-down mouth and anguished clench of his face.

Hussey, smeared in sunscreen, is left to maintain the impetus as Australia contemplate a surprising mini mid-order collapse. Michael Clarke chases a wide delivery from Bresnan and gives Rashid catching practice at backward point; the all-rounder Marcus North plays on against Onions; the wicketkeeper Brad Haddin is (very dubiously) given out lbw after a delivery from Bresnan which looks to be scooting past leg stump. Even Hussey is fortunate to survive. On 75, he drives Mahmood uppishly and is relieved when the sheer pace of the ball takes it through the bowler's grasping fingers. Mahmood feels it squirm through his hands like a fine rain of sand. Hussey digs himself in the ribs with a gloved fist, as though mild self-flagellation and public reproach will remind him not to be so careless again. He promptly gets his head over every ball, like an old-fashioned accountant studiously bent across a ledger. Hussey flicks and drives, and occasionally cuts and pulls. The Lions probe away, like a dentist looking for cavities, without breaking him down. His century comes with a back-foot off-drive against Rashid. Bell pursues it and slides inelegantly into and across the rope, losing his cap, his sunglasses and some of his dignity in the effort. It is Hussey's fiftieth first-class hundred,

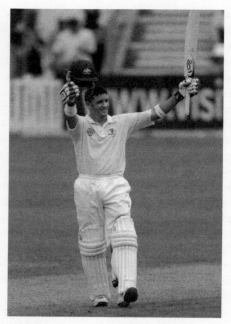

*An example of basic tactics and technique from the solidly reliable
Michael Hussey, who celebrates a century at Worcester after
refusing to let the bowlers dominate him.*

reached off 153 balls and with 15 fours. Notably with Johnson, who
makes a lusty 47, including a six off Rashid that clears the roof of the
Supporters Club shop and lands in the car park, Hussey navigates the
Australians into the safe waters of 300.

The heat of the day is ebbing at last, but New Road still feels alive and
is filled with clear light as the final overs of the last session begin. The
crowd starts to thin out and head home, taking with them the knowledge
that Australia aren't, after all, going to be easy meat. On this evidence
there isn't much dash, audacity or felicity of expression about them. But,
when the Ashes begin, only the end product matters.

Those who love Worcester and its cosy country-green atmosphere brood
about its future when the tipping rains come and the Severn slops over its
banks, making it as watery as Arthur's Avalon. Somehow it always

survives; however high the tidemark, however long the dark water remains. Eventually it drains away, the mud and silt is cleared, and the grass grows handsomely again. It is rolled and cut and manicured. The bad winter is forgotten. As it must, though, New Road is changing. The pavilion is now a modern structure, glassy and muted grey and box-tidy, as if it's been assembled in big pieces rather than built or put together by hand. 'You'll hate the new pavilion,' I was told earlier in the season. 'It's bloody ugly.' Actually, it isn't ugly at all. By the time I leave New Road, I've already grown accustomed to it. The most important thing is that the view from beyond its far boundary will always remain the same: the great spread of greenery, the Severn with its swans and boats, the spire of St Andrew's spearing the sky and the cathedral's grace, the round central west window watching the cricket like a single, unblinking eye. It's poignant enough to know that Bradman passed this way and became integral to the landscape. In his day it was traditional for the Australians to visit King John's tomb in front of the cathedral's high altar. The tourists touched the head of the lion, which lies tangled around his feet, for good luck. As the custom died out, I decide to visit on the Australians' behalf. The King in effigy is carved in Purbeck marble on his coffin-shaped slab and flanked by the figures of St Oswald and St Wulfstan. He wears a large crown and carries a sceptre, long ago broken. Semi-precious stones, originally set into the crown and on to the cuffs, belt and gloves, were removed, also long ago. I am conscious of the fact Bradman once stood in the same small spot – a king beside a king. In standing here too, listening to the echoes of organ music beneath the vaulted ceiling, I know, without doubt, who was the greater royal.

Umpires: J. H. Evans, J. W. Lloyds
Toss: Australia

Australia first innings

P. J. Hughes	c Denly	b Harmison	7
S. M. Katich	c Onions	b Harmison	95
R. T. Ponting*	c Solanki	b Onions	1
M. E. K. Hussey	b Harmison		150
M. J. Clarke	c Rashid	b Bresnan	4
M. J. North	b Onions		1
B. J. Haddin†	lbw	b Bresnan	7
M. G. Johnson	c Davies	b Bresnan	47
B. Lee	b Harmison		6
N. M. Hauritz	c Denly	b Onions	11
S. R. Clark	not out		10
Extras	(6b, 10lb, 3nb)		19
Total	(all out, 96.4 overs)		**358**

Fall of wickets: 1-19, 2-24, 3-165, 4-185, 5-186, 6-197, 7-306, 8-315, 9-348, 10-358

England Lions bowling	O	M	R	W
Onions	23.4	3	70	3
Harmison	25	3	80	4
Bresnan	17	1	46	3
Mahmood	17	2	74	0
Rashid	14	1	72	0

England Lions first innings

J. L. Denly	b Lee		66
S. C. Moore	c Haddin	b Lee	120
I. R. Bell*	lbw	b Lee	0
V. S. Solanki	b Lee		8
E. J. G. Morgan	lbw	b Lee	4
S. M. Davies†	c Clarke	b North	53
A. U. Rashid	c Hussey	b Clark	66
T. T. Bresnan	b Johnson		5
S. I. Mahmood	b Lee		0
S. J. Harmison	not out		7
G. Onions	c Hughes	b Clark	8
Extras	(5b, 2lb, 8nb)		15
Total	(all out, 96 overs)		**352**

Fall of wickets: 1-172, 2-172, 3-198, 4-209, 5-209, 6-295, 7-315, 8-316, 9-344, 10-352

Australian bowling	O	M	R	W
Johnson	26	1	118	1
Lee	27	6	76	6
Clark	16	2	40	2
Hauritz	18	1	80	0
Clarke	4	0	15	0
North	5	1	16	1

Australia second innings

P. J. Hughes	c Morgan	b Harmison	8
S. M. Katich	c Moore	b Rashid	37
R. T. Ponting*	c Rashid	b Harmison	15
M. J. North	not out		191
M. J. Clarke	c Onions	b Solanki	80
M. E. K. Hussey	retired hurt		62
B. J. Haddin†	not out		25
Extras	(11b, 8lb, 1nb)		20
Total	(4 wickets declared, 103 overs)		**438**

Fall of wickets: 1-17, 2-41, 3-90, 4-260

England Lions bowling	**O**	**M**	**R**	**W**
Onions	19	2	74	0
Harmison	17	3	55	2
Mahmood	18	2	56	0
Bresnan	18	6	60	0
Rashid	22	2	109	1
Solanki	5	0	32	1
Denly	4	0	33	0

England Lions second innings

J. L. Denly	c Haddin	b Johnson	36
S. C. Moore	c Ponting	b Johnson	16
I. R. Bell*	c Katich	b Hauritz	20
V. S. Solanki	b Lee		28
E. J. G. Morgan	not out		28
S. M. Davies†	not out		18
Extras	(4b, 11lb, 1nb)		16
Total	(4 wickets, 47.2 overs)		**162**

Fall of wickets: 1-29, 2-62, 3-105, 4-115

Australian bowling	**O**	**M**	**R**	**W**
Johnson	9	2	48	2
Lee	8	1	38	1
Clark	9	2	11	0
North	5	0	17	0
Hauritz	12.2	4	22	1
Katich	5	0	11	0

Result: Match drawn

Man of the match: B. Lee

CHAPTER NINE

INSTEAD OF A TELEGRAM

*James Taylor, who dashes for a single at incredible speed, like a
mouse scampering along a skirting board.*

Scarborough: Friend's Provident, First Under-19s Test: England v. Bangladesh, 6–9 July

There is nothing to match cricket by the sea, and the sharp sense of holiday freedom it brings. And the coast – at least for me – is Scarborough, which turns its face towards the billowy winds of the North Sea, where I instinctively feel at home. Part of the reason is the way it looks as much as how it feels to be here. There is a place where the sea directly meets the saw-tooth-shaped cliffs and a swell of foam, as if frosting the waves, repeatedly strikes the high, worn rock. Along the coast are whitewashed buildings with red-tiled roofs that cling to the resort's two bays and the mauled outline of the Norman castle, which, caught in silhouette at twilight, looks as though it belongs in an adventure story for boys from the 1950s. Squawking gulls, scavenging and silver-shone against the glint of the sun, wheel and dip around it and from a distance resemble rising flecks of ash from a fire. Wilfred Owen saw exactly this scene when he came to Scarborough in 1917 and wrote some of his war poetry from a turreted room in one of the sea-front hotels.

Arriving in Scarborough each year is like walking through the rooms and passageways of an old, familiar house. It's important to check that nothing significant about it has changed during the winter; that the town, in fact, is almost exactly as I left it on a hot weekend the previous September. And so it is today. Everything is in its place and just as it ought to be. The tea rooms and the secondhand bookshops are still in business. The banners, strung across the High Street, proclaim another season of the town's Spa Orchestra and the Peasholm Park concerts. The views across the bays are unblemished, and the sea between them is like a burnished shield. Along the hard edge of the horizon, there's a freighter, no more than a pencil smudge, heading southwards. A few smaller boats cut through the chop and spit in the middle distance. With the tide out, the beach is wide and long and as smooth as a polished table; perfect for the donkey rides and the erratic games of cricket that will fill it less than a fortnight from now when the holiday season properly begins. The candy-striped rock and trinket shops are freshly painted and selling the usual cheap kitsch – inflatable beach balls, plaster seagulls, gaudy commemorative plates, plastic fish and paperweights which become snowstorms in a glass after shaking. The cafés with steamy windows advertise all-day breakfasts. The taste of salt and the vinegary scent of fish and chips hang in the air.

Every trip to Scarborough has within it something of every other trip. But I wish I could have come here decades ago with the urbane, pipe-smoking J. M. Kilburn, the cricket correspondent of the *Yorkshire Post* for more than forty years. Kilburn began writing for the newspaper in 1934 and retired just as Kerry Packer began to brand and commercialise cricket with entrepreneurial zeal and Midas's fortune. Kilburn was tall, slightly hawk-nosed and scrupulously correct in manner and bearing; a patrician of the press box. The preservation of the aesthetics and nobility of the game were important to him. He blanched at anything overtly showy or meretricious in case cricket came out of it badly, and he disparaged gamesmanship in any form. According to those who knew him, he could be austere and puritanically formidable about protecting it. He did once, however, reveal a mischievous streak. When Sir Donald Bradman and Douglas Jardine were both writing about the 1953 Ashes series, Kilburn deliberately arranged the press seating at Headingley so that the two of them were placed beside one another. He then positioned himself – and his friend Bill Bowes – close enough to eavesdrop on what was said when the architect of Bodyline and its victim were forced to share the same square yard of space. The greeting was not exactly Stanley meets Livingstone.

JARDINE: Good morning.
BRADMAN: Good morning to you.

Seven hours of near-perfect silence followed. The protagonists of the 1932–33 series covered the Test – a dullish, low-scoring draw – with funeral-like expressions, barely glancing in one another's direction and grateful to go their separate ways at the end of it.

Kilburn felt privileged to have seen Jack Hobbs and Frank Woolley, Wilfred Rhodes and Hedley Verity. He was grateful not to have seen close-up the era of coloured clothing, the white ball, floodlights and 'crash helmets', which he abhorred. He didn't care much for the one-day game – even when the Gillette Cup was played as a 65-overs-per-side competition. When Yorkshire won it in 1965, he hurried off to make sure he was home on Saturday night so as to be on the golf course early and on time the following morning. Worse, he regarded the John Player League as blasphemous. At heart, though, Kilburn was a romantic.

Cricket had to be played with pleasure to be able to give pleasure. His practical function was to report matches; but his fundamental role was to transmit to the reader the emotion the game stirred in him. He boiled it down into the maxim: 'Beauty we see in cricket because cricket is beauty.' Scorecard figures never captured the splendour of an innings or the line of beauty in a spell of bowling for him. But his stylishly tight descriptions of both always did.

It's appropriate for Scarborough to stage the Under-19s Test. For Kilburn was born on 8 July 1909. He's 100 years old this week. The resort became his spiritual Yorkshire home (he was born in Sheffield and lived in Harrogate), and North Marine Road was his favourite ground. He wrote the definitive account of its Festival and even married a Scarborough girl called Mary. Fittingly he met and began courting her at the Festival dance. It was Kilburn who wrote: 'Whenever a pilgrimage through the cricketer's England may begin it must surely end, if the traveller has any sense of the appropriate, at Scarborough in Festival time . . . To have made one visit is almost certain infection for the desire to return. Two visits made is virtually the establishment of a habit . . .' With the Festival seven weeks away, the pull of Scarborough is still too strong to resist. That it dovetails with Kilburn's centenary seems as though Fate, rather than the ECB, arranged the fixtures. Even without the trimmings of the Festival – the ground sealed in the heat of high August, the white and sea-green striped tents, deckchairs in primary colours, sunburned faces and the Yorkshire flag curled around the flagpole – North Marine Road is as Kilburn described it: 'Always new yet never changing'. I adhere to my own specific Festival rituals, which repetition never dulls. I take a slow walk to the match, passing the hotels and boarding houses with the sea at my right shoulder. I buy my newspapers from the corner shop. I sit on the dark-brown benches five rows or so below the tea bar at the Trafalgar Square End of the ground. Early in the afternoon, I read the *Yorkshire Post*. And I think of JMK.

North Marine Road's black metal gates are already open, but the tea bar is closed. There are fewer than 100 spectators, who mill around in search of scorecards, which a tannoy announcement finally reveals are still being printed. There's no sign either of Dickie Bird, usually found wandering on a route from the pavilion to the members' area behind the bowler's arm or on a sea-front bench, where he talks about the summer Frank Tyson hospitalised him here with a bouncer. 'My fault,' he always says. 'I made the mistake of hitting him for two successive fours, you see. After he hit me, he came down the pitch and said, "Try and hit that one for four, you bastard." What might Tyson have made of C. I. 'Buns' Thornton? He was a nineteenth-century hitter so extraordinarily fierce that he struck a ball 140 yards at the Oval, 132 yards and then 140 yards at Canterbury and 162 yards during net practice at Brighton. He never waited for any delivery to reach him. Thornton, who wore neither gloves nor pads, took long strides down the pitch to meet it instead. Photographs of him reveal an unspectacular face – small mouth, tired-looking eyes and sideburns like strips of leather. He wore an ill-fitting cap and a knotted tie cut off fractionally below the breast bone. In 1886 he came to Scarborough with the Gentlemen of England to play I Zingari (Italian dialect for 'the gypsies') and eyed the terraced housing which faces Trafalgar Square. His 107, compiled in an hour and 10 minutes, comprised 12 fours and 8 sixes, one of which shattered the second-storey window of one of the homes. Another cleared the rooftops and chimneys. 'Really,' a lady is supposed to have said to him after hearing the story of the shot which landed in Trafalgar Square. 'Tell me, Mr Thornton,' she asked, 'were you playing at Lord's or the Oval?' Thornton's improbable feat wasn't equalled for seventy-nine years. The Australian Cec Pepper, playing for the Forces, was urged by Arthur Wood, the wicketkeeper of H. D. Leveston-Gower's XI, to 'try for those houses'. Five minutes later the ball vanished behind them. Some of the houses today are in need of a paintbrush and several gallons of whitewash.

The crowd is tight to the other three sides of North Marine Road. Seating in the pavilion is also on the same level as the dressing rooms. Five years ago I saw Ricky Ponting make a classical century for Somerset here on his Championship debut. Every shot was effortless and majestic. On the second morning, he made 50 of the first 55 runs scored. One six in particular, climbing over wide long on, looked as if it might carry on rising and never fall to earth again. The stroke brought up his hundred. Ponting looked capable of outstripping some of the highest scores on the ground: Hobbs's unbeaten 266 for the Players against the Gentlemen in 1928, Hutton's 241 in the same fixture twenty-five years later or the 202 Herbert Sutcliffe took off Middlesex in 1936. Even the most partisan Yorkshireman put aside county loyalty, grateful instead just to watch Ponting bat. And then, for a microsecond, Ponting lost his focus and his wicket. He gave it away loosely to the spinner Richard Dawson. Like a mourner unwilling to leave a graveside, Ponting didn't move at first. When he did so, he took the pavilion steps two at a time, stomped into the dressing rooms, threw his bat against a wall and simultaneously uttered a long, loud oath which could be heard throughout the pavilion. The oath rhymed with clucking bell. There are few secrets on such an intimate ground.

Occasionally sea fret rolls in and spreads across the outfield like a muslin veil. In 2007 it stopped play against Warwickshire. It was impossible to see the stumps from 25 yards away. A distant foghorn gave the impression that North Marine Road was a boat adrift on the ocean. There's no threat of a repeat today. A breeze is blowing from the town, and a purplish band of cloud hangs menacingly over deep mid-wicket.

In cricket the walk to the wicket tells you a lot about a batsman. Kilburn used to say of Hobbs that he 'trod softy' but 'so assuredly' that he brought with him the guarantee of runs. Len Hutton, he added, left the pavilion with the brisk efficiency of a businessman determined to clear a backload of work. I particularly remember Ian Chappell, who came into bat as though he were leading a bayonet charge; often, he did. Kevin Pietersen always looks as if he's about to peel off his gloves like a fairground boxer and challenge the bowler to a bare-knuckled fight; often, he does too.

England win the toss, and when the openers, Josh Cobb and Jaik Mickleburgh, emerge there is no question that Bangladesh's bowlers are soon going to be over-familiar with the full circumference of the outfield. Mickleburgh, of Essex, made his first-class debut in 2008 and has a highest score of 72 against Warwickshire at Chelmsford. Cobb, however, is the more striking presence. Not only because last August he made 148 not out, batting at number seven for Leicestershire against Middlesex at Lord's, in a match which began only three days after his eighteenth birthday. Not only because it made him Leicestershire's youngest century maker and the youngest batsman to score a century at Lord's too. And not only because his photograph appears in the current *Wisden*, which describes him as 'outstanding among the prospects'. It's because Cobb carries himself as though he expects to make runs. This is his Under-19s debut; no one, though, would know it without being told. The firm set of his face and body and his purposeful stride exudes cold authority, a fact conspicuous when he begins middling the ball against Bangladesh's two pace bowlers; though, it has to be said, the word pace ought to be encased in inverted commas.

Neither Abu Jayed nor Alauddin Babu are quick enough to pitch short, which happens often, or sufficiently accurate to prevent the fast flow of runs from Cobb and Mickleburgh, who cracks Jayed for a six that almost punches a hole in a burger van parked on the concrete walkway. Next, with a touch so light that he could have been using a feather rather than his heavy bat, Cobb flicks Jayed square off his toes for four. After just 1 hour and 1 minute, the partnership has reached 72, and the Bangladesh captain, Mahmudul Hasan, submissively switches to spin at both the Pavilion and Trafalgar Square Ends. Resting his hands on his hips and breathing hard, as if he's just broken the tape after a half-marathon, Hasan's ambitions narrow to limiting the damage and sweeping up the wreckage of the earlier bowling as tidily as he can. When a shower interrupts the scoring, the tourists welcome it the way the bruised fighter welcomes the escape of the bell at the end of a round. The respite is brief. Within ten minutes the rain has passed, and Cobb is driving, steering and cutting them to all parts again. His half-century arrives in 52 balls.

To date a total of 101 Under-19s have gone to play for England in Tests, one-day internationals or in Twenty20 competitions. Nine – including Mike Atherton, Michael Vaughan and Andrew Flintoff – have become captain. The batting order against Bangladesh Under-19s in the First Test at Headingley five years ago included Alastair Cook, Joe Denly, Ravi Bopara and Luke Wright. Past form, as well as the law of averages, dictate that at least one name on today's scorecard will claim a place in the 2013 Ashes series, which adds to the significance of this Test and puts into perspective the difficulties facing Hasan in chaining England down. His options are limited. He can only replace one flighty bowler with another, swapping off spin for wristy leg-breaks.

Ali and Ahmed make way for Hossain and Rahman, who in turn surrender the ball to Haque and Hasan himself. Hasan is the most skilled at temporarily fastening down England with an occasional change of pace. He bowls a much flatter trajectory and holds his line, which means Cobb and Mickleburgh have to make room before working him away. Hasan also adopts a less attacking field. He pushes his men into the deep, allowing singles but reducing the number of boundaries. It is difficult to know how Bangladesh will conjure a wicket. But it comes from the most unlikely source – a self-inflicted wound by Mickleburgh five minutes before lunch. In the 33rd over he treats a friendly ball from Rahman, who has switched to the Pavilion End, as though it is a trial of strength. Mickleburgh is goaded into accepting a challenge. In trying to hit the ball as hard as 'Buns' Thornton, he treads on the slick grease of farce. Mickleburgh winds himself up – high backlift and chest on – until his right leg slips beneath him. He drops to the ground, bringing up dust and flecks of lime, and collides with his stumps on the way down. Mickleburgh is splayed in the crease as rigidly as a puppet snared in its own strings. The dislodged bails lie beside him. He requires treatment before being embarrassingly shepherded off the field. England are 139 for 1.

During lunch there is thunder and stabs of flashed, crooked lighting and then rain and intense sunshine, which leaves a rainbow clinging to the hill in the far distance behind the pavilion. There is a waifs-and-strays look about the Bangladesh team, which wanders into its upper tier in search of something to eat. One of the players, in a wide-brimmed sun hat, starts to examine the photographs on the wall. A signed portrait of Lord Hawke instantly grips him, as surely as if the Yorkshire patriarch had ordered him to heel. He points to Hawke's thickly distinguished moustache, and spreads two fingers across his own top lip in imitation. The photograph of Len Hutton, hung on the balcony, is more revealing still. At first he glances at Hutton, smiling weakly and posing stiffly at the crease in front of the pavilion, and then lets his eyes wander across the dusty glass. With animated wafts, he begins pointing at the date beneath the photograph: 1948. It immediately registers with him that the backdrop against which he has been fielding all morning has barely changed in more than sixty years. He calls over a team mate, who studies the picture too, almost pressing his nose against the frame. At the start of the morning I'd watched two of Bangladesh's coaches walking around the ground with a pocket camera. I asked whether either of them had been to Scarborough before. Their English is limited; my Bengali non-existent. We communicated through predictable hand-gestures to such an extent that I was soon holding their camera and taking a photograph of them. I *think* the coaches said that no one in the squad had seen, let alone visited, England before – a jolting reminder that Bangladesh, as a cricket nation, is still a work in progress. It only qualified for its first World Cup in 1999. It only played its first Test in 2000. In the span of cricket's history, it scarcely represents the blink of an eye. Bangladesh's current captain, Mashrafe Mortaza, is just seven years older than Hasan of the Under-19s. There is not much history for Bangladesh to draw on, which explains why the teenagers cluster around Hutton as though he's a fossil from the Palaeolithic period.

Also in the pavilion is a white-haired man with his grandson, who is, I guess, eleven or twelve years old. The old man gives him a tour of the photographs, talking as though Hutton was only yesterday stroking a century for Yorkshire during the Festival. 'He was my hero. I saw him when I was your age,' he says to his grandson, whose expression is quizzical in response. 'Did he bat like Kevin Pietersen?' he asks. 'Better than Pietersen,' replies the grandfather, as if there no point in debating it. 'And he was more consistent too.' The boy moves half a pace closer to the photograph and stares at Hutton, immaculate in whites unblemished by advertising, and who holds a clean bat with the maker's name marked in

What sweat and concentration bring. The reward of a
double century for Josh Cobb against Bangladesh at Scarborough.

nothing more than modest capitals instead of today's elaborately garish stuck-on logos. The bat itself has been cut from the thinnest strip of willow. Hutton's batting gloves look flimsy by contemporary standards; no more than a piece of soft cloth and a sliver of padding on the fingers. The boy looks up at his grandfather and says dismissively: 'But you always say the past was better.'

After lunch Cobb continues in his clear-sighted and quietly serene way. Around him England begin to shed wickets as though it hardly matters. Hampshire's James Vince, who defied Andrew Flintoff for so long at Aigburth, goes lazily through a drive and gives Ali the gentlest of catching practice at mid-off. *Wisden*'s Schools Cricketer of the Year for 2008, James Taylor, doesn't last much longer either. At the end of May, Taylor made his debut century for Leicestershire and saved them from defeat after following on against Middlesex at Southgate. He is only 5 feet 5 inches tall. His helmet always looks half a size too big for him, as though it might slip over his eyes. Against the West Indies earlier in the summer, he survived only five balls before Darren Sammy trapped him lbw, which made it impossible to judge his potential. Against the Bangladeshi attack, he prods the ball down early on and dashes for singles at incredible speed. He's rather like a mouse scampering along a skirting board. After judging the pace of the pitch, he is soon cutting and pulling and out-scoring Cobb. He makes a stylish 21, more a cameo than an innings, before casually lofting Mominul Haque to Hasan at extra cover. Without him the match suddenly dulls; there's a dead patch in mid-afternoon which no one adequately fills. Luke Wells never gets off the mark. He chases a wide, hopeful ball from Babu and is caught at first slip by Anamul Haque. Four England wickets have gone for only 67 runs, and Bangladesh have barely had to scrap for any of them. At least Cobb remains, imperturbable but gradually more cautious. He moves out of the 80s and into the late 90s with twelve successive singles, a painful labour indeed before reaching his century. The England coach, Andy Pick, watches him from behind glass in the pavilion. 'As he's close to his hundred,' he says, 'I'll go and tempt Fate.' Pick sits on the front row of the balcony, and, eventually, Cobb breaks free of self-imposed shackles. He sends a full ball from Babu over wide mid-off for four, the signal for Pick to rise to his feet. His arms are soon aloft. From that moment on, there is no doubt that Cobb will make a double hundred. The spinners, led by Hasan, try to beguile him in the air and off the surface, which is too slow and unresponsive for them. Cobb's defence is stone-solid too. He smothers the spin or waits for it on the back foot and plays the ball as late as possible. In this mood he could tackle the bowling with a piece of driftwood from the beach. At 5.10 p.m., he's on 186. Five minutes later – after striking Ali for two successive sixes to long on and long off and running a speedy two to wide mid-on – he's reached 200. The sixes aren't in the master-class category of Thornton or Pepper. Both, however, thump loudly against the white tip-up seats at the Pavilion End behind the bowler, who swivels only head, neck and eyes to follow them and is reluctant to watch the final drop of the ball. He gives the helpless shrug of the defeated. The sky has broken into clear blue by now, the sun is intense, and two huge gulls begin to glide around the long benches near the main gate, as if saluting Cobb with a royal fly-past. The right wing of one of the gulls almost clips me across the ear. 'Buns' Thornton became one of fathers of the Scarborough Festival, and the Borough eventually rewarded him with the freedom of the town. Cobb must make do with applause, the hot memory of today's achievement and the almost synchronised swoop of the gulls.

I leave North Marine Road with Cobb and Kilburn on my mind. Kilburn died in 1993, so there is no telegram from the Queen for him this week. But in its place he'd be satisfied to know that someone else will always endorse his firm view of Scarborough. 'Once visited,' he wrote, '. . . it takes hold of you inexorably . . . the spell is laid never to be broken.' For the nineteen-year-old Josh Cobb, it is sure to be true now.

INSTEAD OF A TELEGRAM

Umpires: N. G. C. Cowley, M. A. Gough
Toss: England

England first innings

J. J. Cobb	c Mahmudul Hasan	b Alauddin Babu	220
J. C. Mickleburgh	hit wicket	b Sabbir Rahman	57
J. M. Vince	c Saikat Ali	b Sabbir Rahman	22
J. W. A. Taylor	c Mahmudul Hasan	b Mominul Haque	21
L. W. P. Wells	c Anamul Haque	b Alauddin Babu	0
S. G. Borthwick	c Amit Majumder	Sabbir Rahman	14
Azeem Rafiq	c Saikat Ali	b Shaker Ahmed	28
H. Riazuddin*	c Amit Majumder	c Mominul Haque	95
T. Poynton†	b Alauddin Babu		0
C. P. Wood	c Mahmudul Hasan	b Alauddin Babu	14
N. L. Buck	not out		9
Extras	(5b, 7lb, 5nb, 5w)		22
Total	(all out, 121.4 overs)		**502**

Fall of wickets: 1-139, 2-168, 3-205, 4-206, 5-250, 6-300, 7-409, 8-417, 9-436, 10-502

Bangladesh bowling	O	M	R	W
Abu Jayed	15	3	77	0
Alauddin Babu	17	2	73	4
Saikat Ali	2	0	14	0
Shaker Ahmed	20	2	77	1
Noor Hossain	12	0	61	0
Sabbir Rahman	30	5	76	3
Mahmudul Hasan	11	3	34	0
Mominul Haque	12.4	2	65	2
Amit Majumder	2	0	13	0

Bangladesh first innings

Amit Majumder	c Cobb	b Wood	2
Saikat Ali	c Buck	b Borthwick	33
Asif Ahmed	c Vince	b Azeem Rafiq	23
Mominul Haque	c Cobb	b Buck	90
Anamul Haque†	c sub	b Buck	31
Mahmudul Hasan*	lbw	b Wood	5
Sabbir Rahman	c Azeem Rafiq	b Borthwick	57
Noor Hossain	b Borthwick		2
Alauddin Babu	c & b Borthwick		6
Shaker Ahmed	b Borthwick		2
Abu Jayed	not out		4
Extras	(6lb, 9nb)		15
Total	(all out, 70.4 overs)		**270**

Fall of wickets: 1-8, 2-62, 3-103, 4-186, 5-195, 6-204, 7-221, 8-247, 9-253, 10-270

England bowling	O	M	R	W
Wood	19	3	59	2
Buck	12	1	38	2
Azeem Rafiq	21	2	89	1
Riazuddin	1	0	8	0
Bothwick	17.4	4	70	5

Bangladesh second innings (following on)

Amit Majumder	c Vince	b Wood	4
Saikat Ali	b Azeem Rafiq		58
Asif Ahmed	lbw	b Buck	0
Mominul Haque	lbw	b Azeem Rafiq	80
Anamul Haque†	b Azeem Rafiq		39
Mahmudul Hasan*	c Vince	b Azeem Rafiq	46
Sabbir Rahman	c Borthwick	b Azeem Rafiq	4
Noor Hossain	c Taylor	b Azeem Rafiq	12
Alauddin Babu	b Buck		24
Shaker Ahmed	b Wood		1
Abu Jayed	not out		0
Extras	(4b, 1lb, 2nb, 1w)		8
Total	(all out, 83.5 overs)		**276**

Fall of wickets: 1-1, 2-5, 3-102, 4-171, 5-186, 6-190, 7-232, 8-247, 9-272, 10-276

England bowling	O	M	R	W
Woods	15.5	5	44	2
Buck	15	4	31	2
Vince	4	0	24	0
Borthwick	13	0	64	0
Azeem Rafiq	30	7	90	6
Wells	6	1	18	0

England second innings

J. M. Vince	not out	16
J. J. Cobb	not out	31
Extras		0
Total	(0 wicket, 6.2 overs)	**47**

Bangladesh bowling	O	M	R	W
Alauddin Babu	2	0	9	0
Saikat Ali	2	0	25	0
Shaker Ahmed	1.2	0	7	0
Noor Hossain	1	0	6	0

Result: England won by 10 wickets

CHAPTER TEN

IT'S A CLEARING SHOWER
IN THESE PARTS

*Cheltenham College – the perfect place for those who
regard watching cricket as a heavenly pursuit.*

Cheltenham: LV County Championship Division Two: Gloucestershire v. Derbyshire, 12–15 July

The low, mellifluous notes of the chapel organ, and the high soprano of the choir, filter across the damp outfield. Like the peal of the cathedral bells at Worcester, it is appropriate background music for those who regard watching cricket as a heavenly pursuit. Even under the heaviest clouds, spread like a smoky-coloured army blanket, Cheltenham College is still striking on the eye: leafy and dignified. The ornate carving and precise lines of neo-Gothic architecture makes it so: two low chapels of thick gold stone with buttresses, and the makeshift pavilion (actually the College's gymnasium) with its twin spires and small black-faced clock. The façade, which isn't spoilt or scarred by the temporary tiers of seating in front of it, resembles a late-Victorian railway station. I half expect a train to chug past it and a guard with mutton-chop whiskers to blow a shrill whistle. A dozen snow-white tents and marquees on the periphery of the boundary give the opposite wing of the ground the sophisticated feel of a well-heeled, well-organised village fête. Behind them in the middle distance are vivid strips of clipped grass and the pale-tipped Cotswold hills, which shelter the spruce town. What marks the College out most of all as miniature theatre for cricket is the ambience that the landscape generates. History and tradition fit together here without a loose or fragile joint.

It's in settings like this one that the flagging County Championship, which seems to be dying inside, might profitably be revived and widely loved again. A sense of place is important in cricket. The four-day game especially demands to be played in surroundings that befit its style and tempo; certainly not against the backdrop of cavernous and three-quarter-empty Test venues, such as Edgbaston, Headingley or Old Trafford, where a cover drive sounds like a shot fired in an underground vault. It is better captured on the canvas of the pastoral and the picturesque, where spectators are within touching distance of what's happening on the field, where it's possible to browse for a longed-for book (or to find a book that you didn't know existed) at the secondhand stalls, and where old dogs can lie under their owners' chairs and doze or be walked gently around the boundary. The match can then drift along like a slow-moving river. I know this description sounds impossibly, and perhaps cloyingly, romantic; a kind of an undisturbed, cricketing Eden that possibly never existed and has no place in today's slick, Twenty20-charged atmosphere. But there is something consoling and so utterly civilised about Championship cricket when all these factors perfectly align. They do at Cheltenham College during the Festival. The town takes pride in its fortnight of cricket (this season comprising two Championship matches and three Pro40 League games), which begins with Gloucestershire against Derbyshire. No one at the start of the summer would ever have anticipated it as a 'top of the table' fixture. But that's what it has become. The favourites, Kent, have misfired so far, and Gloucestershire, who finished bottom in 2008 after abjectly failing to win a match, lead Division Two with 87 points. Derbyshire, whose recent Championship record is as glum and black as a misery memoir, sit three places but just 20 points below them.

Cheltenham is wearing its Sunday best for them both. Blue-and-white vertical banners advertising the Festival decorate rows of lamp-posts. Hanging baskets and window boxes are festooned with petunias in purples and reds, which spill brilliantly from the Regency architecture of its spacious Promenade. The ordered parks are palettes of colour too. The only thing missing is a clear sky. A slow splash of rain turns into a fine slide of drizzle, and then into a downpour, which soaks the College and lowers the spirits. Each drop is as big as a penny piece. The red collapsible seats skirting the ground begin to glisten like wet flint. The dark roof of the makeshift pavilion drips rain on to the weathered brick. The whole pallor of the ground turns a sickly grey, leaching away the light and leaving it too dark to cast a solitary shadow.

There are still people who refuse to budge beside the sightscreen, as though establishing squatter's rights to the plum place that an early arrival has granted them. A gaggle of us, far less hardy and resilient, take the more sensible option. We ask for refuge in the beer tent, peering out occasionally from the flapping doorway in the canvas to perfunctorily check the clouds, which seem to be getting lower, as if closing in on the ground. The mood is gloomy and resigned. 'Don't worry,' say a middle-aged husband and wife, who have come prepared with umbrellas stamped with Gloucestershire's crest, 'it's just a clearing shower in these parts. The sun will be out soon, you'll see.' I have no confidence in the couple's prediction. Rain is still running nosily off the tent roof, and I expect no play before lunch. I'd originally planned to watch these two counties in the corresponding match in June. I wanted to see Chesterfield's herbaceous borders and trellises, the lime and horse chestnuts trees, the trim bandstand and boating lake and the

Chinese pagoda. The opening day, however, was washed out. Much of the second was too. Chesterfield's crooked spire (the devil is supposed to have wrapped his tail around it in a fit of pique) was only half glimpsed from a passing train. I'd begun to think one of these counties was weather-cursed. But, within five minutes, the couple's reassuring forecast proves miraculously accurate. The rain drifts across the ground and goes off to spoil someone else's day. The sky is tinged gloriously blue for the first time since breakfast. The ground-staff smartly remove the covers and sweep only a thin amount of surface water off the outfield from the Chapel End. Improbable though it seemed when I was hiding in the tent to stay dry, the start of the match is delayed by only fifteen minutes. And when Derbyshire, who win the toss, dispatch their openers down the pavilion steps, the sun is high and burning. A decent crowd is already beginning to file four at a time through the gates with bags and radios tuned to *Test Match Special* from Cardiff, where England are fighting to avoid defeat in the First Test. The couple with the Gloucestershire umbrella are beside the sightscreen, and now use it for shade rather than shelter. Where else in the world but in England could this happen?

Gloucestershire's bowlers' first task is to cope with a damp ball. More crucially, the fielders are afflicted with dreaded dropped-catch syndrome. In the first 3 overs Derbyshire's Australian captain, Chris Rogers, and Wayne Madsen, a South African who holds an Italian passport, are allowed to live twice. Madsen, making his debut, pokes and prods about like a reluctant Sunday gardener. He plays a slack shot and edges Steve Kirby to third slip. James Franklin moves to his right to take the catch and grimaces in acute self-disgust as the ball wriggles free from him. In the next over, Rogers nicks Kirby to Hamish Marshall at second slip and the chance is grassed too. The pugnacious Rogers makes the most of his reprieve. With a cold, efficient disdain, he flicks full length deliveries, swept in on middle and leg, off his pads, drives with panache through extra cover and mid-off and rapidly takes the score past 30. Rogers is a solid-looking left-handed batsman with fair skin and ginger hair and a liking for the harder pitches on which he grew up in Perth. Nothing could be further from those baked conditions than slightly soggy Cheltenham this morning, but the outfield is small, and the ball regularly beats the fielder once it goes past him; Rogers exploits it. Within 8 overs Gloucestershire are calling on Jon Lewis, the most reliably consistent figure of their attack and the bowler most likely to take advantage of swing as well as seam on a surface offering hope for whoever plants the ball on a decent length. Lewis is one of those bowlers who always seems to have far more potential than he entirely fulfils. 'He has played for England, hasn't he?' I hear one man, holding a long red pencil and a full-sized scorebook on his lap, ask another sitting two seats away from him. 'Of course,' says his friend, without glancing up from his creased copy of the *Sunday Telegraph*. 'About four or five times, I think.' In fact Lewis has made only one Test appearance – against Sri Lanka at Trent Bridge three years ago. His other caps have come in one-day internationals. But the vagueness about what he's formerly achieved encapsulates the fate of so many players for whom Test cricket becomes a brief flirtation with fame. Sometimes ex-Test cricketers are like former soap actors who appear for a few episodes in *Coronation Street* or *Eastenders* before being written out of the plot. The public recognises their face afterwards – perhaps even their name – but can't quite remember where it was seen or why. Lewis nonetheless looks too impressive for Division Two. He has a long, elastic frame, which has been prone to injuries, but still extracts lift and movement and is mulish in pursuit of a wicket. He's a clever bowler too, able to weigh up a batsman's weaknesses and dig away at them.

Rogers and Madsen, who were looking comfortable before Lewis's arrival, are less assertive now. It's no surprise when Madsen, already groping twice outside the off stump for deliveries which cut and swing from off, edges Lewis and brings a classic wicketkeeping catch out of Steven Snell. He measures 6 feet – tall for someone with the gloves – but his height restricts neither his mobility nor his agility. Snell dives instinctively to his right and takes a one-handed catch in front of first slip. The loss of Madsen doesn't affect Rogers' confidence at all. He assumes control again, seeing the ball early and working it away late, or leaning into his drives to send them hurtling down the appreciable slope, which runs from the pavilion. Rogers brings up Derbyshire's 50 in the 17th over and his own half-century – which includes nine fours – shortly afterwards with an uncharacteristic, partly mistimed lunge that squirts away behind backward point. He celebrates reaching his milestone by hitting Kirby for two more fours in the same over. At lunch Derbyshire are 93 for 1, and Gloucestershire seem shorn of ideas about how to respond.

* * *

One of the sadnesses of cricket during the past forty years has been the reduction in the number of first-class venues in which it is played. Even as late as 1978, I can count twenty-six towns, cities or resorts (excluding the Minor Counties and the Universities) that now no longer host a county club unless it is for a beer match or benefit. Among the late and much-lamented are Eastbourne, Harrogate, Hastings, Newark, Weston-Super-Mare, Burton, Bradford and Worksop. From the 1969 *Wisden*, I can add even more, including Buxton and Middlesbrough, Dover and Glastonbury. It's as if cricket's own version of a flinty-eyed and unfeeling Dr Beeching stared at a map of England one summer's day and tut-tutted his disapproval. Not liking what he saw, and regarding it as an unnecessary extravagance of choice, he put his cold, dead hand on the fixture list and wiped a lot of it away. In specific acts of desecration some grounds don't exist at all now. Hastings' Priory Meadow, which overlooked the grey, pock-marked walls of the castle and rows of five-storey town houses, long ago became an ugly spread of bland shops. The planners' inadequate sop in recognition and remembrance of times past is the statue of a floppy-hatted batsman at the end of a flowing stroke. It is stuck between the usual suspects – the ubiquitous High Street retailers. The ball the batsman has supposedly just struck is embedded high into the wall of one of the stores. But the grass on which Gilbert Jessop once scored 112 not out in exactly an hour, a century in 68 minutes and 119 in 55 was bulldozed and concreted. The excuse given for it is progress.

Sentiment only occasionally interprets the task of money-making, which is why out-grounds have withered. Upping sticks, taking the tent from county headquarters and repitching it elsewhere is time-consuming, bothersome and costly. Yorkshire, for example, who were once itinerants, now only break from Headingley to camp at Scarborough, where it makes financial sense to do so. The coastal holiday crowds are far larger and more diverse than those attracted to the sombre skyline of Leeds. Yorkshire are investing extensively in Headingley. Why, under those circumstances, would it want to stretch capital and resources to remodel Harrogate or Bradford as fit places to stage first-class matches again? The out-ground, however, creates a solid intimacy between spectator and player that the larger, more steeply banked arenas were never built to foster. I feel part of, rather than apart from, what is going on in front of me at Scarborough and Cheltenham. There's a friendlier, cosier air too. I check this season's fixtures. Eight counties will not play away from their 'headquarters' at all. Even Chesterfield was only restored to Derbyshire's calendar three years ago after being struck off in 1998. At least Cheltenham is sacrosanct. It is part of the loam and marrow of the summer. With a lineage stretching back to 1872 – when Gladstone was still occupying 10 Downing Street – it is the longest-running Cricket Festival on an out-ground, and no other Festival anywhere in the world runs for twelve days or longer. The supporters' souvenir tent in front of the Chapel End is selling T-shirts with the date of the Festival's formation stamped boldly and proudly across the chest, like the vintage on an aged and fine bottle of wine. Only fashions change. If you ignore the advertising boards and the clothes – men in bowler hats or boaters, women in long dresses toting dainty parasols – photographs of the Edwardian Festival look almost identical to today's.

The architect of the Festival was James Lillywhite, a canny operator and wheeler-dealer not unlike Nottinghamshire's William Clarke. *Wisden* chummily described him as a 'right good fellow'. Like Clarke, Lillywhite had only one good eye. Also like Clarke, he was another cricketer and businessman and knew how to exploit those twin, spiked interests of his nature. He produced his own annual *Cricketers' Companion*, which rivalled *Wisden* and outlived him for eight years after his death in 1882. Lillywhite, who was once part of the fabric of Sussex cricket, became College coach in 1856 on the salary of fifty-two guineas per year – the equivalent of nearly £40,000 today. By 1877 he was paid £120 (£65,000) to run two Festival games within six days. Lillywhite was obliged to cover all 'local expenses', which he easily cleared. There's a studio portrait of Lillywhite which captures the exuberant, slightly eccentric streak of his personality. He is wearing a three-piece white suit, a black-and-white striped tie, a brown bowler hat and a brown pair of square-toed shoes. He's leaning to his left, as if tilting to accommodate the sway of a ship. His left hand is buried in his trouser pocket. His right hand is raised to his eyes, as though adjusting a pair of rimless pince-nez spectacles. He looks like a Variety Hall comedian. Lillywhite nonetheless was a serious entrepreneur without whom Cheltenham would never have become Cheltenham any more than Glyndebourne would have become one of the homes of opera without John Christie. In the first Festival game, W. G. Grace took seven wickets and humbled Surrey to an innings defeat. Its best stories, however, are about characters rather than performances. Charlie Parker, on his final Festival appearance in 1935 –

three months short of his fifty-third birthday – bowled disappointingly against Middlesex before heading off to a nearby pub for the solace of several pints. He listened in anonymous silence to a Middlesex member berating and demeaning the Gloucestershire side as humble and unworthy, like a collection of village idiots. When Parker's humour and patience finally ran dry (unlike his glass) he clenched his left hand into a tight fist, took two steps across the room and punched the man on the jaw. He calmly returned to his table, drained his pint and said: 'Time to go.' During the same Festival, Reg Sinfield scored a century against South Africa. In the final innings, with the tourists moving serenely towards a winning target of 290, Sinfield looked down and saw a ladybird crawling up the front of his shirt. He went to his captain 'Puggy' Page and insisted: 'Give me the ball. I feel lucky.' Sinfield took two wickets in one burst and then another three. His 5-31 enabled Gloucestershire to win by 87 runs. 'I always likes ladybirds,' said Sinfield, ungrammatically, but with sincerity, afterwards.

A savage shot in heavenly surroundings. Hamish Marshall takes advantage of the downhill slope to punish a loose delivery at Cheltenham's intimate and beautiful ground.

Sinfield would have felt at home today. The ladybirds are here in battalions. It has turned into a blissful afternoon, but Derbyshire begin to enjoy it too much and consequently become complacent. Last summer Worcestershire made a Festival record of 672-7 declared; Vikram Solanki hit 270 of them. In 2006 Glamorgan heaped up 647 for 7 before declaring too, and Mike Powell fell one run short of a triple hundred. Sweetly dreaming of similar match-winning totals, Derbyshire find themselves shaken awake by an abrupt collapse; one of those dramatic reversals of fortune that convulse a match and jerk it out of shape. The entirely unexpected begins when Lewis gets a ball to leave Garry Park, and Snell pockets his second catch without difficulty. Dan Redfern lasts only ten balls before falling to Kirby; Marshall atones for his earlier error by taking the ball faultlessly. Rogers, the prize wicket of the moment, is on 81 when he decides to go on to the back foot and try to crack Lewis through the covers. He misjudges the pace and gets a bottom edge on to his stumps. His head drops in dejection and he walks glumly off; truly the Knight of the Woeful Countenance. He knows he's needlessly squandered an exquisite chance of a hundred and more. Finally, the West Indian Wavell Hinds becomes another victim of the Kirby–Marshall combination after fending the ball into the slips. From 112 for 1, Derbyshire have sunk to 119 for 5 in only 7 overs. It should have been worse. Gloucestershire could have penetrated to the very core of the batting. Greg Smith has made just 2 when Lewis squares him up and gets another edge. At second slip Craig Spearman spills it horribly. The bowler is halfway through an appeal before letting it die away in embarrassment.

The reason for Derbyshire's sudden malaise is swing. In particular Lewis makes maximum use of a ball that is nearly 50 overs old and is bending in the air far more than it did during the morning. The science of swing is hard to explain definitively. On the inside the ball has a condensed core of rubber, cork and yarn. On the outside, it is from 5.5 ounces to 5.75 ounces in weight, 8.82 to 9.02 inches in circumference, with 78 to 82 stitches to each seam, and is thickly coated with nitrocellulose. But why one specific ball swings and another does not is arbitrary and unfathomable. The ball is supposed to swing under heavy cloud and in a humid atmosphere. There are still mysterious periods when conditions that should be bespoke for swing don't produce so much as a shiver after it leaves the bowler's hand. This season Division Two is a laboratory where experiments on a new ball, the Tiflex, take place. It is expected to swing more than the traditional Duke and is described as an 'absolute rock'. There is still no accounting, however, for the fact that a bowler such as Lewis can swing it all over the place in one game and not at all in the next.

Whether the ball swings or not, Smith, a South African, deals with it expertly after a dour hour during which Gloucestershire handcuff him. A crisp, back-foot cover drive for four off Franklin is Smith's release. He has a commanding stance – feet well apart and a stiff spine. Since making an unbeaten 94 against Surrey in the second match of the season, he's totalled a mere 117 runs from six Championship innings, a statistic hard to believe when his touch returns and he begins browbeating the bowlers. Smith would prefer to bat higher in the order. But it's just as well for Derbyshire's sake that he's at number six and can act as the robustly effective last line of defence-cum-attack. Without him, the death rattle would have spread through the innings. Smith tackles the bowling with unpitying harshness, hitting seven fours in his first 50 and another four in his next. He roars through the last session. The boundary that brings up his hundred is struck to wide long off from the spin of Chris Taylor. He'd been more ruthless in the previous over when Banerjee tried to tease him with a floating ball. Smith responded by taking a stride down the pitch and provocatively hitting him back over his head for six. The ball was momentarily lost in flight. Only the crack as it landed against the sightscreen announced its arrival at the Chapel End. Smith's 126 enables Derbyshire to get past 300.

There are grumbles – some entirely justified – that the skills gap between the counties in the First and Second Divisions has widened every summer since 2000, when the County Championship was split with the force of a woodsman's axe. This cleaving apart has created the haves and have nots, a truism which the current season emphasises. The First Division comprises five of the Test venues: Durham, Lancashire, Nottinghamshire, Warwickshire and Yorkshire. In the Second Division the crowds are smaller, the grounds generally less impressive and the ability to recruit diminished. There are also serious questions about whether, eventually, even the most tolerant membership will be satisfied if their side is relegated into Division Two or can't escape from it. The Second Division isn't as intense as the First. Often there isn't the bowling depth to worry the new, let alone the well-set, batsman. The teams in it – and Gloucestershire and Derbyshire are prime examples – don't have much glitz or glitter about them either.

In mid-afternoon, I still saw Smith play one shot that alchemised into pure gold. It was a late cut off Anthony Ireland. The delivery came to him fractionally outside off stump, and Smith anticipated it to the extent that he was in position for the stroke when the ball had travelled only half its distance. His right foot was planted firmly back, and the bat was raised in preparation for the slicing motion long before he brought it cleanly down. Smith did so deftly, as though trying to make the runs soundlessly. He gently cocked his wrists and caressed the ball to the third-man boundary. The shot was so late that Smith almost played it posthumously. Even the partisan locals at the Chapel End were full of admiration for it and him. These small, fleeting acts count. When Smith late-cuts so stylishly, the fact he did it in Division Two is immaterial. The result of this match won't be chiselled on to fine marble to preserve it for posterity. The newspaper reports will dry and go dusty and be forgotten too. But, as the result or the figures of the individual performances hazily fade and cease to matter, I'll retain, freeze-framed, the image of Smith's stroke in my mind – a bright little fragment of beauty.

At the close, as the marquees darken, I stay on, determined to wring the last of the warmth out of the early evening. When I head off at last, I can't resist turning around for a lingering glance at the chapel. The organ music drifted away and died hours ago. But I swear I can still hear it; and I can still hear it more than an hour later.

Umpires: B. Dudleston, P. Willey
Toss: Derbyshire

Derbyshire first innings

C. J. L. Rogers*	b Lewis		81
W. L. Madsen	c Snell	b Lewis	7
G. T. Park	c Snell	b Lewis	25
D. J. Redfern	c Marshall	b Kirby	4
W. W. Hinds	c Marshall	b Kirby	0
G. M. Smith	c Snell	b Franklin	126
D. J. Pipe†	b Banerjee		22
G. G. Wagg	c Snell	b Ireland	31
T. D. Groenewald	c Marshall	b Franklin	26
J. Needham	not out		1
P. S. Jones	c Marshall	b Franklin	0
Extras	(3lb)		3
Total	(all out, 88.4 overs)		**326**

Fall of wickets: 1-34, 2-112, 3-117, 4-117, 5-119, 6-183, 7-231, 8-321, 9-326, 10-326

Gloucestershire bowling	O	M	R	W
Franklin	18.4	3	59	3
Kirby	14	3	50	2
Lewis	17	4	40	3
Ireland	14	2	79	1
Banerjee	19	0	84	1
Taylor	6	1	11	0

Gloucestershire first innings

Kadeer Ali	b Wagg		25
C. M. Spearman	c Pipe	b Jones	7
H. J. H. Marshall	run out		7
A. P. R. Gidman*	lbw	b Jones	55
C. G. Taylor	c Pipe	b Groenwald	6
J. E. C. Franklin	b Smith		14
S. D. Snell†	b Jones		2
J. Lewis	c Needham	b Jones	6
S. P. Kirby	c Hinds	b Smith	9
V. Banerjee	not out		5
A. J. Ireland	b Groenwald		16
Extras	(5lb, 6nb, 1w)		12
Total	(all out, 56.2 overs)		**164**

Fall of wickets: 1-21, 2-34, 3, 74, 4, 89, 5-121, 6, 121, 7-127, 8-138, 9-138, 10-164

Derbyshire bowling	O	M	R	W
Jones	18.2	6	44	4
Wagg	14.4	3	49	1
Groenewald	13.2	1	48	2
Smith	7	3	12	2
Needham	2	0	6	0

Derbyshire second innings

C. J. L. Rogers*	c Snell	b Franklin	3
W. L. Madsen	not out		170
G. T. Park	c Snell	b Lewis	9
D. J. Redfern	lbw	b Marshall	31
J. Needham	c Spearman	b Kirby	5
W. W. Hinds	b Kirby		54
G. M. Smith	c Lewis	b Ireland	34
D. J. Pipe†	not out		0
Extras	(8b, 7lb, 2w)		17
Total	(6 wickets declared, 89 overs)		**323**

Fall of wickets: 1-3, 2-28, 3-117, 4-126, 5-243, 6-321

Gloucestershire bowling	O	M	R	W
Lewis	11	3	24	1
Franklin	14	4	28	1
Kirby	19	5	58	2
Ireland	16	3	51	1
Banerjee	18	3	95	0
Taylor	2	0	9	0
Marshall	2	0	11	1
Gidman	7	2	32	0

Gloucestershire second innings

C. M. Spearman	c Pipe	b Jones	27
Kadeer Ali	b Jones		44
H. J. M. Marshall	b Groenewald		0
A. P. R. Gidman*	b Groenewald		60
C. G. Taylor	c Pipe	b Groenewald	9
J. E. C. Franklin	b Needham		109
S. D. Snell†	c Rogers	b Needham	13
J. Lewis	c Rogers	b Needham	0
S. P. Kirby	c Rogers	b Wagg	16
V. Banerjee	c Needham	b Wagg	8
A. J. Ireland	not out		2
Extras	(9lb, 2nb, 1w)		12
Total	(all out, 95.4 overs)		**300**

Fall of wickets: 1-71, 2-76, 3-76, 4- 91, 5-185, 6-213, 7-213, 8-261, 9-276, 10-300

Derbyshire bowling	O	M	R	W
Jones	27	7	64	2
Wagg	33	4	96	2
Groenewald	20	4	64	3
Needham	14.4	3	51	3
Smith	1	0	16	0

Result: Derbyshire won by 185 runs

CHAPTER ELEVEN

ON THE SHOULDERS
OF GIANTS

*Lumpy Stevens, left, climbed out of bed with the dawn chorus to choose
his own pitch and became the most deadly under arm bowler of his day.
'Silver Billy' Beldham, right, executed the cut with a wrist that
'seemed to turn on springs of the finest steel'.*

Ridge Meadow: Southern Electric League Division Two: Hambledon v. Hook and Newnham Basics, 18 July

Nothing separates the two cradles of English cricket on this fine Saturday afternoon except the small matter of 71 miles. At Lord's England face Australia in the Second NPower Test. At Ridge Meadow, Hambledon face Hook and Newnham Basics in the Second Division of the Southern Electric League. There are 30,000 squeezed into Lord's, spilling out of the Compton and Edrich Stands, the Grand Stand and the glass-fronted hospitality boxes. There are twenty-three, plus one energetic mongrel, beside the advertising boards and parked cars, which lie in an open field at Hambledon. But, whatever the geographical distance between St John's Wood and the Hampshire village, the importance of each match and the intensity of the cricket is – at least in relative terms – just the same.

The old-fashioned television with its teak surround and curved screen, fixed to the wall of Hambledon's low wooden pavilion, relays the Ceefax scores from Lord's. The signal is poor, and so letters and numbers are frequently lost in transmission. It's like looking at a jigsaw with a quarter of the pieces missing. On occasions, working out which batsman is at the crease, let alone the number of runs scored and wickets taken, becomes an impossibly frustrating job. In truth, however, no one from either Hambledon or Hook takes much notice of what is happening at Lord's. The Test isn't central to anyone's thoughts. Their own game is too significant to allow the Ashes to encroach on it.

Hambledon are second from bottom of the table and need points to revive them and hold off the prospect of relegation. Hook hover in its nether regions and ambitiously eye higher things. Whatever Andrew Strauss and Ricky Ponting do over the next six hours, and however much it seminally shapes the rest of the summer, won't impact on Hambledon and Hook. The Test will be treated as almost inconsequential until the match here is over, which supports the view of John Arlott, also a man of Hampshire. Arlott observed solemnly that: 'Village cricket is a serious matter.'

Hoary stereotypes nonetheless cling to it. The village game is parodied and satirised as if the fictional comic turns in A. G. Macdonnell's *England, Their England* – Fordenden against the boozy, rubicund and class-conscious literary gents – were living still. But there is a lot more to contemporary village cricket than sandwiches and cake and barrels of beer. Nor does it comprise two motley, shabbily dressed crews of ageing, flabby men with wobbly knees and arthritic backs, who share pads and bats and gloves, swopping them on the way out of the pavilion and getting half-dressed on the outfield. And nor does the pitch – often set in the most ravishing scenery – resemble an unkempt and rutted back garden. None of it is true at Hambledon, where there are standards and traditions to be maintained and the past is tangible in the present because the village embraces the almost sacred earth of Broadhalfpenny Down and the skilled prose of John Nyren to describe it.

There were matches spread across the chalky South Downs before Hambledon cut and pitched its first set of stumps. But it became the crucible in which the game developed, and the original 'gentlemen of Hambledon' became its arch practitioners. From the 1770s Hambledon flayed the opposition of whatever stripe and gave its players the handsome enticement of a five-guinea win-bonus per match – the modern parallel is a lottery windfall – when the basic salary in George III's England was the 'pittance' scrapings of a copper or two. Often 20,000 walked or rode horses or climbed on clattering wooden-wheeled carts to reach Broadhalfpenny Down and watch Hambledon, who whipped All England on twenty-nine occasions, as if the pride of the country were novices. So much minor detail is known about Hambledon because Nyren wrote about its players in *The Cricketers of My Time*, which Arlott described as 'the finest study of cricket and cricketers ever written'. Nyren's father, Richard, was not only captain, groundsman and 'head and right arm' of the club, but also landlord of the Bat and Ball Inn, which sat – and still sits – beside Broadhalfpenny Down. The team were tradesmen and workers, initially drawn from a 10-mile radius of the ground: builders, bakers, potters, farmers. Those who came to see them drank punch strong enough, at sixpence a bottle, to 'make a cat speak' and barleycorn ale that flared 'like turpentine' at twopence per pint and which 'put the souls of three butchers into one weaver'. The players and officials were clubbable too. The minutes of its meetings record Hambledon's penchant for combining cricket and alcohol irrespective of the risk of elephantine hangovers. One entry reads: 'A wet day: only three members present: nine bottles of wine.' A late-eighteenth-century song, composed in the club's honour, implores:

> Then fill up your glass!
> He's the best that drinks the most.

Nyren published his book half a century after he'd seen – or been told about – the characters and events of which he wrote. He might consequently be accused of over-sanctifying them or be guilty of an old man's rheumy romanticism, misted and rose-hued by nostalgic yearning.

It was in Nyren's authorial interests to be lyrical about Hambledon, of which he said: 'No eleven in England could compare.' But the statistical evidence of presence and power is undeniable. This was the revered Team of All the Talents. There was 'Lumpy' Stevens, who climbed out of bed with the dawn chorus to choose a pitch of rough turf, which he preferred with a downward slope to accommodate his own vicious speciality – the shooter. He bowled it underhand at a zippy pace, frequently bruising and chipping the shinbones of whoever faced him. There was Tom Walker, who tested the then experimental 'round arm' action in 1788 – forty years before the MCC legalised it – and found himself accused of being 'a chucker'. It was said that Walker 'moved like the rude machinery of the steam engine'. The protests against him were the eighteenth-century equivalent of the approbation heaped on Ian Meckiff for throwing in Australia during the late 1950s and again in the early 1960s. 'Some strong things were said about his suspect bowling action,' wrote Jack Fingleton with gross understatement in describing the ramifications of the Meckiff controversy. 'You know,' said one of Fingleton's friends, 'if that chap was delivering a boomerang instead of a ball, it would come right back to his feet.' Well, Nyren could have reported on similar angry responses about Walker. A law against 'jerking' was passed specifically because of him.

With a more 'graceful arm', there was Hambledon's tricorn-hatted David Harris, capable of making the ball steeple off the surface almost perpendicularly with his underarm deliveries, which struck the bare, hard-veined hands of the batsman like skimmed rocks. He is supposed to have 'ground' fingers 'to dust', 'pulverised' bones and 'scattered' blood all over the field, which sounds as if he carried the gladiatorial element of the game to the point of savagery like a swordsman in a Kurosawa film. In fact, Harris merely released the ball from the level of his armpit with a 'twist' of his hand. Nyren wrote: 'When preparing for his run . . . he stood erect like a soldier at drill'; hardly Dennis Lillee, let alone Jeff Thomson. With the bat, William 'Silver Billy' Beldham's favourite stroke was the cut, which Nyren said he executed with a wrist that 'seemed to turn on springs of the finest steel'. He averaged 43 runs per match for thirteen years. It hardly sounds Bradmanesque until one vital statistic is added and burnishes his reputation. The average score for a batsman in those primitive days was less than 20.

The landscape around Hambledon largely remains as Nyren first saw it. Staring across Broadhalfpenny Down, long since the home of another club, Brigands CC, it requires only minimal imagination to see Stevens and Harris, Beldham and 'the chucker' Walker as rough but noble figures in dark breeches, silk socks and billowing white-grey vests. The past feels tangible in the heavyweight silence here. It's a spiritual site of communion, like a Civil War battlefield still redolent of the conflicts it once saw.

Across the road the walls of the Bat and Ball Inn are shrines to Hambledon's brief, shining moment of cricketing fame. Among the collection is a portrait of Nyren in his black coat and collar. White receding hair reveals the polished dome of his forehead. He looks like a nascent school-master. There is the 'Hambledon bat', which is the ebony colour of a blacksmith's mallet. And there is a print of a game on Broadhalfpenny Down in 1777. It evokes the England of old thatched cottages and clear-watered streams and wildflower meadows. In the far distance are hidden corkscrew paths trimmed with the oak, the beech and the elm. It's the sort of country scene found on the lid of a tin of shortbread. The red-brick inn is visible along the road, and a church steeple pokes beyond a hill in the far distance. Someone – perhaps the demon Harris – is about to run in and bowl and bring blood and panic to the batsman, who is taking guard.

An unprepossessing grey obelisk, opposite the Bat and Ball Inn, is simply carved with two curved bats resting on two stumps. The bland inscription reads:

> This stone marks the site
> of the ground
> of the Hambledon Cricket Club
> Circ 1750–1787

Since 1850 Hambledon's club's home has been at Ridge Meadow. Well before the Great War, the writer E. V. Lucas described the route to it as 'steep and stony as one of Bunyan's toilsome ways'. Today it is a pleasant drive through a dark arch of trees – the branches interlock like spindly fingers – into the heart of the Meon Valley. The village is quintessentially English: neat square cottages and a Saxon church with lichen-covered gravestones and patches of wildflowers. Ridge Meadow is a mile closer to the village than Broadhalfpenny Down and sits on the crest of a shallow rise. It is circled by stumpy trees and wide hedges. The clouds, like froth, are hanging low over it, almost brushing the turf. I feel I could reach out and drag the tail of one of them to the ground. Thick woodland and cornfields fill the rest of the landscape. The wind is getting up into a swell. The club's flag – white capital lettering on a blue background – and a Union Jack fly straight from matching poles on either side of the pavilion balcony.

The chocolate box image of English cricket during the pomp of Hambledon's team of all the talents. It neither conveys the intense competitiveness nor the often brutal, bloody business of winning matches in that era. The exact location – and date – of the painting is unkown.

Every player is explicitly aware of what it means to be a modern 'man of Hambledon' and to stand on the shoulders of giants. The blue-blood past is inescapable. The date of the formation of the club – circa 1750 – is stitched on to the team's shirts, caps and the flag. One of the original parchment 'cards of the match', from June 1777, is displayed beside the away team's dressing room as a deliberate reminder of the club's aristocratic lineage. Attractively stylish handwriting in fading sepia ink records Hambledon's dominance of the era. England were bowled out for 166 and 69; Hambledon made 405, including 167 from the number ten batsman, Aylward, to win by an innings and 170 runs.

Sometimes history does set the bar at an impossible height.

* * *

Hambledon's captain is twenty-one-year-old James Scutt, a painter and decorator who talks about the club and what it represents with devotional zeal. Scutt is a six-footer, and broad too. He has closely cropped fair hair and wide hands. This is his second summer as skipper. The first brought promotion. Life in Division Two, however, has proved more exacting and less forgiving of mistakes. Hambledon have also experienced difficulties common among most village teams. Personnel changes at a rapid pace. The older players – in their late thirties and forties – succumb to joint injuries. The younger players get married, find new jobs, move on or discover that a commitment to cricket has to be replaced by a commitment to family. Pre- and immediately postwar, before car exhaust fumes choked the air, the English village was a static community, which only visibly changed as one agricultural season passed into another. Everyone worked close to home, and most lived and died in the same cottage. The village team was drawn from narrow boundaries. The village sides of today are scattered affairs. Scutt, who first opened the batting for Hambledon at fourteen, spends much of his week on his mobile phone sorting out and rearranging his team around holidays, weddings and other social affairs.

The age range spans fifteen to thirty-eight; but the second-oldest player is only twenty-three. The fifteen-year-old is Ollie Mills, son of the club's chairman, who bats at number five. Hambledon have a new overseas player this summer too: Australian all-rounder Blake Dean, hired from Grade cricket in New South Wales, has replaced pace bowler Simon Milenka, who returned to Queensland's Gold Coast Dolphins in 2008. The arrangement suits both Hambledon and Dean. Hambledon pay for Dean's travel to and from England and for his accommodation. In return he not only plays but also coaches. 'Our policy is to take someone for two years,' explains Scutt. 'And they have to be young because we think they'll fit in better with the rest of the team. But it takes them time to adjust to the conditions here – the climate and the soft, grassy pitches. They're nearly always more effective in their second season.'

Dean and Scutt open the batting after Hambledon, who have won only two games from eleven this summer, lose the toss and are put in on a wicket flecked with green. Soon Hook are ruing the decision. Dean and Scutt deal effectively with back of the length bowling. Dean is especially impressive. If, as Shakespeare insisted, a rose is a rose is a rose, then a back-foot drive through the covers is just as supremely elegant whether Dean executes it at Ridge Meadow or at Lord's. When Hook's nineteen-year-old Jason Hobday drops a delivery short, Dean leans effortlessly away from it and punishes him hard with an instinctive and poetic backlift and follow-through. The ball thunders off to the ropes. The Australian brings up the 50 with a pull shot that further illustrates his strength off the back foot. Dean almost claimed his first century for the club earlier in the month. He was on 99 when Scutt's error ran him out. 'I did apologise,' says the captain, shaking his head at the stabbing memory.

Hambledon get the bonus of a let-off. Scutt top-edges Hobday, and the ball floats towards the covers like a child's balloon. What follows is high farce. Cover point leaves it for backward point; backward point leaves it for cover point. When the fielders realise that neither has moved for the straightforward catch, the two of them set off simultaneously and at full pelt. Somehow they manage to avoid smashing into one another – backward point veering away a split-second before the expected collision – as the ball drops harmlessly between them. But Hobday's revenge is swift. He brings the ball back into Scutt and clean bowls him for 18 in the 13th over.

It is important to work out the longitude and latitude of the terrain at Ridge Meadow. The outfield slopes away on either side of the wicket, but predominantly towards one corner to the left of the pavilion. In fact, when long leg fields there I can't see his body from below the knees. When I stand in the same position, I can't see the bottom half of the stumps either. Whoever scuttles off in pursuit of the ball disappears from view for a second or two, like someone leaving a room, before his torso and head reappear to hurl it in. It is unsettling as a fielder to negotiate this slope for the first time, as if faced by a high fortification. Now well used to the geography, Dean makes use of it. He knows a firm clip there will probably go for four.

With his upright stance and piercing eye, he looks impossible to shift unless he makes a mistake. He does so in the 31st over against the left-arm spin of Kevin Poulter. Poulter is forty-eight, a veteran of more than twenty summers with Hook. His run to the stumps – eight shortish steps and the ball cradled in his hands – as well as the sweep of his delivery action are in the mould of Norman Gifford, the Worcestershire and England spinner of the 1960s and '70s. When he holds one ball back, bowling it flatter, Dean tries to drive (again off the back foot) and is bowled for 70. The middle and lower orders scratch around, and only a late flurry from the tail – the last three batsmen push and nurdle 46 between them – manages to raise the total to 187 for 8 off 50 overs. Mills is unlucky. He succumbs to one of the best deliveries of the afternoon – a doosra from Anik Divecha that entices him out of his crease.

Scutt stands in front of the pavilion in T-shirt, shorts and a pair of flip-flops, smoking a cigarette he rolls himself. He is pensive. He doesn't look or sound entirely convinced that Hambledon's total will be sufficient. 'Well done boys,' he says anyway, clapping his hands as if banging together two dustbin lids.

For a cricketer, the phrase 'tea is taken' is one of the most evocative in the English language. Somehow the tea itself always tastes stronger, fuller and richer when it is poured from a brown pot or a tall silver urn (and not, as George Orwell believed, 'always tasteless' as a consequence). The full cups and mugs have a practical use today. The weather is turning colder, greyer. The players stand in clusters, sheltering from the gathering breeze, and wrap both hands around whatever they're drinking from for warmth and comfort. Their spikes dig into and rake the wooden boards of the pavilion.

The sky abruptly darkens, and shortly before Hook begin to bat there's a roll of thunder and a prolonged shower. Using the captain's prerogative, Scutt dispatches his team to push on the covers. He watches them do it while smoking another of his slim cigarettes. The grey-haired umpires emerge and glance up at the heavens, as if asking a question. 'The weather comes from behind the pavilion. It's light over there,' says one of Hambledon's officials optimistically. 'Don't get too cosy in there,' he adds, pointing to the players who are standing in front of the television. 'You'll be out there again five minutes from now.'

No sooner have Hambledon put the bulky covers on, then Scutt orders his team out again to wheel them back into the long grass. The shower slows, if only slightly, and gives the umpires the excuse to start Hook's innings. Two overs are lost through the delay, but the openers, captain Ben Thane and Neil Marsh, seem more perturbed by a grey, misty dimness, which shrouds the ground like a thin fog, than the fact the rain is lashing down on them. Even bowling with a damp ball, Hambledon exert control from the beginning. Blake Dean and Dan Hewitt are accurate and nippy. Hewitt's slender frame and long-legged approach, which allow him to crack the ball on to the pitch like a whip, cause Thane and Marsh discomfort. Hewitt has a hairstyle – an extravagant, frizzy mop – that seems to have been borrowed from Bob Willis, circa 1982. He comes down the hill in the same jerky, straight-armed manner too.

Within 13 overs, Hook are 30 for 3. The runs have mostly come from an undistinguished catalogue of false shots, streaky cuts and fluked edges, and Hambledon are starting to think about a rare win. But, after Hook add 17 to their total without further loss, the weather intervenes again. The cloud sinks lower still, and the rain is more persistent. 'Don't know why they've come off,' says a Hambledon old-timer in a fleeced blue jacket, leaning back on a bench seat in front of the pavilion. 'I once played in snow in early May here. Don't know they're born, this lot.' Hambledon's Second XI have been washed out only half an hour's drive away, and refugees from the abandoned fixture arrive at Ridge Meadow to offer advice. Everyone is peering at the sky. An hour passes before the cloud, which has stubbornly refused to shift all day, breaks apart like a drop of dye in water, and reveals a giddy brightness.

Groucho Marx, glancing at a complicated financial report, said: 'Why, a child of four could understand this. Run out and find me a four-year-old child.' The mathematics of rain-affected cricket falls into the same category. The umpires do their calculations – stiff sums about run rate and time and overs bowled, which makes the Duckworth Lewis Method look as straightforward as a two-digit sum on an abacus. The bottom line is this: Hook are now chasing 131 to win and have 13 overs to score 83 with 6 wickets left. The match, once so one-sided, begins to change in unpredictable gusts. Hook slip to 80 for 7 before Thane and Anik Divecha summon the shots to whittle down the target and give Hambledon palpitations. With two short waves of his hand, as if the effort wearies him, the umpire at the Pavilion End signals another ferocious four from Thane to the scorers, who sit in a small, flat-roofed wooden box like birders in a hide.

Hook need 53 runs off 9 overs and then only 33 off 5 – almost a run a ball, which is entirely achievable on this ground and its runaway slope. At last the light is sparkling and tips the nearby hills with gold.

Hook's players camp on the boundary's edge, yelling and whooping each precious run home, as if shouting a horse past the finishing post, and watching the scoreboard tick over in their favour. A downcast, resigned silence settles, like dust after an explosion, on the Hambledon members. It appreciably deepens when Hook's Lye launches a certain four to long off. The ball disappears towards the dark hedges – a hard black dot against rich blue. Hook's team are already raucously celebrating it when Tanios Watfa, making his first-team debut for Hambledon, lunges and stretches and takes the catch six inches from the floor. It is hard to know who is the more shocked: the catcher or his victim. Watfa bounds off the floor, lifting the ball aloft like a gleaming trophy.

On 102 for 8 Hambledon are improbably back in the game. With the overs running out, Scutt bravely and brazenly takes the ball and bowls spin from the Pavilion End. Only four runs have been added when Thane, after a resourceful innings of sensible nudges and extravagant hitting, clubs Chapman towards deep mid-wicket. The ball glides across the summer air, and everyone's first thought is whether Hewitt can block it to prevent the boundary. He gallops in, devouring in one step the ground that most others would take three to cover. He's within seven feet of the ball when he takes off, his hands outstretched. He arrives at the very moment it is about to kiss the grass. He pushes his hand underneath the ball and scoops it up before tumbling like a gymnast at the end of a practised fall. There's a cathedral-like hush in the two seconds it takes for the rest of his team to comprehend that he's taken a clean, legitimate and extraordinarily brilliant catch; better, indeed, than anything at Lord's today. Hook are 106-9. Hewitt has wrenched his knee, and he limps away holding it, head slightly bowed like an injured stork.

The last-wicket pair, Williams and Poulter, opt to limit their shots, dabbing and cutting and are occasionally blessed with a fortuitous edge that brings them runs and relief. Hook need 22 off 3 and implausibly mine 16 off the next 12 balls. When the last over starts – to be bowled by Scutt – there's just 6 to win. At Lord's England long ago finished the third day of the Test on 311-6. No one here is giving it the slightest thought.

Still in his sleeveless sweater, Scutt tinkers with his field, pushing it out and then pulling it in again, acutely aware that Hambledon's season could rest on the ball he is about to deliver. Defeat now would be morale-sapping; perhaps ruinously so. The captain marches to his mark and begins the seven strides that will carry him to the crease. Poulter is on strike, bat thumping against the ground. The ball Scutt bowls is elaborately tossed up, inviting Poulter to hit it. At the end of its flight it dips and drops. Poulter swishes the bat without moving his feet. The stumps rattle behind him and the bails dance and twirl in the air before landing. Scutt stands feet apart and hands upraised in exultation; the pose of Andrew Flintoff after he's taken a five-for in a Test. Hambledon seem to have astonished themselves. 'Did you have trouble seeing the ball?' I ask Poulter. 'I always have trouble seeing the ball,' he replies.

Arlott was right. Village cricket is a serious business. Never say it doesn't matter. It emphatically mattered here. And it mattered later in the Bat and Ball when Hambledon replayed it – every shot, every edge, every ball that took or almost took a wicket.

It must have been the same for 'Lumpy' Stevens, Silver Billy and the devilish Harris.

Umpires: G. Burgess, J. Green
Toss: Hook

Hambledon innings

J. Scutt*	b Hobday		18
B. Dean	b Poulter		70
J. Lavous	lbw	b Hobday	0
G. Marshall	c & b Poulter		23
O. Mills	st Buckingham	b Divecha	0
D. Hewitt	lbw	b Divecha	2
I. Chakrabarti	c Marsh	b Poulter	9
H. Moseley	b Williams		19
N. Scutt	not out		14
R. Chapman	not out		13
Did not bat: T. Watfa			
Extras	(9b, 6lb, 4w)		19
Total	(8 wickets, 50 overs)		187

Fall of wickets: 1-57, 2-59, 3-121, 4-122, 5-124, 6-124, 7-137, 8-170

Hook bowling	O	M	R	W
Hobday	10	2	36	2
Williams	9	1	47	1
Lye	8	0	33	0
Divecha	10	2	26	2
Poulter	10	6	11	3
Thane	10	0	19	0

Hook innings

B. Thane*	c Hewitt	b Chapman	40
N. Marsh	c J. Scutt	b Dean	0
A. Robinson	b Hewitt		0
B. Allnutt	b Dean		0
M. Love	b Hewitt		10
J. Hobday	lbw	b Chapman	6
J. Buckingham	c & b Chapman		15
C. Lye	c Watfa	b Chapman	2
A. Divecha	b Mills		11
G. Williams	not out		11
K. Poulter	b J. Scutt		7
Extras	(2b, 10lb, 12w)		24
Total	(all out, 33.1 overs)		124

Fall of wickets: 0-1, 2-17-3-30, 4-47, 5-47, 6-76 7-80, 8-102 9-106, 10-124

Hambledon bowling	O	M	R	W
Hewitt	10	3	17	2
Dean	10	2	19	2
Chapman	7	0	36	4
Mills	5	0	34	1
J. Scutt	1.1	0	6	1

Result: Hambledon won by 6 runs (recalculated target)

CHAPTER TWELVE

RIDING THE CHARABANC
TO LORD'S

*Nothing surely felt as sweet as the taste of champagne for Hampshire
– winners of the 2009 Friends Provident Trophy final at Lord's –
and especially for Dominic Cork, who was named as Man of the Match.*

Lord's: Friends Provident Trophy Final:
Hampshire v. Sussex, 25 July

The sights and scents of on-rushing autumn used to accompany Cup final Saturday at Lord's. Held back until early September, the match always brought with it incipient evidence of one season slowly turning into another. Leaf by leaf crumbled the gorgeous year. There was jewelled dew and mist in the morning, and the smell of peaty, damp earth and late-cut grass. Already the evenings were noticeably shorter and often chillier too, as if a wet cloth was hanging in the air. The Cup final back then was both longed for and dreaded. The splendour of a full house at Lord's came tinged with melancholic regret and conscious awareness that its very arrival signalled that summer was all but over. The day was savoured like the last half-glass of good wine.

No such emotions surround Lord's today. It's as if someone in the fixture-planning department at the ECB tossed the Friends Provident Trophy upwards and determined the date of the final on the basis of where it landed randomly on the calendar. The game is earlier than it has ever been. Still to come are three Ashes Tests, seven one-day internationals, seven rounds of County Championship matches and the Twenty20 semi-finals and finals. The fifty-over final, wedged into this crush as though being deliberately camouflaged, blurs into the hectic background. The Trophy is struggling to make an impact against the money, prestige and hype of the Twenty20 Finals, an occasion not unlike Guy Fawkes Night – sparks and the cracking of shots everywhere. There is no doubt where the balance of power between the two domestic competitions now lies. But the atmosphere at Lord's is no less expectant or heady, and there are few empty seats despite the fact this is Hampshire's third final since 2005, and Sussex's second in three years. In fact, there's haste to be in place for the 10.45 a.m. start. A couple who look like characters from a seaside postcard argue at the head of the stairs leading to the top tier of the Compton Stand. She is portly and florid, with a spread of thick lipstick and wears a pink floral dress and blue cardigan. It is fitted tightly across her fleshy arms. He is small and slight in a loose white shirt, turned up at the cuffs to reveal narrow wrists. She (carrying three bags) isn't travelling as fast as he (carrying nothing but a rolled-up copy of *The Times*) would like. 'Come on, Hilda,' he urges. 'We'll be late.' She stops, panting and flushed and rearranging the bags in her plump hands. 'We will not be late, and this is not a bloody route march,' she replies tartly and stares at the Cyclops eye of the Media Centre above her.

On the outfield Dominic Cork is taking slip catches struck towards him by Duncan Fletcher, who began a consultancy coaching role with Hampshire before the semi-finals and ends his temporary duties today. Everyone but Cork is soon in the dark sanctuary of the dressing room. He remains, still working the stiffness out of his ageing limbs on one of the old wickets in front of the Grand Stand. He bowls one over and then another and finally a third before shaking the sweat off his creased face. He looks across at the clock beneath the Old Father Time weather-vane, its black iron hands at 10.37 a.m. He reacts like a bridegroom worried about being late for his wedding. He makes a 50-yard dash to reach the pavilion steps, goes through the Long Room and up more steps before reaching the dressing room. Just two minutes later the bell orders him on the return journey. He jogs down those same worn steps and back through the picket gate, so white it seems to have been enamelled for the occasion. The match programme describes Cork as 'the old warhorse', which is meant as flattery but makes him sound like Boxer in *Animal Farm* and emphasises his age and longevity: 3 counties, 37 Tests, 32 one-day internationals and 3 previous Lord's finals. His thirty-eighth birthday is in three weeks' time. Hampshire signed him on a two-year contract after Lancashire decided to release him. So far Cork's figures haven't swallowed up extravagant amounts of printer's ink: 14 wickets at 30.3 in the Championship and a modest highest score of 36. Just as well that his value isn't measured strictly in statistics. Hampshire hired Cork as much for his high-wattage personality, so he could rouse the team and bring it an aggressively competitive edge. Cork does so as naturally as breathing. He is by nature as vocal as a street barker, provocative and needling. Some swear by him. Others swear at him.

He will bowl the first over of the morning from the Nursery End because, after Sussex's Michael Yardy spun the coin, and watched it roll down the Lord's slope like a fairground penny in a slot, Dimitri Mascarenhas called heads instead of tails. He tried to sound upbeat about the loss, but wearily volunteered that he would have batted first too. Non-threatening clouds canopy Lord's, occasionally spilt by wide, calming bursts of blue. Conditions look benign for run making.

Cup final day puts memories in motion: the usually restrained

Geoffrey Boycott batting as though he'd been implanted with the cavalier gene of Keith Miller and making 146 for Yorkshire in 1965; Lancashire's captain Jack Bond learning to fly as he reached out with his right hand to drag down a drive from Kent's Asif Iqbal, cutting him off in the prime of a classic innings in 1971; the rotund body and moon-face of John Dye, his hair thin and his whites smeared with the red stain of the ball after bowling 7 overs for just 9 runs for Northamptonshire in 1976. When the Gillette Cup became the NatWest Trophy, there was Geoff Miller's late lunge into the rising dust to ensure Derbyshire beat Northants after losing fewer wickets in 1981. And, after the sponsors changed again and turned it into the Cheltenham and Gloucester Trophy, there was the climax of 2006 when Lancashire, chasing just 172, edged within 17 runs of their target after slouching to 72-6. Lancashire came so close because of one man's patient, unflustered and unbeaten 35. That man was Cork, who is now tugging at the Prussian-blue sweat band on his left wrist and thinking about the two gestures he wants to make during the next eight hours – one to Lancashire for pushing him out of Old Trafford and the other to Sussex in retribution for rendering his contribution pointless and anguished three years ago. Late-arrivals are fumbling for their seats as Cork leans into his run, his spare physique slightly bowed, as if he needs to cut through a gale to reach the crease.

The fifty-overs competition is criticised for being too long and predictable. The criticism usually comes from those whose boredom threshold is set at a low mark. There is certainly a template to follow, which begins with a steady start and brief acceleration, consolidation in the sometimes stodgy middle overs and the climax of an anything-goes slog. But the game breathes and shifts course and builds drama. There are enough overs for a batsman to create a nuanced innings and for bowlers to put their back properly into their work. Teams who start badly in Twenty20 have no escape; the game soon slips away from them. Teams who start badly in the Friends Provident have room for manoeuvre and can still win the match rather than just make a decent fist of it. The Power Plays, like a game of Battleships, also add strategic thought. Most significant of all, the winners are the best one-day team in the country. Twenty20 is like flash-lightning, and anyone bowling four inspired overs or tearing through fifty balls with the bat can ride an individual tempest to carry the match away from the best and brightest of teams. For temperament and talent alone are no defence against inspiration when it is turned on so spontaneously and needs to be only briefly sustained. The best one-day teams reveal depth and mettle over 50 overs. Just to reach Lord's, Hampshire and Sussex have played eight group games and survived the pressurised torture of the quarter- and semi-finals. To win today takes even more nerve.

Cork is running in now, his right wrist cocked, as if he's about to fire, rather than bowl, the ball at Ed Joyce. The left-handed Joyce tucks the delivery smartly off his legs for a single backward of square, and the Sussex supporters acclaim it as though he's struck a six into the middle rows of the Grand Stand. Cork's expression sags and he watches the ball retrieved with one hand on his hip. Two balls later Chris Nash drives him down the slope for four; Cork puts both his hands on his hips this time and tosses his head skyward, as if he can't believe how easy he is making it for Sussex to rid themselves of those early jitters. Seven runs come from his opening over, and Sussex look jaunty. Nash, as though using a round bat, squirts inside edges to the boundary and almost sends the ball careering into his own stumps after misjudging the pace of the pitch off Cork. The psychological advantage already belongs to Sussex, who beat Hampshire in a dress rehearsal – a Pro40 League game at Arundel – the previous Sunday. To judge from the early overs, the residue of the defeat is lingering on Hampshire's mind. The beauty of cricket, however, is the way in which it fluctuates so abruptly.

Cork has the body of a thirty-seven-year-old man, but the effervescence of a teenager on a night out. Appealing for a catch or an lbw decision is like a long, wounded squawk, as if someone has hit him on the toes with a builder's mallet. It's accompanied with stage theatrics. These begin with the acrobatic, gun-turret swivel so Cork directly faces the umpire and is followed by the pleading pop-eyed gaze and outstretched arms, which turn him into a human form of the Angel of the North. If these well-oiled, showboating dramatics prove unsuccessful, he looks away to his right and raises his chin slightly in disgust before slinking away, like a spurned, hurt suitor who can't believe his heart has been broken when his case and cause are so justified.

Sussex are 30 without loss, and ostensibly in scant danger, when Cork's voice fills the Lord's air. When he claimed a hat-trick for England, against the West Indies at Old Trafford in 1993, it began when Richie Richardson deflected a delivery on to his own stumps after shaping to leave it alone. In the 6th over Joyce does exactly the same thing. Rather than bending away from him, the ball jags in and catches the blade of the bat before taking the bails. The celebratory yelp from Cork is piercing, like a scream amplified through a rock-concert speaker.

The ECB has given the teams dispensation to play centrally contracted players, an act of generosity made hollow in Hampshire's case because Kevin Pietersen has undergone an Achilles operation in mid-week and will not pick up a bat again for the foreseeable future. He arrives at Lord's as a spectator on a pair of crutches. The parochial argument about the advantage Hampshire might have gained with Pietersen is understandably submerged beneath the acres of newsprint about the more pressing consequences of how England will possibly cope without him for the remainder of the Ashes series. The ECB's benevolence does enable Sussex to slot in Matt Prior at number three. He's back at Lord's five days after the Second Test against Australia – England's first win over them here since Hedley Verity took 14 for 80 in 1934. Any notion that Prior will make a difference is soon dispelled. Cork sprints to get back to his mark again, as if sensing his moment has come. His first ball to Prior belts him on the pad like a clenched fist and allows Cork to expand his lungs again. His shout is turned down. The second ball takes the slope. Prior moves on ponderous feet, and edges to wicketkeeper Nick Pothas. Sussex are 30 for 2, and Cork has wrenched the initiative from them. There is something of the magpie about Nash in the way he steals runs almost through sleight of hand or stealth to reach 21. But, exactly like Prior, he finds himself caught on the crease in Cork's 6th over. The delivery strikes him on the top roll. Cue another of Cork's rebel yells. Whatever the debate about height, the umpire Neil Mallender calculates instantly – as though his brain is wired directly into the Hawk-Eye computer – that the ball would have hit the stumps. Sussex are 39 for three, and Cork has taken each wicket in a spell of 11 balls.

The breeze has gathered its energy in short, heaving gusts and pushed most of the cloud cover to the west. What remains casts slender, fast-moving shadows across the pitch, as though someone is opening and then closing a pair of curtains. The new batsmen are Sussex's most experienced campaigners: Yardy, who has promoted himself in the order to repair the cracking hull of his team, and Murray Goodwin. Yardy immediately finds Cork strolling towards him to offer welcoming words; presumably not 'Good morning, Mr Yardy'. For the opposition Cork is an irritant, like a

Life in the 'old warhorse' as Dominic Cork dominates
Lord's with his personality as well as his aggressive, dogged bowling.

fly that swoops around your head and which you can't, however hard you chase it, swat to oblivion. What Sussex sorely need is a period of calm. What Sussex get is another grievous and unnecessary set back. Only four runs have been added to the total when the over-anxious Goodwin thinks he can snatch a single off Mascarenhas. He finds Chris Tremlett running him out with a hit as direct as a ray of light. The Hove faithful try a reviving chorus of 'Sussex by the Sea', pitifully and half-heartedly sung and as out of tune as a pub piano. Sussex's fifty doesn't arrive until the 16th over, and Yardy watches his fellow batsmen come and go rapidly, as though each of them has somewhere else he'd rather be: Luke Wright makes 20 before Tremlett bowls him; Dwayne Smith takes two paces down the pitch and lifts Sean Ervine beyond wide long off for six before surrendering to the leg spinner Imran Tahir. No one stays with Yardy for long until the bespectacled Rory Hamilton-Brown arrives with the score on 111-6. With his vivid blond curls and nineteenth-century face, Hamilton-Brown looks as though he's part of the Pre-Raphaelite

Brotherhood. But he is more doughty than dashing in making an invaluable 32.

In the knowledge that he needs to bat through the innings, or otherwise the final won't stretch beyond late afternoon, the left-handed Yardy is intent on reducing risk. There is a rigorous austerity about his batting. He pares it down and works the ball where he can. At one stage he goes 20 overs without a boundary. There are two thumping fours off Tahir that oblige Jimmy Adams, at silly mid-off, to check the small print of his insurance policy. The helmeted Adams jumps out of the way, as if avoiding thrown knives. He sensibly retreats into the covers.

Adams's understandable nervousness about having his flesh turned to pulp reminds me of a cold spring morning I spent with Brian Close four months earlier. We were sitting in the open air so Close could chain smoke. I'd asked him about his 'suicidal tendencies', the almost insane desire he demonstrated for fielding so near to the bat – usually at short leg – that he almost crushed the batsman's toes. With blissful indifference, he all but ignored the personal danger in the same way he now ignores the blunt warning on the front of his packet of Superkings: 'SMOKING KILLS'. 'There were times,' he admitted mischievously, 'when I might have been, or possibly should have been, killed'. He remembered the closing stages of a Championship game against Kent at Gravesend, which Yorkshire needed to win. Close went in tight at silly mid-off against Alan Brown and urged his spinner, Don Wilson, to 'give it some air'. Brown took the agricultural route, the ball clipped the crown of Close's head and, according to him, 'soared over the pavilion for six'. Even allowing for the apocryphal element of the story, the ball certainly hit Close. He instinctively rubs the spot on his head at the very moment he delivers the punch-line. I asked him whether he'd ever been afraid. With a burning cigarette still in his hand, he climbed out of his chair and, at nearly seventy-nine years old, adopted the low, crouching position of his playing days. He got down without a twinge or grimace. 'I reckoned,' he said, 'that the only place the ball could hit me was on the front of my head [he slaps his palm against it] or either shoulder [he slaps the right and then the left] or on the legs [he slaps each of those too]. But how can a ball hurt you? It's only on your flesh for a split second.' I resist mentioning to Close that you could argue the same thing about being run over by an articulated lorry; but that you'd be in pieces across the front grille all the same. I was about to ask the obvious question when he anticipated it, as if through telepathy, and answered it. 'No, I wouldn't wear a bloody helmet. You don't need one.'

Yardy is exemplary in taking the strain almost entirely alone now. In the closing overs he rattles Sussex past a semi-respectable 200. Cork returns and claims his fourth wicket with a slower ball, which persuades Robin Martin-Jenkins to swish and give Chris Benham routine catching practice at deep backward point. After his final over Cork, with figures of 4 for 41, stands on the boundary in front of the Compton Stand, where some of the Sussex supporters verbally abuse him. One man in particular stands up and begins raging at Cork. He is middle-aged, stripped to the waist and with wind-burned skin. He is foully, abysmally drunk. His vocabulary is predictably base. 'You're a fucking loser,' he hollers at Cork, ignoring the evidence of the scoreboard for expediency's sake. 'You always lose against Sussex because you are a fucking loser.' The man begins to stab his finger into the air. Spittle streams from his mouth. Cork playfully cups a hand behind his ear and good-naturedly mouths that he can't quite hear what's being said to him. He pretends to clean out his ears with both index fingers. He then scratches the back of his head, as if itched by a puzzling thought. The man's rage peters out. He gives up and drops back into his seat, where he begins to doze off the vat of ale he's already consumed. He spends so long in one slumped position that he nearly petrifies. He misses the closing stages of the Sussex innings – a limping 219 with Yardy, eternally vigilant, on 92 not out from 127 balls. Lord's rises to acknowledge him. Just before Yardy reaches the pavilion gate, shyly raising his bruised bat, one figure emerges unannounced on his right shoulder and offers his hand with authentic warmth and respect. It is Dominic Cork.

It's difficult to go anywhere at Lord's during the interval. The crowds seep out from the stands and head towards the Nursery End, where most of the food and drink, as well as the souvenir shop, are found. It's rather like trying to simultaneously fight your way through the New Year sales and slogging through the mud at the Glastonbury Festival. Beer is spilt, the backs of legs trodden on, plastic bags knocked out of people's shaky hands. The Lord's shop can only be toured one inch at a time. There is also a queue of spectators waiting to hand over £5 for the privilege of having their photograph taken with the Friends Provident Trophy and Mike Gatting, who, wearing his pale cream suit and with his grey miniature beard, looks like a cross between Colonel Sanders and someone who might sell you a ninety-nine with an extra flake. The line for the toilets could plausibly stretch as far as Baker Street tube station.

I try to work out the peculiar logic of buying a £45 ticket and then deciding to watch the game on the big screen behind the Media Centre. Several hundred do so, however; probably because it's closer to the beer and champagne stalls. The easiest thing to do is to return to my seat, which I do with utter relief. I collapse gratefully into it, as though I've returned exhausted from a long voyage rather than from hunting out a copy of a new and only recently published guide to Lord's.

When Michael Lumb and Jimmy Adams come out to bat, the ground isn't even half full. The bright white seating glows like rows of polished teeth. Lumb has been to two previous Lord's finals without scoring a solitary run. He avoids three ducks in a row with a single, and yet hardly anyone is there to witness it or see some of the pressure drain from his face as the cameras capture his expression and project it on to the screen.

Hampshire only need to stroll at 4.3 runs per over; Adams, though, seems intent on reaching the target before the cocktail hour. His backlift is eye-catching. A stride or two before the bowler delivers the ball, Adams raises his bat in two separate and distinct jerky movements, which leaves the blade high above his left shoulder. He resembles an executioner about to bring an axe down on a prisoner's ropey neck. He does so to release his hands away from his body, which avoids being 'tucked in'. The result is scarcely artistic, but, irrespective of its lack of style, the substance of the method works for him. He lashes at James Kirtley, striking him for three fours in one over to mid-wicket, long off and backward point. The Lord's pitch becomes better. The Hampshire openers are actually in more danger from themselves than Sussex's bowlers. Filching an audacious single Adams and Lumb collide midway down the wicket, bouncing off one another like dodgem cars; Adams's bat is torn from his grip.

The partnership is approaching its century, and Sussex have fallen into the sickening drop of a trough, when Adams, on 55, gets a shoddy decision. He's given out lbw from a ball by Luke Wright which pitches outside leg at the Pavilion End. No one is better equipped to replace him than the square, muscled bulk of Michael Carberry, who has made three hundreds in his last four innings. He is seeing the ball supremely early and with a pitiless, clear eye. In this form, the ball must seem to Carberry to be a diamond as big the Ritz and travelling at him in super-slow motion; as though, in fact, he can stroke or strong-arm it anywhere he chooses. He plays with a flash and a gleam, like bright water, and makes 30 off 23 deliveries. The final has already slipped well and irrevocably away from Sussex when Carberry tries to pull Yasir Arafat and gets a leading edge on to his helmet. Arafat, grateful for small mercies, hares up the wicket to take the catch himself.

A minor drama follows. Nick Pothas damages the groin that has been troubling for a fortnight and plays on with his right leg as stiff and as barely functional as Long John Silver's wooden peg. He's still able to take a stride down the pitch and dispatch Yardy for two lofted boundaries. At 5.51 p.m. the honour of hitting the winning runs falls to Chris Benham. Sussex long ago faced the gloomy facts of defeat before he finishes them off with a boundary to the Mound Stand ropes. The Sussex supporters, clustered around where I am sitting, went long ago in sombre silence, leaving behind scorecards and programmes and departing without a backward glance. Even the man rotted by drink, who hurled those poisoned words at Dominic Cork, lurched away to find a bar to prop him up an hour before the end.

I remember being able to walk on to the outfield at the end of a Cup final. The wicket was roped off, and the crowd stood respectfully in front of the pavilion, as if it were a high altar, and watched the presentations on the balcony. Now a sonorous voice over the public address makes brimstone warnings about laying so much as a toe on to the Lord's grass – purely for reasons of personal safety and public order, you understand – and stewards in lime green vests protect the ropes more successfully than Sussex have managed to do all afternoon.

A pantomime follows. The Hampshire fans, most of whom occupy the Edrich Stand, need a pair of binoculars to view the presentation which takes place on the self-assembled stage in a near-deserted corner of Lord's 150 yards in front of them. Their clearest view of the event is via the large screen rising behind them. The obvious candidate wins the Man of the Match award. There was a time when a stellar performance in the Cup final would usher a player into the winter tour party, perhaps as a dark horse. Cork instead has the satisfaction of fully making up for the scarring failure against Sussex in 2006. He knows, too, that Lancashire will have been watching. Cork will bowl better and more effectively on occasions, but take fewer wickets. The luck went with him, and yet he deserved it because of the indefatigable example he set. Next season the ECB will be waving cash at the counties to encourage them to field two players under twenty-two years old and three more who are under twenty-six. In this clumsy gerrymandering, players of Cork's vintage could find themselves excluded. He has shown up the obvious flaw of the plan.

I stay until Hampshire drift by the Compton Stand with the glinting Cup. The straggler in the procession is Cork, clutching a stump and with his medal draped from a ribbon around his neck. I head for the printer's shop to collect a completed scorecard. My ticket for the match attractively displays the badges of the eighteen counties, from Derbyshire's crown and flower to Yorkshire's white rose, as well as the emblems of Scotland and Ireland. In reality the past ten finals have been largely dominated by Gloucestershire, Somerset and today's two counties. Northamptonshire haven't reached the fifty-overs final since 1992; Middlesex since 1989; Nottinghamshire since 1987; and Glamorgan since 1977, so long ago that average house prices were £13,500, a bottle of milk cost 12 and half pence and Margaret Thatcher was still two years away from becoming Prime Minister. But when any of these four counties reaches the Cup final, there will be a rush for tickets, coaches and hotels. For it is a supporters' excursion, like an old-fashioned charabanc ride to the seaside with hats and banners and bulging picnics. The crowds come to be swept up into the enjoyment of the occasion, and to fall asleep on the way home. The final is cricket's Grand Day Out – apart from, and unlike, any other. It ought to be defended by the very people who often condemn it through faint praise. Of course, I am thinking of the ECB.

Umpires: N. J. Long, N. A. Mallender
Toss: Sussex

Sussex innings

E. C. Joyce	b Cork		15
C. D. Nash	lbw	b Cork	21
M. J. Prior†	c Pothas	b Cork	0
M. W. Goodwin	run out		1
M. H. Yardy*	not out		92
L. J. Wright	b Tremlett		7
D. R. Smith	c Carberry	b Imran Tahir	20
R. J. Hamilton-Brown	c Mascarenhas	b Imran Tahir	32
Yasir Arafat	c Pothas	b Mascarenhas	9
R. S. C. Martin-Jenkins	c Benham	b Cork	4
R. J. Kirtley	not out		3
Extras	(9lb, 2nb, 4w)		15
Total	(9 wickets, 50 overs)		**219**

Fall of wickets: 1-30, 2-30, 3-39, 4-43, 5-77, 6-111, 7-171, 8-186, 9-203

Hampshire bowling	O	M	R	W
Cork	10	1	41	4
Mascarenhas	9	0	27	1
Imran Tahir	10	0	50	2
Tremlett	10	0	40	1
Ervine	6	0	31	0
Dawson	5	0	21	0

Hampshire innings

M. J. Lumb	c Prior	b Wright	38
J. H. K. Adams	lbw	b Wright	55
M. A. Carberry	c & b Yasir Arafat		30
S. M. Ervine	c Nash	b Wright	15
C. C. Benham	not out		37
N. Pothas†	not out		35

Did not bat: L. A. Dawson, A. D. Mascarenhas*, D. G. Cork, C. T. Tremlett, Imran Tahir

Extras	(2lb, 4nb, 5w)		11
Total	(4 wickets, 40.3 overs)		**221**

Fall of wickets: 1-93, 2-110, 3-137, 4-154

Sussex bowling	O	M	R	W
Kirtley	5	0	26	0
Yasir Arafat	10	0	54	1
Martin-Jenkins	4	0	21	0
Wright	9	1	50	3
Nash	3	0	15	0
Hamilton-Brown	3.3	0	27	0
Yardy	6	1	26	0

Result: Hampshire won by 6 wickets

Man of the match: D. G. Cork

CHAPTER THIRTEEN

THE MAN IN THE UNMARKED GRAVE

Edmund 'Ted' Peate, whose cricketing life was scarred by a single miscalculation, and, right, his burial plot in Yeadon cemetery near Leeds.

Edgbaston: Third NPower Test:
England v. Australia, 30 July–3 August

The small, rectangular cemetery in Yeadon is well hidden on the outskirts of the village, as though it doesn't want to be found. A plain Victorian arch is attached to a disused, blank-windowed chapel, and a rising tarmac path, which divides two plots of gravestones. Some of the gravestones are cracked. Others are tipped over. Age and weather have worn smooth, and made indistinct, the inscriptions of love and grief and loss, which were once so tenderly composed and finely chiselled. The landscape around this West Yorkshire cemetery – sealed off by a low stone wall – is as barren as the Brontë moors. Today it is almost as wild too. Wind bends the branches of the trees, and spearing rain lashes into the already sodden ground.

On my way to Edgbaston, I make a minor detour here to make a courtesy call on the man without whom the term 'Ashes Test' would not have existed. Edmund 'Ted' Peate is in an unmarked grave. The local council's records starkly describe his patch of neatly cropped grass as Section A, Plot No. 241, as if someone is about to build on it. There is nothing to commemorate Peate, who even in death seems unloved and uncared for, and whose cricketing life was scarred by a solitary mistake made in a single, infinitesimal moment when rational judgement and hand-eye-feet coordination miserably failed him.

In a portrait photograph Peate holds the ball in the well of his left hand. He has over-large ears and a straggly, walrus-like moustache, which grows over his top lip and hides the downward turn of his mouth. His black hair is swept back and oiled, and tufts out at the sides. His sorrowful eyes are sunken in hollow sockets. He wears a button-down white shirt and a tie that seems to have been abruptly snipped off at quarter length with a pair of blunt scissors. He is a reluctant sitter, restless and uncomfortable, as if impatient to be off as soon as the photographer had finished with him. Peate was a practised slow left-arm bowler, once described by W. G. Grace as 'the best . . . of England'. In 1882 it was his good fortune to claim 214 wickets – despite missing two weeks of the season with a strained ankle. It was his misfortune to be a batting rabbit in the solitary England v. Australia Test of the same summer.

Peate took more than 1,000 career wickets for Yorkshire and England and twice claimed 14 in Championships matches. But if he's remembered at all – and a lot of hardened Yorkshiremen remain vague about him or are unaware of his career – it is because of his calamity at the Oval; a result of calculation rather than grim mischance. He is infamous rather than famous. In a team comprising Grace, Barnes, and C. T. Studd, who was making his debut, England needed what appeared to be the formality of 85 runs to win a low-scoring Test. Grace compiled 32 before England, shaky on 66 for 5, lost 4 wickets for 9 runs. Enter Peate, the last man, in front of a 20,000 crowd scarcely able to comprehend that England might actually *lose* for the first time to the country that *The Times* described condescendingly – but entirely in tune with the period – as 'Our Colonial visitors'. With just 10 runs required, Peate – batting average barely above 13 – had a straightforward task. His job was to push the odd, well-judged single and give the strike to his partner, Studd. But Peate wouldn't play the supporting role allocated to him. He had wanted to be the laurelled hero instead. He struck his first ball off Harry Boyle to square leg for two and hurried back to cling on to the bowling. With the good manners and breeding of Cambridge and Eton ingrained in him, Studd said nothing to rebuke Peate. Studd was only twenty-one, and Peate had taken 4 wickets in the first innings and another 4 in the second. Studd naively thought there was method in his madness and deferred to the superior experience of his partner. Studd had no idea Peate had once played in a troupe called Treloar's Cricket Clowns, or that the clown element still remained in him.

In the same over, Peate – no doubt imagining himself chaired back to the dressing room – tried a haymaking slog at another ball. He was clean-bowled, and England lost by 7 runs. One spectator was found dead on the spot – a heart attack induced through shock. Afterwards in the dressing room Grace gave the Peate the 'dead eye' and his captain, A. N. Hornby, chastised him for gross incompetence. Why, asked Hornby angrily, didn't Peate leave the run-making entirely to Studd? 'I couldn't trust Mr Studd,' replied Peate tartly and unrepentantly. What came next is well-known historical fact – as familiar as Harold taking one in the eye at Hastings and Henry VIII swopping and chopping up his wives. Four days later the *Sporting Times* published its mock obituary of English cricket – the body to be cremated and the Ashes taken to Australia. But another, more obscure, lamentation on the defeat appeared in *C W Alcock's Cricket: A Weekly Report of The Game* on the morning after Peate's stumps were uprooted. It read:

SACRED TO THE MEMORY OF ENGLAND SUPREMACY
IN THE CRICKET FIELD WHICH EXPIRED ON THE
29th DAY OF AUGUST, AT THE OVAL:
ITS END WAS PEATE

The end of Peate himself was sadder still. He drank and ate himself
to oblivion. Peate put on so much weight – swelling to 16 stones – that
he lurched to the crease like a beached seal, and Lord Hawke brusquely
sacked him from Yorkshire. Nine days after his forty-fifth or forty-fourth
birthday – his obituary gave one date and the inscription on his pine coffin
another – Peate died of pneumonia on 11 March 1900. He left nothing to
his wife and children, who were saved from the poorhouse and the soup
kitchens through charitable collections and donations.

Almost no one visits Yeadon cemetery with flowers for Peate. There are
no plans to provide a headstone bearing his name and the crest of Yorkshire's
white rose, which is crushingly sad when I pace the graveyard and stare at the
only thing still belonging to Peate: his own few square yards of grassy earth.
I contemplate the *what if* of his innings at the Oval. *What if* he'd blocked and
given Studd the bowling? *What if* he'd struck Boyle for two fours? *What if*
he'd won the match on his own? Of course, the competition between
England and Australia would still be as sharp and bitter. And, of course, the
jarring turns and high boiling points of successive series would still have
happened. But what we recognise as the symbol of it would be different – if,
indeed, there was a symbol at all. There'd be no Ashes and consequently no
urn in which to keep them. Instead of being half mocked, Peate ought to be
celebrated. His fatal swish at the ball intensified the rivalry. It was a non-shot
which rang across 12,000 miles.

As it is, with the rain coming down harder still on Yorkshire, I notice
the cemetery's caretaker in a bright-yellow oilskin jacket sitting on his
lawnmower. Sheltering beneath a spread of trees, he looks at me with
half-pitying, puzzled eyes, as if I qualify as deranged for being here on
such a wretched afternoon. I think about asking him whether he knows
who occupies Section A, Plot No. 241 and his significance to the Ashes.
Instead, I merely nod in his direction, leave quietly and head for
Edgbaston. The rain is dripping off me.

The rain is still dripping off me the following morning. It falls in cold,
hard spikes over Birmingham and leaves a pewter-coloured archipelago

of lakes across the outfield, which are deep enough for Ophelia to drown in. An amalgam of boredom, restlessness and frustration forces the spectators to spill out of the wet, uncovered seating to seek shelter in the crowded bars. Otherwise there's nothing else to do apart from take one dreary circular stroll after another around Edgbaston, a dour, unappealing ground, badly in need of sprucing up, and redolent of the late 1970s. The big screen at the City End is replaying highlights of the 2005 Test here on a long, endless and all too familiar loop. There is Michael Vaughan grimacing beneath his wide-brimmed sun hat at dropped catches, involuntary edges, byes and no balls in the closing overs of the match. There is Australia's number eleven Michael Kasprowicz improbably stealing runs with inside and outside edges. Finally there is Geraint Jones rolling across and forward to take the gloved leg-side catch from Kasprowicz, curled up and glancing away, as though protecting himself against a blow from a hammer. And then there is Kasprowicz again during the slow-motion replay; his hand clearly off the handle of the bat as it makes contact with the ball. England win by two runs, and neither this evidence, which incontrovertibly contests its legitimacy, nor Australian tears can wash out a word of it.

The Test produced the defining image of that series: Andrew Flintoff crouching beside the kneeling Brett Lee in the moment immediately after Australia's defeat. He stretches out his huge left arm before letting it drop consolingly on to his opponent's right shoulder. The video ends with this image, and briefly freezes it too. Flintoff looks like a missionary comforting a broken refugee after a natural disaster. How near, and yet how long ago, it all seems now; 2005 manages to feel simultaneously close and also curiously distant, as if belonging to far away, almost ancient time. This is probably because the personnel has changed so much. Vaughan has gone, of course. Flintoff is noticeably heavier and older. Australia have lost half a team: Warne, McGrath, Hayden, Langer, Gilchrist and – temporarily at least – Lee, who is injured. Those who bother to stop and glance at the film of 2005 do so for only a frame or two before moving on. It was pure theatre back then. Watching it again today is actually tiresome, like listening to a story heard so often that repeated telling has stripped all the drama and nervous tension out of it. But the Ashes is a bonfire always waiting for a struck match, and it was lit here in 2005.

Why the Ashes matter, and why each series is fuelled by pride, vanity, ego, bragging rights and faraway memories of Empire, colonial control and class is more conspicuous in the crush of the Edgbaston store rather than on the City End screen. With no prospect of play, the store draws customers easily to it. A sales assistant, her polished nails coloured treacle black, is restocking the rack of Bodyline T-shirts. The brisk trade in these stems in part from a mischievous need to goad the Australians as much as to commemorate the Ashes series that has endured longer, and more controversially, than any other. The T-shirt is fashionable cadmium red and displays the names of each member of the MCC's 1932–33 tour on a wheel of stark white letters beneath an arched 'BODYLINE'. The eye inevitably seeks two names: Douglas Jardine and Harold Larwood, architect and chief perpetrator of the flesh-bruising, bone-breaking tactic of bowling at leg stump with a congested leg-side field specifically to torment and tame Donald Bradman. The fine details of that feuding Australian summer of long ago – even the fact England won 4-1 – may be hazily indistinct even to those who buy the T-shirt purely for the purpose of expressing a bit of black humour. But the symbolic nature of Bodyline and the significant, stormy way in which it ratcheted up Ashes friction to its tipping point is relevant in explaining the depth of the modern rivalry between England and Australia. Wearing the T-shirt – I watch as an overweight man slides his purchase out of its thick plastic bag and immediately slips it over his flabby beer belly – is an act of silent sledging. England crushed Australia in 1932–33 and satisfied the ruthless part of Jardine's intelligent brain. Schopenhauer once said that the expression of the outer man revealed the inner one. Jardine seemed imperturbable, serious and determined – exactly the qualities required to design and implement and then to persevere with the dangerous ploy, which he defended right until his premature death. Bodyline is always raked up and replayed at some point whenever the Ashes take places; and Australia are always striving to avenge it just one more time.

I have chosen to sit in the R. E. S. Wyatt Stand. Wyatt, who was Jardine's vice-captain, obeyed orders and first unleashed the packed leg-side field, instructing Larwood to bowl to it, during a warm-up game before the opening Test; Jardine, a practising disciple of Izaak Walton's *The Compleat Angler*, had gone fishing 'up country', far from the scent of cordite and the sound of Bradman's rage. The highly principled Wyatt was opposed to Bodyline, but, like everyone else who found it ugly, repellent and unnecessary – arguing that Larwood was at his absolute peak and could have intimidated the Australians to defeat through shattering orthodox pace alone – he remained stonily mute in deference to his captain.

I buy one of the shirts to give to Larwood's daughter Enid before she returns to Australia with a more fitting tribute to her father's talents locked in her suitcase. I tell her she won't be allowed home unless she wears it on the aeroplane. The basic pillars of Larwood's story are well known now: callously ostracised by the MCC after refusing to apologise for bowling Bodyline; never to play another Test; persuaded to emigrate to the country which had once reviled and threatened to slice and dice him into minuscule pieces; revered and given his due and an MBE at the end of his life. Posthumous forgiveness came at Lord's on the Royal Friday of the Second Test. Larwood was inducted into the ICC Hall of Fame. Enid collected the dark-blue cap with vivid yellow braid. She is a short, trim woman in her early seventies with dark, bobbed hair. She was born in Nottingham, but emphatically regards herself as Australian after emigrating with her family in 1950. Her own cricket hero is Steve Waugh. She'd already been in England almost six weeks and had also unveiled a plaque honouring her father in Blackpool, where he played before the war and briefly lived after it was over. Everywhere Enid went she was asked about Bodyline and Bradman. 'Strange, isn't it,' said Enid, holding her father's Hall of Fame cap in her stretched fingers. 'He'd have been staggered to know he's still being talked about like this.'

The best Ashes series are like melodramatic novels, which unfold with an unstoppable, tearing narrative energy. Which is why, more than seventy-five years after Larwood bowled his last delivery in Australia, there are teenagers with dyed blond hair and heavy middle-aged men walking around Edgbaston wearing Bodyline T-shirts as proudly as an England blazer. Under Birmingham's miserably leaden skies it is hard to imagine anyone, circa 2084, dressed in a T-shirt with Strauss, Onions and Anderson emblazoned across it. Perhaps in time there will be a market for a Ted Peate T-shirt instead.

Everywhere I've gone this summer, the Met Office's forecast has been as reliable as a badly drawn map. Whether long or short term, the weather gurus with satellite photography and sophisticated gadgetry have proved erratic at best, useless at worst and contradictory in between. The fickleness of the climate seems as much a penumbral mystery to them as it is to those of us who can't tell the difference between the Orographic Lift and the Beaufort Scale. The Met Office didn't predict the intense heat

I experienced at Grace Road or at Worcester. It didn't pin down the erratic cloud bursts at Cheltenham or the early evening's imperfect light at Trent Bridge either. By the law of averages, however, it has to be right once. It proves depressingly so on the opening day of this Test. At 5 a.m. the sky is relatively clear. Only a few strands of cloud, like thinning grey hair, are stretched across it. At 7.30 a.m., the showers start, and a rainbow hangs behind the Eric Hollies Stand. At 10 a.m. the sky is almost perfect again. But at 10.30 a.m. – just as the forecasters had predicted – it is pouring. In mid-afternoon the umpires, Aleem Dar and Rudi Koertzen – with Andrew Strauss and a cheerless-looking Ricky Ponting beside them – emerge for the umpteenth pitch inspection. The walk to the middle is accompanied by boos and slow hand-clapping and irritable shouts of 'Get on with it'. There's been no rain for two and a half hours, and the sun is casting hard-edged shadows. Dar and Koertzen fix their gaze on the bowlers' saturated run-up at the City End. At one point Ponting takes a ball and throws it into the grass. There is scarcely any bounce; the ball fails to rise above ankle high, as though Ponting had hurled it into a bucket of plasticine. The talk between them goes on. The four figures are grouped together like men huddled over an open bonnet who can't decide how to restart a stalled car. The crowd knows nothing and is, disgracefully, told nothing either. The booing and slow hand-claps begin again.

Why did the ECB award this Test to Edgbaston when it is the only major Test venue not to have a modern drainage system? When tickets cost £75 or more, and you've travelled 12,000 miles, it is no consolation to be told that the outfield will be dug up in 2010 to install one. 'And why,' asks an Australian with a Merv Hughes-like white moustache, 'is there the sudden urgency to get on the field when they've done bugger all for the past six hours?' It's a rhetorical question because he brandishes his ticket the way an advocate would brandish an exhibit in a courtroom. 'Because it says on the back of this that we don't get a refund if they bowl twenty-five overs,' he adds bitterly, tugging at the stretchy fabric of his Cricket Australia green-and-gold shirt. 'I bet they bowl twenty-six. His prediction is almost right. There are two hours' play, starting at 5 p.m., and England struggle through 30 lethargic overs, bowling as though stiffness is still in their joints and sleep is still in their eyes. The public address system is fifteen minutes behind the news that has already been passed from neighbour to neighbour around Edgbaston. Brad Haddin, the Australian wicketkeeper, fractured the fourth finger of his left hand in the final practice session only five minutes before the start. The teams were already announced, and Ponting had won the toss. But Strauss preserves the spirit of the game by allowing Australia to replace Haddin with the uncapped Graham Manou. I contemplate what the icy Jardine would have done in the same circumstances. I doubt he'd have been so charitable. Australia leave out Phillip Hughes because of indifferent form – he's been especially vulnerable against the short ball – but he warns England in advance by making the announcement on his Twitter page. I also contemplate what would have happened in 1932–33 if, rather than sending laborious cables, the MCC and the Australian Board of Control had been able to instantly Tweet one another about Bodyline in the same way.

> ABC: Bodyline bowling has assumed such proportions as to menace the best interests of the game . . . In our opinion it is unsportsmanlike.
> MCC: We deprecate your opinion that there has been unsportsmanlike play.

Those cables were sent five days apart. The ABC agonised a further week before responding to the MCC's cold rebuff. Instant communication might have stirred more trouble at the start, but led to less stress and fewer lingering recriminations later on.

England's generosity extends further than letting Manou replace Haddin. The bowlers feed the two makeshift openers, Simon Katich and Shane Watson, a myriad selection of friendly deliveries – half volleys, balls straying outside leg stump or dropped short of a length and begging to be pulled and also the odd full toss with 'hit me' written all the way through it like a stick of rock. England either forget or abandon the simple principles of wicket-to-wicket bowling. After an hour Australia are already 62 without loss. By the close the score is 126 for 1. The only wicket is Graeme Swann's. He removes Katich lbw with an arm ball. The weather is glorious, and the light like crystal, and yet the bails are tucked into the umpires' pockets at 7 p.m. and the crowd – even the Australians – file away feeling cheated after paying so much for such a meagre amount of cricket.

On the way out of Edgbaston I eavesdrop a conversation about Strauss. A tall, mop-haired man in a windcheater expresses the opinion that he is a 'lousy' captain. 'He's not like Michael Vaughan,' he says. 'He never gets his field right.' It is difficult to argue against him when, after Swann removes Katich, Strauss posts a long on against Watson rather than bringing him up to tempt the batsman into striking him over the top. He also takes Swann out of the attack when the spinner is England's most dangerous bowler. I think back to the opening match of the season at Lord's. The afternoon before I went into the Tavern bar near the Grace Gates and sat down randomly at a table. I hadn't noticed Strauss in his blue blazer and crested tie sitting only two feet away. He was sifting through a heap of correspondence and fan mail, which had piled up during the tour of the West Indies. There were requests to endorse products, invitations to attend various functions and photographs to sign. The TV hanging on the wall was tuned into *Sky Sports News*. Strauss's face appeared on the screen. The barman turned the volume up a notch or two. At the sound of his own voice, Strauss raised his eyes to check whether any of the half dozen of us scattered around the bar were looking at him looking at himself. For a minute he tilted his head and wore the expression of someone who was half surprised, half inquisitive, as though he couldn't quite place where he'd given an interview or what he'd said during it. Strauss looked slightly embarrassed and began to sign the photographs on the table in front of him, as if doing so would make us all turn away from him.

No one expects anything else on day two other than the sight of Australia compiling a first-innings score substantial enough to bat England instantly out of the match. On the eve of this Test Strauss answered candidly when asked whether he thought the present Australian team possessed an aura – a word which the *Shorter Oxford Dictionary* describes as a 'subtle emanation or exhalation; a surrounding glow'; Strauss shook his head and said no. Pessimists at Edgbaston are certain of two things. First, Strauss should have gone into a darkened room and slapped himself across the forehead immediately afterwards. Second, that the scoreboard will glow like a magnesium flame in retaliation at such a slur. The pitch looks full of runs. The air is fresh and slightly cold and there are only flakes of cloud to encourage the bowlers. In fact, there is a creamy glaze to the sky. At 11 a.m. Graham Onions begins his run from the City End with three men on the boundary and more than half the seats around me in the Wyatt Stand unfilled. There are grumbles about why Onions is bowling at all. Shouldn't Strauss have given the ball to James Anderson? By 11.05, those of us who'd bothered to arrive on time are grateful for being punctual and also grateful Strauss chose Onions. The screenwriter William Goldman's cynical assessment of Hollywood, 'Nobody Knows Nothing', applies equally to Test cricket, it seems.

The opening ball of the day is always watched in silence. It's a question of respect, like entering a church and not speaking. Onions gets tight to the stumps. Of all the England bowlers, he's the one who works most on the basis of plain, orthodox geometry – the straight line. He begins with a full delivery arrowed at middle stump. Waiting for it, Watson barely shuffles, as if there's an iron block tethered to his front leg. The ball strikes him on the roll of the pad. The appeal is prolonged and throaty. The lbw decision from Dar is instant. Watson heads off to the pavilion with the blank, slightly nonplussed expression of the sleepwalker. The din of the crowd rolls around the bowl of the ground and is carried to the queues of people waiting with tickets and bags outside it. There's a sudden urgency to get inside, like rushing to catch a train that is already pulling away from the station. The left-handed Michael Hussey is already taking guard, picking his way around the field with a nervous pair of dark eyes and his hands tense on the handle. After a scratchy run – scores of 3, 51 and 27 – Hussey needs a major innings. Onions is back at his mark, the ball tight in his grip. The second delivery is bowled against a wall of noise, which propels Onions to the crease like a gust of wind at his back. He bowls another accurate delivery, and, without thinking, Hussey raises his bat to let it go, as though standing back to allow a lady through a door before him. The ball clips the top of his off stump. Pandemonium follows. The crowd yells and screams and whoops. Onions' clenched fist punches the air before he vanishes beneath the England fielders smothering him. In his distress Hussey turns and retreats at hyper-speed, almost running back to the pavilion. 'Cricket,' wrote John Arlott, 'is a game of the most terrifying stresses . . . the loneliest game I know.' The mortification across Hussey's face is the proof of it.

In two balls everything changes. The momentum swings towards England, who seem to have the hex on Australia. At the non-striker's end Ricky Ponting lets his chin drop against his chest. The late-comers sprint into any vacant seat to watch the hat-trick delivery, staring at the scoreboard to confirm the damage of the first two balls. Michael Clarke, the new batsman, is too shrewd to be hustled. He makes Onions wait.

Responsible for one of the most dramatic starts to a day in Test cricket, Graham Onions seems unable to believe the impact he's made with his opening two deliveries on the second morning.

He taps his bat against the pitch, walks around the crease, pretends to readjust and then readjust again the sleeves of his shirt, his gloves and his grip. He's deliberately wasting time, calming himself and the crowd, who are whipped up and frenzied, as if waiting for the climax to a bull-fight. Onions is straining to be let loose at Clarke, who is now flexing his shoulder muscles to swallow up a few more seconds before settling reluctantly into his stance. When he does so, Onions sets off immediately, the thin strip of his tongue almost hanging out. He's like a greyhound in intense, focused pursuit of the hare. The ball is shorter than his two previous deliveries and it climbs towards middle and leg. Clarke moves inside it, making certain his bat and gloves are out of the way. The bowler and the batsman make vivid eye-contract – one hard stare reciprocated with another. The tempest – for now at least – has passed.

The Australian team of 2005 would beat this England side. The England of 2005 would beat the current Australians too. But it matters to no one caught up in the five-minute wonder of Onions' achievement, which emphasises why Ashes cricket is the purest, most compelling, rigorously competitive and unmissable form of the game.

Seen as a whole, the 2005 series was an unforgettable spectacle, embedding itself in both popular consciousness and culture that summer. It affected almost everyone because even those who didn't watch or care about it found themselves on the periphery of, or directly pulled into, conversations about the outcome. Four years ago the result at Edgbaston blew away a glib assumption made months beforehand. To take Australia on was supposed to be impossible for England. After Edgbaston, there was no longer an atom of truth in it. The myth of Australian invincibility was broken like a hypnotist's trance. Shaken out of it at last, England dominated the ferocious quarrel, and Australia could not dismiss it lightly as a glitch. The holders were ground down and went home with faces which looked as though tears had lately dried on them. This Edgbaston Test can be just as pivotal – if England accept the chance Onions has given them.

Ponting strives to reassert his authority and becomes Australia's leading run maker in Tests with a push for two off Flintoff. It proves to be Australia's only mini-triumph of an extraordinary morning, in which the middle order flies apart like shattered glass. Onions tempts Ponting into a rash hook, and the ball takes the edge. The Australian captain looks down the pitch and lingers in the faint hope of a reprieve. He mouths something in reproach to himself, his lips moving like a ventriloquist's dummy. If the first act of today's drama belong to Onions, then the second and third acts are Anderson's alone. From the Pavilion End, he sublimely swings a ball more than 40 overs old. No one, perhaps not even Anderson himself, knows precisely why. Australia are in a bad way. Clarke goes lbw after a dancing appeal. There is a two-second wait as umpire Koertzen replays the delivery in his mind. He raises his finger with a painful slowness; it's like a coffin lid creaking open. Marcus North is caught behind. Mitchell Johnson, like Hussey, goes first ball. Haddin's replacement, Manou, is beaten by Anderson's out-swinger and then bowled by one angled into him from wide of the crease. Anderson takes 4 wickets in 13 balls and Australia are 203 for 8 at lunch. A revival, led improbably by Nathan Hauritz and the last man, Ben Hilfenhaus, who each reach 20, can't push the Australian total much beyond 260. Within an hour of the restart England are batting, surviving the early loss of Alastair Cook, and dominating Australia again. Cook lasts only four balls before edging Peter Siddle and giving Manou a bootstrap-low diving catch on his debut. England nonetheless have Strauss, who is on one of the best and most reliable streaks of his life. There is no swing *à la* Anderson for the Australian bowlers, and Strauss sprays shots around Edgbaston, chiefly off the back foot, on his way to an unbeaten half-century. Ravi Bopara gives another comet-like appearance – burning brightly but briefly before dragging a ball from Hilfenhaus on to his stumps for 23. Nothing disturbs Strauss, though. When bad light stops play as six o'clock approaches, England are 116 for 2, and the bookmakers are scything down the odds on a 2–0 series lead.

The Edgbaston Test, washed out entirely on its third day, finishes tamely as a draw. It ends with a shrug and an acceptance early on that Headingley and the Oval will decide the series. But there is a deeply depressing coda to the story, which the ECB will soon have to confront.

More tears, said St Teresa, are shed over answered prayers than unanswered ones. Cricket in England has tried to become the 'new football' in its enthusiasm to be fashionably trendy, all-embracingly popular and populist. In doing so it has troubled its own house, inheriting the ill wind of football's unsavoury aspects.

It isn't so much the wearisomely tuneless and tediously repetitive chanting of the Barmy Army, like the thudding beat of a migraine, or the garish fancy dress that is no longer original but instead boorish and stale, the novelty long since drained from the act. The most concerning thing about watching a Test in England is the abuse and rank obnoxiousness of spectators who drink too much and behave like the swaying, gape-mouthed characters in Hogarth's *Gin Lane*. The drunks constantly leave the sober on the very edge of embarrassment and dread. On radio and TV the base vulgarity of the hecklers is often euphemistically described by commentators, behind glass and distant from it, as mere 'banter' or a sign of the crowd being 'in good heart'. If you happen to be next to it, the nastiness and deliberate malice accompanying the words and actions – beer spilt, innocent people jeered at or castigated, players dismissed in loud shrieks as 'wankers' and 'fucking useless' – are just repulsive. Sitting behind me on the first day were four 'fans' (another term imported from football) who boasted of spending nearly £50 apiece on twelve pints of strong lager. By late afternoon the slurred but perpetual expletives and the hallucinations began.

Australia's players were transformed in their eyes as venal, a Leviathan of grotesque proportions, and drink allowed them the spurious entitlement to ridicule and rant. Beery pockets of 'fans' spread like an infection. Stewards could do nothing to control either them or their epic drinking. On the second day there were another three 'supporters' who smuggled white wine into the ground in silver bags, which was squeezed, as though it was orange juice, into large glasses all morning and afternoon. At four o'clock, after insulting a steward on the perimeter of the pitch and the Australian bowler Peter Siddle, who was fielding at third man, as well as the Australians in the crowd around them, one of them was so drunk he could barely stand. Rising slowly off his seat to celebrate a boundary, he teetered like an apprentice stilt walker. The alcohol seemed to have sunk deep into his bones as well as his bloodstream. The sour smell of drunkenness hung in the air. 'We don't watch the cricket to listen to this,' said an Australian woman in her sixties, pursing her lips in utter contempt, almost too choked to speak. 'Disgusting,' she said before retreating to safety behind the Wyatt Stand.

There are now people who come to Tests simply to drink and to get drunk and who have no knowledge of, or empathy for, cricket. There is no deep immersion in the game, but simply a desire for the alcohol which accompanies it. The ground for them is just a pub, open all hours. The drinking itself is not to blame. It is the excess. They regard it as a felony to consume only small amounts. At Edgbaston it was possible to buy from sellers who walked around the concourse with boxes of beer strapped in large rucksacks on their backs. It won't take much – a remark that injures, a drink upturned into someone's lap, a young child accidentally barged or stamped on – to provoke violence. This is a hard truth, attributed to statistical inevitability and the liberating effects of booze. But it places a chill on the people around them. If the ECB ignores the drinking culture, or allows it to go unchecked, it will at some stage find itself trying to explain away a profoundly serious incident.

For if you dabble with high explosive, you are likely to blow up yourself up.

Umpires: Aleem Dar, R. E. Koertzen
Toss: Australia

Australia first innings

S. R. Watson	lbw	b Onions	62
S. M. Katich	lbw	b Swann	46
R. T. Ponting*	c Prior	b Onions	38
M. E. K. Hussey	lbw	b Onions	0
M. J. Clarke	lbw	b Anderson	29
M. J. North	c Prior	b Anderson	12
G. A. Manou†	b Anderson		8
M. G. Johnson	lbw	b Anderson	0
N. M. Hauritz	not out		20
P. M. Siddle	c Prior	b Anderson	13
B. W. Hilfenhaus	c Swann	b Onions	20
Extras	(5b, 7lb, 1nb, 2w)		15
Total	(all out, 70.4 overs)		**263**

Fall of wickets: 1-85, 2-126, 3-126, 4-163, 5-193, 6-202, 7-202, 8-203, 9-229, 10-263

England bowling	O	M	R	W
Anderson	24	7	80	5
Flintoff	15	2	58	0
Onions	16.4	2	58	4
Broad	13	2	51	0
Swann	2	0	4	1

England first innings

A. J. Strauss*	c Manou	b Hilfenhaus	69
A. N. Cook	c Manou	b Siddle	0
R. S. Bopara	b Hilfenhaus		23
I. R. Bell	lbw	b Johnson	53
P. D. Collingwood	c Ponting	b Hilfenhaus	13
M. J. Prior†	c sub (Hughes)	b Siddle	41
A. Flintoff	c Clarke	b Hauritz	74
S. C. J. Broad	c & b Siddle		55
G. P. Swann	c North	b Johnson	24
J. M. Anderson	c Manou	b Hilfenhaus	1
G. Onions	not out		2
Extras	(2b, 4lb, 9nb, 6w)		21
Total	(all out, 93.3 overs)		**376**

Fall of wickets: 1-2, 2-60, 3-141, 4-159, 5-168, 6-257, 7-309, 8-348, 9-355, 10-376

Australia bowling	O	M	R	W
Hilfenhaus	30	7	109	4
Siddle	21.3	3	89	3
Hauritz	18	2	57	1
Johnson	21	1	92	2
Watson	3	0	23	0

Australia second innings

S. R. Watson	c Prior	b Anderson	53
S. M. Katich	c Prior	b Onions	26
R. T. Ponting*	b Swann		5
M. E. K. Hussey	c Prior	b Broad	64
M. J. Clarke	not out		103
M. J. North	c Anderson	b Broad	96
G. A. Manou†	not out		13
Extras	(4b, 6lb, 3nb, 2w)		15
Total	(5 wickets, 112.2 overs)		375

Fall of wickets: 1-47, 2-52, 3-137, 4-161, 5-346

England bowling	O	M	R	W
Anderson	21	8	47	1
Flintoff	15	0	35	0
Onions	19	3	74	1
Swann	31	4	119	1
Broad	16	2	38	2
Bopara	8.2	1	44	0
Collingwood	2	0	8	0

Result: Match drawn

Man of the match: M. J. Clarke

CHAPTER FOURTEEN

THE POET OF
PENRHYN AVENUE

Small acts of craftsmanship – and years of experience –
underscore Robert Croft's value to Glamorgan

Colwyn Bay: Glamorgan v. Northamptonshire: NatWest Pro40 League, 9 August

Nowadays it is difficult to believe that 40-overs cricket was once the gleaming future. It was 1969, the summer of the moon landings. Lord's own giant leap was to alter the shape and construction of the game by inaugurating the Sunday 'Players' League'. I was almost eleven years old, watching the matches on the family's ancient, 16-inch black-and-white television, which sat in its polished teak case in the far corner of the living room. The images it broadcast were so ghostly and smoky that NASA could have been transmitting Warwickshire v. Lancashire from the Sea of Tranquillity rather than leafy Nuneaton. I had no idea that I was witnessing something revolutionary. I had no idea, either, of the sober debate, ricocheting often bad-temperedly around the counties, about the desirability of allowing the competition to take place at all and what it might do to the whole game.

It's true that the more things change the more they stay the same. I found evidence of it in a large cardboard box earlier in the season during the Cheltenham Festival. On the secondhand bookstall I came across two towers of old magazines, *The Cricketer* and *Playfair Cricket Monthly*. The bookseller was virtually giving them away – 25p each, or five for a pound. I picked up a dozen, attracted by the monochrome cover photographs – John Edrich, Garry Sobers, John Snow – and occasionally the front-page blurb designed to entice the reader to pull it down from the newsagent's rack. One of the blurbs in *The Cricketer* contained Alan Gibson's *Journal of the Season* for 1979, which demanded to be read. In it he falls victim for the umpteenth time in his eventful, journalistic life to a 'trifling delay at Didcot' junction and is half an hour late for the start of Oxford University v. Yorkshire at the Parks. 'Everyone was laughing,' he writes, 'and smacking each other on the back, and there was a large 0 on the board below "Last Man".' Gibson discovers Geoffrey Boycott has been caught and bowled in the first over by a theology student. 'Countless hours of prayer from the community must have been responsible for getting Boycott out,' he adds pricelessly. But the articles which drew my eye the most were in the editions of *Playfair Cricket Monthly* from the closing months of 1969. The impact of the Players' League, and what it meant for cricket, was already apparent.

The magazines are as dense and inky grey as twelfth-century parchment. There is page after page of poorly illustrated text and statistics, like a bank's annual report to its shareholders. The advertisements promote 'Cricket Flannels of the Highest Quality', *I-Spy* Cricket books and Haig 'Don't be Vague' whisky. *The Radio Times* boasts of the BBC's commitment to its cricket coverage in a voice that suggests it would be shocking impudence for anyone else to lay a clammy hand on the summer game. In the minuscule 'For Sale' columns someone is selling Jack Hobbs's own bat 'signed and used by him in the Fourth Test in 1921' (I check: Hobbs made 27 and 13 against Australia in Melbourne, and England lost by 8 wickets). Today there'd be a bidding war for the bat on eBay. The editorial content of these issues is gloomily dominated by one thing, always highlighted in thick capital letters and carrying a question mark, as if fumbling for an answer.

IS THE SUNDAY LEAGUE THE BIG BONANZA?
WHAT IS THE FUTURE OF THREE DAY CRICKET?
CAN WE TAKE A BALANCED LOOK AT WHAT HAPPENS NEXT?

The Sunday League, so important to me when it began four decades ago, is dismissed in *Playfair Cricket Monthly* as 'Pop-age cricket' and 'biff-bang' which can grievously harm the health and well-being of sacred Tests and the foundations of the County Championship. Like a High Court Judge solemnly lifting the black silk death cap on to his head, E. W. Swanton warns that the 'price to be paid for it could be too heavy'. As the claret-voiced megaphone for cricket's Establishment, Swanton encapsulates in that straightforward sentence the fear that the shorter form of the game might become *too popular* and destabilise everything around it. J. M. Kilburn was just as dismissive. For him, the Sunday League was 'tea party entertainment' and a 'TV variety show', which was not to be taken seriously. An avuncular by-line photograph of his friend Bill Bowes – white hair, wire-framed dark glasses and a 1950s-style telephone in his right hand – accompanies his view that 'the public will not pay to watch once the novelty wears off'. The *Playfair* editorial thunders out its lofty concern that 'one-day cricket will not breed Test material . . . A surfeit of one-day matches might, in the end, kill the goose that has laid the golden eggs.' Rather than this being cricket's eureka moment – and the chance to restock the bare coffers of the counties – the anonymous writer offers a doomsday scenario. He sounds as ridiculous as the Gothic novelist Horace Walpole, who was sure that late eighteenth-century balloons would be 'converted into new engines of mass destruction'. Also expressed in *Playfair* is some maudlin hand-wringing over the 'proliferation of Instant Cricket' and the 'esoteric arguments' about whether 'it's real cricket' in the first place.

It was certainly real to me at the time; very real, in fact. On the way home from Cheltenham I read Bill Bowes' piece twice. From my kitchen window I can see the roof of the house in Wharfedale where he lived for the final decades of his life as a journalist covering Yorkshire and England. The house juts out between a clump of trees. He used to walk his dog along the narrow curve of the lane. Having felt an affinity with Bowes, and taken a special interest in his writing because of our shared geography, I'd assumed he would have taken a more tolerant and less reactionary stance than Swanton. After all, Bowes bowled Bodyline. 'It was not such a tremendous success,' he said of the opening season of the Players' League, 'that the Yorkshire club want to rush headlong into an extension of the one-day type of game'. Yorkshire's Yearbook reveals a different a story. The champion county took £6,000 from thirty days of Championship matches, and £5,000 from only seven Players' League games. All summer the gates were slammed shut on Sunday. The 1960s may have swung a little, but not sufficiently to make the Sabbath anything other than as dully staid and stiff as a Victorian starched collar. The shops were closed. The pubs were shut by early afternoon. There was nowhere to go. The combination of 'lightning cricket' and the relaxation of the licensing laws at every ground enticed the crowds because it offered relief from an otherwise boring afternoon. Even if you didn't like the game, the bar was still open.

Forty years on it is easy to criticise Swanton and Bowes for expressing nothing more than cracker-barrel opinions. We have the advantage of knowing how things turned out, and can consequently ridicule such pessimism without contradiction. But I realise that Bowes' hesitation in recognising the merits of 40-overs cricket exactly reflects my own opinion of Twenty20 as the Devil incarnate, replete with sharpened horns and a toasting fork. I am already thinking that cricket as I know it won't be the same ten years from now. Bowes was wrong. The 40-overs game no more killed cricket than the typewriter killed the fountain pen or the pencil. So perhaps I am wrong too. It's proof, though, that we are always waiting for the worst to happen.

* * *

When the Players' League began, the counties often took matches to out-grounds, such as Ebbw Vale or Harlow, Stourbridge or Western-Super-Mare. I have chosen Colwyn Bay in the hope of recapturing some of the spirit of those distant days. The match is also being played on a Sunday – rare nowadays when Pro-40, like everything else, is rearranged and shuffled for the benefit of Sky Sports. The only difficulty is finding the ground, which isn't signposted on the long promenade. It isn't even in Colwyn Bay, with its dilapidated-looking Victoria pier, stretching like a withered finger into the sea, but in Rhos-on-Sea which seamlessly adjoins it. The ground hides behind a low brick wall on Penrhyn Avenue and is fringed with the back gardens of neighbouring houses. Walking around the boundary, I can hear the chopped, muffled voices from TVs in front rooms and the rattle and clatter of dinner plates being washed and put away. There's a mixture of blue bucket seats and white garden chairs, which creates the atmosphere and chummy flavour of a particularly grand village match on the green from an era predating the Players' League. The pavilion resembles a large, 1970s-style house on one of the posher suburban estates. The most striking sight is the three-tiered grass embankment behind the bowler's arm, which rises towards rows of bungalows with grey roofs and grey cladding and the small windows that lead your gaze into private lives. Although this is North rather than South Wales, far away from the Boat House where his imagination was laid down in ink, the place reminds me of Dylan Thomas's starless and moonless Llareggub Hill, where 'time passes' in slow procession without leaving a footprint. The sea lies at the end of the Avenue, and there is no wind to turn the offshore turbines, which stand in a slip cordon against the hard line of the horizon. Each blade is like an outstretched arm.

Early arrivals have been filing in since 10.30 a.m. (half an hour before the gates were due to open) to lay towels and bags and sunhats on the best seats beside the sightscreens. On a wet day there'd be nowhere to shelter here except under the odd, sparse tree. But today the sun is out and the cloud swims by, as if only tipping its hat at us before hurrying off. Glamorgan and Northamptonshire are mid-table in Division Two. The edge nonetheless belongs to Northants, who are preparing for a 'big day out'. A fortnight ago Northants defeated the Friends Provident Trophy winners, Hampshire, to reach Twenty20 Finals Day at Edgbaston. It is held six days from now, and the opening batsmen in particular – Stephen Peters and Niall O'Brien – set off as though Colwyn Bay is a dress rehearsal for fast scoring. Northants, who win the toss, motor along at a rate of 5–6 runs an over. The Glamorgan seamer Ryan Watkins is treated a like a net bowler capable of being struck anywhere with impunity. There is a slight stutter in Watkins' trundling, over-long approach to the stumps, as if he's still making up his mind en route about where to put the ball. No matter where he lands it, O'Brien drives him straight or through the covers. Watkins' 5 overs cost 42 runs.

O'Brien and Peters each bring up half-centuries as early as the 15th over; O'Brien off 52 balls and Peters from an even 50. The partnership is so absorbing that no one follows the last rites of the Fourth Ashes Test, eventually completed at 2.04 p.m.. As Australia level the series 1–1 at Headingley, I am sitting behind two elderly couples who come to Colwyn Bay each summer. The husbands, both wearing Ashes 2009 baseball caps, position themselves either side of their wives, who talk incessantly of holidays and shopping and the town's hotel. Neither shows a modicum of interest in the match. Their husbands, familiar to such indifference, lean forward, as if peering around a corner, and hold conversations across them.

'We've no attack,' says one.

'No attack at all,' says the other.

'Going to be a long day,' says the first.

'A very long day,' says the second.

'This team can bat.'

'This team can bat very well.'

Finally the public address system leaks out the news of England's innings and 80 runs defeat.

'Don't know what they'll do at the Oval,' says the man to my left.

'I don't know what they'll do either,' says his friend.

'Call up two new players, I think.'

'Call up three new players if you ask me.'

Even expressing such banalities, the Welsh accent has a soft, sing-song lilt, perfect for story-telling. But the bored, distracted wives, who have heard it before, gather up bags and sweaters and depart for the shops.

'Where are they going?'

'To the shops.'

'There's a match here . . .'

'There's a match to be watched here . . .'

The line of the conversation is only broken as O'Brien advances down the pitch and lifts the spin of Robert Croft perilously close to our heads. The ball pounds against and dents the metal sign advertising a frozen foods firm attached to the wall of Penrhyn Avenue.

'Lucky neither of them got hit with that,' says one of the men.

'There'd have been no shopping then,' adds his friend.

Another parallel between the original Sunday League and the arrival of Twenty20 was the dire prediction of the death of the spinner, as though he'd suffer cricket's equivalent of a public stoning. The slow bowler was reckoned to be nothing but casual fodder; certain to become extinct in the fast churn of the new competition. He'd toss the ball up and watch it vanish behind him. At the end of 1969, however, two of the top four bowling performances in the Players' League belonged to spinners: Ray East's 6 for 18 for Essex against Yorkshire; and Don Wilson's identical figures for Yorkshire against Kent. Croft also proves that the small feats of craftsmanship which spinners can perform are frequently more precious than just lobbing on one seamer after another. Northants have taken the score on to 153 without loss when Croft deceives O'Brien with an arm ball, trapping him lbw on the back foot for 82. The new batsman, South African Andrew Hall, lasts only two deliveries. Croft tempts him into half-cutting, and he plants an inside edge on to his stumps. Glamorgan, who have looked lackadaisical until this point, perk up still further when Peters, on 69, complacently flicks another ball from Croft into mid-wicket's hands. Alex Wakely is also enticed into a loose shot, which he spoons back to Croft with a scrambled seam. In 17 balls, he's taken 4 wickets for just 11 runs, and Northants have crumbled at the edges to 173 for 4 with 12 overs left.

Croft will be forty next May and has given a life of devoted labour to Glamorgan. He is blockishly rectangular – thicker around the waist and jowls than on his Championship debut in 1989. It's said that advancing age always catches men by surprise. Croft self-evidently is putting off the day when it surprises him. As others of his generation announce their retirement – John Crawley, Andrew Caddick and Mark Butcher are among the most prominent already this summer – Croft has signed another two-year contract, like a cricketing actor for whom the scent of greasepaint is too intoxicating to give up just yet. More curtain calls await. Only after Croft's regulation eight-over spell ends do Northants reassert themselves. The captain Nicky Boje thumps one six off Jamie Dalrymple into a maple

Clive Lloyd – a coiled athletic grace was the hallmark of his quite brilliant batting. He hit the ball with supreme force.

on the square-leg boundary and another into a knot of trees 15 feet further along the rope. The ball breaks a branch, scatters leaves and sends small birds fleeing. His 43 enables Northants to reach 268 for 7 – a respectable but not unachievable target on a compact ground. The women return from shopping. 'Are we losing?' one of them asks merely to be polite.

All afternoon the public address has been plugging the fact that Glamorgan's replica Pro40 shirts, once £40, are now available for half-price. It's indisputably a buyers' market. Within another month, the shirts will be worth less still. What began as the Players' League and almost immediately became the John Player League – and then dressed in the name of whichever transient sponsor put up most money – is in its final season. The competition is moribund; condemned as out-of-date and redolent of the era in which it was created. It is useful no more, and unfashionable too. And so Glamorgan's Pro40 shirts are at best a potential collector's item and at worst a piece of pointless, out-of-date tat. The end of Pro40 was forecast almost as soon as Twenty20 began crackling like a lit fuse, and no administrator wore funereal black after the decision to purge it from next year's calendar was made. It was portrayed instead as an act of kindness, like putting an ageing family pet to sleep. Today's programme includes what is tantamount to its obituary. 'The games,' it says in pointing out the imminent death of 40 overs, 'are a reminder of bygone days . . . and commentary from John Arlott [and] Jim Laker.' The article ends with the line: 'For now, though, it's probably time to raise a glass to 40-overs cricket and say "Thanks for the memory!"' I will miss it because the competition fostered my childhood devotion to cricket, and kept it alive on television before, after and in between Tests. It inspired my father to watch cricket too. The Sunday League converted him the way a hell-fire evangelist preacher can convert the most strident non-believer.

Those early days were dominated by Lancashire, who won the first title. Whenever Clive Lloyd came into bat, I only had to shout 'He's in' for my father to know exactly who I meant. Immediately he'd put down his newspaper or stop whatever else he was doing to watch him. Lloyd carried his tree-trunk bat as though it was as light as a piece of kindling and wore darkly framed, oversize spectacles that glinted beneath the brightly stitched red rose on his cap. There was a coiled athletic grace and a sharp vitality about him. What is more, it was as if his lean limbs were elastically jointed, which allowed him to stretch them and extend his reach beyond comprehension. In the field he swooped with a fluid dive. He prowled the covers, moving effortlessly to rake the ball up with his long fingers, before sending it back with a bullet's speed and accuracy to the wicketkeeper, Farokh Engineer. At the crease he hit the ball with supreme force, generated by his high backlift and the threshing motion of his full follow-through. He went after the bowling like a shark in pursuit of a poor swimmer. The ball never survived. My father thought watching Lloyd was worth his TV licence. Within two summers of following the Sunday League, its tactics and fielding positions, which had previously been as incomprehensible and strange-sounding to my father as equations in nuclear physics, were embedded into his heart as much as his brain. Within three summers, he was engrossed in *any* cricket anywhere – a Test, the Roses match, the Gillette Cup – that appeared on the screen. He'd check the *Radio Times* to hunt them out and plan for them. In retirement one of his pleasures was to sit through every ball of a Test. The Sunday League began all this for him.

Colwyn Bay has no giddy expectations about the size of the total Glamorgan are capable of mustering. The early consensus is that Northants have enough on the board to win comfortably enough. Of primary interest now is watching Monty Panesar bowl. Panesar is back in Wales for the first time since he batted out the last 11 overs of the First Test at Cardiff with James Anderson to force the draw. It was improbable for two reasons. First, Panesar bats about as well as Ricky Ponting bowls. Second, the Australians had all day to take only eight wickets and muffed the chance; something I suspect would never have happened in the invade-and-conquer dynasties of Taylor, Border or Waugh. The maker's name Panesar repeatedly showed Australia added to his cult status. His form so far this summer hasn't otherwise troubled the headline writers but, rather like minor royalty, he endears himself to his public merely by turning up. Clad in a tight black turban, Panesar paced the grass path behind the pavilion during Northants' innings and ate his pre-packed sandwiches slowly, safe in the knowledge that more batting heroics were never going to be necessary here. During the short innings break, he turns his arm over on the outfield and signs autographs. When he goes to field on the Embankment boundary, there are more books, scraps of blank paper, miniature bats and a steady queue to pester him. Fielding duties don't overstretch Panesar. He doesn't have to chase hard or often. Mostly he's required to drop on bended knee and take the ball in the classic manner of the MCC coaching manual. There's still an expectation that somehow it might slip from his hands, thud off his thigh or go straight through him for four. He isn't naturally elegant or convincing and he takes the ball as though lacking both his thumbs. His eyes seem to wander too, and his body visibly tenses, as if he'd rather just be bowling. Which is why, whenever he sweeps up the ball without a hitch and returns it over the stumps, there's a relieved cheer and the chant of his name from the Embankment End.

At the start Glamorgan rattle along, as if free-wheeling downhill. The openers keep pace with the rate for 10 overs before Lee Daggett removes Will Bragg for 18 and Mike Powell for a single in quick succession. When Dalrymple goes too, leaving Glamorgan's total wheezing on 103 for 3 and already beyond the halfway point of the innings, Northants' command looks unshakeable. The number five batsman is twenty-year-old Tom Maynard, son of the coach, Matthew. He is taller and broader and more imposing than his father; his forearms are meaty, as though he splits wood with a lumberjack's axe during his spare weekends. In the 21st over Panesar is brought into the attack rather belatedly, like someone arriving late at a party. Straight away Maynard launches him to the mid-wicket boundary with a shot that takes one rabbit hop into the boards. Panesar looks listless. There is no venom in his bowling. The ball is pushed through flat. The seam doesn't cut through the air with the same twirl that Croft managed earlier. It's as though Panesar doesn't want to chafe the skin on his spinning finger. He's really only half-glimpsed as a bowler in this game. He lasts only 2 tired overs – which cost 18 runs – before finding himself back on boundary patrol.

It makes no difference who bowls at Maynard. This is a broadsword innings. He attacks everything fired at him irrespective of length. Dalrymple is repeatedly pummelled through the covers. Boje is driven over the sightscreen and into Penrhyn Avenue, where the ball bounces off the roof of a stationary car with a destructive crunch. Another poetic drive to long off against Johan van der Wath spears over the rope and smacks against the 'Visit Wales' hoarding, almost pushing it over. Even the loss of his partner, Gareth Rees, who reaches 73 before skying a catch to backward square leg, doesn't shake Maynard out of his lethal rhythm. His fifty comes off 33 deliveries. He needs only another 24 balls for a century, which he reaches with a second six off van der Wath. This 57-ball spree is Glamorgan's fastest-ever List A hundred. With neat symmetry, the previous holder was his father, who scored his ton in 58 balls and did so thirteen years earlier, when his son was still learning joined up handwriting and playing with his Lego. The crowd glance at Maynard and then at the scoreboard. Glamorgan, who needed 107 off 10 overs and then 68 off 5, are closing in on Northants like a fire-engine reaching the fire. With 2 overs left, and only 24 needed, Maynard tries a Dilshan-like half-starfish in an effort to deflect van der Wath to fine leg. When it goes wrong the flair of improvisation looks instead a knuckle-headed shot, as fatuous as sawing off a branch that you're sitting on. Maynard is bowled; and he is furious with himself.

When Peters and O'Brien were whacking the ball to all parts, Maynard fielded in front of me on the Penrhyn Avenue boundary. One of the men wearing his souvenir Ashes cap said to him: 'You'll need to get a hundred today, my friend.' Maynard turned and appeased him with the reply: 'I'll get a hundred. And not out too.' Had he made it through to the end, there's no doubt Glamorgan would have won. But it would be unjust to criticise him. Maynard batted as vividly as a poet writes. I still can't believe that 40-overs cricket is being jettisoned. The match has generated more than 500 runs, including a century that glowed like white neon, and the outcome remained in doubt until the penultimate over. I leave knowing one thing: my father would have loved it.

The two friends in baseball caps begin packing up.

'It's been a long day,' says one of the wives.

'A very long day,' says the other. 'But at least we enjoyed the shopping.'

Umpires: N. L. Bainton, V. A. Holder
Toss: Northamptonshire

Northamptonshire innings

S. D. Peters	c Cosker	b Croft	69
N. J. O'Brien†	lbw	b Croft	82
A. J. Hall	b Croft		2
A. G. Wakely	c & b Croft		8
R. A. White	b Kruger		35
N. Boje*	c & b Harrison		43
J. J. van der Wath	c Dalrymple	b Kruger	15
D. J. Willey	not out		6
D. S. Lucas	not out		0
Did not bat: M. S. Panesar, L. M. Daggett			
Extras	(3lb, 4nb, 1w)		8
Total	(7 wickets, 40 overs)		**268**

Fall of wickets: 1-153, 2-155, 3-162, 4-173, 5-236, 6-248, 7-267

Glamorgan bowling	O	M	R	W
Harrison	7	1	46	1
Watkins	5	0	42	0
Kruger	8	0	54	2
Coster	7	0	40	0
Croft	8	0	43	4
Dalrymple	5	0	40	0

Glamorgan innings

G. P. Rees	c Daggett	b Boje	73
W. D. Bragg	b van der Wath		18
M. J. Powell	b Daggett		1
J. W. M. Dalrymple*	c & b Boje		11
T. L. Maynard	b van der Wath		108
M. A. Wallace†	c & b Boje		5
R. E. Watkins	b Lucas		10
R. D. B. Croft	c Hall	b van der Wath	6
D. A. Cosker	not out		6
D. S. Harrison	not out		12
Did not bat: G. J. P. Kruger			
Extras	(5b, 3lb, 4w)		12
Total	(8 wickets, 40 overs)		**262**

Fall of wickets: 1-51, 2-60, 3-103, 4-137, 5-145, 6-215, 7-238, 8-247

Northamptonshire bowling	O	M	R	W
van der Wath	8	0	55	3
Lucas	5	0	36	1
Daggett	8	0	52	1
Hall	8	1	31	0
Boje	7	0	49	3
Panesar	2	0	18	0
Willey	2	0	13	0

Result: Northamptonshire won by 6 runs

CHAPTER FIFTEEN

THE CRIMSON PETAL
AND THE WHITE

The outstanding agility of the modern fielder is typified by Lancashire's
Steven Croft as he claims a catch off Anthony McGrath.

Headingley: LV County Championship Division One:
Yorkshire v. Lancashire, 19–22 August

Some things seem improbable at the time, but inevitable in retrospect. So it was this summer with the retirement of Michael Vaughan, a departure ostensibly abrupt and rushed to the extent that there was no time for to say a proper goodbye to him. Like the magician's assistant in a stage trick, Vaughan was there one moment and gone the next.

I think about Vaughan as I sit at Headingley waiting for the start of the 248th Roses match. I remember his hesitant footwork at the start of the summer in the nets at Lord's, where his bat was almost always a critical quarter of a second late with its appointment with the ball. A week later I saw him again on this ground – a cold, bright day in April when Yorkshire were playing a practice match among themselves. There were only a dozen spectators here, which included an elderly couple huddled together in coats and scarves. The man, his skin as worn and nut-brown as an old Gladstone bag, poured his wife tea from a Thermos, holding the flask and the cup for her in small, woollen-gloved hands. Dressed entirely in black, a bobble hat pulled over his ears like an old-fashioned swimmer's skull cap, Vaughan fielded in front of the boundary with the construction of Headingley's new £21 million pavilion clanking behind him. He was closest to the din of cement mixers, the vigorous hammering and the grinding noise of concrete being smoothed, the residue of it rising like fine flour across the building site. Two enormous skeletal cranes swung towards one another, like the arms of a slow-moving puppet, and lifted girders and boards skyward. The former England captain seemed incongruously out of place – too grand and elegant for such grim surroundings. I thought then that Vaughan had travelled almost as far from the tumult of the 2005 Ashes – the operatic finish and the ticker-tape shower of the Oval – as it was possible to get without tipping off the edge of the first-class game. And, as I watched, I asked myself how long someone like him would be content and prepared to tolerate the comparatively thin gruel of the County Championship.

Pride is one of the basic propellants of human instinct, and it explains why Vaughan, at thirty-four, clung on, as though patience and perseverance alone would restore the form that age and the physical and psychological fatigue of constant cricket was incrementally stealing from him. For a while he was like Conrad's Captain Black tackling the typhoon:

'Facing it, always facing it.' There was a goal before him: return to the England team and what he hoped would be his first-ever appearance in an Ashes Test at Headingley. When, eventually, this seemed so unlikely as to make striving for it insanely pointless, he abandoned it and sensibly moved on. By then he was averaging only 19.87 from 8 first-class innings. His run of scores read: 12, 24, 20, 5, 16, 39, 43. He particularly struggled in late spring and early summer, when the surfaces were green and damp and skewed towards the bowlers. Vaughan was always at his best against pace and bounce. The harder the pitch and the faster the delivery, the more fluently Vaughan made his shots. The parched grounds of Australia in 2002–03, where he made 633 in Tests at 63.30, perfectly fitted his natural game. But he'd noticeably begun to find scoring awkward against medium-pace trundlers; the boys of the 70-odd-mile-per-hour brigade who were hard for him to force away and could occasionally dart a difficult one off the strip and take his wicket. He pushed and prodded and missed, as if groping blindly for a light switch in the dark. His bad knee throbbed like toothache too.

Whenever I went to Headingley I found the Yorkshire membership split over Vaughan. Some thought him too aware of his own self-worth. To them he was conspicuously using the county to lever himself back into the Test arena for the equivalent of the politician's last hurrah before abandoning them again. He'd already begun to publicise his alternative career as a modern artist, driving paint-daubed balls into a blank canvas to re-create his most notable innings. The effect is something Jackson Pollock might have produced if he'd been born in Mytholmroyd or Heckmondwyke. Others were more conciliatory and less cynical towards Vaughan, and aware also that all of us, at one time or another, indulge in acts of self-delusion, chasing something unreachable. We only stop chasing when common sense belatedly intervenes. So the reaction to Vaughan's departure – ten days before the opening Test against Australia at Cardiff – consequently depended on whichever side of the argument you took. But the defects of great men are the consolation of dunces, and so there was no gloating about his resignation. Without the prospect of a Test recall, there was no longer any reason for Vaughan to prolong his career except to add easy runs at the end of the summer. Vaughan had already achieved enough anyway to make his reputation secure. He won more Tests as England captain than anyone else: 26 from 51 matches. He made almost 6,000 Test runs at an average of 41.44. What distinguished

Vaughan is a quality that his figures can only imply but never adequately reflect. It was his outwardly calm temperament. Regularly Vaughan diminished problems to their true size, which is a rare thing for a captain under fire. Where there is no vision teams perish, but Vaughan always provided it. There have been England captains who merely looked to be renting the job; Vaughan possessed it. Bad is the plan that can never be altered, but it takes sensitive antennae to recognise tactical change is necessary well before it becomes plainly obvious to everybody else, and gutsy strength with which to implement it. To see a captain at his finest – Mike Brearley, for instance – is to watch someone pulling the levers of some wondrous machine. In unison the field moves at his bidding, the bowler responds to these changing tactical coordinates, and the batsman bites at the hook floating in front of him. Vaughan wasn't Brearley. But he was an instinctive leader – active rather than reactive. He used this intuition one last time in deciding when to quit.

Nothing should befit a man more than the manner of his leaving, so the only regret about Vaughan is the ragged nature of his departure. When he offered to continue in one-day matches for Yorkshire, the county flat-batted the idea. As the news of his retirement broke – in the *Sunday Telegraph*, which pays Vaughan for his weekly column – he left himself out of a Twenty20 match against Derbyshire at Headingley. He practised in the nets before retreating to the players' balcony in his civvies, where he sat beside his four-year-old son, Archie. It was a messy and incomplete farewell and, like a clock that stops one minute before noon, lacked the perfect synchrony that Vaughan warranted: a proper and definitive full stop. Vaughan deserved to play his last match in front of an appreciative audience at Headingley or Scarborough or at Lord's. And his last shot ought to have been the cover drive, which was the emblem of his game. Instead his final domestic innings ended when his stumps were splayed by a shocking full toss at Grace Road from Leicestershire's Andrew Harris, who will be able to say until his last, gasping breath: 'Here, take the hand that once bowled England's most successful captain.'

Headingley's building work continues. Ugly, bare, square pillars and a cat's cradle of scaffolding remain. The cranes are still dragging girders and thick concrete blocks. Strong-armed men in yellow hard hats and fluorescent jackets are visible between the tangle of metal and grey, flat stone. During the fourth Ashes Test, which finished only ten days ago, a large billboard urging the patriotic to 'Roar England On' was attached to the scaffolding for cosmetic purposes. This corner of West Yorkshire still came across on television as exactly what it is: an unsightly construction site with a bit of cricket poking out in front of it.

At 10 o'clock, as Headingley begins to fill, the clang of a workman's hammer sounds a hollow echo across the ground, like a gong calling monks to prayer. This is a dowdy, mongrel of a place. Even J. M. Kilburn found Headingley unappealing on the eye. Kilburn was delicate in describing its faults. 'The touch of sentiment so strongly impressed upon other grounds,' he wrote, 'has seldom fallen significantly upon the Headingley atmosphere.' Were Kilburn to return here now, he'd be terser and less charitable about it. The ambitious, virtuous idea is to turn Headingley into the 'Lord's of the North' and so preserve its Test status, which is already threatened by Durham's gleaming Riverside, Hampshire's Rose Bowl (soon to be remodelled and improved too) and also challenged across the Pennines at Old Trafford, which is also a building site this summer. Given the state of Headingley's Rugby Stand, which has two gurning faces – one staring at the cricket, the other at both codes of rugby – building such an ostentatious pavilion is rather like tacking the Brighton Pavilion on to a Lowry-like terraced house. The part instantly becomes greater than the whole. At last, though, Yorkshire recognise how urgently change is necessary. The Rugby Stand, however, looks like a ramshackle oil tanker run aground. It so obviously belongs to the glum, austere era of postwar England that I half-expect Fred Trueman to emerge from the dressing room and begin marking out his run from the Kirkstall Lane End before verbally abusing the batsman with his standard repartee: 'This 'un will go through you like a streak o' piss,' or 'A good ball's wasted on rubbish like you.'

On the outfield Yorkshire – unfortunately without the Lancastrian Vaughan or the belligerent Trueman – are using two catching cradles as nets and warming up with a game of football. Exactly why is unknowable. When did coaches begin to believe that kicking a football was an appropriate way to prepare for cricket? I long for the Saturday afternoon when I turn up at Old Trafford or Anfield and watch Manchester United or Liverpool pitch two sets of stumps and arrange a five-four field in the penalty area for a half-hour of cricket before a Premier League game.

The beginning of every Roses match cultivates one hope: that the old, clannish feud just might muster a result which lingers in the frieze of memory long after its final ball. The match you remember and talk about for years. The match savoured for something dramatic, fit to stand alongside George Hirst's 9 for 23 in 1903, Graham Lloyd's 225 from only 151 balls in 1997, Darren Lehmann's 252 in Yorkshire's Championship-winning season of 2001. The match in which someone blows away the ancient, caked-on dust of this fixture and uses fresh ink to write his own name in next year's *Wisden*. Anything will do. It certainly happened in the Twenty20 Roses game in mid-June. Yorkshire's Jacques Rudolph hurled the ball back from the Western Stand boundary at the exact moment that a pigeon took off from mid-on. The pigeon had climbed to a cruising altitude of 30 feet – and was still rising – when Rudolph's high return struck it clean on the beak. The last thing it saw on God's earth was the white seam of the ball. A museum is planned for Headingley's new pavilion, and the pigeon ought to be stuffed and put in a glass case like the sparrow at Lord's, which in July 1936 made the worst decision of its short life; rather akin to leaping into the road in between heavy traffic. The bird flew across the flight path of a ball bowled by Jehangir Khan. The ball won. The men of Yorkshire, who like to think of themselves as harder than granite, don't sentimentalise such things. Rudolph picked up the fallen, limp bird by the wing and laid it to rest beside the advertising boards.

Roses matches usually produce *something*. The Australian Ted McDonald bowled leg theory – four men in the leg trap and no slips – five summers before Douglas Jardine ordered Harold Larwood to bruise Donald Bradman's flesh with Bodyline; McDonald took 11 wickets. A year earlier 78,617 wedged themselves into the three days of a high-scoring draw at Old Trafford. In 1968 Brian Statham, in his last first-class match, poignantly claimed 6 for 34, and Yorkshire were bowled out for 61. Geoffrey Boycott, as Yorkshire captain, once had to make a public apology when remarks he made 'off the record' about Lancashire bowling deliberately wide to slow down the scoring rate became tabloid fodder. Leg theory was outlawed after Harold Larwood used it too effectively; 78,000-plus people would only turn up to a Roses match today if a) entry was free, and b) the beer was free too; and players of Boycott's calibre prefer not to be interviewed these days unless it's to sell, endorse or plug something. But there is the outside chance of a Statham-like performance – or at least a miserably small total – after Lancashire win the toss and decide to bat on a slow, dry pitch.

Yorkshire had gone twenty matches, stretching back to last June, without a Championship win until Adil Rashid spun them to one a week ago against Hampshire at Basingstoke. Spasms of self-doubt are now replaced with a refreshed belief. Within 11 balls Tim Bresnan's swing tempts the opener Steven Croft to edge the ball into Gerard Brophy's right glove. Paul Horton follows him two deliveries later. Horton, twisting on the crease as though on casters, doesn't get sufficiently behind a full ball from Matthew Hoggard and squirts it into gully. Lancashire are two for two. As the Western Stand isn't used during the County Championship, and because almost half of the Kirkstall Lane End remains out of bounds, seats are in demand, and there's a big-match atmosphere in the summer air. Lancashire have no option but to buckle down for three sessions of physical endurance. V. V. S. Laxman escapes with edgy strokes, which he watches with relief roll down to third man, before he is able to start playing some shots. After each one he has the habit of delicately patting the pitch with the bottom curve of his bat. His arm is stiff and fully outstretched. He looks like a painter touching up a canvas with small daubs of colour from a loaded brush. The morning ambles by. Lancashire lose Mal Loye, who perishes because he can't decide whether to paddle Rashid around the corner or take the cover off the ball in dispatching him to the fence. He does neither. The ball floats off the back of his bat to Bresnan, who lunges forward and safely catches it behind square. In the afternoon Rashid bowls an assortment of artless long-hops and balls which are so full of guile and flight that Shane Warne would be proud to put his name to them. In one over the new batsman, Mark Chilton, plays at Rashid as if each delivery is a trap. There are strangled shouts and curses from the fielders, who see Chilton sway indecisively, half forward or half back but never sure-footed. Like a salesman who never gives you a searching look at what he's selling, the best and most beguiling spinners leave the batsman guessing until the ball pitches. Rashid is still an apprentice in a trade which can take a decade or more to properly learn. No matter. But half a century from now old men will feel privileged to tell their grandchildren that younger eyes saw his raw, early years.

This pitch isn't really bowler friendly, and Lancashire are tethered as much by their own tentativeness as the laboured accuracy of Yorkshire's bowling. Laxman, for example, reaches his half-century with a push into the covers off Bresnan before impetuosity overtakes him. He comes out of his crease to put Rashid in his place, mis-drives and scoops his shot to

Hoggard at mid-on. The scoring becomes so slow that at one stage I think I'm narcoleptic. Half an hour drifts by, and the scoreboard doesn't twitch.

The run famine continues. Lancashire take 88 overs to reach 200, and Chilton drops anchor. Even when his new partner, Francois du Plessis, goes down on one knee to sweep David Wainwright into the West Stand for six, the stroke doesn't galvanise the game. Wainwright's retaliation is to trap him lbw, a decision which du Plessis greets with dismay. He's 3 feet out of his crease when the ball strikes the pad. When Luke Sutton goes too – a ball from Bresnan scratching the outside edge of his bat – Lancashire are 159 for 6 and ripe for the taking. All summer Yorkshire have found it hard to kill teams off. There's always a traceable tremor in the hand holding the blade. Chilton and Kyle Hogg put on 54, and, despite bringing back Hoggard and switching Rashid to the Football Stand end, Yorkshire can't budge them. Hogg, dropped by Brophy on 18, survives until the closing stages, rashly pulling at a ball from Rashid which the substitute fielder, Azeem Rafiq, holds at mid-wicket. It's been a slow, muted day and satisfying only for the purists and the partisan. It's been cold too, almost befitting Byron's description of an English winter as 'ending in July to recommence in August'.

Not even J. M. Kilburn, cricket correspondent of the Yorkshire Post *for four decades, found Headingley pleasing on the eye. 'The touch of sentiment so strongly impressed upon other grounds,' he wrote 'has seldom fallen significantly upon the Headingley atmosphere'.*

The Roses matches used to be thought of as an exclusively northern affair, which had nowt to do with anyone else. The matches were so intense in the 1920s that the combatants claimed: 'We shake hands on t' first morning and say "How do". Then we say nowt for three days but "Howzat".' That quotation has been attributed to at least two Yorkshire players and subsequently substantiated – through either words or actions – by another twelve dozen, which endorses the hoary stereotype of the Broad Acres as stonily serious to the point of possessing neither charm nor humour. No longer does the south believe that in the People's Republic of Yorkshire it is obligatory to wear flat caps, walk whippets or keep coal in the bath, but the idea of the brusque, chip-on-the-shoulder Yorkshireman remains intact.

It takes one to know one; and so it was Alan Gibson, a Yorkshireman himself, who best and definitively described the Yorkshire character. 'It is the bugbear of Yorkshiremen,' wrote Gibson, 'that they always feel that they have to behave like Yorkshiremen, or like their fixed belief in what a Yorkshireman should be: tough, ruthless, brave, mean.' Others might argue that Gibson was too charitable and ought to have added bloody-minded and self-obsessive to his list. His observation came in the late 1970s during a period in which the bodies were still being counted after a particularly intense decade of bloody 'family arguments' at Headingley; most of them, it has to be said, about Boycott. It was the Yorkshire curse back then to always live in interesting times: Johnny Wardle sacked less than a week after being chosen for the MCC tour to Australia in 1957–58, or Ray Illingworth's abrupt departure over a contractual dispute in 1968 ('He can take any other bugger who feels the same way as him,' said the chairman and ex-captain Brian Sellers), or Boycott's removal as captain ten years later with the acid explanation: 'It is not for what you have done, but because of what you are.' Long service at Yorkshire – especially from the you've-never-had-it-so-good 1950s to the beginning of the Thatcherite 1980s – frequently ended not with a gold watch, but with a hatchet in the back.

Winston Churchill once said of the Balkans: 'They have more history than they can consume.' The same applies to Yorkshire CCC. But no other county has practised so much self-harm. In the past few decades Headingley has been cratered by civil war. It used to be claimed that a stranger always knew he'd arrived here because he could hear the committee rowing or see sparks shoot upward as knives were sharpened.

Brian Close was the cricketing version of Rocky Marciano. He'd absorb five punches for the sake of landing a decent one himself. But nowhere other than Yorkshire could Close have been told so pointedly, and with such obvious malice, by the autocratic Sellers: 'You've had a good innings. I'm going to give you the option of resigning or getting the sack.' He was heaved out of the door with an impatient roughness. In his book *A Century of Great Cricket Quotes*, David Hopps devotes an entire chapter to Yorkshire. Reading it is like sitting through the Headingley equivalent of the Reduced Shakespeare Company's production of *The Complete Works*. Here's the history and comedy, and especially the tragedy and treachery, of Yorkshire cricket condensed into just ten pages. Spite and malevolent score-settling drip like spilt blood from some of these quotes. Most were uttered in the era when Yorkshire were either dominant or coming painfully to terms with the fact that their dominance had ended. The struggle to regain it is on-going, arduous and so far mostly futile.

These are parlous times for Yorkshire. Not one Yorkshire player has figured in the Ashes series this summer, a state of affairs almost unimaginable from the period of Ted Peate onwards. The present team is near the bottom of the table, and a single defeat could see them fall precipitously into Division Two. 'I have not been able to convince myself, as a Yorkshireman, that the sun necessarily shines out of Yorkshire,' said Kilburn tartly on his retirement in 1976. The implication was obvious: others thought differently than him, and Kilburn regarded it as his duty to highlight such a regal attitude as arrogance. He felt it was perpetrated by an implacable old guard, who believed Yorkshire's reputation automatically entitled the county not only to a level of respect bordering on obsequiousness, as well as certain privileges, but also guaranteed a successful future merely on the basis of the past. Far too often Yorkshire resembled the aristocratic family in Tolstoy. Long after the silver had been sold, the servants dismissed and the house left to decay, it continued to have an inappropriately grand edge and a lofty manner about it. Something of it lingers still. A county can't, however, be regarded as being among the nobility when it has won just one Championship in more than forty years. Status of that sort has to be kept in constant repair.

Another curiosity of Headingley is the lack of permanent tributes to its ex-players. It is one of the traditions of cricket grounds to name stands after heroes. Canterbury honours Frank Woolley, Colin Cowdrey and Les Ames; the Oval bows to Bedser and Lock; Old Trafford has the Statham

End; Taunton named its newest stand after Andrew Caddick. At Yorkshire there is nothing for Trueman or Verity, Rhodes or F. S. Jackson, Boycott or Illingworth or Close. In fact I arrived at the ground at the same time Illingworth was drawing his dark-blue Jaguar (with its personalised ILLY plate) towards the entrance. The former Yorkshire and England captain had to politely explain to the student in charge of the gate – born at least three decades after he bowled his first ball here – that he was, after all, entitled to a car-parking space. She glanced at the guest list attached to her clip board, and then glanced at it again, before eventually waving him through. Headingley does hang a white-faced clock over the Western Stand in recognition of Dickie Bird. And I leave through the black wrought-iron of the Len Hutton Gates specifically because his kiss goodbye to Yorkshire had so much in common with Michael Vaughan's. 'To everyone at some time or another,' wrote Hutton in his autobiography, 'comes a day of reckoning when we reach, as it were, the point of no return.' Just like Vaughan, Hutton found himself in physical pain at the end of his career. He took aspirin to 'lull me to sleep' and dull the shredded muscles in his wrecked back. Also like Vaughan, there were no party balloons or streamers, no fuss or flummery, about his retirement. He played 11 matches for Yorkshire in 1955, scoring only 537 runs (which included 194 against Nottinghamshire at Trent Bridge) and retired quietly on medical advice in January the following year. He returned for one final first-class match in 1957 – ironically at Old Trafford – for the MCC. It was a bleak, bitingly cold Whitsun weekend. Hutton scored 76 and 25 to take his total of first-class runs to 40,000. Later he explained why he felt obliged to retire. 'I wanted,' said Hutton, 'to go out on the top note. The perfectionist part in my make-up would not allow me to go on trying the impossible . . . Frankly, I'd rather not play at all than merely potter along, a mere shadow of the Len Hutton the public would rightly expect to see.'

Vaughan's thoughts ran along parallel lines and, exactly like Hutton, he stumbled on the same uncomfortable truth. If he continued to play as no more than a silhouette of his former self, then the public might only remember him that way. Somerset were next on Yorkshire's fixture list, and Vaughan admitted: 'Nothing in me wanted to be playing at Taunton . . . standing at mid-off with Marcus Trescothick belting the ball at me.' And yet, despite Vaughan's insistence, I can't help but contemplate what might have been for him. If he had gone to Taunton and batted on its gloriously pale oatmeal-coloured track – so flat that Somerset racked up

479 in just 85.5 overs to record the second-highest chasing score in the history of the Championship – he might have shaken his dormant summer awake. In writing about Hutton, E. W. Swanton also encapsulated Vaughan's predicament more than half a century later. Hutton was a 'closely prisoned victim of his fame', said Swanton. 'In an age when pressures on great sportsmen were less onerous he would probably have decided . . . to have had done with the burden of five-day Test cricket.' But he knew, Swanton added, that 'it would need only a hundred or two from him . . . to start up a cry for his return'. That return, Swanton concluded, might not be in his own best interests.

Sport is mostly about losing, but there is a pride in doing so gallantly, which is what Vaughan did at the end. 'When I had made the decision,' said Hutton of his own retirement, 'I knew a peace and quietness of mind that had not been my companion for several years.' Michael Vaughan now knows exactly what he meant.

Umpires: J. H. Evans, V. A. Holder
Toss: Lancashire

Lancashire first innings

P. J. Horton	c Bairstow	b Hoggard	2
S. J. Croft	c Brophy	b Bresnan	0
M. B. Loye	c Bresnan	b Rashid	24
V. V. S. Laxman	c Hoggard	b Rashid	50
M. J. Chilton	not out		111
F. du Plessis	lbw	b Wainwright	32
L. D. Sutton*†	c Brophy	b Bresnan	4
K. W. Hogg	c sub (Rafiq)	b Rashid	29
T. Lungley	c Bairstow	b Bresnan	10
O. J. Newby	b Rashid		2
G. Keedy	c Sayers	b Rashid	4
Extras	(3b, 3lb, 2nb)		8
Total	(all out, 122.2 overs)		276

Fall of wickets: 1-2, 2-2, 3-65, 4-92, 5-144, 6-159, 7-213, 8-241, 9-252, 10-276

Yorkshire bowling	O	M	R	W
Hoggard	18	7	40	1
Bresnan	31	13	46	3
Shahzad	18	7	48	0
Rashid	34.2	7	97	5
Wainwright	21	5	39	1

Yorkshire first innings

J. A. Rudolph	c du Plessis	b Hogg	0
J. J. Sayers	lbw	b Lungley	17
A. McGrath*	c Croft	b Lungley	17
A. W. Gale	c & b Lungley		6
J. M. Bairstow	c & b Newby		15
G. L. Brophy†	c Sutton	b Keedy	99
T. T. Bresnan	c Lungley	b Newby	46
A. U. Rashid	not out		157
A. Shahzad	c Loye	b du Plessis	32
D. J. Wainwright	st Sutton	b Keedy	1
M. J. Hoggard	c Horton	b Keedy	8
Extras	(5b, 6lb, 20nb)		31
Total	(all out, 141.2 overs)		**429**

Fall of wickets: 1-0, 2-27, 3-35, 4-68, 5-72, 6-144, 7-312, 8-412, 9-413, 10-429

Lancashire bowling	O	M	R	W
Hogg	33	10	75	1
Newby	24	4	102	2
Lungley	23	2	85	3
Keedy	46.2	11	104	3
Croft	2	0	12	0
du Plessis	11	1	33	1
Laxman	2	0	7	0

Lancashire second innings

P. J. Horton	c Brophy	b Bresnan	15
S. J. Croft	c Brophy	b Rashid	28
M. B. Loye	not out		84
V. V. S. Laxman	not out		65
Extras	(3lb, 1w)		4
Total	(2 wickets, 72 overs)		**196**

Fall of wickets: 1-23, 2-65

Yorkshire bowling	O	M	R	W
Hoggard	10	2	24	0
Bresnan	11	2	30	1
Rashid	24	5	55	1
Wainwright	19	3	67	0
Shahzad	5	3	13	0
Sayers	3	0	4	0

Result: Match drawn

CHAPTER SIXTEEN

FIRST LOVE, LAST LOVE

*Herbert Sutcliffe, the patient genius who based each innings on concentration.
And right, Sutcliffe – aged 79 and in a wheelchair – beside Geoffrey Boycott and
Len Hutton, who both matched him in scoring a century of centuries.*

Wormsley: PCA Twenty20 Masters XIs: England v. Australia, 8 September

Age wearies and the years condemn, but we still see old cricketers in our mind at the point at which a stroke was played, or a ball bowled, that made our senses come alive. We preserve them in the high summer of their life.

After Geoffrey Boycott reached his 100th hundred at Headingley in 1977 he was asked to pose with two Yorkshire batsmen who had made a century of centuries long before him. On the outfield Boycott stood to the left and Len Hutton to the right. In the middle was Herbert Sutcliffe, who was seventy-nine and among the last of the Victorians. He was sitting in a wheelchair. The hands, which held a bat prolifically for twenty-one years between the wars, lay in his lap. The fingers were slightly crabbed. His sturdy black shoes were planted on the metal footrests of the wheelchair. His hair was silvery and thinned to narrowed strands, exposing the high dome of the forehead. The grooved lines of his face, from cheek to mouth, were particularly prominent. A white rose decorated the buttonhole of his black suit. Sutcliffe took the eye not only because he was in the centre of the frame – as if sitting for a portrait – but also because he looked eminent: as grand and distinguished as to be almost kingly, like a man sure of his worth and his hierarchical place. But in the crowd that day at Headingley were people who didn't see an elderly figure in a wheelchair. To them Sutcliffe wasn't ancient. Irrespective of how many decades had slipped by, and irrespective of his frailty, he remained to them as young and fit and padded up. That was how Sutcliffe had looked when he'd made the greatest impression on those fortunate enough to watch him play. And so this is how he had stayed – dark, swept-back straight hair with the bright sheen of oil and with a ruler parting, unblemished skin firm on the bones, forearms and wrists muscled and strong, footwork quick and solid. He was dapper too. The sleeves of his shirt were rolled four times to create wide, symmetrical cuffs, which stopped at the elbow. Appearance mattered to him. R. C. Robertson-Glasgow said of Sutcliffe that he 'would rather miss a train than be seen in disorder and breathing heavily'.

I've seen film of Sutcliffe. He emerges as a patient batsman, each innings based on concentration and the elimination of risk. He didn't stroke his runs in the manner of Jack Hobbs. Mostly, he dug them out. Sutcliffe was obdurate in defence because his radar, tracking the line and flight of the ball as though it were an enemy aircraft, proved almost infallible. He judged its path instantly. In fact, Sutcliffe was so formidably difficult to dislodge that bowlers had to wait for the mistake – a shot uncharacteristically rash or wearied at the end of a long day – to release them from his punishment. Sutcliffe was Boycott well before Boycott existed – a self-made, mentally tough and thinking cricketer who became progressively more skilled through practice and focus and application. He aimed for an extraordinary level of perfectionism and drilled deep into himself to achieve it. What he did in the nets he duplicated on the field. There were flourishes but no pomp and circumstance from Sutcliffe, who had a defence as mean as sin. It was said, however, that his 'off-drive wore a silk hat', which is hardly Boycottesque. Bill Bowes called him 'the most resolute batsman I ever saw'. On page 29 of his coaching book, which he wrote and published himself, Sutcliffe includes verses of his own version of Walter D. Wintle's 'If You Think You Are Beaten'.

If you think you're beaten, you are
If you think, you dare not, you don't
If you'd like to do it, but you think you can't
It's almost certain you won't

Full many a wicket is lost
Ere ever a hit is run
And many a duffer fails
Ere ever his batting's begun

Think big and your success will come
Think small and you'll fall behind
Think that you can and you will
It's all in the state of the mind

Cricket's battles don't always go
To the stronger or better man
But soon or late the man who wins
Is the fellow who thinks he can

The poem succinctly sums up Sutcliffe's tenacity towards whatever he tackled. 'That's the spirit,' he said, 'you must adopt in every sphere of life.' The will to win 'despite great odds' always permeated his thinking. Sutcliffe died less than six months after posing with Boycott and Hutton. It is courtesy and practice for the obituary page to publish an image, alongside the documentary of the life, which captures the deceased at his handsome peak. When the news of his death was announced, anyone who had seen Sutcliffe bat visualised him like this anyway. A friend of mine, of the same vintage as Sutcliffe, explained it to me. 'I saw him immediately in my mind as I'd seen him at Headingley, Bradford and Sheffield. He was never old, never frail to me. Your heroes stay as you first saw them.' At the time I was too young to appreciate that imagination could be more powerful in this way than reality; or that hero worship, a little like love, strikes when you least expect it. The full common sense of it came much later to me. And today – when I least expect it – it reoccurs.

Lord Mancroft once claimed cricket was 'a game which the English, not being a spiritual people, have invented in order to give themselves some conception of eternity'. If so, eternity would pass very pleasantly at Wormsley, where, on his own estate, the billionaire Sir John Paul Getty created a monument to his passion. The pitch was a cornfield before Getty had it cut, tilled and hoed and then carpeted with turf, which looks as immaculate as baize. The result – the first country house ground built since the war – can be conveyed in one over-used but appropriate word: beautiful. Wormsley would be beautiful to the eye of the most cynical beholder. Getty listed his occupation in *Who's Who* as 'philanthropist', a description factually accurate but far from strong enough to bear the loading weight it carries. It is rather like describing Wren merely as 'an architect'. With his chequebook, Getty supported entire blocks of England's heritage. He gave £50 million to the National Gallery in 1985 and £5 million to clean the West Front of St Paul's Cathedral; Lord's received £4 million for the renaissance of the Mound Stand and more for the Allen and Edrich Stands. Some might say it is easy to give money away if you already happen to be incalculably rich, and becoming richer still at an hourly rate. But there was discernment in Getty's largesse, and he distributed it out of generosity towards the causes he thought worthy, rather than in pursuit of fame, which he neither courted nor desired, or self-aggrandisement, which he abhorred. These causes exactly mirrored his enthusiasms, and cricket became foremost among them. A dullard, who didn't recognise Getty, once fell into conversation with him and, learning of his interest in cricket, boasted that he owned a full set of *Wisden*. Getty was too modest to say that he owned the company publishing *Wisden*.

As an American he came to cricket raw, belatedly and without prejudicial baggage. In it he found 'solace' and the 'subtle complexities', which at first he wrestled to comprehend. It was like solving a brain-puzzle. In retrospect cricket was the obvious 'game of games' for Getty because it represented then, and represents still, the ideal of rustic England, which was precious to him. By his own admission Getty was an 'old-fashioned' gent. He immersed himself in the black-and-white movies of the 1920s and 1930s, watching and rewatching them, because he was nostalgic for a world of good tailoring and civility, roads uncluttered by cars and stripped of commercialism. He liked to see England as George Orwell described it: a gentle England of 'old maids biking to Holy Communion through the mists of the autumn morning' and a place where 'the beer is bitterer, the coins are heavier, the grass is greener'. He liked to see cricket as the poet Edmund Blunden described it: in a *Cricket Country* sort of way with 'all that summer glory . . . going slow and flashing past' – or, coincidentally, in the way Orwell reviewed Blunden's book. In his review Orwell argues that the test of the true cricketer is to prefer village cricket, where everyone plays in braces, the blacksmith could be called away in mid-innings on an urgent job and, as the light begins to fail, a ball driven for four kills a rabbit on the boundary. He believed Blunden fell into this category.

Getty's Wormsley fuses together the separate halves of Orwell and Blunden into a nostalgic whole. It exists as the embodiment of what Getty believed an English cricket ground ought to look like. Tradition is more important than modernity. If you died and went to Heaven, Wormsley is the place you'd want, and expect, to find there; and with Hobbs and Grace opening the batting and Jack Gregory coming on to bowl from the Marquee End too.

The ground is on a plateau surrounded only by the dense foliage of 35,000 trees and the drop and rise of the hills of Buckinghamshire and Oxfordshire. It is a privilege just to watch the grass grow here. A bank rises from the top half of the ground to create a single, raised tier for the pavilion, which has three black thatched roofs and a pink-washed pediment and clock. Two dozen wide stone steps, roped off on both sides, lead on to the outfield, almost entirely flat, hard-rolled and blemish-free. For weeds don't dare sprout in Paradise. For sentiment's sake Getty placed a red telephone box next to the pavilion, which adds to the illusion that its matches are taking place while debutantes in long dresses are still being courted during white-tie balls, and the BBC is still broadcasting the Home Service.

The first country house ground built since the war – John Paul Getty's
magnificent creation which is beautiful to the eye of
even the most cynical of beholders.

One of the traditions of cricket is the end of season 'beer match' in which watching the play is secondary to the gastronomic, alcoholic and amiably social aspects of the afternoon; no one pays much attention to the scoreboard. There is more champagne than beer at Wormsley. The spirit is nonetheless identical. Families arrive with wicker baskets and fold-up metal tables. White cloths are spread, and food appears: smoked salmon, pâté, a spread of bread and cheese and fruit. Wine bottles are arranged like a close-in field. Clear glasses catch the sun. A knife and fork glint in it too. A blanket is laid on the grass. A dog dozes, spreading its lean body in the sun, as though settling down in front of the fireside back home. Sheep graze in a nearby field. More than two hours before the start of the PCA Twenty20 Masters I sit in a blue linen deckchair on the long-off boundary. It is hot enough for late July. The occasional pearl-coloured cloud drifts across the sky, but soon wilts and breaks apart in the heat of the dry day. Getty introduced the red kite to his estate. The birds are like dust-specks in the distance until one of them, riding the invisible surf of the thermals, emerges from the high trees stacked behind the pavilion and glides in a descending half arc over the roof. It flies no more than 50 feet above my head before rising and disappearing down into the valley.

It is close enough to see the individual feathers on its broad bronze-and-white wings, the blackness of the tips and the fawn ochre of fanned, forked tail. Near the arrow point of its grey head the left eye of the bird is a small glassy button. The cricket? Well, who really cares?

The two teams include well-known names – a mixture of those still playing, recently retired and retired long ago: Stuart Law, Paul Nixon, Darren Gough, Graeme Hick, Greg Blewett, Rodney Hogg, Dominic Cork, Philip DeFreitas. Australia's captain Law wins the toss and decides to bat. Gough opens the bowling, and the opener Ian Harvey drives him for four. The ball is soon dispatched to all corners. The bowlers aren't able to stop the forward march of the Australian total, and no one minds. 'Please watch the ball at all times,' a tannoy announcement warns. 'It can be very hard on the head.' His words float away on the warm air as Harvey, with a full wheel of the bat, lifts a delivery from the spinner Peter Such on to the roof of the marquee behind the sightscreen, where the suited corporate sponsors lunched. The ball lands with a soft thud. Harvey continues to tan the hide off the ball, as if he had some grudge against it. If it comes at him short – which it often does – he casually pulls it to mid-wicket, where it hops and takes one bounce over the head of spectators, who are obliged to put down their wine and duck, as if avoiding something thrown at them. If a delivery is pitched up he fires it straight back. The ball frequently sinks into the grass bank and rolls back into the hands of the fielder it has convincingly beaten. England's attack is chopped and changed. DeFreitas, who had been keeping wicket, comes on to bowl. Cork, who had bowled off a benign, shortened run, takes the gloves from him. With eight fours and three sixes, Harvey makes sure the tempo never flags. Like everyone else, he knows he's here to be a showman, which is a role he plays well. He twirls his bat at the end of a stroke, as though ending his signature with the flourish of underlining it. By the end, he's made 73 in a stiff total of 196 for 5. Harvey's audience, however appreciative of his efforts, is more concerned about the next glass of decent crisp white.

Getty died in 2003, aged just seventy-one, after long bouts of ill health. One of the things he liked most about cricket, he said, was talking to old cricketers, which was another justification for creating Wormsley. One of the things he disliked about it was coloured clothing, which makes it incongruous to see England dressed in navy and Australia in the familiar green and butter yellow, rather than bright white, and the sightscreens painted lamp black. At tea I walk as far as I can around the boundary before reaching signs, which are staked in front of a wide, closed-off area, that warn in capitals: 'INVITED GUESTS AND PLAYERS ONLY'. This roped entrance is as firmly patrolled as the pavilion at Lord's.

There is no scorecard or glossy programme on sale. The lack of them leaves the crowd – about 1,500 of us – memorising the teams as best it can. Either I hadn't heard him announced at the beginning of the afternoon, or his inclusion was overlooked. Whatever the reason for it, at 5.15 p.m. I experience what I realise is the frisson of my own 'Herbert Sutcliffe moment' (akin to my J. M. Kilburn moment with Mark Ramprakash at the Oval). 'From the Marquee End,' says the man on the tannoy matter-of-factly, 'Jeff Thomson.' Sometimes a name, a place or a half-glimpsed face wrenches you straight out of the present and drops you into the distant past; just as my friend, like Edward Thomas remembering Adlestrop, found he was dropped back into smoky Yorkshire of the 1920s whenever Sutcliffe was mentioned. I immediately see Thomson in 1974. He is twenty-four years old and has long, feather-cut, beach-blond hair. He is pummelling England to dust on the glazed surfaces of Brisbane and Sydney and Perth. His action, the like of which I've never seen before, whips the ball like a catapult from powerful shoulders at the batsman. The arc of his right arm begins from the back of his right thigh. The arch of his bent back almost forms a V shape before release. The position at the point of release, however, is flawlessly side-on. The last, long stride is like a threat. And the ball as it hits the pitch is the fulfilment of it. Defending Thomson's most lethal deliveries on these hard pitches, which accentuate his speed, is like fending off a blow from an iron club. A batsman who is nervous or slow – or both – will be caught off the edge or be struck on the chest, abdomen or head. There are no helmets, and he sees no ethical difference between bowling short at a tail-ender and doing so at numbers one to eight. The batsman facing him experiences the symptoms of sweating fear – the fear of being struck more pronounced than the fear of being embarrassed by a low score.

Thomson once claimed that he preferred to see a batsman's 'blood on the pitch' rather than his stumps shattered and scattered. Thomson then denied ever saying it at all, let alone so graphically, but conceded later that he meant it and didn't mind 'scarin' the hell' out them. The job of fast bowling was strenuous on the body, he said, and his aim was to get it over with as quickly as possible. He wasn't over-fussed about detail or method. Asked about his attitude towards it, Thomson defined it with a description lacking philosophical gloss. 'Aww, mate,' he said, 'I just shuffle up and go wang.' The simplicity of the approach is disarming, as if to make you believe the delivery he set out to bowl was never the one he sent down. But 'the wang' splintered or split the batsman in two. Ian Chappell remembers how, shortly before West Indies began their 1975–76 Australian tour, the tail-ender Lance Gibbs pulled him aside for a conversation.

> GIBBS: I can sort out Lillee. He has a wife and kids like me. But you're responsible for that mad man Thomson. You must convince him not to kill me.
> CHAPPELL: But, Gibbsy, I'm not captain.
> GIBBS: I don't care. I'm holding you responsible.

Whether Chappell placed a sympathetic word or two into Thomson's ear on Gibbs's behalf is unrecorded. But he survived the First Test in Brisbane (not out in both innings), the Second in Perth (run out for 13), the Third in Melbourne (again not out in both innings), the Fourth in Sydney (not out once) and the Fifth in Adelaide. It wasn't until his last innings of the Sixth and final Test that Gibbs succumbed. The scorebook reads:

L. R. Gibbs   c Marsh   b Thomson   0

Gibbs got off lightly. High-speed cameras from the University of Western Australia clocked Thomson's speed during the Perth Test. One ball was timed at 160.45 kmph – the equivalent of 99.6990078 mph.

Thomson is still shuffling up. He just doesn't have the 'wang' any longer. After all, he is almost sixty years old. I don't recognise him as he comes down the pavilion steps and ambles across the outfield. Half of the field is cloaked in dark shadow. The rest is in blazing sun. In the glare of it Thomson's hair – as long as it ever was in his youth – looks parchment white. He walks on flattish feet, as if his arches have fallen. The run-up – once fourteen paces long – is awry. Thomson takes ten steps to bowl his first ball; eight for his second; six for his third; back to ten for his fourth. The arc of his back is almost half an O rather than the V it used to be.

Straight away Nixon smites a short ball for four. The ball is tossed back to Thomson, and he half polishes it on his trousers and then looks at the result to see how well he's done his work. Once he would have responded to Nixon's impertinence with a promise to himself to fasten the batsman to the sightscreen with a ball that came up off a length. Now he gives a desultory shake of his head and bowls a fuller delivery, which Nixon picks off through the covers. At the end of the over – which includes a wide – Thomson slides off to long leg. When he returns, his second over is almost identical to the first – there is even another wide too – until the third ball. Thomson claims a wicket. The opener Jason Gallian perishes the way so many others perished against Thomson decades before. He steers a short ball into the gulley; Law pockets the waist-high catch.

Thomson doesn't bowl again. As the sun begins to dip, and only the blazing curve of it remains, I wait in vain for him to come back. 'Jeff Thomson's figures,' says the announcer at the end, 'are two overs, no maidens and thirteen runs for one wicket'. England finish 23 adrift of Australia, despite a half-century from Nixon, comprising eight fours and two sixes, and a stylish 20 from Hick, who looks capable of coming out of retirement at any moment of his choosing to score a Championship hundred. But the highlight is Thomson's 12-ball cameo. I ignored the evidence of my own eyes. In between deliveries – in fact, often as each ball was bowled – I saw Thomson as he used to be rather than the way he is now: the sleek long run to the crease, the single swift sling of the right arm, the ball rearing towards the batsman, who stumbles back to play it as best he can. And as he bowled I thought about one imponderable. How would Herbert Sutcliffe have batted against him?

Umpires: R. Julian, M. Steer
Toss: Australia

Australia Masters innings

I. J. Harvey	lbw	b Such	**73**
C. J. L. Rogers	c Gallian	b Bicknell	**1**
M. J. Cosgrove	c Cork	b Giddins	**52**
L. Vincent†	c Hick	b Such	**1**
M. R. Foster	c Gallian	b Headley	**14**
S. G. Law*	not out		**19**
G. S. Blewett	not out		**24**

Did not bat: J. R. Thomson, R. M. Hogg, S. H. Cook, I. S. L. Hewett, B. Osbourne, P. Law

Extras   (6lb, 6w)   **12**

Total   (5 wickets, 20 overs)   **196**

Fall of wickets: 1-6, 2-98, 3-103, 4-145, 5-153

PCA Masters XI bowling	O	M	R	W
Gough	3	0	27	0
Bicknell	2	0	15	1
Cork	1	0	11	0
Giddens	4	0	52	1
Such	4	0	37	2
Headley	3	0	20	1
DeFreitas	3	0	28	0

PCA Masters XI innings

P. A Nixon	c Vincent	b Cook	**54**
J. E. R. Gallian	c S. G. Law	b Thomson	**6**
G. A. Hick	c Foster	b Hewett	**20**
D. J. Cork	b S. G. Law		**27**
P. A. J. DeFreitas†	b Hewett		**0**
M. P. Bicknell	b S. G. Law		**9**
D. Gough*	st Vincent	b Cosgrove	**9**
M. J. Saggers	not out		**16**
D. W. Headley	st Vincent	b Osbourne	**5**
P. M. Such	not out		**11**

Did not bat: E. S. H. Giddens

Extras   (2b, 4lb, 10w)   **16**

Total   (8 wickets, 20 overs)   **173**

Fall of wickets: 1-26, 2-77, 3-88, 4-89, 5-101, 6-126, 7-136, 8-149

Australia Masters bowling	O	M	R	W
Hogg	2	0	16	0
Thomson	2	0	13	1
Cook	4	0	29	1
Hewett	4	0	32	2
Cosgrove	3.5	0	23	1
S. G. Law	3	0	30	2
Osbourne	0.1	0	0	1
P. Law	1	0	24	0

Result: Australia Masters won by 23 runs

CHAPTER SEVENTEEN

A MORAL LESSON FROM
LORD HARRIS

*Richard Vigars, an intelligent and highly skilled competitor who
epitomises Yorkshire grit – despite being born in London.*

Lord's: NPower Village Cup Final:
Streethouse v. Glynde and Beddingham, 14 September

In an elegant and eloquent way – similar to the silkiness of his batting – Tom Graveney once wrote about his first sight of Lord's. He went there by steam train. 'The only way,' he explained, 'that Gloucestershire ever travelled' in those pre-motorway days, when a journey from the West Country to London could take a laborious six hours on single-lane roads. Graveney had only ever seen Lord's before on the black-and-white of Pathé or Movietone News at, as he quaintly put it, 'what we called the pictures and you would call the cinema'. He admitted that the combination of steam and 'the picture house' made his story sound almost 'prehistoric'. But his coloured description of Lord's, and especially the emotions he felt passing through the imposing pale stone of the Grace Gates and walking into the pavilion, is as fresh and relevant now as when he experienced them in that postwar summer of 1948. Graveney talked about his 'strong sense of wonder' and 'awe' at being in 'the place where Compton and Edrich had broken all batting records the previous year'. His most telling phrases come next and emphasise how mere bricks and mortar and a circle of well-mown grass so powerfully affected him. He momentarily shrank in physical size, as if cowering, and thought of himself as unworthy to be there. 'I wondered what I could possibly be doing on this great ground,' he said. 'To judge by the glances some of the gatemen were giving me as I entered they were wondering the same thing, and the net result was that I felt very overawed and inadequate.'

As Gloucestershire's junior pro, Graveney, then twenty-one, carried twelve long, leather cricket bags to the visitors' dressing room like an Everest sherpa. By the time he could blunt his curiosity, and began browsing in the Long Room, his inferiority complex was 'magnified to gigantic proportions, blotting out practically everything else'. Graveney gazed around him at the gallery of faces captured in oil and framed in gilt. The paintings, he went on, 'added a kind of hallowed reverence to the already overpowering feeling' that some mistake had been made. He was insignificant; he didn't deserve to be at Lord's at all. He was the archetypal hick from the Gloucestershire sticks with sallow skin and a skinny body and a dry West Country accent, which sounded roughly alien and out of place in the leafy refinement of NW8. Who was he to walk where Grace and Hobbs, Fry and Bradman had been before him? Graveney was convinced someone would soon tap him on the shoulder and tell him crisply to be on his way, as if dismissing the grocery boy. 'The generally intimidating atmosphere and, perhaps most of all, the cool glances I received from the members as I went out to bat, all conspired to make me feel very uncomfortable,' he added. 'In fact, it took me a long time to feel at home at Lord's; to feel as if the great ground and I were friends.'

Graveney's detailed and candid account outlines the disparity between the sweet dream of playing at Lord's and the reality of doing so – the pressure to perform, the urgency to prove a point and not to let yourself or your team down, the prospect of being suffocated by grandeur and history. Everyone who has ever held a bat or bowled a ball with intent has scored a century here or taken five wickets – most have achieved both – and then seen the sign-painter take a brush of gold leaf and caress their name on the honours' boards fixed to the dressing-room walls. It's a harmless fantasy, and it can be indulged in with impunity, like pretending you once spent a night with Marilyn Monroe. As for Lord's, the wishful thinking of what we might have done here – if only the call had come – can lie privately intact and undisturbed. We'll never take guard here or mark out our run, and the consequences of doing so won't be preserved for ever in the pages of *Wisden*. That's a good thing for most of us. It prevents us from making damned fools of ourselves. As I watch the teams from Streethouse and Glynde and Beddingham inspect the pitch an hour before the thirty-eighth Village final, I think of Graveney and the personal anxieties which dogged him. The visceral grab of Lord's was so strong for Graveney that he retained it, and was able to recall it perfectly. And so I wonder at which point, after the semi-finals, Streethouse and Glynde at last appreciated what it really meant to play here; and to what degree each individual has already experienced the trepidation and sense of displacement that Graveney did sixty years ago. With the privilege comes the pressure. For now sits expectation in the air.

At least Graveney came to Lord's in the knowledge that he would come again. Streethouse and Glynde – two teams comprising plasterers and carpenters, students and bankers, forklift drivers and warehousemen – will probably get this day in isolation; this one, single shot at walking down the wide turn of the staircase, through the Long Room with its high windows and then down the pale concrete of the pavilion steps, where the gate will be swung open for them by a man in a suavely tailored, cream-coloured jacket. It is true there are no foreign lands; for only the traveller is foreign. But at this moment the foreign travellers of Streethouse and Glynde – familiarly comfortable with the small, tree-lined pitches of villages and the modest tiled roofs of nearby houses – can only feel the nervousness that comes with being a stranger in a strange land. Whoever copes with it best will win today.

From the 300 clubs that entered this summer's competition, the two finalists beautifully represent polar opposites. The final is billed in *The Times* as The Council Estate against The Viscount's Estate. Glynde and Beddingham can trace its cricket lineage as far back as the late eighteenth century. These separate East Sussex villages – just a mile apart – overlook the soft rise of Mount Caburn on the South Downs. A tributary of the Ouse courses past the tangle of the club's banked boundary. Nearby Virginia Woolf sank and drowned after filling her overcoat pockets with stones and wading into the neck of the main river in 1941. Glynde village is part of the estate of the Seventh Viscount Hampden. His home is Glynde Place, which has tall Sussex chimneys, a spread of greenery imposing enough to make Lord's look like a pocket-handkerchief garden and sculptured hedges, which the clip and buzz of shears have turned into the smooth contours of topiary. A mile away is Glyndebourne, the manicured home of English opera – the combination of high notes and high living. With its music come dinner jackets and bow ties, wicker hampers and champagne on the lawn.

Streethouse is a former mining community of modern 1960s and '70s housing hemmed in between Wakefield and Featherstone, strongly redolent of rugby league. Traffic, rather than murky water, runs through it. White smudges of sprayed paint and black marker-pen graffiti scar the walls of the Working Men's Club – a flat-roofed, ugly building that was designed and built in the era when architecture's progressive thinkers decided all new structures ought to be blocky and grey and look as though someone had thrown them up in five minutes. Some of its window frames are rotting. Dark-brown paint beneath the roof is flaked or chipped. Litter lies among the over-long grass flanking the entrance.

Streethouse's ground was once a 4-acre swamp, which only began to be transformed after a dozen volunteers, gathered around a pub table in 1962, made the pledge to make it playable and to sustain a team on it or 'bare their arses' as a consequence. These disparate places are exactly alike in spirit, however. Cricket contributes not only to giving each village part of its identity, but – more importantly – also establishing it as a proper flesh-and-blood community. The Rules and Conditions of the Cup (section four) define a village as 'rural . . . surrounded on all sides by open country and consisting of no more than 5,000 inhabitants'.

The name Rhodes figures prominently among Streethouse's population of 1,222 and in the cricket club. Paul is chairman. His brother Graham looks after the pitch. His sister Pam is secretary. Brothers Mark (number five on the scorecard) and Gary (number nine) make sure the family tree continues into the present generation, and probably the next as well. Glynde (population 558) have a pair of brothers in the team too: Robert Mouland, a right-handed middle-order bat, and Stuart, the wicketkeeper. The club also has the most prolific opening pair in this season's competition. Joe Adams, twenty-two, and Dominic Shepheard, a twenty-five-year-old fitness instructor, have scored 940 runs between them in seven matches. In round four Adams made 177 against another Sussex side, Findon, who lost the 2007 final. He shared 260 for the first wicket with Shepheard, who is the competition's leading wicket taker too. He has 20 of them so far. Streethouse and Glynde know nothing about one another apart from the line scores of the previous rounds. On statistics alone, Glynde are narrow favourites.

The first Village final in 1972 drew a crowd of almost 3,000; some of them simply curious to see whether the two teams, Troon from Cornwall and Astwood Bank of Warwickshire, really were harmlessly shambling country bumpkins. Even back then there weren't enough blacksmiths to fill a column of the *Yellow Pages*, and no one arrived at Lord's with a piece of rough rope tied around his waist to hold up his flannels. To those who didn't know much about the village game, or who retained a quaintly romantic ideal of it, the competitiveness of the final and the skill of the cricketers jolted them out of the misty-eyed assumption that it was all about gently sloping greens with a thatched pub on the boundary's edge and agricultural, cross-batted heaves. In part, the old image remains because there are people who want to believe it. But the stereotype isn't true, and Streethouse and Glynde will disprove it again.

The crowd – about 2,000 – are sprinkled among the Allen, Tavern, Mound and Edrich Stands. The colour and atmosphere here is a curious mixture of a Pro40 League match, Founder's Day at a good public school and Ladies Day at Ascot. Streethouse wear neat light-blue blazers with gold embroidered badges on the breast pocket. Wives and girlfriends are dressed for the occasion too. There are shimmering silk dresses in primary colours, well-made plain jackets matched with floral, floating skirts and high heels and handbags. Supporters, who have arrived on coaches in crested T-shirts or zip-up fleeces, are already queuing for pints or searching for the bar beneath the curve of the Tavern Stand. At this early stage no one, apart from the teams, has taken much notice of the clouds, which are glowering and low, or the fact that the pitch is barely a shade lighter than the outfield. That meteorological and horticultural combination suggests bowling first is the best option. That is exactly what Streethouse's Richard Vigars does after Glynde's Adam Davies calls 'tails' and the flipped fifty-pence coin lands on its back. Davies isn't bothered. Glynde always prefer to bat first, he says.

It is quiet enough during the opening over to hear the sound of nervous hearts beating on the outfield. Adams faces Vigars, who looms out of the Nursery End from a seven-pace run. Vigars runs his own cricket equipment business. He is a Londoner who was transplanted to Yorkshire as a boy. His hair is shaved tightly into a natural arc across a broad forehead. He has a firm, chiselled face and narrow eyes. To everyone at Streethouse he is 'RV', and represents the gem-like flame of the club. He once played in Lancashire's Second XI, alongside John Crawley and Ronnie Irani, and began his Streethouse career eleven years ago. He's led them to nine Pontefract League titles. He gets Glynde off the mark with an uncharacteristic, third-ball wide, which is evidence of the anxiety of the occasion rather than the standard of his bowling. There is another example of it when he over-pitches, and the delivery slips down the slope. With a wristy twist of the bat, Adams clips it to the long mid-wicket boundary in front of the Grand Stand.

In the next over Shepheard, facing Stuart Bellwood, leans back and scythes the ball for four. Given the prolific drive of the Adams–Shepheard partnership, and the fact 10 runs have come from as many deliveries, the conclusion is that Streethouse's fielders will face a tough morning. The assumption is wrong. Bellwood gets one to leave Shepheard and the straightforward, light edge drops into Paul Langley's gloves. Shepheard goes reluctantly, as though not believing his innings can possibly be so short. From the Tavern Stand comes the chant of a single word, 'Yorkshire', the pronunciation deliberately elongated to stress its syllables.

What follows are 10 overs of attritional sweat in which survival and the task of adapting to the pace and movement off the green pitch – as well as to the Lord's slope – is paramount for Glynde. Adams stands noticeably tall in his shot-making. His front-foot movement is long and decisive, and his back straightens as he comes forward to meet the ball. But he isn't finding the middle of the bat yet. The pitch is difficult to read, and so his shots deflect off thick inside edges or are struck just below the sweet spot. At one point Glynde go 23 balls without scoring. Part of the reason is Scott Bland, an energetic twenty-one-year-old with a whippy action who gets a lot of sideways purchase, angling the ball into and then away from Adams and the new batsman, Callum Smith. Only solid temperament carries Adams and Smith through these testing overs. Lesser batsmen would have become impatient and made impetuous errors. Adams and Smith wait for wayward deliveries, eventually bringing up 50 in the 12th over. The partnership looks unbreakable until Bland is rewarded for accuracy and perseverance. Smith drives on the full straight back at the bowler, who is at the end of his follow-through and listing to his left. The ball travels with speed towards him at below waist height, and he takes it amazingly cleanly. Smith is half incredulous. He tips his head back, as though calculating that the sheer force of his shot alone ought to have jarred the ball free from Bland's cupped hands. But the catch sticks, and the final is anyone's again.

Glynde, 91 for 2 at the halfway stage, are dependent on Adams. The secret of good batting is to behave as though the previous ball – if it beats the bat – either didn't happen or doesn't matter. Adams does so, proving unflappable as he brings up his half-century in 68 balls and takes his total for this season's competition past 500. At last he is batting on a high flame and burning his shots and finding gaps on the Tavern boundary, which is only 40 yards away. Vigars tries the medium pacer Martin Rhodes from the Pavilion End in an effort to dislodge Adams. Rhodes is three strides into his run when the Lord's tannoy, with imperfect timing, announces the bowling change, and interrupts his sprint to the crease, rather like the person on business from Porlock interrupting Coleridge at his desk. Rhodes's concentration, wound up for *his* moment, temporarily snaps, and Adams slices him down to the third man for four.

Nearing the end of Glynde's 40 overs, and with the 200 approaching, Vigars brings himself back on and removes Adams, clean-bowled for 79. The new batsman, Dale Tranter, is twenty-seven years old today. Glynde supporters serenade him from pavilion to crease with a chorus of 'Happy

Birthday'. Vigars clips his stumps first ball. The Streethouse supporters serenade Tranter with another chorus of 'Happy Birthday' from crease to pavilion. Glynde reach 207 for 9, which includes 41 from Dominic Harris, who looks a most unlikely combination of two Lancashire batsmen from the 1970s. He is as short as Harry Pilling (around 5 feet) but hits the ball with the gusto of Clive Lloyd. Harris even swings one delivery from Vigars for six, dropping it into the belly of the boisterous Tavern crowd. There is no lofty artistry about what he does because none is necessary. He stands still and, with a scattershot approach, clubs the ball hard enough to generate sparks. Harris was on 15 when Langley – and everyone else, including the batsman – believed he'd stumped him. The umpires adjudged that wicketkeeper hadn't broken the wicket cleanly, and recalled Harris, who was already walking away and pulling off his gloves. His cameo is critical. Without it Glynde's total wouldn't be so daunting. As it is, Streethouse will bat with the weight of history against them. Only two teams have ever chased down more than 200 to win the final.

Well polished, and with the sponsors' scarlet ribbons already tied on its swirl handles, the Cup and decorative base stands on a table in the Long Room directly beneath the whiskered portrait of the Fourth Lord Harris (Eton, Oxford, Kent and England). The table is covered in a dark-blue cloth and carries the MCC's insignia. It's supposed to be bad luck to touch the trophy before or during the match. Standing in the Long Room, I notice the out-going batsmen superstitiously don't even glance at it. The Cup and the portrait are positioned almost directly opposite the pavilion doors, and I think of Lord Harris slyly nodding in approval at the Corinthianism of the final, which represents what he held most dear: the ethics and amateur status of cricket. After all, it was Harris who reacted to Wally Hammond's decision in 1922 to sign for Gloucestershire, rather than Kent, with Old Testament wrath and preposterous over-reaction. 'Bolshevism is rampant, and seeks to abolish all laws and rules, and this year cricket has not escaped its attack,' said Harris. It was his belief that Hammond, born in Dover, was obliged through the requirement of birth and moral etiquette to play for Kent. To do otherwise became in his eyes not only a heinous betrayal of one's county, but also a betrayal of the honour of cricket. As a man of Kent, Harris is open to the charge of bias. But no one ever challenged or doubted his devotion to the Noblest of Games. He was a stickler for correct behaviour. A year before his death, in 1932, he made a speech which contained the kernel of his personal manifesto. Harris did more than outline what he thought was the meaning, purpose and the intrinsic values of cricket. In its most quotable passage he also concisely articulated the personal responsibility of each cricketer in upholding cricket's virtues.

> You would do well to love it. It is more free from anything sordid, anything dishonourable, than any game in the world. To play it keenly, honourably, generously, self-sacrificing is a moral lesson in itself . . . protect it from anything that would sully it, so that it may grow in favour with all men.

Lord Harris, a guardian of the game's most precious attribute – its sense of duty and honour.

Another of the Village Cup's Rules and Regulations (section six) stipulates that: 'All clubs . . . are expected to uphold the Spirit of Cricket, as defined in the MCC's Laws of Cricket.' While pure serendipity brings the Cup and Harris's portrait side-by-side in the Long Room, it is beautifully appropriate for them to share the same space. For the competition embodies the things Harris championed. I'm sure he would have liked the scene in front of him as Streethouse's openers, Jonathan Hughes and Paul Langley, stand under the lintel of the pavilion door. Hughes is a thirty-one-year-old banker. Langley is forty-six and earns his living making saw blades. The older man drapes an arm over the younger one, as if to reassure him.

In early afternoon the sky has cleared into blue. By the time the Streethouse innings is about to begin, the clouds have rolled back over Lord's, leaving just thin tongues of light and bright daubs of colour across the outfield. Hughes starts well. He clips a four off Shepheard towards third man. Instead of settling him down, the exhilaration of the shot persuades him to chase the next ball, which he glances into Stuart Mouland's gloves. He returns to the pavilion and slowly ascends the steps he has only recently descended, as if mounting a scaffold. Out of politeness, the suited members sitting on the Long Room's high chairs don't make eye-contact and half turn only to follow Hughes's route back into the dressing room after he has already walked past them. Coming so quickly, this first fall of plaster could easily presage the collapse of the top order. For a while, though, Langley and Callum Geldart stay up with the rate. Geldart punches Mark Beddis over the fence for a mid-wicket six. Beddis, the lone Yorkshireman in Glynde's side, resembles Ryan Sidebottom – left-arm, shoulder-length dark hair and the same slightly crouched lean into the top of his run. He even begins his run with the ball close to his hip.

Early on Streethouse manage to deal with him, and whatever else Glynde offer up, until there is a swift clatter of wickets: 60 for 1 becomes 98 for 5. Only Langley is resisting, and Vigars comes out to join him. With Streethouse beginning to flat-line, Glynde look rather too pleased with themselves, as if the final already belongs to them, and neither Vigars nor Langley can possibly wrench it from them. But what becomes self-evident over the next hour is the mature competitiveness of a pair of intelligent and highly skilled practitioners. Langley and Vigars are a two-man insurgent army. At first the ball is met cautiously. Gradually gaps are exploited, and the bowlers become irritable. But Glynde still don't seem to believe Streethouse can get close to them until first Langley and then Vigars begin to ransack runs. In the 31st over Langley yanks a ball from Tranter for six, and Vigars responds to his partner's example. With three arcing sixes he roughs up the distraught spinner Ollie Bailey and takes 18 off one dismal over. With 4 overs left Streethouse are 177 for 5. With

2 to go Langley and Vigars need only 18 to win. There's a cantankerous heroism about both of them. At last Glynde look panicky.

The sky, the colour of weathered silver in mid-afternoon, has turned lamp-black, and thick, pressing clouds have extinguished almost all the light from Lord's. The stark whiteness of two batsmen and the fielders are caught in this landscape like images on a negative. The electric bulbs in the scoreboard over the Allen and Compton Stands glow in this awful gloom as intensely as shop-sign neon. Davies drops the ball into Beddis's hand and guards the boundaries. The first delivery of the penultimate over is a dot ball. The second is struck for two. Vigars does his sums – 16 to win off 10. And then, in the intoxicating high of the moment, he plays across the line and is clean-bowled for 41. Streethouse's supporters slump into a funereal silence, which soon becomes more solemn still. This over represents the final twist of the game. For with the last delivery of it, Langley, on 68, darts across the line too and, exactly like Vigars, is bowled. The ball splinters part of the off stump. Beddis uproots it and carries the broken piece of wood off to the Tavern Stand, where he presents it as a souvenir to his father. For Streethouse, the final is over. For Glynde, the champagne flutes are already being raised in the front rows of the Allen Stand.

As it is the end of the season, Lord's allows the crowd to spill in front of the pavilion for the presentations, which take place on its wide top step. The table with the blue cloth cover is carried out. The Cup is gently and respectfully placed in the middle of it, and square ruby boxes of medals appear. Glynde's players march towards the trophy, each one with grass-stained whites. I wonder whether these marks of their triumph will ever be washed off, or instead preserved. My gaze becomes fixed on one face, which I doubt I'll ever forget. Richard Vigars is miserably wretched. However hard he tries to hold it in, the grief still escapes and lies as evidence on every line of his face. Still wearing his pads, he stands on the outfield, as though looking in on a drama in which he no longer has a part to play. There is a compact symmetry about his pose: arms folded tight against his chest, feet apart and toes pointing at ten to two. An elderly woman in a thick pale coat and dark glasses gives him a well-meaning, consoling hug. Her comforting words accentuate the anguish. Vigars bites his lip and lowers his sad eyes. At the exact moment Glynde are given the Cup, he half averts his gaze.

Like life, sport is chiefly about coping with defeat or coming to terms with the cutting pain of disappointment. Vigars has always wanted to win the Village Cup. In the past he's cancelled holidays to play in its early rounds. Now he's like Tantalus. What he most wanted moved away from him at the very point at which he reached out to grab it. The medal he collects is no consolation. In different circumstances – with 4 wickets and the third-highest score – he could have been man of the match. Instead, he drags himself up the pavilion steps, as though carrying a heavy bundle, and vanishes into the Long Room. No words, however finely wrought, will console him tonight.

He can only wait for the pain to pass.

Umpires: C. Jones, P. Hinstridge
Toss: Streethouse

Glynde and Beddingham innings

J. P. Adams	b Vigars		79
D. B. Shepheard	c Langley	b Bellwood	4
C. B. Smith	c & b Bland		32
R. P. Mouland	lbw	b Vigars	10
O. B. Bailey	b Hughes		13
D. Harris	lbw	b Hughes	41
A. Davies*	not out		12
C. Blunt	b Hughes		0
S. W. Mouland†	c Langley	b Vigars	3
D. J. Tranter	b Vigars		0
M. M. Beddis	not out		2
Extras	(1b, 2lb, 2nb, 6w)		11
Total	(9 wickets, 40 overs)		**207**

Fall of wickets: 1-10, 2-80, 3-129, 4-134, 5-167, 6-200, 7-200, 8-205, 9-205

Streethouse bowling	O	M	R	W
Vigars	9	1	60	4
Bellwood	5	2	24	1
Bland	9	2	32	1
M. Rhodes	8	0	55	0
Hughes	9	0	33	3

Streethouse innings

J. G. Hughes	c S. Mouland	b Shepheard	4
P. C. Langley†	b Beddis		68
C. J. Geldart	c S. Mouland	b Tranter	34
M. P. Rhodes	lbw	b Tranter	0
M Robinson	b Shepheard		5
P. McMullan	b Adams		10
R. Vigars*	b Beddis		41
P. Haselden	not out		4
S. Bellwood	not out		4
Did not bat: G. G. Rhodes, S. A. Bland			
Extras	(4b, 12lb, 9nb, 6w)		31
Total	(7 wickets, 40 overs)		**201**

Fall of wickets: 1-4, 2-60, 3-61, 4-72, 5-98, 6-191, 7-192

Glynde and Beddingham bowling	O	M	R	W
Shepheard	9	0	34	2
Beddis	7	1	34	2
Tranter	8	0	36	2
Bailey	8	0	52	0
Adams	8	1	29	1

Result: Glynde and Beddingham won by 6 runs

Man of the match: J. P. Adams

CHAPTER EIGHTEEN

THE CAPTAIN IN THE
BAGGY GREEN

*Ricky Ponting, so familiar in the Baggy Green that he looks
incongruous in Australia's one-day, canary-yellow baseball cap.*

Riverside: NatWest One-day International:
England v. Australia, 20 September

Australia's forty-second captain is standing in front of the pavilion boundary with the index finger and thumb of his left hand locked around his chin. His brows are half-pinched in concentration. His dark eyes are like small glass beads. He is staring in the direction of the squat turrets of Lumley Castle, which rise above the thicket of trees in the middle distance. Ricky Ponting looks as though he's straining to remember something only recently forgotten, and which is now stuck in the mud of his memory. Perhaps he is trying to work out where he has come from, what he's supposed to be doing here and where he is due to go next. Given his and Australia's workload, he could be forgiven for thinking any of those things. With the start of this long season's seventh, and final, one-day international less than half an hour away, Ponting is already changed into his bilious sunflower-yellow uniform. The colour doesn't suit him. What doesn't suit him, either, is the matching baseball cap. It isn't only because of the oversize peak, which juts out like a duck's beak and shadows three-quarters of his round, tanned face. It isn't only because the cap looks slightly too tight on him. It's because Ponting is so familiar in the traditional Baggy Green that he looks incongruous and almost unrecognisable in anything else. Seeing Ponting without the Baggy Green is like seeing Fred Astaire without his white tie and tails. Somehow it doesn't look right; he seems scruffily underdressed. The cap has always seemed to be part of Ponting's physical being, as if he has been wearing it from a ridiculously early age. The Baggy Green defines who he is.

His cap is battered-looking through overuse. The colour has faded. There are wear and tear scuff marks close to the crown, and the stitching in some of the panels is in need of repair. The gold thread of the embroidered badge no longer has a sheen about it. And the cloth on the right-hand side of the peak is worn away, leaving a hard, white, bald rim where Ponting has repeatedly tugged at it or run his fingers along the edge. The exhausted condition of the Baggy Green is important because of what it represents both to him and to Australia. Its distressed state is an honourable sign of battles fought and won or lost, and the effort Ponting has put into them. The Baggy Green also binds him to his predecessors. What it symbolises in itself has been romanticised to the point at which one of those predecessors, Mark Taylor, talks about the

Baggy Green as though the cap has alchemical properties. 'There is no doubt,' he says, 'that its aura provides Australian teams with a psychological edge.' Taylor was responsible for making sure the Australian team always wore the cap during the first session on the field of every Test, a custom he began in 1994 against England at Brisbane. It was also Taylor who initiated the ritual of presenting the Baggy Green to the debutant on the opening morning of the Test. It is passed on with ceremony and solemnity, as if anointing the recipient into High Church.

It wasn't always regarded as important, let alone iconic. For Bill Brown, part of Donald Bradman's 1948 Invincibles, the cap was purely a functional piece of kit and something to be 'flung' after use into his bag. Neil Harvey gave away all but one of his Baggy Greens; he only kept the cap from the '48 series. Earlier in the summer, a week after the ICC inducted him into its Hall of Fame at Lord's, Harvey and I stepped into the same hotel lift. He was nineteen when he came to England with Bradman. His hair was as dark as coal, swept upwards and back and parted low on the left. His jaw was strong and made him look like a Hollywood matinee idol. He's seventy-nine now. The hair is as silver as mercury. The jawline is jowly, and there are liver spots across the backs of his hands. 'I kept none of my sweaters either,' he said to me. 'I gave them all away'. Rodney Hogg swapped his 1979 Baggy Green for a policeman's truncheon, handcuffs and an identification number. He isn't alone. Jeff Thomson, Max Walker, David Hookes, Ashley Mallett and Doug Walters also used the cap as currency to barter for souvenirs from other tours. But a pack of hounds couldn't tear the Baggy Green away from Ponting. He handles the cap with patriotic reverence and always wears it – even to post-Test press conferences – not because it accentuates his commercial brand, but as the embodiment of what it means to be Australian and to play for Australia.

Whatever Ponting forgot he has now remembered. He stops looking at Lumley Castle, turns in a short circle and darts up the pavilion steps in preparation to pad up. Watching his retreat, I think, more than anyone else, that to make him wear anything but the Baggy Green – and especially a mere baseball cap – seems almost an affront to his dignity.

The past few months have been bitter for Ponting. However hard it is to believe, almost a month has already slipped by since England took the Ashes back from him at the Oval. That series now feels so distant as to belong to an entirely different summer altogether. Indeed, Michael Vaughan's win in 2005 is sharper and still more memorable in the mind at the moment (in a way, curiously, that it wasn't at Edgbaston). This is probably because of the number of matches pressed on to both teams since. No motive, other than the raw pursuit of money, led the administrators to arrange two Twenty20 internationals, as well as this interminable round of ODIs, almost as soon as the Ashes urn was taken out of Andrew Strauss's hand and put back into its glass case. The convenient excuse is that the ODIs are preparation for the Champions Trophy, which begins in South Africa in two days' time. Like Potemkin's Village, this defence has the benefit of offering an attractive and half-believable front while behind it lurks nothing but hot air. The surfeit of these 50-over matches confuses memories of the Ashes to the extent that it is now difficult to remember them vividly. Yes, England won 2–1. Yes, the celebrations were more muted compared to 2005 (Vaughan's achievement was a culmination; Strauss's repeat of the feat seemed more like a beginning). And yes, Ponting will examine the statistics without ever quite believing Australia were beaten. He'll think about the First Test at Cardiff, where an improbable, Trevor Bailey-like clinging on by Jimmy Anderson and Monty Panesar denied him. He'll think about Australia's rout of England at Headingley, where the Fourth Test was over in two and a half days. He'll think about the fact that six Australian batsmen occupied the top seven places in runs scored, and totalled seven centuries to England's two. And at the end he'll conclude, as he must, that England's bowlers won the Ashes for them. His own attack of Johnson and Siddle, Hilfenhaus and Hauritz only once took 20 wickets.

In defeat Ponting was immediately bracketed beside the distant figure of Billy Murdoch, the only other Australian captain to lose two Ashes series in England. Murdoch's teams were beaten in 1880, 1884 and again in 1890. *Wisden* called him 'incontestably the finest batsman' of the teams he captained, which gives him something else in common with Ponting. The similarities end there. In everything else – especially physical bearing and appearance on the field – the two men are markedly different. Murdoch once stood on a slight slope beside the 6 feet 2 inch W. G. Grace without looking noticeably shorter than him. He was wide-shouldered too, and wore the bushy moustache of a First World War general. Murdoch's wicketkeeper-batsman's pads were filthy enough to suggest he'd been gardening in them. The willow of his bat was darker than a creosoted fence. A. G. Steel, the England captain, said of Murdoch that 'his better judgement was too frequently hampered by the ceaseless chattering and advice of one or two men who could never grasp the fact that in the cricket field there can only be one captain'. Steel was also generous in his assessment of Murdoch's 'thoughtful' tactical acumen. Ponting wouldn't allow 'ceaseless chattering' in his ear and he doesn't possess the superior gift of strategy. Seldom is his captaincy alone highly praised. When he could bowl Glenn McGrath at one end, and Shane Warne from the other, penetrative and perceptive thinking was almost superfluous anyway. There was no need for Ponting to scheme out so much as a rudimentary battle-plan. Even against Strauss, scarcely more sophisticated as a tactician, Ponting often got it wrong. He did at Cardiff in the last session against Anderson and Panesar. He did again at the Oval in opting not to pick Hauritz's specialist spin. What he got right was his attitude to defeat.

Exactly like Ricky Ponting, Billy Murdoch was 'incontestably' the best batsman in his Australian side. Also like Ponting, he lost more than one Ashes series in England.

Sportsmen are venerated to such a degree that accepting them as suffering mortals, just like the rest of us, can at times be difficult. The crowds booed and goaded Ponting like a black-caped, waxed-moustached villain during the Ashes. Those who did so believed the public pillory was a legitimate place in which to put him; and also that, because he comes across as gruff, aggressive and chippy, he would be impervious to whatever bullying was dished out. In *To Kill a Mocking Bird*, the older Scout recalls what her father Atticus once said. 'One time,' she remembered, 'Atticus said you never really knew a man until you stood in his shoes and walked around in them.' At the Oval no one wanted to stand in Ponting's shoes because of what the thought of doing so must have been like. He'd lost – again. He'd have to comfort Australia and congratulate England – again. He'd have to bite back his own despair – again too. There was nowhere for Ponting to hide, and no one to share what as captain he had to bear alone. But he was sensitively aware about what he needed to say, and how he needed to act, to match the circumstances. His response was gracious and gracefully restrained; so much so, in fact, that the decency of his words and the nobility of his bearing in expressing them lanced and made humble the ignorant rabble who'd turned nearly every walk to the crease into a tiring and wearisome trial of his temper. It took five Tests, but Ponting beat them in the end.

On the way to the Riverside, Nature sends a sign of the changing seasons. Across the A1 fly three flocks of migrating grey geese in loose formation, clearing the bright fields of shorn corn and heading east towards the North Sea. Today's weather, though, is unseasonably warm for late September. The sky is piercing blue, and nothing more than thin strands of cloud cling, like fingers, on its edges. The early start – 10.15 a.m. – makes the toss critical, like one of the old-fashioned one-day finals at Lord's, where the bowlers could have the match won before noon's autumnal shadow fell across the Warner Stand. There is dampness in the pitch, and Strauss unhesitatingly makes first use of it. This series was quickly emptied of almost all meaning. Australia won it a week ago at Lord's, and now lead 6–0, which sends a gruesome message about England's form and shot-through confidence. It isn't as though any of Australia's wins have been fluked either. Only the opening match, at the Oval, was close enough to be genuinely described as a contest. England lost the second at Lord's by 39 runs; the third, at the Rose Bowl, by 6 wickets; the fourth, also at Lord's, by 7 wickets; and the fifth and sixth at Trent Bridge by 4 wickets and then 111 runs. Statistical evidence alone convicts England as abysmal. The visual evidence is worse. England have looked like untutored novices with the bat and been unable to chain down the Australian batsmen with a decent line or length. Without Kevin Pietersen, still *hors de combat*, the very qualities necessary for ODIs – powerful and inventive strokes and the vision to make them – are sorely lacking in England. At Trent Bridge just three nights ago, the crowd was heading home more than two hours before Australia went through the motions of claiming the final wicket. Advance ticket sales nonetheless ensure a sell-out at the Riverside. Behind me in the North East Terrace sits a thin, pale-skinned and ageing woman in a wide-brimmed England sunhat. The sunhat is flat on her slender head. Her hair pokes from the side like snapped bunches of straw. She's bought two £40 tickets. One for herself and another for her rucksack, which she places beside her and then pats as if it's a small dog. She talks in a high voice, like the squeak of chalk against a blackboard, about the need to have 'some space' around her. Beside me are two bearded students dressed in replica football shirts – one Chelsea, the other Newcastle United – and here purely for the purpose of drinking lager. Already, two pints apiece are being toted in flimsy and wet cardboard containers. For them, the match will dissolve into wavy, drunken lines before mid-afternoon. The woman with two seats tries to begin a conversation, which soon becomes as pointless as talking to the drunk in Kafka. Well aware of England's capacity for collapse, she is relieved that Strauss has chosen to bowl. 'At least,' she says, aloud and to no one in particular, 'we're guaranteed to get some play after lunch.' She chatters on to herself, annoyingly, like the tsk, tsk, tsk noise that leaks out of an iPod.

From the first ball Anderson makes the ball swing and kiss the top before darting off at an angle. With his fourth he claims Australia's first wicket. The delivery leaves Shane Watson, his bat and hands high in tame defence, and he edges the catch to Graeme Swann in the slips. Ponting makes an earlier than expected entrance. 'I don't like him,' says the student in the Newcastle shirt, who has his hair crimped in a tight, unfashionable wave across his skull 'But he's OK when he starts to get some runs. Then he's worth watching.' Apart from this sliver of respect, which is expressed grudgingly, Ponting's reception is welcoming. There is actually some cheering for him. After the Ashes ended, he did what Billy Murdoch would have found impossible. He went home to Australia for two weeks. On his return he's made scores of 48, 126 and 6. The century, at Trent Bridge, included the most stupendous straight six, which landed close to the TV commentary box in the Radcliffe Road Stand. The shot was notable for its economy. The drive derived its power from timing rather than muscular slogging. Seen side on, the free flow of the bat and the checked follow-through, which ended level with the shoulder blade, made it look as though Ponting had merely pushed the delivery back towards the bowler. But the ball soared in a triumphal arch over the boundary and bashed against the seating. Here, the ball is moving around too much to allow Ponting early scope for a repeat into the Finchale End. He has to watch each delivery with a hawkish eye and get forward to it, which suits his natural game. When Anderson strays six inches outside the line of off stump Ponting nonetheless provides a model example of how to play swing. Whereas most batsmen would have been tempted to throw their hands hard at the ball, he eases gently into the shot and drives it a yard past point to the rope. On other occasions the bowler is fooled into believing he's about to trap Ponting lbw. He comes towards him with a long stride and shapes to play across the line. The straight ball looks as if it will rap him on the pads in front of the stumps until, at the last moment, Ponting powerfully whips his bat around and inside it and sends the delivery scuttling to the leg-side boundary. He lifts his back leg, like a stork, as he makes contact. After Ponting plays him exactly this way, Anderson tosses his head back and lets out an anguished, frustrated shout. Ponting merely turns his back and begins to remark his guard with the toe of his boot, scraping it against the grassless track and raising a small cloud of dust.

With the score on 17, Australia lose wicket number two after Graeme Onions, making his ODI debut, entices Paine to give a catch to Matt Prior. The responsibility placed on Ponting increases. There can be a splenetic fury about his batting; but not in these circumstances. He is cautious, as though negotiating the opening session of a Test. The runs come with torturous slowness because of the difficulty of the pitch, and the swing Anderson achieves in the air. But if Ponting is beaten, he ignores the bowler's minor triumph over him. It's as if these small defeats never happened. He has the patience to wait and the experience to know that he'll get his own back eventually – even after Anderson and Prior appeal for a catch against him. Framed in the shadowed rectangle between the lip of his helmet and the rim of his metal, meshed guard, Ponting's eyes betray no emotion. He blankly outstares the bowler. Another, far louder and longer, appeal follows after Anderson brushes the top of Ponting's left pad. Anderson adds to it with a leap and a begging turn towards the umpire. Again, the Australian captain is imperturbable. He responds with a trademark drive, more rapier than bludgeon, in which he meets the full ball and pushes it, as though setting it off downhill, past Anderson. At the end of the stroke Ponting stands straight and still, and his left elbow is in the classical raised pose. Generally his footwork is faultless and he is a good judge of length. Each ball is returned with a high backlift. The pageantry of his batting derives from the shots he makes. Even the nudges and flicks are done with planned, conscious thought, as though Ponting is able to get his feet precisely where he wants them in pursuit of the bowler. His half-century, which takes 57 deliveries, is reached with his eighth four and dispatched with the flourish of a pull behind square leg. Paul Collingwood lacks the speed to discomfort someone of his class with the short ball; bowling one to him is as pointless as trying to bash a square peg into a round hole. When Collingwood does let go of a half-tracker, the quicksilver Ponting is already in place to take advantage of it. He is moving across the crease and bringing the bat down from gully, a fraction before it strikes the pitch. The ball takes two long hops to the fence and hits the advertising boards beyond the boundary. But even a genius can make mistakes. Swann, bowling in his sunglasses from the Lumley End, flights a ball from wide of off stump and spins it back. In attempting to drive it, Ponting's left leg goes too far across, and his hands reach for a delivery which grips and comes in at him. His horrible miscue spoons to Collingwood at short mid-wicket, who dives forward to take it.

Without Ponting, Australia's innings comes apart. Swann is the main beneficiary of uncharacteristic lapses, which suggests either Australia are weary, and thinking ahead to the Champions' Trophy or believe the pitch is more spiteful than it now seems. Whatever the reason, Swann bowls Cameron White with the stock off spinners' ball. He persuades James Hopes to twist forward and get a looping leading edge, which he catches himself. He draws Mitchell Johnson into an error, beguiling him in the air, and bowls Brett Lee through the gate. As Australia sink limply to 176 all out in the 46th over, Swann finishes 5 for 28. There isn't much for Australia to bowl at.

* * *

Fielding in the slips, Ponting's mannerisms soon become apparent. He bites his nails a lot – despite the fact he is simultaneously chewing gum. He rubs his left forearm with his right hand. If a batsman has a narrow escape, he plants both hands on his hips in frustration, and his mouth drops open. If a ball shoots for four, especially after a bad piece of bowling, he gazes down at the floor, as though the answer to his problems might be found there. If one of his bowlers beats the bat, or induces a false stroke, he lifts his hands above his head and claps them, as though he's waving a flag. This is the 100th England–Australia ODI, and the running total reads: Australia 58 and England 37. There have been two ties, and two no results. The outcome here is scarcely in doubt. Brett Lee and Ben Hilfenhaus are ill-disciplined, and give away too many extras – wides and no balls – and let Strauss and Joe Denly get off to a jump start. Ponting's hands spent a lot of time on his hips. And his mouth is nearly always open.

This has been an arduous tour – packing and unpacking, moving from one blank hotel room to another – and Australia look red-eyed and tired, as though the end cannot come soon enough for them. Of course, nothing can ever be taken for granted where England are concerned. As if not wanting an early finish, England react to the dizzying possibility of a win in the same way someone with vertigo would react to a high building. The ground begins to swim and sway beneath them. Five wickets are lost for 33 runs. England move from 129 for 1 to 162 for 6. The worst offender is Strauss, impaled on a spike of his own making after rushing into an ugly reverse sweep. England just about hobble inelegantly past Australia's score. The man who is more comfortable in the Baggy Green pulls at the peak of his baseball cap and shakes a few hands.

'Ever tried? Ever failed?' asked Samuel Beckett. 'Try again. Fail again. Fail better.' Ponting has and does. In his book *On Top Down Under*, which chronicles Australia's captains, Ray Robinson wrote that 'nerve counts as much as know-how, sometimes more' in determining success. Ponting has nerve, and this is most evident in his batsmanship. His Test average before taking the captaincy was 55.97. His average now is 55.79. It's unfortunate that a combination of jitteriness and impulsiveness has led to some high-profile botched decisions as a captain. These have partly obscured his batting figures, which are the true stamp of his gift. That he isn't the most cerebral captain is immaterial in judging him adequately as a prolific run maker. To discuss him in the same breath as Bradman, let alone to compare the two, is flawed and irrational thinking only because Bradman was and remains so uniquely separate from anyone else who ever held a bat. The range of his talent was so immense that he redefined his art the way Turner redefined painting. But Ponting is certainly the closest thing Australia has to Bradman right now; and the experience of watching him (along with Sachin Tendulkar) is also the closest we can come to knowing how it must have felt to have actually seen Bradman. Like Bradman, Ponting is capable of doing something striking to any ball.

Just two days before going to the Riverside I met a ninety-two-year-old woman in Oxfordshire. She was physically frail but mentally alert. She told me about watching the second Bodyline Test at Melbourne in 1932. As though the scene were being played in front of her at that very moment, she saw and described the long, curved walk Donald Bradman took to the wicket to let his eyes adjust from dressing-room darkness into mid-morning's harsh light. She saw, too, Bradman carefully taking guard. She also remembered the still silence, draped like a shroud, over that first delivery and the expectation Bradman carried with him after missing the opening Test in Sydney. Finally, she saw again Bradman lurch across his crease to pull an atrocious long-hop from Bill Bowes to the fence. She recalled the way in which, instead, the greatest batsman cricket has ever known got an inside edge, which dropped on to his stumps. As he walked stiffly back to the pavilion, readjusting his Baggy Green, the scorers' pencils scratched the most improbable line of the entire series into the book: 'Bradman b Bowes 0'.

It was evident from the way in which she spoke about Bradman that to have seen him even so fleetingly counted as a privilege, like catching sight of a rare bird for a second or two before the flap of its wings carried it away. As Bradman didn't just break records, but splintered them, he had the benefit of being venerated while his career was in full bloom. But often a player is only properly valued at the end. Ponting's worth, especially in England, isn't always appreciated as fulsomely as it ought to be. There is still time, however. Allan Border captained Australia four months short of his thirty-ninth birthday. Bradman was forty during the 1948 Invincibles tour, and blew out the candles on his cake while playing against the Gentleman of England at Lord's. Ponting isn't yet thirty-five. There's a lot more to come; and we need to enjoy it while we can.

Umpires: Asad Rauf, N. J. Long
Toss: England

Australia innings

S. R. Watson	c Swann	b Anderson	0
T. D. Paine †	c Prior	b Onions	4
R. T. Ponting *	c Collingwood	b Swann	53
M. J. Clarke	run out		38
M. E. K. Hussey	c Denly	b Bresnan	49
C. L. White	b Swann		1
J. R. Hopes	c & b Swann		11
M. G. Johnson	c Anderson	b Swann	10
B. Lee	b Swann		0
N. M. Hauritz	c & b Shah		3
B. W. Hilfenhaus	not out		2
Extras	(1lb, 4w)		5
Total	(all out, 45.5 overs)		**176**

Fall of wickets: 1-0, 2-17, 3-96, 4-110, 5-112, 6-138, 7-158, 8-158, 9-163, 10-176

England bowling	O	M	R	W
Anderson	7	0	36	1
Onions	9	1	28	1
Bresnan	6.5	0	25	1
Collingwood	7	0	37	0
Swann	10	1	28	5
Bopara	1	0	7	0
Shah	5	1	14	1

England innings

A. J. Strauss*	c Hilfenhaus	b Hauritz	47
J. L. Denly	run out		53
R. S. Bopara	lbw	b Watson	13
O. A. Shah	c Paine	b Hopes	7
P. D. Collingwood	not out		13
E. J. G. Morgan	c Paine	b Lee	2
M. J. Prior†	c Ponting	b Hilfenhaus	11
T. T. Bresnan	not out		10
Did not bat: G. P. Swann, J. M. Anderson, G. Onions			
Extras	(4b, 2lb, 9nb, 6w)		21
Total	(6 wickets, 40 overs)		**177**

Fall of wickets: 1-106, 2-129, 3-133, 4-137, 5-141, 6-162

Australia bowling	O	M	R	W
Lee	10	3	33	1
Hilfenhaus	6	1	38	1
Johnson	5	0	29	0
Hauritz	8	0	30	1
Hopes	6	1	29	1
Watson	5	0	12	1

Result: England won by 4 wickets

Man of the match: G. P. Swann

A VERY PERFECT
GENTLE KNIGHT

Albert Chevallier Tayler captures on canvas Canterbury at its finest –
Kent against Lancashire in 1906.

Against the china-blue of a cloudless sky, and tightly wrapped in light bright enough for August, the cathedral tower is bleached white, as though it were built from mother of pearl rather than stone. It is the final day of this season, and I carry into it an underlying and disorientating sense of something being already over and lost. The summer is gone, which seems inconceivable on such a tearfully beautiful morning. By six o'clock the last match will have come and gone too, and the last scoreboards will be ready for printing in next year's *Wisden*.

There is only one fitting place to finish this pilgrimage, which began at Lord's in bitter, blowy April: Canterbury, where Chaucer sent his own pilgrims. The game – a Pro40 contest between Kent and Northamptonshire – is unimportant. The result will decide nothing, and no one who has come to watch it much cares – if at all – about who wins or loses. It is merely important to be here for the season's dwindling hours and to say a lingering and proper goodbye, as if waving a good friend off on a long winter's journey. Stretching gloomily ahead is a seven-month wait before the St Lawrence Ground's gates will open again. The crowd wants to make the most of what is left of the season, however modest and inconsequential.

In *The South Country*, a book he wrote about his tour of the southern counties, the poet Edward Thomas believed 'the end' of every walk 'should come in heavy and lasting rain', as though rinsing the landscape clean and washing away the traveller's tracks would leave the ground fresh for whoever follows him. It won't happen today. There isn't even the usual crystal chill of late September to dampen the air. The trees aren't bare yet, either, but well clothed, and the broad, still-green leaves give relieving shade to the deckchairs beneath them. A single seagull circles the outfield, as if on a reconnaissance mission. Perhaps it is the same gull which, earlier in the summer during the England Lions game here against Australia, revealed its predatory instincts by swooping down and scooping up a dislodged bail before flying off with it jammed in its pointy beak and cheekily alighting on the pavilion roof. The gull clung on to the bail like a precious trophy.

I decide to sit in the top tier of the Frank Woolley Stand, where two white butterflies are chasing and dodging one another between the pillars. It seems appropriate, as if paying tribute to one of my grandfather's heroes. The writer Ian Peebles called Woolley 'the most graceful of the efficient, and the most efficient of the graceful' batsmen. The manner in which Woolley scored almost 60,000 runs epitomised Chaucer's 'very perfect gentle Knight,' a description which also applies to my grandfather. I'm near two men with binoculars, who scan the landscape like sea captains studying a distant horizon, a bulky chap with a baseball cap, who balances a huge red scorebook across his knees and is writing down the names of the Northamptonshire batsmen in light pencil, and a father and son. The father is portly and middle-aged with short, greying sideburns. He is dressed in a white T-shirt with C. L. R. James's most famous quotation printed across it: 'WHAT DO THEY KNOW OF CRICKET WHO ONLY CRICKET KNOW?' The son is wearing a pair of gold, square-framed spectacles and examines his programme and scorecard. Each of us in the Woolley Stand shares the same curious need to pay our respects to the end of another season.

The pavilion bell brings out the umpires. The sound it makes is like pushing open an old-fashioned shop door, the clapper clanging against thin cast metal. Northamptonshire's Stephen Peters and Niall O'Brien flog Kent's bowlers towards the pavilion, the cars parked on the grass in front of the Old Dover Road – one six bounces off a bonnet – and the rickety Les Ames Stand, which looks as though a medium wind might turn it into splintered wreckage, like the Hesperus. After 10 overs, Northants are 96 without loss. What follows – a decent total and a poor Kent response – is immaterial. During the dead patches of the afternoon the crowd relives the memories and scenes of the summer. The Official Replica Ashes Urn and the cut-glass trophy England were given at the Oval are discreetly on display in a corner of the ground. It's possible to have a photograph taken with a life-size cardboard cut-out of the England team. As if through execution, Andrew Strauss's head has been removed from his body. Place your own head in the vacant space and you, too, are holding the urn beside Collingwood and Swann, Flintoff and Prior. It's rather like one of those seafront attractions in which you can pretend to be a fat woman in a striped swimsuit from a Donald McGill postcard. Most spectators stare at the urn and are quietly overawed by the smallness of it.

And so the day quietly slips away, and slowness falls upon it.

It's been A Very English Summer for me, and the landscape of the St Lawrence Ground encapsulates it both within and beyond its boundaries. The Colin Cowdrey and Woolley Stands sit beside a pavilion almost unchanged since A. Chevallier Tayler painted it to commemorate Kent's County Championship of 1906. Tayler chose to capture in detail a solitary ball of this ordered Edwardian era: 1.25 p.m. on 10 August – the second day of Kent against Lancashire. Wide of the crease, Colin Blythe is bowling Kent towards an innings win. His left arm is hidden by the rotation of his body. The batsman, Johnny Tyldesley, grips the bat high on the handle. A thick black band has been pulled tight through the belt loops of his whites. At the end of 2005 – the same year its historic, spreading lime tree was blown over in a storm, which reduced it to nothing more than a wide stump – Kent announced Tayler's painting would be sold. A replacement lime was planted close to the spot where the other once grew, and a copy of Tayler's oil hangs over the pavilion bar. I guess Kent's members are so familiar with the scene of Blythe bowling to Tyldesley that Tayler's painting is nothing more to them now than a wide strip of framed wallpaper. As it is no longer fresh, it is no longer 'seen'; and the 'ways of seeing' it – other than casually, as if out of the corner of the eye – are greatly diminished. It is a silent work, which speaks to no one – unless, of course, the viewer sees it for the first time. 'The way we see things,' wrote the critic John Berger, 'is affected by what we know or what we believe . . . [and] to look is an act of choice.' As I look out of choice at what Tayler painted – irritating the thirsty men who are trying to elbow a way through me towards the bar – the sight of it draws one thing more tightly into focus. No sport so urgently feels the tug of war between modernity and tradition than cricket. It is – and perhaps always will be – in a struggle with itself over whether the game in its modern form is relevant and really matters to the public; whether it can be tinkered with or improved to compete with the more flashy, snazzy sports; and whether without such improvements it might weaken and wither or be blown away like the Kent lime. Other sports go through the same debates; but cricket's always seems the most fraught and anguished and frequently bring about more dramatic shifts of thinking and planning, which football and rugby, for instance, have been spared. Football shook off its image of working-class cloth caps and mufflers with barely noticeable change to the essential rules. Rugby – albeit reluctantly at first – embraced professionalism. Cricket is constantly more revolutionary than gradually evolutionary in creating new competitions or laws. But for all this remodelling cricket still has a cultural nostalgia about it, which contributes to its perpetual charm and inspires devotion. Raving sentimentalists, such as me, believe parts of it should be preserved like milk on the doorstep or red telephone boxes purely so we alone can enjoy them. We want it to be motes and beams when everything else is steel and glass. We believe – as C. P. Snow pointed out – that: 'Drinking the best tea in the world on an empty cricket ground . . . is the best final pleasure left to man.' Then reality bites.

'The golden age is always well behind us; we catch sight of it with young eyes when we see what we want to.' Neville Cardus wrote those lines in 1930. The truth Cardus exposed – that Golden Ages often have tin underneath them – still applies; and applied also during and immediately after the months Tayler was putting together the preliminary sketches for his painting at Canterbury. The summer of 1906 was no different from any other in cricket. It was dominated by talk about 'necessary change'. Proof that themes reccur in different disguises is found in the editor's notes of the 1907 *Wisden*. The editor, Sydney Pardon, criticised what he called 'various persons, who ought to have known better'. Pardon said these 'persons . . . jumped to the conclusion that cricket was losing its attraction to the public, and needed drastic alterations'. The targets of Pardon's attack were – in no particular order – Gilbert Jessop, who advocated shorter boundaries; W. G. Grace, who wanted the County Championship split into two Divisions; and Kent, which argued that 'in the case of a cricketer coming to this country to make a livelihood out of the game the period of qualification should be extended'. *Wisden* ever so gently condemned the brainwaves of Messrs Jessop and Grace without causing them too much offence; for to do so would have been like spitting at nobility. But Pardon added: 'There is a very strong feeling that the free importation of ready-made players does not make for the good of the county cricket.'

The ground on which these arguments stand is always being ploughed and reploughed. The future of the County Championship, overseas players and tagging more gimmicks on to cricket (similar in spirit to Jessop's well-meaning but bone-headed notion) have been discussed on the letters pages of *The Times*, the airwaves of *Test Match Special* and everywhere else this summer. Were Pardon around now, he would be writing about them again and throwing in his threepenny worth about the sustainability of central contracts and the emergence of the freelance cricketer (the soldiers of far fortune), the lack of cricket on terrestrial television, the appeal (and whether it can truly last) of Twenty20 as opposed to Tests, the fact cricket's central seat of power has moved from North London to Mumbai, the workload and pay of the players and the strategy and attitude of the administrators – particularly towards the cricket lover. Like any other era, the current one can't be judged and estimated properly until it is over. But recently cricket has arrived at a point in its journey where the road diverges. The road taken has always been influenced by the bright star of commercialism and the jingling coins of sponsorship. Only in the loosest sense of the word's dictionary definition can this be described as a strategy for the future. And, when the principles of navigation are so obviously base, there is no need for either a map or the vision to read it imaginatively. The dangers are obvious, and yet avoidable.

The future has a habit of turning out in ways we least expect. I look at Tayler's painting again and think about the next unsketched and unpainted frame. Where did Blythe pitch the ball? Which shot did Tyldesley play in response? Most of all I think of this preserved moment as evidence that cricket has survived so much and can survive much more still. It survived the change from under-arm to round-arm bowling. It survived dwindling crowds after the postwar boom. It survived Mr Kerry Packer – and prospered because of him too. It will survive whatever else happens to it; I am convinced of that, and comforted by it too.

One of the simplest, but saddest, sentences ever written is the line 'What begins also ends.' But it's true today. I am reluctant to turn away from Canterbury. The finality of doing so is like walking out of a room, hearing the door close behind you and then the soft click of the key in the lock. More than an hour ago Northamptonshire beat Kent by 99 runs. The ground is almost deserted now. The players left toting swags of kit, the evening is gathering in, and a ghostly half moon hangs over the Ames Stand. I leave the warmth of the pavilion and go over to the sapling lime on the far boundary. I pick up two fallen leaves as souvenirs and press them between the pages of my notebook. Only then do I head towards the gate. On the way out I stand next to the grey stone obelisk, which commemorates Colin Blythe, who died – aged thirty-eight – on the Forest Hall to Pimmern military railway line near Passchendaele in November 1917, another victim of the Great War. The sight of Blythe's name chiselled in stone takes me back to where I began – my grandfather, whose route home from France cut through the Kent countryside which Blythe never saw again. Like me, he disliked the bleak, inhospitable and depressing winter months. Both of us moved together towards another summer, half wishing our lives away. 'It'll be back again soon, boy,' he'd say when we parted at the end of our holidays together. He said the same thing to me in early September 1973.

But I knew with a certainty that I can't explain – either then or now – that I would never see or speak to him again. Armed with this dreadful knowledge, which I felt unable to share with anyone, I watched his face intently as his bus pulled out of the station. He waved at me from a window seat on the left-hand aisle. I waved back at him long after the tail lights of the bus dissolved into the early-morning traffic, and the exhaust fumes drifted away, like black smoke, on an autumnal wind.

My grandfather died two weeks later. I inherited his ribboned service medals, which I framed, and the brass compass he took to war and then into the mines. The glass face is cracked because of some unknowable minor calamity. I can still see the detail of his face, and the glinting gold of his wedding ring on his third finger. I can still hear his voice and feel the touch of his wrinkled hand on my bony shoulder. I can still see myself too – young and pale and self-consciously hunched over. Above everything else, I can still remember being suddenly infused with an extreme sense of loss that day – a loss for an event which had not yet occurred, but which I was helpless to stop.

All this, from long ago, passes through my mind as I walk away from Canterbury and leave it behind me. I am already longing for the same thing my grandfather would have longed for: yet another season.

Come quickly summer; come quickly.

Frank Woolley at his zenith. Ian Peebles called him 'the most graceful of the efficient and the most efficient of the graceful' batsmen.

AUTHOR NOTES
AND
ACKNOWLEDGEMENTS

While researching a biography of Harold Larwood, I spoke to Geoffrey Moorhouse, who had dug around the archives at Lord's more than a quarter of a century earlier. At the end of our conversation about Bodyline – and specifically the Case of the Vanishing MCC Report of the 1932–33 Tour – I told him how much I admired *The Best Loved Game*, which is his account of watching cricket during the summer of 1978. I added that I hoped, one day, to write a similar book, but in the vague shape and tone of J. B. Priestley's *English Journey*.

'Priestley was very helpful and generous to me,' he replied. 'He reviewed my first book for the *Guardian* in the mid-1960s. The book was inspired by *English Journey* too.' Geoffrey Moorhouse was just as helpful and generous to me. 'Good luck with it,' he said. 'I'll look forward to reading your version.'

At the beginning of November 2009, I finished *A Last English Summer* and planned to send a proof copy to him early in 2010. At the end of the same month – the day after *Harold Larwood* won the William Hill Sports Book of the Year Award – I was sitting with my wife, Mandy, in the Green Room of BBC's *Today* programme. I was waiting to be interviewed and thinking about what I might say. Mandy was reading *The Times*. She leaned across and silently handed me the newspaper. I read that Geoffrey Moorhouse had died just three days before his seventy-ninth birthday.

I had thought about him a lot during the summer and particularly recalled a phrase he used about his own work: 'Most of it is travel writing or travel writing in disguise.' I had so wanted him to think that *A Last English Summer* was travel writing in disguise too.

That's why Geoffrey Moorhouse and, of course, J. B. Priestley, head the list of acknowledgements.

Many others made very significant contributions. At Quercus, I was extremely grateful to be able to lean on the skill and experience of Jon Riley, the backing of David North, the work of Josh Ireland and David Watson and the enthusiasm of Richard Milbank. As ever, my agent, Grainne Fox, was indispensable in ways that would take another 1,000 words to properly explain.

Thanks for support, encouragement and practical assistance also go to: Bob Appleyard, Trevor Bailey, Dickie Bird, Geoffrey Boycott, Alex Butler, Stephen Chalke, Brian Close, Lucy Dupuis, Mark Eklid, Matthew Engel, Andrew Gidley, Tony Greig, John Grimsley, Brian Halford, Rod

Hamer, Paul Jones, Steven Lawrence, Jim Lyon, Sheila McQueeney, Chris de Mellow, Jennie de Mellow, Benj Moorhead, Lord David Puttnam, Paul Rhodes, Tom Richmond, John Stern, Nigel Stockley, Tim Sutcliffe, Enid and Iain Todd, Derek Underwood, Chris Waters, Tim Wellock, Simon Wilde, Glenys Williams and Peter Wynne-Thomas. Apologies to anyone who has been omitted through oversight (which is a euphemism for my own forgetfulness).

In my days as a novice newspaper reporter and later as a nascent sub-editor, I often came across golden wedding stories in which the celebratory couple were always asked: 'What's the secret of a happy marriage?' As far as I can remember, no one ever said watching cricket together. But Mandy – a cricket devotee too – lived *A Last English Summer* as much as I did. Some might describe their partner as 'their sun, their moon, their guiding star'. She's my Lord's, my Trent Bridge and especially my Scarborough.

And she knows that's a compliment . . .

Duncan Hamilton,
Wharfedale, 2010

POSTSCRIPT

The writer Thornton Wilder once said that time was a river in appearance only. 'It is,' he argued, 'a vast landscape and it is the eye of the beholder that moves.' Well, the eye of the beholder had to operate at rapid, blinking speed at the end of the summer.

The ordinary cricket watcher long ago accepted the fact that the game's landscape would shift with the seasons and be arranged to provide 12 months of almost unbroken coverage for the benefit of television and the satisfaction of accountants. He also accepted that most of what happened would pass him by, only half-glimpsed, in a jumble of images and a churn of statistics. As a consequence, some don't bother to attempt to follow the constant noisy rush of tournaments and ODIs because it fatigues the senses (so goodness knows how much it wears down and wearies the players) and because there are a limited number of hours that anyone can stay awake. However, cricket, like Burlesque theatre, never seems to close. Entertainments can always be rustled up to fill the stage specifically created for them.

After I said my lachrymose goodbye to Canterbury, I still hadn't expected so much to change so immediately.

*The ECB announced that the curtain raiser to the 2010 season, MCC against the Champion County – Durham, again – would be played in Abu Dhabi under lights and with a pink ball. (I'd like to have taken R. C. Robertson-Glasgow with me to witness it unfold).

*Hampshire v Sussex proved to be the farewell to 50-over finals at Lord's.

*The 40-over format was not only pardoned but given fresh, vigorous new life.

*Andrew Flintoff decided to reveal an entrepreneurial bent and become a 'freelance' – a bat and bowler for hire.

*The ECB made adjustments to the distribution of Championship points for 2010.

*Yorkshire decided to name an enclosure in their new Pavilion after Fred Trueman.

*The Lancashire League is persisting with professionals – though some clubs have recruited local players to fill those roles; Ramsbottom found a new sponsor and also won the Worsley Cup.

As for the main cast of characters. . .well, this is what happened next.

James Anderson (Lancashire) The Ashes highlight for Anderson turned out to be 5-80 on the second morning at Edgbaston. He failed to take a wicket at either Headingley or the Oval. In South Africa he took 16 wickets at 34.25. Along with Stuart Broad, he had to defend himself against allegations of ball-tampering during the Test at Newlands. He dismissed his action as being 'a bit lazy and absent minded'.

Sulieman Benn Benn took four wickets in his two Tests in England (both of which the West Indies lost). During the tour of Australia, he was suspended for two one-day internationals after an on-the-field squabble with Brad Haddin and Mitchell Johnson. It began after he collided with Johnson, the non-striker, in an attempt to field the ball. Benn pleaded not guilty to any offence. The match referee, Chris Broad, thought otherwise.

Ian Blackwell (Durham) One of the cricketers of the summer. Blackwell made 801 runs (40.05) and took a personal best of 43 wickets (23.53) after making, at 30 years old, the pivotal move of his career (which he also described as 'the hardest thing I've ever had to do') from Somerset. He even took five wickets for seven runs against his former county at the Riverside. 'I couldn't have written a better script,' he said of his season.

Nicky Boje (Northamptonshire) Had to suffer the agony of missing out on promotion by a single point – Essex beating Leicestershire to clinch it for themselves – but scored 801 runs and took 30 wickets.

Tim Bresnan (Yorkshire) He unfortunately got himself involved in what was described as a 'foul mouthed Twitter rant' on the social-networking site after a fellow user mocked up an image that made him appear over-weight. 'Don't mind my mates dishing it out,' he wrote, 'but who the **** are you.' He subsequently apologised. It was the only small blight on an otherwise impeccable season which saw him play two Tests against the West Indies and win an incremental ECB contract.

Stuart Broad (Nottinghamshire) He took more wickets than any other England bowler during the Ashes summer – 18 – which included 5-37 in the first innings at the Oval and 6-91 at Headingley, where he scored 61 of his 234 runs in a defiant second innings contribution when the Test was already a foregone conclusion. He finished the Ashes series top of the Professional Cricketers' Association MVP rankings.

Michael Carberry (Hampshire) With 1,251 Championship runs – only Jimmy Adams made more for the county (1,280) – Carberry won himself a place on the England Performance Programme. And when Paul Collingwood was temporarily injured during the South African tour, Carberry was called up as cover for the remaining Tests and then taken on the tour of Bangladesh.

Josh Cobb (Leicestershire) He made 445 runs from 12 first class matches and was rewarded with a contract extension, which ends in 2012.

Paul Collingwood (Durham) After scoring exactly 250 runs in the Ashes series, Collingwood's tour of South Africa was even more profitable. He made 344 runs (highest score 91) at 57.33.

Dominic Cork (Hampshire) He took 27 Championship wickets at 28.40 with a best of 5-14. Cork was presented with his county cap – a particularly poignant moment because it was given to him before the Division One game against his former club, Lancashire, at the Rose Bowl.

Robert Croft (Glamorgan) He bowled more first class deliveries – 4,421 – than anyone else in first class cricket in 2009. His nearest rivals were James Tredwell (4,091) and Danish Kaneria (3,587). Finished with more than 50 wickets and over 500 runs and won Glamorgan's first class Player of the Year award.

Michael Di Venuto (Durham) A career best of 254 not out against Sussex – and a double hundred which flayed the Nottinghamshire attack – contributed to Di Venuto's 1,601 runs at 80.05, which made him irresistible to watch and invaluable to Durham, where he has now won a trophy in each summer since joining them in 2007.

Luke Fletcher (Nottinghamshire) He went on to make eight Championship appearances and take 29 wickets at 27.58. After scoring only 26 runs in nine innings from all competitions, Fletcher also unexpectedly proved himself with the bat. Coming in at number nine, he scored 92 against Hampshire at the Rose Bowl. He earned a place on the England Performance Programme during the winter.

Andrew Flintoff (Lancashire) Only 48 hours after the lap of honour at the Oval, Flintoff underwent a knee operation and then began his new role as 'freelance' one day and Twenty20 specialist after turning down the ECB's offer of an incremental contract. In his most recent autobiography *Ashes to Ashes*, published in the autumn of 2009, he admitted: 'The one thing that burns away at me is that I never actually peaked in my career.'

Chris Gayle He remained West Indies captain and made a quite brilliant – if futile – 165 not out against Australia in the Adelaide Test. *See also Shane Watson

Rory Hamilton-Brown (Sussex) At 22 years old and after only six Championship matches, he left Sussex after being recruited by Surrey as their new captain for 2010.

Steve Harmison (Durham) His 6-20 against Notts at Trent Bridge in July forced him back into the England side for the last two Tests. Left out of the party to tour South Africa, the 31-year-old Harmison responded by signing a contract which ties him to Durham until 2013.

Matthew Hoggard (Yorkshire) 'All I got after 15 years,' said Hoggard after learning that he wouldn't be offered a new contract at Headingley, 'was a cup of coffee in the chief executive's office'. Hoggard added that he felt as if he'd been 'effectively sacked'. At 32, he took more wickets (43) than any other Yorkshire bowler, including a hat-trick in the penultimate match at Sussex. After what he described as the 'shock' of his departure, he agreed to sign for – and captain – Leicestershire in 2010.

Phillip Hughes Only regained a place in the Australian team for the Second Test against Pakistan in Sydney in January, 2010. Ended the previous year with a century for New South Wales against Victoria.

Mike Hussey After his 121 in a losing cause against England at the Oval, Hussey scratched around for form and his place in the side was said to be in jeopardy. Those who had doubts about him – Shane Warne was critical of his batting – had to shed them after 134 not out which was the basis of Australia's win against the odds over Pakistan in the Second Test at Sydney. Hussey said Warne's verdict on him proved to be a spur.

Sanath Jayasuriya After 444 ODI appearances – making him the world's most experienced batsman in this form of the game – he lost his place for the Sri-Lanka–Bangladesh TriNations series and was told he would have to force his way back into the side as a spinning all-rounder.

Simon Katich Australia's top run scorer in 2009 with 1,111 runs. Katich ended the year well but frustratingly with scores of 92 against the West Indies in Brisbane and 99 in Perth. Another 98 followed in the Melbourne Test with Pakistan before he made exactly 100 against them at Hobart.

Robert Key (Kent) Key led Kent to the Division Two Championship and to the Twenty20 finals for a third successive season. Shortly after the end of the season he signed a new long-term contract after newspaper speculation about his future (Surrey were said to be interested).

Steve Kirby (Gloucestershire) Finished the summer with more Championship wickets than anyone else at the club – 64 at 22.18 – as the director of cricket John Bracewell reflected on 'First Division bowling and Second Division batting' which frustratingly defined Gloucesteshire's season. Expressed his 'total elation' at being called up for England Lions' tour of the UAE in early 2010 and said he wanted to be a good 'death bowler' for the team.

Justin Langer (Somerset) He led the county to third place in the Championship. They were also runners-up in the Twenty20 Cup. But Langer's summer will be remembered for the leaked 'dossier' he provided for Australia's Test team in which described English cricketers as 'lazy', 'shallow' and 'flat'. In particular he was critical of James Anderson, who he said could be a 'bit of a pussy' if things went against him. Langer gave up the Somerset captaincy, retired as a player and subsequently took a coaching job with the Australian Test side.

V. V. S. Laxman (Lancashire) With Lancashire struggling at 45-3 in their final match of the season against Warwickshire – and the prospect of relegation still looming over them – Laxman made a typically stylish 113 despite a back injury. It took his tally for the summer to 857 Championship runs, including four hundreds.

Brett Lee Lee's frustration at missing the Ashes series through injury was partly assuaged by a pyrotechnical performance for New South Wales Blues in the Champions League final against Trinidad and Tobago. He rescued the innings with a powerful 48 off 31 balls and then took two for 10 – including a remarkable return catch – to win Man of the Match. An elbow problem unfortunately interrupted his comeback again and he announced his retirement from Test cricket in February 2010.

Jon Lewis (Gloucestershire) Lewis again proved precious to Gloucestershire. He came top of the Championship averages for them with 57 wickets at 20.10.

Graham Lloyd (Accrington) Another memorable season of run making – he made 842. The Lloyd family was further represented at the end of the season when Graham's father, David, appeared against Lowerhouse. He made four not out.

Sajid Mahmood (Lancashire) He ended the season with 38 wickets at 29.42 and was named in England's one-day and Twenty20 squads for the tour of South Africa and then the Lions squad for matches in the United Arab Emirates. 'I've gone back and worked on certain areas of my bowling,' he said. 'I have been trying to perform a lot more consistently.'

Lasith Malinga He didn't take a wicket from 112 balls bowled in the one-day series against India and subsequently lost his place. He was due to play for Tasmania in Australia's Twenty20 Big Bash tournament, but had to pull out because of international commitments.

Angelo Mathews His 'wonder' catch is still being watched on YouTube. Missed his maiden Test century by only one run against India at Mumbai. 'There were tears in my eyes,' he admitted after 'creasing' his bat before pursuing a second run and losing the race with Sachin Tendulkar's throw to the wicketkeeper.

Tom Maynard (Glamorgan) Made only five Championship appearances and finished with 115 runs – including an unbeaten 51.

Ajantha Mendis After a disappointing end to the year, he was left out of Sri Lanka's TriNations tournament against Bangladesh and joined his IPL side Kolkata Knight Riders for preliminary training.

Muttiah Muralitharan In the end-of-year Test series against India, Muralitharan took 9 wickets, but at a cost of nearly 600 runs. He admitted he may retire before the World Cup in 2011. 'I am 37-years-old,' he said, 'and cannot bowl as much because I get tired after 15 or 16 overs.'

Graham Onions (Durham) His 7-38 against Warwickshire, and another 6-31 to punish Somerset, began what became the most memorable season of his career. He took 5-38 at Lord's on his debut against the West Indies. He finished the Ashes series with 10 wickets from three Tests (his best figures were 4-58 at Edgbaston). He then revealed a sharp instinct for survival under extreme pressure during the winter tour of South Africa, where as last man he twice survived 'at the death' of the Centurion and Newlands Tests to force a draw. He also took eight wickets.

David Ormerod (Accrington) Again the club's best bowler with 66 wickets at 16.51.

Monty Panesar (Northamptonshire) Took just 18 Championship wickets at 59.44 in 13 matches. Lost his England central contract and moved to Sussex during the winter on a three-year contract. To mark his ten years at Northamptonshire, he donated £10,000 to the county.

Brenton Parchment (Ramsbottom) Made 697 runs at 33.9 and took 55 wickets at 18.36. He returned to Jamaica to help them defend their four-day title.

Stephen Peters (Northamptonshire) One of only two Northants batsman to score more than 1,000 runs – the other was their Player of the Season, Andrew Hall – Peters signed an extension to his contract, which will now expire in 2011.

Kevin Pietersen (Hampshire) The injury to his Achilles tendon persisted and kept him out of both the rest of the Ashes series and the Champions Trophy. His form in South Africa was worrying – just 177 runs from seven innings with a highest score of 81 and an average of 25.28.

Ricky Ponting Within six weeks of the Ashes defeat, Ponting and Australia had retained the ICC Champions Trophy in South Africa. Ponting finished as the tournament's top run scorer with 288 from five innings. His highest score was 111 not out in the semi-final against England. He said it was no consolation for losing the Ashes. He also led Australia to Test series wins over West Indies and Pakistan (who were whitewashed). In the last Test, against Pakistan at Hobart, he made 206 in the first innings – watched by his parents and the Australian Prime Minister – and 89 in the second.

Mark Ramprakash (Surrey) Turned 40 at the end of another successful summer in which he scored more than 1,300 Championship runs and was strongly championed – mostly by the public – for a Test place at The Oval. The job went to Warwickshire's Jonathan Trott instead. 'The selectors have said to me the door is always open but it appears to be closed,' he reflected. 'People say to me all the time, "Ramps, how come you're not being selected. You have scored over 6,000 runs in the last four years and average over 90?" It seems unfair.'

Adil Rashid (Yorkshire) Rashid took 26 Championship wickets at 31.46, but Yorkshire's director of professional cricket Martyn Moxon became concerned at the lack of overs he had bowled competitively over a 12-month period. He subsequently asked England to outline their long-term plans for the spinner's development. He was released from England's senior squad in South Africa to join up with the England Performance Programme and went on to the England Lions tour of UEA rather than to Bangladesh.

Chris Rogers (Derbyshire) Comfortably the most successful – and consequently valuable – of Derbyshire's batsman. Rogers scored almost 1,500 Championship runs and over 2,000 in all competitions. His former colleague Justin Langer – who presented Rogers with his Baggy Green on his Australian debut – even called for him to be recalled to the Test squad. At the beginning of 2010 he fractured his hand in an Australian club game.

Jacques Rudolph (Yorkshire) For the third successive season Rudolph was Yorkshire's leading run scorer. He made 1,334 runs at 51.30. He was switched to open the innings in an effort to give Yorkshire a better start to matches – despite reservations from Geoff Boycott – and it consequently weakened the middle order. There is no news about the burial of the pigeon.

Ramnaresh Sarwan The Guyana Cricket Board named Sarwan as Player of the Year for 2009 after his 850 runs in nine Tests, including four centuries.

Ryan Sidebottom (Nottinghamshire) There was no Ashes glory for Sidebottom. There was, however, a benefit awarded to him for 2010 and the arrival of his first child (a girl) in November. He retained his England central contract and went on the tour to South Africa, playing in the final Test. In the Championship he took 31 wickets at 24.51.

Roy Silva (Accrington) He took 31 wickets at 23.93 with a best of 4-44. He was not retained for the 2010 season.

Greg Smith (Derbyshire) Derbyshire's end-of-season report in *Wisden Cricketer* perfectly encapsulated Smith's performance. He went, it read, from 'promising talent to reliable performer'. The result left him only 23 short of 1,000 runs for the Championship season. He also took 32 wickets in the Second Division. He was awarded both his county cap and a new two-year contract.

Will Smith (Durham) 'Just about every game went according to plan,' said Smith of Durham retaining the Championship in his first season as captain. He made 700 runs at 33.33, a figure which reflected the burdens of his new job. But he did hit 150 against Hampshire in the penultimate match.

Andrew Strauss (Middlesex) 'At times,' said Strauss of England's Ashes win, 'there were times when I didn't think we would make it.' His success, however, didn't impress the Australians overmuch. Only 4 per cent of state and international cricketers, surveyed by the Australian Cricketers' Association at the end of 2009, regarded Strauss as the best opposition captain from another country. The ACA members overwhelming voted for Graeme Smith, who claimed 48 per cent of the vote. Strauss left himself out of the tour of Bangaldesh, which divided opinion among former England captains.

Graeme Swann (Nottinghamshire) He did more than turn himself into England's number one spinner. Swann established himself as one of those almost old-fashioned characters that Neville Cardus would have written about as though he were detailing the quirks and peculiarities of Emmott Robinson. Swann's Twitter introduction would, however, have been alien to

Cardus: 'I play cricket, I'm in a band and I recently stopped wetting the bed.' He was given an England central contract for the first time and finished top of the averages on the South African tour with 21 wickets at 31.38.

James Taylor (Leicestershire) Named both the Professional Cricketers' Association Young Cricketer of the Year and the Cricket Writers' Young Player of the Year. The awards were recognition of his 1,177 first class runs in 16 games at an average of 58.85. He hit three hundreds and six fifties with a best of 207 not out against Surrey at The Oval. At the end of the season he signed a contract extension which will keep him at Grace Road until 2012.

Dilshan Tillakaratne He scored ten international centuries in 2009, which included 1,071 Test runs, more than 1,000 in one-day matches and 471 in Twenty20 games. The success rate, he insists, came as a result of a 'different mindset' after opening the innings. He was named the ICC's Twenty20 International Player of the Year after his 96 not out from 57 balls against West Indies in the World Cup semi-finals at the Oval and also won the tournament's top player award with 317 runs at 52.83.

Marcus Trescothick (Somerset) The Professional Cricketers' Association made him their MVP for 2009 after performances which made the decision almost a formality. Trescothick scored 1,817 Championship runs (more than anyone else) and 2,934 runs in all competitions. He was appointed Somerset's captain for 2010 after the departure of Justin Langer and signed a new three-year contract during the winter. Sadly, he had to return home prematurely from the Champions League tournament after suffering a repeat of the illness which he first revealed in his autobiography.

Michael Vaughan (Yorkshire) As well as continuing his new career as an artist, Vaughan joined *Test Match Special* as a summariser for the winter tour to South Africa. He continues to write for the *Sunday Telegraph*.

James Vince (Hampshire) Named vice-captain of the England Under19 side for the World Cup in New Zealand. He scored 172 runs there at 86.00 with highest score of 76 not out against Hong Kong.

Shane Watson After making 96, 89 and 93 during the Australian summer,

Watson at last scored his maiden Test hundred against Pakistan at Melbourne. He made headlines for other reasons during the West Indies series. He was fined 15 per cent of his match fee for over-exuberant celebrations after removing Chris Gayle. Watson claimed Gayle had provoked him. In the Champions League trophy, he scored centuries in both the semi-final and final.

Chris Woakes (Warwickshire) The pitch at Edgbaston was seldom responsive to seam, but Woakes, 37 wickets for Warwickshire (a best of 5-40) was also buttressed by a career best 131 not out – his maiden century – against Hampshire. Batting at number nine he shared a 222 partnership with Jonathan Trott. He also claimed 6-43 playing for England Lions against the West Indies.

Luke Wright (Sussex) He made 12 ODI and eight Twenty20 appearances for England in 2009. Signed a new three-year contract for Sussex at the end of the summer.

Michael Yardy (Sussex) He steered Sussex to the Twenty20 and the Pro40 titles, but the side was relegated from Division One of the Championship. While learning some harsh truths about captaincy in his first season in charge, Yardy still scored 1,046 Championship runs. Signed a three-year contract for Sussex at the end of 2009.

STATISTICS
OF
SUMMER

County Championship Div 1

	P	W	L	D	Bat	Bowl	Deduct	Points
Durham	16	8	0	8	49	48	1.0	240
Nottinghamshire	16	4	2	10	56	41	0.0	193
Somerset	16	3	1	12	50	43	1.0	182
Lancashire	16	4	2	10	35	44	0.0	175
Warwickshire	16	3	3	10	54	38	0.0	174
Hampshire	16	3	3	10	50	40	3.0	169
Yorkshire	16	2	2	12	46	44	0.0	166
Sussex	16	2	6	8	45	39	1.0	143
Worcestershire	16	0	10	6	30	40	0.0	94

County Championship Div 2

	P	W	L	D	Bat	Bowl	Deduct	Points
Kent	16	8	3	5	43	44	0.0	219
Essex	16	6	3	7	40	43	1.0	194
Northamptonshire	16	6	4	6	40	45	0.0	193
Gloucestershire	16	6	6	4	39	46	0.0	185
Glamorgan	16	2	2	12	56	43	0.0	175
Derbyshire	16	2	3	11	55	45	0.0	172
Surrey	16	1	4	11	54	36	0.0	148
Middlesex	16	2	7	7	43	41	0.0	140
Leicestershire	16	2	3	11	31	35	0.0	138

Division One batting

		Mtchs	Inns	NO	Runs	Best	Ave	100	50	Ct	St
S. Chanderpaul	Durham	5	6	4	472	201*	236.00	3	0	3	0
D.J. Hussey	Nottinghamshire	3	5	0	407	189	81.40	2	1	5	0
I.J.L. Trott	Warwickshire	14	20	5	1207	184*	80.46	4	5	10	0
M.J. Di Venuto	Durham	16	26	6	1601	254*	80.05	6	5	23	0
A.C. Voges	Nottinghamshire	8	10	1	697	139	77.44	1	6	8	0
A.U. Rashid	Yorkshire	7	9	4	387	157*	77.40	2	1	4	0
M.E. Trescothick	Somerset	16	26	2	1817	146	75.70	8	9	21	0
C.M.W. Read	Nottinghamshire	16	22	6	1203	125	75.18	4	6	46	4
N. Pothas	Hampshire	11	15	4	816	122*	74.18	1	6	24	0
M.A. Carberry	Hampshire	12	21	3	1251	204	69.50	4	8	6	0
V.V.S. Laxman	Lancashire	11	16	3	857	135	65.92	4	4	15	0
A.G. Prince	Lancashire	5	10	2	497	135*	62.12	1	3	8	0
O.B. Cox	Worcestershire	1	1	0	61	61	61.00	0	1	4	1
S.C.J. Broad	Nottinghamshire	1	1	0	60	60	60.00	0	1	2	0
C. Kieswetter	Somerset	16	24	3	1242	153	59.14	4	7	48	0
C.D. Nash	Sussex	14	25	3	1298	157	59.00	4	6	3	0
I.R. Bell	Warwickshire	13	21	3	986	172	54.77	4	4	10	0
M.B. Loye	Lancashire	13	21	3	983	151*	54.61	2	6	4	0
W.J. Durston	Somerset	1	2	1	54	54*	54.00	0	1	0	0
J.H.K. Adams	Hampshire	16	28	4	1279	147	53.29	3	9	16	0
D.M. Benkenstein	Durham	16	22	0	1155	181	52.50	5	4	10	0
J.A. Rudolph	Yorkshire	16	27	1	1334	198	51.30	4	6	13	0
M.J. Chilton	Lancashire	15	22	6	777	111*	48.56	1	6	14	0
A.V. Suppiah	Somerset	16	26	1	1201	151	48.04	3	6	18	0
G.R. Breese	Durham	1	1	0	48	48	48.00	0	0	2	0
L.J. Wright	Sussex	8	13	2	527	118*	47.90	2	3	1	0
J.M. Bairstow	Yorkshire	12	19	6	592	84*	45.53	0	6	21	0
M.J. Prior	Sussex	5	8	0	362	140	45.25	1	2	12	0
D.J. Wainwright	Yorkshire	9	12	4	356	102*	44.50	1	1	0	0
J.C. Hildreth	Somerset	15	23	2	934	303*	44.47	2	4	10	0
L.E. Plunkett	Durham	12	12	3	400	94*	44.44	0	3	12	0
G.L. Brophy	Yorkshire	13	21	5	709	99	44.31	0	6	35	2
J.L. Langer	Somerset	15	21	2	831	122*	43.73	2	4	17	0
J.S. Patel	Warwickshire	3	4	1	131	120	43.66	1	0	1	0
E.C. Joyce	Sussex	14	23	1	936	183	42.54	3	3	12	0
J.J. Sayers	Yorkshire	16	27	1	1103	173	42.42	2	5	15	0
P. Mustard	Durham	16	20	6	592	94*	42.28	0	5	61	1
M.H. Yardy	Sussex	16	28	3	1046	152	41.84	2	5	13	0
P.J. Franks	Nottinghamshire	4	4	0	167	64	41.75	0	2	1	0
S.M. Ervine	Hampshire	15	22	2	832	114	41.60	3	3	6	0
A. Shahzad	Yorkshire	13	17	6	445	88	40.45	0	2	4	0
A.D. Brown	Nottinghamshire	16	24	3	849	148	40.42	1	6	18	0
I.D. Blackwell	Durham	16	22	2	801	158	40.05	1	6	4	0
S.M. Davies	Worcestershire	14	26	2	952	126	39.66	2	4	39	2
J.O. Troughton	Warwickshire	16	21	0	823	223	39.19	2	3	10	0
R. Clarke	Warwickshire	13	17	1	619	112	38.68	1	5	22	0
M.A. Ealham	Nottinghamshire	14	20	7	493	70*	37.92	0	2	6	0
M.J. Lumb	Hampshire	15	23	1	834	219	37.90	1	5	8	0
T. Lungley	Lancashire	2	2	1	37	27*	37.00	0	0	2	0
M.A. Wagh	Nottinghamshire	15	24	2	813	146	36.95	3	2	4	0
C.D. Hopkinson	Sussex	9	13	1	443	139	36.91	2	0	2	0
A.D. Hales	Nottinghamshire	6	10	0	358	78	35.80	0	3	2	0
G.M. Andrew	Worcestershire	9	16	5	391	92*	35.54	0	3	0	0
K.J. Coetzer	Durham	6	9	1	284	107	35.50	1	0	7	0
V.S. Solanki	Worcestershire	15	28	1	953	206*	35.29	1	4	13	0
A.W. Gale	Yorkshire	16	25	1	828	121	34.50	2	4	6	0

		Mtchs	Inns	NO	Runs	Best	Ave	100	50	Ct	St
T.R. Ambrose	Warwickshire	16	21	1	686	153	34.30	2	4	37	2
C.R. Woakes	Warwickshire	16	21	7	480	131*	34.28	1	1	3	0
R.J. Hamilton-Brown	Sussex	4	7	1	205	171*	34.16	1	0	5	0
C.C. Benham	Hampshire	5	8	2	205	100	34.16	1	1	5	0
D.K.H. Mitchell	Worcestershire	16	30	0	1022	298	34.06	1	5	17	0
P.D. Trego	Somerset	16	23	5	610	103*	33.88	1	5	5	0
W.R. Smith	Durham	15	23	2	700	150	33.33	2	3	6	0
M.W. Goodwin	Sussex	16	27	3	800	344*	33.33	1	2	6	0
G.J. Muchall	Durham	11	17	2	497	106*	33.13	1	2	13	0
A. McGrath	Yorkshire	16	26	1	825	211	33.00	2	2	10	0
G. Chapple	Lancashire	11	14	2	390	89	32.50	0	3	3	0
S.J. Croft	Lancashire	8	12	2	317	79	31.70	0	2	6	0
B.J. Phillips	Somerset	7	8	2	190	84	31.66	0	1	4	0
J.S. Gatting	Sussex	3	5	0	158	70	31.60	0	1	2	0
L.A. Dawson	Hampshire	14	21	4	536	69	31.52	0	4	10	0
A. Lyth	Yorkshire	4	7	0	220	71	31.42	0	2	1	0
F. du Plessis	Lancashire	13	20	3	531	86*	31.23	0	5	8	0
O.A.C. Banks	Somerset	6	7	2	156	53	31.20	0	1	1	0
Z. de Bruyn	Somerset	16	25	3	686	106	31.18	1	6	3	0
T.T. Bresnan	Yorkshire	10	14	2	372	97	31.00	0	1	5	0
S.R. Patel	Nottinghamshire	15	23	0	712	95	30.95	0	4	7	0
I.J. Westwood	Warwickshire	14	23	3	605	133	30.25	1	4	10	0
J.C. Buttler	Somerset	1	1	0	30	30	30.00	0	0	0	0
P. Chawla	Sussex	6	10	3	206	102*	29.42	1	0	2	0
D.G. Wright	Sussex	3	4	1	88	42	29.33	0	0	0	0
P.J. Horton	Lancashire	16	29	2	776	173	28.74	1	4	16	0
M.M. Ali	Worcestershire	16	30	2	803	153	28.67	2	3	4	0
A.A. Noffke	Worcestershire	6	9	0	258	89	28.66	0	2	0	0
A.D. Mascarenhas	Hampshire	10	11	2	254	108	28.22	1	0	4	0
A.C. Thomas	Somerset	14	15	3	338	70	28.16	0	3	2	0
D.A. Wheeldon	Worcestershire	4	5	0	138	87	27.60	0	1	3	0
S.C. Moore	Worcestershire	14	27	0	738	107	27.33	1	5	5	0
A.N. Kervezee	Worcestershire	8	14	0	381	66	27.21	0	2	2	0
A.G. Botha	Warwickshire	14	19	2	444	64	26.11	0	2	5	0
A.J. Hodd	Sussex	15	22	3	489	101	25.73	1	2	23	3
J.M. Vince	Hampshire	8	11	0	282	75	25.63	0	1	2	0
K.W. Hogg	Lancashire	13	13	1	307	69	25.58	0	2	2	0
L.D. Sutton	Lancashire	16	21	6	377	45*	25.13	0	0	53	3
M.J. Wood	Nottinghamshire	6	9	1	200	86	25.00	0	1	0	0
A.R. Adams	Nottinghamshire	11	13	1	300	84	25.00	0	1	13	0
N.M. Carter	Warwickshire	9	13	0	318	67	24.46	0	2	0	0
T. Frost	Warwickshire	13	20	1	463	94	24.36	0	2	7	0
L.J. Fletcher	Nottinghamshire	8	8	3	121	92	24.20	0	1	0	0
J.P. Crawley	Hampshire	7	12	2	240	81*	24.00	0	1	6	0

Division One bowling

		Overs	Mdns	Runs	Wkts	Best	Avge	5w	10w
E.C. Joyce	Sussex	2.0	0	9	1	1-9	9.00	0	0
J.M. Anderson	Lancashire	51.0	15	109	11	6-56	9.90	2	1
J.J. Sayers	Yorkshire	10.5	0	32	3	3-20	10.66	0	0
T. Frost	Warwickshire	5.1	1	12	1	1-12	12.00	0	0
S.C.J. Broad	Nottinghamshire	48.0	12	106	7	5-79	15.14	1	0
G. Onions	Durham	248.5	61	688	45	7-38	15.28	4	0
K.R. Brown	Lancashire	8.0	0	37	2	2-30	18.50	0	0
A. Flintoff	Lancashire	51.3	15	149	8	4-47	18.62	0	0
D.M. Benkenstein	Durham	42.0	10	150	8	3-20	18.75	0	0
G.P. Swann	Nottinghamshire	55.0	15	127	6	3-52	21.16	0	0
S.J. Harmison	Durham	412.2	109	1154	51	6-20	22.62	4	0
I.D. Blackwell	Durham	430.1	121	1012	43	7-85	23.53	3	0
N.S. Tahir	Warwickshire	232.5	55	711	30	5-67	23.70	1	0
I.J. Westwood	Warwickshire	19.0	2	49	2	2-39	24.50	0	0
R.J. Sidebottom	Nottinghamshire	260.2	70	760	31	5-59	24.51	2	0
L.E. Plunkett	Durham	346.3	65	1217	49	6-63	24.83	3	1
G. Chapple	Lancashire	335.4	87	884	35	6-19	25.25	2	0
V.V.S. Laxman	Lancashire	13.0	4	26	1	1-13	26.00	0	0
A.S. Miller	Warwickshire	61.0	12	184	7	4-76	26.28	0	0
P. Chawla	Sussex	341.5	72	981	36	6-52	27.25	4	1
M.S. Mason	Worcestershire	418.4	125	1186	43	7-39	27.58	2	0
L.J. Fletcher	Nottinghamshire	245.3	62	800	29	4-38	27.58	0	0
C.D. Thorp	Durham	307.4	89	831	30	5-49	27.70	2	0
T. Lungley	Lancashire	40.0	8	139	5	3-85	27.80	0	0
D.K.H. Mitchell	Worcestershire	90.0	13	252	9	4-49	28.00	0	0
D.G. Cork	Hampshire	287.0	69	767	27	5-14	28.40	1	0
A.R. Adams	Nottinghamshire	408.5	102	1224	43	4-39	28.46	0	0
M.K. Munday	Somerset	25.1	0	114	4	2-46	28.50	0	0
S.I. Mahmood	Lancashire	306.3	59	1118	38	6-30	29.42	2	1
M. Davies	Durham	217.1	60	562	19	4-87	29.57	0	0
C.M. Willoughby	Somerset	555.4	161	1621	54	5-56	30.01	3	0
D.J. Wainwright	Yorkshire	244.2	50	797	26	5-134	30.65	1	0
A.U. Rashid	Yorkshire	242.4	37	818	26	5-41	31.46	2	0
S.G. Borthwick	Durham	27.0	2	95	3	3-95	31.66	0	0
B.M. Shafayat	Nottinghamshire	8.0	1	32	1	1-32	32.00	0	0
S. Sreesanth	Warwickshire	109.4	21	418	13	5-93	32.15	1	0
K.W. Hogg	Lancashire	319.2	83	965	30	4-74	32.16	0	0
D.R. Smith	Sussex	301.0	84	814	25	4-58	32.56	0	0
Imran Tahir	Hampshire	487.4	81	1711	52	7-140	32.90	4	0
W.B. Rankin	Warwickshire	316.1	54	1164	35	5-85	33.25	1	0
A.C. Voges	Nottinghamshire	33.3	2	100	3	1-2	33.33	0	0
M.E. Claydon	Durham	210.0	40	734	22	4-90	33.36	0	0
C.D. Collymore	Sussex	396.0	102	1104	33	4-66	33.45	0	0
L.J. Wright	Sussex	210.1	35	710	21	5-66	33.80	2	0
R.A. Jones	Worcestershire	174.0	25	745	22	6-100	33.86	1	0
D.A. Griffiths	Hampshire	255.0	47	949	28	4-48	33.89	0	0
R.S.C. Martin-Jenkins	Sussex	275.4	74	781	23	5-43	33.95	1	0
M.J. Hoggard	Yorkshire	466.1	100	1467	43	5-56	34.11	2	0
A. Shahzad	Yorkshire	409.5	81	1376	40	4-72	34.40	0	0
G. Keedy	Lancashire	487.5	81	1457	42	6-50	34.69	3	0
M.A. Ealham	Nottinghamshire	386.5	117	983	28	5-31	35.10	1	0
R.J. Kirtley	Sussex	50.5	6	177	5	2-59	35.40	0	0
P.J. Franks	Nottinghamshire	116.0	33	323	9	3-52	35.88	0	0
D.A. Stiff	Somerset	268.1	33	1120	31	5-91	36.12	1	0
R.J. Hamilton-Brown	Sussex	37.0	6	109	3	2-49	36.33	0	0
C.R. Woakes	Warwickshire	415.5	92	1350	37	5-40	36.48	1	0

		Overs	Mdns	Runs	Wkts	Best	Avge	5w	10w
D.R. Briggs	Hampshire	85.4	13	295	8	3-62	36.87	0	0
G.J. Kruis	Yorkshire	252.1	56	816	22	3-51	37.09	0	0
D.G. Wright	Sussex	83.5	33	187	5	3-64	37.40	0	0
A.C. Thomas	Somerset	401.1	77	1317	35	5-53	37.62	1	0
Kabir Ali	Worcestershire	97.0	10	416	11	6-68	37.81	1	0
T.T. Bresnan	Yorkshire	352.4	92	909	24	4-116	37.87	0	0
A. Lyth	Yorkshire	19.0	9	38	1	1-38	38.00	0	0
B.J. Phillips	Somerset	158.1	37	456	12	4-46	38.00	0	0
J.A. Tomlinson	Hampshire	318.1	57	1193	30	3-53	39.76	0	0
C.T. Tremlett	Hampshire	173.0	34	564	14	4-49	40.28	0	0
A.G. Botha	Warwickshire	316.3	61	941	23	5-51	40.91	1	0
Naved ul-Hasan	Yorkshire	124.0	23	412	10	3-102	41.20	0	0
S.J. Croft	Lancashire	16.0	3	83	2	2-42	41.50	0	0
O.J. Newby	Lancashire	274.1	35	1058	25	4-105	42.32	0	0
D.J. Balcombe	Hampshire	44.0	7	174	4	2-21	43.50	0	0
O.P. Rayner	Sussex	294.2	48	870	20	4-186	43.50	0	0
G.M. Andrew	Worcestershire	249.3	37	964	22	5-117	43.81	1	0
N.M. Carter	Warwickshire	190.0	30	704	16	5-37	44.00	1	0
T.C. Smith	Lancashire	181.0	41	572	13	6-46	44.00	1	0
L.A. Dawson	Hampshire	73.0	9	312	7	2-3	44.57	0	0
A.A. Noffke	Worcestershire	158.0	38	452	10	4-92	45.20	0	0
A.V. Suppiah	Somerset	212.5	47	682	15	3-58	45.46	0	0
A.D. Hales	Nottinghamshire	40.0	6	140	3	2-63	46.66	0	0
P.D. Trego	Somerset	257.3	57	889	19	3-53	46.78	0	0

Division Two batting

		Mtchs	Inns	NO	Runs	Best	Avge	100	50	Ct	St
P.J. Hughes	Middlesex	3	5	1	574	195	143.50	3	2	4	0
R.S. Bopara	Essex	2	4	2	269	201	134.50	1	1	2	0
H.M. Amla	Essex	3	5	1	410	181	102.50	2	1	2	0
M.R. Ramprakash	Surrey	11	17	2	1350	274	90.00	5	4	5	0
C.J.L. Rogers	Derbyshire	13	21	1	1461	222	73.05	6	4	21	0
J. du Toit	Leicestershire	2	3	1	142	100*	71.00	1	0	1	0
J.L. Sadler	Derbyshire	3	4	3	71	27*	71.00	0	0	3	0
M. van Jaarsveld	Kent	15	24	3	1475	182	70.23	7	7	30	0
J.W.A. Taylor	Leicestershire	15	25	7	1184	207*	65.77	3	6	8	0
M.J. Cosgrove	Glamorgan	9	14	2	757	175	63.08	3	5	4	0
A.J. Strauss	Middlesex	3	5	0	295	150	59.00	1	1	2	0
W.L. Madsen	Derbyshire	9	16	2	809	170*	57.78	3	3	8	0
U. Afzaal	Surrey	16	28	6	1269	204*	57.68	3	7	3	0
R.W.T. Key	Kent	14	24	3	1145	270*	54.52	4	3	15	0
G.O. Jones	Kent	16	25	0	1291	156	51.64	5	5	41	3
A.J. Hall	Northamptonshire	16	25	2	1161	159	50.47	2	6	16	0
J.W.M. Dalrymple	Glamorgan	16	23	3	1009	128	50.45	3	5	17	0
R.J. Harris	Surrey	2	2	0	98	94	49.00	0	1	1	0
J.E.C. Franklin	Gloucestershire	14	22	3	904	109	47.57	3	4	6	0
R.N. ten Doeschate	Essex	14	22	4	823	159*	45.72	2	2	5	0
J. Allenby	Glamorgan	10	16	2	627	137	44.78	1	6	9	0
H.H. Dippenaar	Leicestershire	15	28	4	1074	143	44.75	2	8	4	0
A.P.R. Gidman	Gloucestershire	15	23	0	1028	176	44.69	4	4	9	0
G.P. Rees	Glamorgan	16	24	1	1028	154	44.69	3	4	13	0
S.D. Peters	Northamptonshire	14	25	1	1050	175	43.75	3	5	12	0
J.M. Kemp	Kent	14	21	3	780	183	43.33	2	2	30	0
T. Westley	Essex	6	11	2	383	132	42.55	1	1	3	0
G.M. Smith	Derbyshire	16	27	4	977	126	42.47	1	6	5	0
G.T. Park	Derbyshire	16	27	2	1059	178*	42.36	2	8	14	0
O.A. Shah	Middlesex	8	16	2	591	159	42.21	2	2	5	0
M.A. Butcher	Surrey	5	8	2	251	65	41.83	0	2	10	0
N.J. Dexter	Middlesex	10	19	2	709	146	41.70	2	2	15	0
J.L. Denly	Kent	9	14	1	542	123	41.69	3	1	5	0
D.I. Stevens	Kent	16	23	2	857	208	40.80	3	2	11	0
S.J. Adshead	Gloucestershire	7	10	1	367	156*	40.77	2	0	22	1
M.J. Powell	Glamorgan	16	24	1	933	108	40.56	2	7	7	0
N. Boje	Northamptonshire	15	25	5	801	98	40.05	0	8	7	0
M.L. Pettini	Essex	15	28	6	870	101*	39.54	1	4	10	0
R.A. White	Northamptonshire	16	29	4	986	193	39.44	1	7	11	0
J.S. Foster	Essex	15	24	1	905	103*	39.34	1	6	57	4
H.D. Ackerman	Leicestershire	11	20	1	741	180	39.00	1	4	5	0
C.D. Crowe	Leicestershire	2	4	2	76	41*	38.00	0	0	0	0
D.J. Pipe	Derbyshire	14	18	5	493	64*	37.92	0	3	36	2
S.A. Northeast	Kent	10	18	2	603	128*	37.68	1	2	10	0
M.P. O'Shea	Glamorgan	1	2	0	75	50	37.50	0	1	0	0
D.J. Malan	Middlesex	15	28	3	930	88	37.20	0	8	19	0
H.H. Gibbs	Glamorgan	5	7	0	259	96	37.00	0	2	7	0
M.J. Brown	Surrey	16	28	1	992	120	36.74	2	4	7	0
W.D. Parnell	Kent	5	6	1	183	90	36.60	0	2	0	0
T.P. Stayt	Gloucestershire	1	1	0	36	36	36.00	0	0	0	0
J.N. Batty	Surrey	16	26	0	935	120	35.96	2	1	46	4
C.P. Schofield	Surrey	14	21	3	644	144	35.77	1	3	7	0
P.A. Nixon	Leicestershire	9	17	2	531	173*	35.40	1	2	10	0
A.N. Cook	Essex	8	15	1	493	87	35.21	0	4	11	0
H.J.H. Marshall	Gloucestershire	16	26	2	844	158	35.16	1	5	13	0
W.W. Hinds	Derbyshire	16	26	2	841	148	35.04	2	2	7	0

A LAST ENGLISH SUMMER

		Mtchs	Inns	NO	Runs	Best	Avge	100	50	Ct	St
M.H. Wessels	Northamptonshire	14	23	0	804	109	34.95	1	6	25	1
G.R. Napier	Essex	10	16	6	348	64*	34.80	0	2	3	0
T.J. New	Leicestershire	16	27	4	800	85*	34.78	0	6	28	1
Kadeer Ali	Gloucestershire	16	28	4	834	90	34.75	0	4	10	0
M.J. Walker	Essex	16	29	2	933	150	34.55	2	2	12	0
S.D. Robson	Middlesex	7	13	0	441	110	33.92	1	2	12	0
R.D.B. Croft	Glamorgan	16	21	4	574	121	33.76	1	1	4	0
C.G. Taylor	Gloucestershire	15	22	1	705	111	33.57	1	5	11	0
N.R.D. Compton	Middlesex	14	28	2	860	178	33.07	2	3	8	0
J.K. Maunders	Essex	10	17	0	560	150	32.94	1	2	12	0
I.D. Hunter	Derbyshire	7	7	3	129	47	32.25	0	0	2	0
S.J. Walters	Surrey	11	18	0	573	188	31.83	2	1	15	0
G.K. Berg	Middlesex	13	23	2	668	98	31.80	0	7	9	0
G.P. Hodnett	Gloucestershire	1	1	0	31	31	31.00	0	0	0	0
J.B. Hockley	Kent	4	7	1	185	72	30.83	0	1	5	0
J.K.H. Naik	Leicestershire	5	8	2	184	109*	30.66	1	0	1	0
W.D. Bragg	Glamorgan	9	12	0	367	92	30.58	0	2	4	0
C.J. Jordan	Surrey	8	10	3	213	42	30.42	0	0	4	0
D.J. Redfern	Derbyshire	14	23	1	668	95	30.36	0	5	8	0
J.C. Tredwell	Kent	16	21	5	485	86*	30.31	0	4	12	0
S.D. Stubbings	Derbyshire	7	11	1	296	83	29.60	0	1	4	0
M.A. Wallace	Glamorgan	16	22	0	644	139	29.27	2	0	30	6
C.P. Murtagh	Surrey	2	2	1	29	15	29.00	0	0	2	0
G.G. White	Northamptonshire	1	2	1	29	29*	29.00	0	0	0	0
J.A. Simpson	Middlesex	3	6	0	170	87	28.33	0	1	5	0
J.G.E. Benning	Leicestershire	7	12	2	282	72	28.20	0	1	2	0
S.P. Crook	Northamptonshire	2	3	0	84	55	28.00	0	1	2	0
T.J. Phillips	Essex	3	4	0	111	69	27.75	0	1	2	0
Arun Harinath	Surrey	3	6	0	165	57	27.50	0	1	0	0
A.B. London	Middlesex	4	8	1	190	68	27.14	0	2	1	0
S.A. Newman	Surrey	5	8	0	217	124	27.12	1	0	2	0
S.C. Meaker	Surrey	5	9	1	214	72	26.75	0	2	0	0
M.N.W. Spriegel	Surrey	6	11	0	294	100	26.72	1	2	7	0
S.J. Cliff	Leicestershire	1	1	0	26	26	26.00	0	0	0	0
M.A.G. Boyce	Leicestershire	14	27	2	638	98	25.52	0	4	4	0
R.K.J. Dawson	Gloucestershire	7	10	0	254	50	25.40	0	1	12	0
J.J. van der Wath	Northamptonshire	13	19	1	452	85	25.11	0	3	4	0
A.J. Blake	Kent	4	5	0	125	47	25.00	0	0	1	0
M.A.K. Lawson	Derbyshire	6	5	2	75	24*	25.00	0	0	3	0
N.J. O'Brien	Northamptonshire	8	14	0	346	128	24.71	1	0	32	1
S.J. Cook	Kent	13	13	4	220	60*	24.44	0	1	0	0
E.J.G. Morgan	Middlesex	10	18	1	412	114*	24.23	1	1	12	0
M. Kartik	Middlesex	10	19	5	336	62*	24.00	0	2	11	0
A.G. Wakely	Northamptonshire	11	18	1	394	113*	23.17	1	1	9	0

Division One bowling

		Overs	Mdns	Runs	Wkts	Best	Avge	5w	10w
R.J. Woodman	Gloucestershire	5.0	4	8	1	1-4	8.00	0	0
Azhar Mahmood	Kent	130.3	38	382	21	5-39	18.19	1	0
J. Lewis	Gloucestershire	426.3	110	1146	57	5-73	20.10	1	0
D.S. Lucas	Northamptonshire	393.3	83	1224	58	7-24	21.10	3	1
S.P. Kirby	Gloucestershire	472.4	107	1420	64	5-44	22.18	1	0
H.J.H. Marshall	Gloucestershire	104.0	24	360	16	4-24	22.50	0	0
A.J. Hall	Northamptonshire	310.2	76	911	40	5-29	22.77	1	0
M. Kartik	Middlesex	317.1	103	755	33	5-65	22.87	1	0
Danish Kaneria	Essex	597.5	124	1777	75	8-116	23.69	6	2
J.J. van der Wath	Northamptonshire	364.3	75	1237	50	5-71	24.74	1	0
T.J. Murtagh	Middlesex	443.0	81	1521	60	7-82	25.35	3	0
A.N. Cook	Essex	10.0	0	51	2	1-3	25.50	0	0
I.E. O'Brien	Leicestershire	181.2	38	547	21	6-39	26.04	2	0
J.A. Brooks	Northamptonshire	50.0	5	184	7	4-76	26.28	0	0
M.J. Saggers	Kent	108.5	34	264	10	3-45	26.40	0	0
J.C. Tredwell	Kent	685.2	178	1837	69	8-66	26.62	4	2
D.D. Masters	Essex	557.2	184	1212	45	5-65	26.93	1	0
R.S. Ferley	Kent	75.0	15	189	7	3-73	27.00	0	0
T.D. Groenewald	Derbyshire	273.2	49	921	34	6-50	27.08	2	0
S.D. Udal	Middlesex	368.5	67	1007	37	6-36	27.21	2	1
A. Nel	Surrey	260.4	69	754	27	6-36	27.92	1	0
J. Allenby	Glamorgan	179.3	48	447	16	3-70	27.93	0	0
I.D. Hunter	Derbyshire	181.4	33	593	21	5-46	28.23	2	0
Murtaza Hussain	Surrey	80.0	18	232	8	4-70	29.00	0	0
J.E.C. Franklin	Gloucestershire	292.3	62	903	31	5-30	29.12	1	0
D.A. Cosker	Glamorgan	312.1	83	769	26	6-91	29.57	2	1
N. Boje	Northamptonshire	315.0	81	891	30	4-59	29.70	0	0
R.D.B. Croft	Glamorgan	719.5	153	1680	56	5-65	30.00	1	0
S.T. Finn	Middlesex	418.3	64	1624	53	5-57	30.64	1	0
S.J. Cook	Kent	374.1	88	1047	34	5-22	30.79	3	0
I.D. Saxelby	Gloucestershire	185.2	30	620	20	3-31	31.00	0	0
J.J. Cobb	Leicestershire	10.0	1	31	1	1-8	31.00	0	0
R.H. Joseph	Kent	97.2	9	373	12	6-55	31.08	1	0
W.D. Parnell	Kent	166.3	35	529	17	4-78	31.11	0	0
D.A. Burton	Middlesex	53.2	3	249	8	5-68	31.12	1	0
P.T. Collins	Surrey	137.2	25	504	16	5-75	31.50	1	0
A.J. Ireland	Gloucestershire	167.0	34	664	21	6-31	31.61	1	0
V. Banerjee	Gloucestershire	200.3	38	667	21	4-58	31.76	0	0
A. Khan	Kent	339.1	65	1146	36	5-113	31.83	1	0
R. McLaren	Kent	164.5	37	608	19	4-51	32.00	0	0
A.J. Shantry	Glamorgan	267.3	46	866	27	5-62	32.07	1	0
S.P. Crook	Northamptonshire	48.0	8	193	6	5-71	32.16	1	0
G.M. Smith	Derbyshire	330.2	64	1098	32	5-65	34.31	1	0
G.R. Napier	Essex	271.2	55	1005	29	4-32	34.65	0	0
J.A.R. Harris	Glamorgan	425.2	83	1441	41	4-69	35.14	0	0
J.W.M. Dalrymple	Glamorgan	225.0	27	709	20	3-11	35.45	0	0
P.S. Jones	Derbyshire	398.0	84	1210	34	5-35	35.58	1	0
D.H. Wigley	Northamptonshire	284.1	54	1090	30	6-72	36.33	2	0
A.P. Palladino	Essex	82.0	19	258	7	4-68	36.85	0	0
M.J. Cosgrove	Glamorgan	51.0	7	188	5	3-30	37.60	0	0
G.G. Wagg	Derbyshire	521.3	85	1773	47	6-35	37.72	3	0
J.D. Middlebrook	Essex	99.0	16	345	9	3-87	38.33	0	0
C.J.C. Wright	Essex	437.1	67	1538	40	4-43	38.45	0	0
T.P. Stayt	Gloucestershire	34.0	7	77	2	1-19	38.50	0	0
G.K. Berg	Middlesex	249.1	46	886	23	5-55	38.52	2	0
D.S. Harrison	Glamorgan	198.1	29	732	19	4-60	38.52	0	0

A LAST ENGLISH SUMMER

		Overs	Mdns	Runs	Wkts	Best	Avge	5w	10w
C.P. Ashling	Glamorgan	28.0	3	116	3	2-66	38.66	0	0
J.W. Dernbach	Surrey	395.1	68	1436	37	6-47	38.81	2	0
L.M. Daggett	Northamptonshire	88.0	15	311	8	3-39	38.87	0	0
G.J.P. Kruger	Glamorgan	353.4	59	1283	33	6-93	38.87	1	0
S.J. King	Surrey	39.3	2	156	4	3-61	39.00	0	0
C.G. Taylor	Gloucestershire	86.2	23	242	6	1-6	40.33	0	0
W.A. White	Leicestershire	170.3	18	728	18	3-91	40.44	0	0
A.P.R. Gidman	Gloucestershire	59.1	13	162	4	3-23	40.50	0	0
J.L. Clare	Derbyshire	119.0	27	407	10	3-64	40.70	0	0
G.P. Hodnett	Gloucestershire	6.0	0	41	1	1-41	41.00	0	0
A.J. Harris	Leicestershire	395.1	79	1439	35	5-26	41.11	1	0

Friends Provident Trophy

Group A

	P	W	L	D	T	NR	RR	Points
Hampshire	8	5	2	0	0	1	0.34	11
Nottinghamshire	8	5	3	0	0	0	0.42	10
Worcestershire	8	4	3	0	0	1	0.29	9
Leicestershire	8	2	4	0	0	2	-0.64	6
Ireland	8	1	5	0	0	2	-0.75	4

Group B

	P	W	L	D	T	NR	RR	Points
Somerset	8	7	0	0	0	1	2.0	15
Middlesex	8	4	4	0	0	0	0.14	8
Warwickshire	8	3	3	0	1	1	0.46	8
Kent	8	3	4	0	1	0	-0.4	7
Scotland	8	1	7	0	0	0	-1.78	2

Group C

	P	W	L	D	T	NR	RR	Points
Gloucestershire	8	5	2	0	0	1	0.45	11
Sussex	8	4	3	0	0	1	1.52	9
Yorkshire	8	4	4	0	0	0	-0.15	8
Durham	8	3	5	0	0	0	-0.63	6
Surrey	8	3	5	0	0	0	0.3	6

Group D

	P	W	L	D	T	NR	RR	Points
Lancashire	8	6	2	0	0	0	0.63	12
Essex	8	5	2	0	0	1	0.41	11
Derbyshire	8	3	4	0	0	1	-0.29	7
Glamorgan	8	2	5	0	0	1	-0.77	5
Northamptonshire	8	1	4	0	0	3	0.16	5

Quarter-finals:

Hampshire v Middlesex at the Rose Bowl
Hampshire won by 44 runs

Lancashire v Essex at Old Trafford
Lancashire   won by 67 runs

Somerset v Sussex at Taunton
Sussex won by 6 wickets

Gloucestershire v Notts at Bristol
Gloucestershire won by 6 wickets

Semi-finals

Lancashire v Hampshire at Old Trafford
Lancashire won by 64 runs

Sussex v Gloucestershire at Hove
Sussex won by 34 runs

Final

Lancashire v Hampshire at Old Trafford
Lancashire won by 64 runs

A LAST ENGLISH SUMMER

Batting averages

		Mtchs	Inns	NO	Runs	Best	Avge	100	50	Ct	St
G.L. Brophy	Yorkshire	3	3	2	156	68*	156.00	0	2	7	1
N. Pothas	Hampshire	5	3	2	103	57*	103.00	0	1	2	2
F. du Plessis	Lancashire	9	7	3	407	113*	101.75	2	2	5	0
Z. de Bruyn	Somerset	9	6	2	388	96	97.00	0	5	3	0
J.H.K. Adams	Hampshire	3	3	1	194	76	97.00	0	2	1	0
K.H.D. Barker	Warwickshire	6	4	3	83	30*	83.00	0	0	1	0
M.R. Ramprakash	Surrey	6	6	1	373	121	74.60	3	0	3	0
M.A. Carberry	Hampshire	8	7	3	295	121*	73.75	1	0	5	0
S.J. Walters	Surrey	2	2	0	134	85	67.00	0	1	1	0
J.S. Foster	Essex	9	5	3	133	71	66.50	0	1	11	5
S.A. Newman	Surrey	7	7	0	463	177	66.14	2	2	1	0
C. Kieswetter	Somerset	8	8	2	395	138*	65.83	2	0	4	2
I.R. Bell	Warwickshire	7	6	2	260	108	65.00	1	2	4	0
J.L. Langer	Somerset	8	4	1	195	78*	65.00	0	2	5	0
M.J. Chilton	Lancashire	9	9	3	386	101*	64.33	1	1	2	0
H.D. Ackerman	Leicestershire	5	5	1	243	118*	60.75	1	1	0	0
M.E. Trescothick	Somerset	9	9	1	476	144	59.50	1	4	6	0
M.H. Yardy	Sussex	8	6	1	296	68	59.20	0	4	1	0
N.R.D. Compton	Middlesex	5	5	1	236	131	59.00	1	0	2	0
C.J. Borgas	Scotland	7	6	1	289	78*	57.80	0	3	0	0
V. Chopra	Essex	9	8	0	460	99	57.50	0	5	4	0
M.W. Goodwin	Sussex	8	7	1	345	144	57.50	1	1	2	0
P.D. Trego	Somerset	9	6	3	171	74*	57.00	0	2	1	0
C.M. Spearman	Gloucestershire	8	8	2	337	92	56.16	0	4	3	0
E.C. Joyce	Sussex	9	8	1	385	127	55.00	2	1	2	0
S.J. Adshead	Gloucestershire	9	7	2	268	87	53.60	0	3	9	2
C.C. Benham	Hampshire	8	6	1	267	108*	53.40	1	1	8	0
J.W.A. Taylor	Leicestershire	7	6	1	260	101	52.00	1	0	0	0
J.L. Denly	Kent	8	8	1	363	115	51.85	1	1	3	0
G.W. Flower	Essex	9	8	4	207	54	51.75	0	1	3	0
P.J. Horton	Lancashire	8	8	1	351	111*	50.14	2	0	4	0
C.G. Taylor	Gloucestershire	9	9	2	339	71	48.42	0	3	5	0
S.D. Robson	Middlesex	1	1	0	48	48	48.00	0	0	0	0
S.M. Ervine	Hampshire	8	7	1	288	167*	48.00	1	0	4	0
J.E.C. Franklin	Gloucestershire	6	5	1	190	85	47.50	0	2	1	0
N.M. Carter	Warwickshire	5	5	0	237	68	47.40	0	3	0	0
T. Frost	Warwickshire	2	2	1	47	28	47.00	0	0	1	0
J.W.M. Dalrymple	Glamorgan	7	6	2	187	78*	46.75	0	2	1	0
M.P. Vaughan	Yorkshire	6	6	0	280	82	46.66	0	3	1	0
L.D. Sutton	Lancashire	9	5	3	93	31*	46.50	0	0	11	2
D.M. Benkenstein	Durham	8	8	2	277	77*	46.16	0	2	3	0
L.M. Daggett	Northamptonshire	6	5	4	46	14*	46.00	0	0	0	0
J.O. Troughton	Warwickshire	8	6	0	275	77	45.83	0	4	1	0
M.J. Walker	Essex	9	8	3	229	69*	45.80	0	1	2	0
M.J. Lumb	Hampshire	8	8	1	317	100	45.28	1	3	5	0
S.M. Davies	Worcestershire	8	8	1	315	82*	45.00	0	3	2	6
C.J.L. Rogers	Derbyshire	4	4	0	180	68	45.00	0	2	3	0
S.G. Law	Derbyshire	6	6	1	222	95	44.40	0	2	1	0
K.J. O'Brien	Ireland	6	6	1	220	94	44.00	0	2	2	0
N.J. Dexter	Middlesex	9	9	3	259	79	43.16	0	3	4	0
A.G. Botha	Warwickshire	7	5	3	86	37*	43.00	0	0	4	0
D.J. Wainwright	Yorkshire	4	3	2	43	15*	43.00	0	0	4	0
S.P. Crook	Northamptonshire	3	3	0	128	72	42.66	0	1	0	0
J.M. Kemp	Kent	6	6	2	170	69	42.50	0	1	2	0
G.T. Park	Derbyshire	7	6	2	169	43*	42.25	0	0	2	0
H.H. Dippenaar	Leicestershire	7	6	1	211	65	42.20	0	2	0	0

STATISTICS OF SUMMER

		Mtchs	Inns	NO	Runs	Best	Avge	100	50	Ct	St
G.M. Hamilton	Scotland	8	8	1	295	75	42.14	0	3	3	0
E.J.G. Morgan	Middlesex	8	8	0	337	161	42.12	1	2	1	0
W.T.S. Porterfield	Gloucestershire	8	8	0	334	74	41.75	0	2	6	0
P.J. Franks	Nottinghamshire	7	5	2	125	50	41.66	0	1	0	0
B.J.M. Scott	Middlesex	9	8	6	83	29*	41.50	0	0	8	2
M.M. Ali	Worcestershire	8	6	0	249	125	41.50	1	1	3	0
B.J. Wright	Glamorgan	7	6	2	161	65	40.25	0	1	2	0
T.C. Smith	Lancashire	8	8	1	281	87*	40.14	0	3	4	0
A.N. Cook	Essex	2	2	0	77	65	38.50	0	1	1	0
P.J. Hughes	Middlesex	8	8	0	308	119	38.50	1	2	1	0
I.J.L. Trott	Warwickshire	8	7	0	269	120	38.42	1	1	4	0
M.A. Ealham	Nottinghamshire	7	5	2	115	42*	38.33	0	0	1	0
K.J. Coetzer	Durham	4	4	0	153	61	38.25	0	1	0	0
R.M. Pyrah	Yorkshire	8	7	3	153	67	38.25	0	1	2	0
C.B. Keegan	Sussex	1	1	0	38	38	38.00	0	0	1	0
G.P. Rees	Glamorgan	5	5	1	151	123*	37.75	1	0	0	0
O.A. Shah	Middlesex	5	5	0	188	82	37.60	0	2	2	0
N. Boje	Northamptonshire	6	6	1	188	56	37.60	0	2	1	0
W.W. Hinds	Derbyshire	7	7	0	263	95	37.57	0	3	1	0
P. Mustard	Durham	7	7	0	259	92	37.00	0	3	6	1
A. Lyth	Yorkshire	3	3	0	110	83	36.66	0	1	0	0
M. van Jaarsveld	Kent	8	8	1	252	132*	36.00	1	0	4	0
M.H. Wessels	Northamptonshire	6	6	0	213	57	35.50	0	1	4	0
B.F. Smith	Worcestershire	7	5	0	177	70	35.40	0	2	4	0
J.C. Hildreth	Somerset	9	9	0	313	151	34.77	1	1	0	0
J.P. Crawley	Hampshire	5	5	0	169	100	33.80	1	0	3	0
A.V. Suppiah	Somerset	9	5	2	101	48	33.66	0	0	3	0
W.I. Jefferson	Nottinghamshire	8	7	1	202	93	33.66	0	2	1	0
M.A. Wagh	Nottinghamshire	9	9	1	266	85	33.25	0	3	2	0
C.D. Crowe	Leicestershire	5	2	1	33	20	33.00	0	0	3	0
J.A. Rudolph	Yorkshire	8	8	0	264	118	33.00	1	1	7	0
C.D. Nash	Sussex	3	3	0	96	41	32.00	0	0	2	0
M.J. Brown	Surrey	8	8	0	252	66	31.50	0	1	1	0
M.A.G. Boyce	Leicestershire	6	6	0	187	80	31.16	0	1	1	0
V.S. Solanki	Worcestershire	8	8	2	187	49*	31.16	0	0	3	0
G.O. Jones	Kent	8	8	2	187	57	31.16	0	1	7	1
A.C. Thomas	Somerset	9	3	2	31	28*	31.00	0	0	2	0
S.D. Parry	Lancashire	2	1	0	31	31	31.00	0	0	0	0
P.R. Stirling	Ireland	6	6	0	180	80	30.00	0	2	2	0
A.C. Voges	Nottinghamshire	9	8	2	180	48	30.00	0	0	2	0
G.M. Smith	Derbyshire	7	7	2	148	43	29.60	0	0	6	0
M.P. O'Shea	Glamorgan	2	2	0	59	49	29.50	0	0	0	0
L.A. Dawson	Hampshire	8	6	2	117	51*	29.25	0	1	6	0
D.O. Brown	Gloucestershire	3	2	1	29	19*	29.00	0	0	2	0
G.R. Napier	Essex	8	6	1	144	42	28.80	0	0	1	0
W.K. McCallan	Ireland	6	5	1	114	40	28.50	0	0	1	0
M.N.W. Spriegel	Surrey	7	7	1	170	64	28.33	0	2	5	0
M.J. Cosgrove	Glamorgan	6	6	0	170	72	28.33	0	2	1	0
R.E. Watkins	Glamorgan	1	1	0	28	28	28.00	0	0	1	0
R.A.White	Northamptonshire	6	6	0	166	51	27.66	0	1	2	0
S.D. Stubbings	Derbyshire	3	3	0	83	50	27.66	0	1	0	0
D.K.H. Mitchell	Worcestershire	8	6	1	138	59	27.60	0	1	1	0
A.R. Cusack	Ireland	3	3	1	55	41	27.50	0	0	1	0
D.I. Stevens	Kent	3	3	1	55	37*	27.50	0	0	1	0
W.R. Smith	Durham	8	8	0	220	77	27.50	0	2	2	0
B.C. Brown	Sussex	7	3	2	27	18*	27.00	0	0	5	1

A LAST ENGLISH SUMMER

		Mtchs	Inns	NO	Runs	Best	Avge	100	50	Ct	St
L.J. Wright	Sussex	6	5	0	134	46	26.80	0	0	2	0
P.A. Nixon	Leicestershire	6	4	1	80	50	26.66	0	1	2	1
M.J. Prior	Sussex	2	2	0	53	50	26.50	0	1	2	0
A.D. Hales	Nottinghamshire	8	8	0	212	106	26.50	1	1	2	0
R.R. Watson	Scotland	8	8	1	183	67	26.14	0	1	3	0
R.N. ten Doeschate	Essex	9	3	1	52	41	26.00	0	0	1	0
I.D. Blackwell	Durham	8	8	0	204	64	25.50	0	2	3	0
T.G. Burrows	Hampshire	3	1	0	25	25	25.00	0	0	3	0
F.D. Telo	Derbyshire	1	1	0	25	25	25.00	0	0	0	0
M.A.G. Nelson	Northamptonshire	4	4	0	100	74	25.00	0	1	0	0
S.D. Udal	Middlesex	8	7	1	148	79*	24.66	0	1	4	0
Naved ul-Hasan	Yorkshire	6	6	1	121	53*	24.20	0	1	4	0
W.A. White	Leicestershire	7	4	2	48	27	24.00	0	0	2	0
A.G. Wakely	Northamptonshire	3	2	0	48	32	24.00	0	0	0	0
G. Chapple	Lancashire	6	3	2	24	18*	24.00	0	0	3	0
J.S. Gatting	Sussex	9	8	0	192	50	24.00	0	1	2	0
G.R. Breese	Durham	8	7	1	143	47	23.83	0	0	1	0
A. McGrath	Yorkshire	8	8	0	189	67	23.62	0	2	1	0
J.E.R. Gallian	Essex	3	3	0	70	38	23.33	0	0	0	0
A.J. Hall	Northamptonshire	6	6	1	116	81	23.20	0	1	1	0
T.L. Maynard	Glamorgan	6	6	1	116	59*	23.20	0	1	4	0
R.J. Hamilton-Brown	Sussex	9	7	1	139	43	23.16	0	0	2	0
R.D. Berrington	Scotland	2	1	0	23	23	23.00	0	0	1	0
G.M. Andrew	Worcestershire	5	3	2	23	23*	23.00	0	0	0	0
B.A. Godleman	Middlesex	6	6	0	137	82	22.83	0	1	1	0
A.R. White	Ireland	6	6	2	91	50*	22.75	0	1	3	0
A. Shahzad	Yorkshire	4	4	1	66	43*	22.00	0	0	2	0
U. Afzaal	Surrey	8	8	0	175	58	21.87	0	1	3	0
Danish Kaneria	Essex	8	2	0	43	23	21.50	0	0	0	0
H.J.H. Marshall	Gloucestershire	9	9	0	193	56	21.44	0	1	5	0
G.G. Wagg	Derbyshire	7	7	3	85	21	21.25	0	0	2	0
N.J. O'Brien	Northamptonshire	5	5	0	106	45	21.20	0	0	4	0
A.G. Prince	Lancashire	9	9	0	190	78	21.11	0	1	2	0
C.P. Schofield	Surrey	8	7	3	84	31	21.00	0	0	3	0
M.J. Di Venuto	Durham	4	4	0	84	29	21.00	0	0	0	0
S.R. Patel	Nottinghamshire	9	9	2	145	48*	20.71	0	0	4	0
W.R.S. Gidman	Durham	5	3	1	41	18*	20.50	0	0	1	0
D.C. Nash	Middlesex	1	1	0	20	20	20.00	0	0	1	0
M.A. Wallace	Glamorgan	7	6	1	100	60	20.00	0	1	6	3
D.T. Johnston	Ireland	2	2	0	40	39	20.00	0	0	0	0
J.B. Hockley	Kent	7	7	1	120	50	20.00	0	1	1	0
A.A. Noffke	Worcestershire	6	4	0	79	29	19.75	0	0	1	0
D.F. Watts	Scotland	6	6	0	116	45	19.33	0	0	3	0
S.D. Snell	Gloucestershire	1	1	0	19	19	19.00	0	0	1	0
D.J. Redfern	Derbyshire	7	7	0	130	53	18.57	0	1	4	0
I.D. Fisher	Worcestershire	7	4	2	37	31*	18.50	0	0	1	0
J.J. Sayers	Yorkshire	6	6	0	111	51	18.50	0	1	1	0
T.R. Ambrose	Warwickshire	7	6	1	91	36*	18.20	0	0	12	2
A.D. Mascarenhas	Hampshire	3	1	0	18	18	18.00	0	0	2	0
D.A. Cosker	Glamorgan	7	5	1	72	50*	18.00	0	1	2	0
A.D. Brown	Nottinghamshire	9	9	0	161	89	17.88	0	1	2	0
S.J. Croft	Lancashire	9	7	2	89	35*	17.80	0	0	7	0
C.M. Wright	Scotland	2	2	0	35	28	17.50	0	0	0	0
W.D. Parnell	Kent	6	3	0	51	22	17.00	0	0	4	0
G.K. Berg	Middlesex	7	6	0	102	33	17.00	0	0	2	0
I.J. Westwood	Warwickshire	7	6	1	85	33	17.00	0	0	0	0

STATISTICS OF SUMMER

		Mtchs	Inns	NO	Runs	Best	Avge	100	50	Ct	St
M.L. Pettini	Essex	9	8	0	131	57	16.37	0	1	3	0
A.R. Adams	Nottinghamshire	8	5	1	65	30	16.25	0	0	1	0
M.J. Powell	Glamorgan	7	7	0	113	33	16.14	0	0	1	0
A.P.R. Gidman	Gloucestershire	8	8	0	129	43	16.12	0	0	1	0
J.P. Bray	Ireland	5	5	0	80	41	16.00	0	0	3	0
Y. Arafat	Sussex	6	4	1	47	24*	15.66	0	0	3	0
Azhar Mahmood	Kent	7	5	1	62	25	15.50	0	0	2	0
R.S.C. Martin-Jenkins	Sussex	8	5	3	30	19*	15.00	0	0	1	0
G.D. Elliott	Surrey	8	8	1	105	30*	15.00	0	0	5	0
J.J. van der Wath	Northamptonshire	1	1	0	15	15	15.00	0	0	0	0
C.M. Willougby	Somerset	2	1	0	15	15	15.00	0	0	0	0
R.D.B. Croft	Glamorgan	1	1	0	15	15	15.00	0	0	0	0
C.R. Woakes	Warwickshire	7	2	0	30	25	15.00	0	0	2	0
R.W.T. Key	Kent	8	8	0	119	27	14.87	0	0	3	0
C.M.W. Read	Nottinghamshire	8	6	0	89	57	14.83	0	1	5	3
S.C. Moore	Worcestershire	8	7	1	85	51	14.16	0	1	3	0
C.D. Whelan	Worcestershire	7	3	2	14	10*	14.00	0	0	3	0
G.J. Muchall	Durham	7	7	0	98	31	14.00	0	0	1	0
A.W. Gale	Yorkshire	5	5	0	69	33	13.80	0	0	0	0
L.E. Plunkett	Durham	8	7	1	82	30	13.66	0	0	3	0
Kadeer Ali	Gloucestershire	6	6	0	80	63	13.33	0	1	4	0
R.A.G. Cummins	Northamptonshire	2	2	1	13	12*	13.00	0	0	0	0
F.T. McAllister	Ireland	2	2	1	13	13*	13.00	0	0	3	0
D.J. Pipe	Derbyshire	7	7	0	91	27	13.00	0	0	6	0
J. Lewis	Gloucestershire	9	7	1	77	32	12.83	0	0	4	0
G.J. Batty	Worcestershire	8	6	0	77	31	12.83	0	0	2	0
D.J. Malan	Middlesex	8	8	1	89	43	12.71	0	0	4	0
A.U. Rashid	Yorkshire	7	6	1	63	35*	12.60	0	0	2	0
C.D. Thorp	Durham	3	3	1	25	20*	12.50	0	0	1	0
J.F. Mooney	Ireland	4	4	0	49	22	12.25	0	0	3	0
G.C. Wilson	Surrey	8	8	2	73	34	12.16	0	0	9	3
M.A. Parker	Scotland	3	3	2	12	8	12.00	0	0	0	0
B.J. Phillips	Somerset	8	3	0	36	24	12.00	0	0	1	0
S.J.S. Smith	Scotland	7	6	1	59	23*	11.80	0	0	3	4
R. Strydom	Ireland	5	4	0	47	27	11.75	0	0	0	0
D.S. Lucas	Northamptonshire	5	4	1	35	32*	11.66	0	0	1	0
N.F.I. McCallum	Scotland	8	7	0	81	50	11.57	0	1	2	0
B.A. Stokes	Durham	2	2	1	11	11*	11.00	0	0	1	0
O.A.C. Banks	Somerset	8	3	1	22	21	11.00	0	0	2	0
S.I. Mahmood	Lancashire	9	2	0	22	15	11.00	0	0	4	0
R. Clarke	Warwickshire	6	3	0	33	16	11.00	0	0	3	0
M.J. Saggers	Kent	1	1	0	11	11	11.00	0	0	0	0
C.E.W. Silverwood	Middlesex	9	4	0	44	26	11.00	0	0	2	0
Kabir Ali	Worcestershire	1	1	0	11	11	11.00	0	0	0	0
M.E. Claydon	Durham	7	4	0	43	19	10.75	0	0	0	0
A.D. Poynter	Ireland	5	5	0	53	29	10.60	0	0	2	0
A. Nel	Surrey	6	4	2	21	8	10.50	0	0	0	0
R.M. West	Ireland	6	5	2	31	17	10.33	0	0	1	0
D.G. Cork	Hampshire	8	3	1	20	16*	10.00	0	0	3	0
C.D. Hopkinson	Sussex	1	1	0	10	10	10.00	0	0	0	0
C.J.O. Smith	Scotland	1	1	0	10	10	10.00	0	0	1	0
S.J. Cook	Kent	5	3	1	20	9*	10.00	0	0	1	0
B.M. Shafayat	Nottinghamshire	1	1	0	10	10	10.00	0	0	3	1
J.H. Stander	Scotland	8	7	0	69	27	9.85	0	0	2	0
K.W. Hogg	Lancashire	9	4	0	38	20	9.50	0	0	2	0
J. Allenby	Leicestershire	4	3	1	19	13	9.50	0	0	0	0

A LAST ENGLISH SUMMER

		Mtchs	Inns	NO	Runs	Best	Avge	100	50	Ct	St
M.S. Panesar	Northamptonshire	5	4	1	28	17	9.33	0	0	1	0
W.B. Rankin	Warwickshire	5	1	0	9	9	9.00	0	0	1	0
W.A.T. Beer	Sussex	9	3	0	27	14	9.00	0	0	4	0
A.J. Hodd	Sussex	1	1	0	9	9	9.00	0	0	0	0
P. Connell	Ireland	5	4	3	9	6*	9.00	0	0	0	0
N.S. Poonia	Scotland	1	1	0	9	9	9.00	0	0	0	0
D.G. Wright	Sussex	3	2	0	18	13	9.00	0	0	0	0
S.T. Finn	Middlesex	8	4	1	26	13	8.66	0	0	0	0
L.J. Fletcher	Nottinghamshire	7	4	2	17	7	8.50	0	0	0	0
J.J. Cobb	Leicestershire	4	2	0	17	13	8.50	0	0	0	0
I.E. O'Brien	Leicestershire	4	1	0	8	8	8.00	0	0	1	0
I.D. Hunter	Derbyshire	4	3	1	15	15	7.50	0	0	0	0
G.A. Rogers	Scotland	6	6	1	37	13	7.40	0	0	0	0
S.M. Guy	Yorkshire	5	4	1	22	22	7.33	0	0	9	3
A.J. Harris	Leicestershire	4	2	1	7	5*	7.00	0	0	0	0
J.G.E. Benning	Surrey	1	1	0	7	7	7.00	0	0	0	0
J.A.R. Harris	Glamorgan	7	5	0	35	21	7.00	0	0	1	0
D.J. Willey	Northamptonshire	6	5	0	32	19	6.40	0	0	2	0
G.J. Kruis	Yorkshire	8	4	1	19	11	6.33	0	0	1	0
R.J. Sidebottom	Nottinghamshire	4	3	1	12	8*	6.00	0	0	0	0
M.S. Mason	Worcestershire	5	3	1	12	9	6.00	0	0	1	0
D.S. Harrison	Glamorgan	6	4	1	17	17	5.66	0	0	1	0
R.S. Ferley	Kent	5	3	0	17	7	5.66	0	0	0	0
J.C. Tredwell	Kent	8	5	0	27	18	5.40	0	0	0	0
S.D. Weeraratna	Scotland	6	4	1	15	8	5.00	0	0	1	0
J.F. Brown	Nottinghamshire	2	2	1	5	5	5.00	0	0	0	0
C.J. Jordan	Surrey	2	1	0	5	5	5.00	0	0	1	0
S.J. Cliff	Leicestershire	3	2	0	10	9	5.00	0	0	0	0
M.M. Iqbal	Scotland	1	1	0	5	5	5.00	0	0	1	0
J.N. Batty	Surrey	2	2	0	9	9	4.50	0	0	3	0
J.D. Middlebrook	Essex	5	1	0	4	4	4.00	0	0	0	0
D.R. Briggs	Hampshire	2	1	0	4	4	4.00	0	0	0	0
G. Onions	Durham	1	1	0	4	4	4.00	0	0	1	0
V. Banerjee	Gloucestershire	9	5	2	11	6	3.66	0	0	4	0
J.D. Nel	Scotland	8	5	1	13	7	3.25	0	0	0	0
G.D. Drummond	Scotland	3	3	1	6	5	3.00	0	0	0	0
R.M. Haq	Scotland	2	1	0	3	3	3.00	0	0	0	0
T.D. Groenewald	Derbyshire	7	6	1	15	5*	3.00	0	0	0	0
C.W. Henderson	Leicestershire	4	2	1	3	2	3.00	0	0	1	0
A.J. Tudor	Surrey	3	2	0	6	6	3.00	0	0	2	0
A.J. Ireland	Gloucestershire	5	3	1	5	5*	2.50	0	0	1	0
R.S. Bopara	Essex	1	1	0	2	2	2.00	0	0	0	0
S.A. Piolet	Warwickshire	3	1	0	2	2	2.00	0	0	2	0
D.J. Balcombe	Hampshire	2	1	0	2	2	2.00	0	0	0	0
P.T. Collins	Surrey	5	1	0	2	2	2.00	0	0	0	0
S.D. Peters	Northamptonshire	2	2	0	2	1	1.00	0	0	1	0
C.J.C. Wright	Essex	8	2	0	2	2	1.00	0	0	1	0
J. du Toit	Leicestershire	2	2	0	2	1	1.00	0	0	1	0
T.T. Bresnan	Yorkshire	2	2	0	2	2	1.00	0	0	0	0
G.J.P. Kruger	Glamorgan	4	2	1	1	1	1.00	0	0	1	0
T.P. Stayt	Gloucestershire	3	3	1	1	1	0.50	0	0	1	0

STATISTICS OF SUMMER

Bowling averages

		Overs	Mdns	Runs	Wkts	Best	Avge	5w	10w
G.P. Swann	Nottinghamshire	8.3	1	24	3	3-24	8.00	0	0
N.R.D. Compton	Middlesex	1.1	0	8	1	1-0	8.00	0	0
V.S. Solanki	Worcestershire	1.0	0	9	1	1-9	9.00	0	0
T.T. Bresnan	Yorkshire	17.0	3	63	7	4-35	9.00	0	0
N. Killeen	Durham	10.0	0	48	5	5-48	9.60	1	0
I.D. Saxelby	Gloucestershire	15.2	1	60	5	4-31	12.00	0	0
L. Evans	Durham	4.0	0	13	1	1-13	13.00	0	0
D.J. Pattinson	Nottinghamshire	9.0	1	45	3	2-19	15.00	0	0
C.P. Schofield	Surrey	73.0	2	307	20	5-32	15.35	1	0
C.D. Whelan	Worcestershire	31.5	0	156	10	4-27	15.60	0	0
A.D. Mascarenhas	Hampshire	28.0	2	128	8	4-39	16.00	0	0
R.M. Haq	Scotland	14.0	1	50	3	2-37	16.66	0	0
J.M. Anderson	Lancashire	6.0	0	17	1	1-17	17.00	0	0
J.E.C. Franklin	Gloucestershire	44.3	3	188	11	3-18	17.09	0	0
O.J. Newby	Lancashire	14.0	1	86	5	4-41	17.20	0	0
D.T. Johnston	Ireland	13.3	1	35	2	2-5	17.50	0	0
P.S. Jones	Kent	9.0	0	35	2	1-9	17.50	0	0
C.D. Nash	Sussex	20.3	1	106	6	4-40	17.66	0	0
S.R. Patel	Nottinghamshire	63.0	3	249	14	6-13	17.78	1	0
B.A. Stokes	Durham	6.0	0	36	2	2-22	18.00	0	0
A.C. Thomas	Somerset	67.0	1	361	20	4-22	18.05	0	0
D.G. Cork	Hampshire	71.4	5	292	16	4-18	18.25	0	0
U. Afzaal	Surrey	21.3	0	111	6	2-2	18.50	0	0
M.P. O'Shea	Glamorgan	3.0	0	19	1	1-19	19.00	0	0
A. Richardson	Middlesex	6.0	0	19	1	1-19	19.00	0	0
S.J. Cook	Kent	38.0	2	154	8	4-37	19.25	0	0
G.J. Kruis	Yorkshire	68.1	8	253	13	3-24	19.46	0	0
D.D. Masters	Essex	79.0	16	256	13	3-19	19.69	0	0
A.A. Noffke	Worcestershire	40.0	2	140	7	3-37	20.00	0	0
P. Connell	Ireland	39.0	4	241	12	5-19	20.08	1	0
G.J. Batty	Worcestershire	62.0	4	225	11	5-35	20.45	1	0
A.G. Botha	Warwickshire	47.5	1	225	11	3-27	20.45	0	0
M.S. Mason	Worcestershire	39.0	2	123	6	2-23	20.50	0	0
P.D. Trego	Somerset	69.2	4	374	18	4-17	20.77	0	0
J. Lewis	Gloucestershire	69.0	7	313	15	4-34	20.86	0	0
Z. de Bruyn	Somerset	43.0	3	190	9	3-24	21.11	0	0
B.V. Taylor	Hampshire	73.2	1	342	16	3-37	21.37	0	0
G.M. Smith	Derbyshire	54.0	1	279	13	4-53	21.46	0	0
M.A. Carberry	Hampshire	12.0	1	45	2	2-11	22.50	0	0
Imran Tahir	Hampshire	30.0	1	113	5	2-36	22.60	0	0
S.P. Kirby	Gloucestershire	35.2	3	136	6	3-33	22.66	0	0
G. Chapple	Lancashire	52.0	8	204	9	2-16	22.66	0	0
R.M. Pyrah	Yorkshire	71.0	3	387	17	4-54	22.76	0	0
Danish Kaneria	Essex	67.1	4	296	13	5-32	22.76	1	0
S.I. Mahmood	Lancashire	75.5	7	322	14	3-17	23.00	0	0
L.M. Daggett	Northamptonshire	40.0	1	185	8	4-51	23.12	0	0
V. Banerjee	Gloucestershire	75.0	2	335	14	3-47	23.92	0	0
W.K. McCallan	Ireland	39.0	0	192	8	3-26	24.00	0	0
D.J. Malan	Middlesex	26.3	1	145	6	2-4	24.16	0	0
Y. Arafat	Sussex	56.0	5	291	12	3-44	24.25	0	0
G. Keedy	Lancashire	71.0	1	317	13	4-43	24.38	0	0
W.B. Rankin	Warwickshire	29.0	4	149	6	2-18	24.83	0	0
J.W. Dernbach	Surrey	21.2	2	125	5	3-23	25.00	0	0
D.S. Lucas	Northamptonshire	27.3	0	125	5	2-39	25.00	0	0
G.W. Flower	Essex	31.0	0	130	5	2-9	26.00	0	0
D.J. Willey	Northamptonshire	12.0	0	78	3	2-44	26.00	0	0

A LAST ENGLISH SUMMER

		Overs	Mdns	Runs	Wkts	Best	Avge	5w	10w
C.M. Wright	Scotland	20.0	0	53	2	2-28	26.50	0	0
C.B. Keegan	Sussex	7.0	0	53	2	2-53	26.50	0	0
D.G. Wright	Sussex	22.0	3	80	3	2-24	26.66	0	0
S.D. Udal	Middlesex	62.0	3	267	10	3-32	26.70	0	0
D.J. Wainwright	Yorkshire	37.0	2	161	6	3-33	26.83	0	0
A.R. Cusack	Ireland	21.0	3	108	4	2-9	27.00	0	0
N.M. Carter	Warwickshire	43.3	2	190	7	3-40	27.14	0	0
D.S. Harrison	Glamorgan	49.0	2	272	10	3-31	27.20	0	0
J. Allenby	Leicestershire	16.2	0	82	3	2-49	27.33	0	0
M.A. Ealham	Nottinghamshire	46.0	4	196	7	4-40	28.00	0	0
D.K.H. Mitchell	Worcestershire	30.5	0	168	6	2-7	28.00	0	0
S.A. Piolet	Warwickshire	25.0	2	112	4	3-53	28.00	0	0
S.D. Parry	Lancashire	17.0	1	56	2	1-17	28.00	0	0
I.D. Blackwell	Durham	76.2	2	337	12	3-26	28.08	0	0
C.W. Henderson	Leicestershire	28.0	0	113	4	3-44	28.25	0	0
T.C. Smith	Lancashire	64.1	4	314	11	3-52	28.54	0	0
A.J. Ireland	Gloucestershire	34.0	1	172	6	3-12	28.66	0	0
R.R. Watson	Scotland	41.1	1	201	7	2-29	28.71	0	0
I.E. O'Brien	Leicestershire	32.4	3	173	6	2-32	28.83	0	0
R.S. Bopara	Essex	7.0	0	29	1	1-29	29.00	0	0
M.L. Turner	Somerset	7.2	0	30	1	1-30	30.00	0	0
R.J. Kirtley	Sussex	61.5	2	362	12	6-50	30.16	1	0
A. Nel	Surrey	49.4	5	244	8	3-39	30.50	0	0
K.W. Hogg	Lancashire	76.0	10	307	10	3-21	30.70	0	0
G.R. Napier	Essex	63.5	7	308	10	3-35	30.80	0	0
A.C.F. Wyatt	Leicestershire	11.0	0	62	2	1-31	31.00	0	0
A.R. White	Ireland	6.5	0	31	1	1-16	31.00	0	0
T.D. Groenewald	Derbyshire	54.3	5	251	8	3-33	31.37	0	0
J.F. Mooney	Ireland	14.0	0	95	3	2-45	31.66	0	0
P.T. Collins	Surrey	33.0	3	159	5	3-56	31.80	0	0
N. Boje	Northamptonshire	42.5	1	192	6	4-14	32.00	0	0
T.P. Stayt	Gloucestershire	14.0	1	96	3	2-51	32.00	0	0
S.T. Finn	Middlesex	55.0	5	323	10	3-67	32.30	0	0
D.A. Cosker	Glamorgan	55.5	3	261	8	3-26	32.62	0	0
L.A. Dawson	Hampshire	54.0	0	294	9	4-48	32.66	0	0
I.D. Hunter	Derbyshire	33.2	3	164	5	2-36	32.80	0	0
R.S. Ferley	Kent	45.0	1	230	7	3-34	32.85	0	0
J.C. Tredwell	Kent	69.0	4	329	10	6-27	32.90	1	0
D. Evans	Middlesex	34.4	1	199	6	2-58	33.16	0	0
J.W.M. Dalrymple	Glamorgan	42.0	3	166	5	2-27	33.20	0	0
S.D. Weeraratna	Scotland	37.0	1	233	7	2-14	33.28	0	0
J.S. Patel	Warwickshire	60.3	5	234	7	2-23	33.42	0	0
C.E.W. Silverwood	Middlesex	62.0	3	301	9	3-26	33.44	0	0
W.D. Parnell	Kent	43.5	4	235	7	3-27	33.57	0	0
M.E. Claydon	Durham	55.2	5	270	8	2-34	33.75	0	0
K.H.D. Barker	Warwickshire	45.1	1	239	7	2-21	34.14	0	0
S.M. Ervine	Hampshire	33.0	0	172	5	3-50	34.40	0	0
G.J.P. Kruger	Glamorgan	25.0	1	138	4	2-69	34.50	0	0
A.U. Rashid	Yorkshire	40.0	1	207	6	2-42	34.50	0	0
A.P.R. Gidman	Gloucestershire	45.0	0	210	6	2-29	35.00	0	0
A.V. Suppiah	Somerset	6.0	0	35	1	1-8	35.00	0	0
G.R. Breese	Durham	56.0	3	246	7	3-42	35.14	0	0
Naved ul-Hasan	Yorkshire	59.0	3	283	8	3-75	35.37	0	0
G.K. Berg	Middlesex	37.0	0	213	6	2-27	35.50	0	0
G. Onions	Durham	7.0	0	36	1	1-36	36.00	0	0
L.J. Fletcher	Nottinghamshire	48.3	3	219	6	2-35	36.50	0	0

STATISTICS OF SUMMER

		Overs	Mdns	Runs	Wkts	Best	Avge	5w	10w
C.R. Woakes	Warwickshire	42.2	4	220	6	1-15	36.66	0	0
I.D. Fisher	Worcestershire	50.0	0	260	7	2-42	37.14	0	0
R.J. Sidebottom	Nottinghamshire	29.0	1	112	3	2-39	37.33	0	0
L.E. Plunkett	Durham	56.2	0	302	8	2-28	37.75	0	0
Azhar Mahmood	Kent	53.5	5	270	7	2-26	38.57	0	0
R.S.C. Martin-Jenkins	Sussex	58.0	4	309	8	3-49	38.62	0	0
C.T. Tremlett	Hampshire	18.0	1	117	3	3-76	39.00	0	0
M.A. Chambers	Essex	6.0	0	39	1	1-39	39.00	0	0
J.D. Middlebrook	Essex	30.0	3	117	3	2-54	39.00	0	0
C.J.C. Wright	Essex	58.4	3	318	8	3-27	39.75	0	0
A.J. Harris	Leicestershire	28.0	0	161	4	1-25	40.25	0	0
G.D. Elliott	Surrey	48.0	2	285	7	4-14	40.71	0	0
O.A.C. Banks	Somerset	38.0	0	210	5	3-40	42.00	0	0
D.J. Balcombe	Hampshire	20.0	0	127	3	2-62	42.33	0	0
D.J. Redfern	Derbyshire	19.2	0	85	2	2-30	42.50	0	0
R.J. Hamilton-Brown	Sussex	40.2	0	214	5	3-37	42.80	0	0
B.J. Phillips	Somerset	54.1	5	259	6	3-23	43.16	0	0
S.A. Patterson	Yorkshire	38.2	2	175	4	2-47	43.75	0	0
R. Clarke	Warwickshire	35.0	3	175	4	2-24	43.75	0	0
J.H. Stander	Scotland	66.0	2	394	9	3-45	43.77	0	0
M.A.K. Lawson	Derbyshire	47.3	1	220	5	2-36	44.00	0	0
G.G. Wagg	Derbyshire	55.0	4	265	6	2-51	44.16	0	0
M.N.W. Spriegel	Surrey	32.0	0	178	4	2-44	44.50	0	0
W.R. Smith	Durham	8.0	0	45	1	1-29	45.00	0	0
C.D. Crowe	Leicestershire	32.0	0	137	3	2-36	45.66	0	0
B.J. Wright	Glamorgan	8.0	0	46	1	1-19	46.00	0	0
A. Shahzad	Yorkshire	30.0	2	140	3	2-29	46.66	0	0
C.D. Collymore	Sussex	8.0	1	47	1	1-47	47.00	0	0
J.A.R. Harris	Glamorgan	59.1	4	283	6	2-44	47.16	0	0
W.A. White	Leicestershire	35.5	0	236	5	2-54	47.20	0	0
P.S. Eaglestone	Ireland	6.0	0	50	1	1-18	50.00	0	0
H.T. Waters	Glamorgan	11.0	1	50	1	1-24	50.00	0	0
C.G. Taylor	Gloucestershire	27.0	0	101	2	1-25	50.50	0	0
J.L. Clare	Derbyshire	14.1	0	52	1	1-24	52.00	0	0
A.C. Voges	Nottinghamshire	19.2	0	107	2	1-9	53.50	0	0
M.J. Cosgrove	Glamorgan	18.0	0	109	2	2-50	54.50	0	0
W.R.S. Gidman	Durham	37.0	5	164	3	1-32	54.66	0	0
C.D. Thorp	Durham	22.0	3	110	2	2-47	55.00	0	0
R.H. Joseph	Kent	30.0	0	166	3	3-55	55.33	0	0
L.J. Wright	Sussex	47.0	2	228	4	2-24	57.00	0	0
S.J. Croft	Lancashire	11.1	1	57	1	1-4	57.00	0	0
C.M. Willoughby	Somerset	35.0	1	176	3	1-16	58.66	0	0
W.A.T. Beer	Sussex	64.0	0	295	5	2-29	59.00	0	0
A.R. Adams	Nottinghamshire	50.0	3	236	4	2-33	59.00	0	0
M. Hussain	Surrey	10.0	0	60	1	1-60	60.00	0	0
G.D. Drummond	Scotland	24.0	2	122	2	2-56	61.00	0	0
A.J. Tudor	Surrey	19.0	1	122	2	1-20	61.00	0	0
S.C. Meaker	Surrey	27.0	1	185	3	1-24	61.66	0	0
S.J. Harmison	Durham	41.0	1	254	4	1-44	63.50	0	0
K.J. O'Brien	Ireland	30.0	1	204	3	1-20	68.00	0	0
A.J. Shantry	Glamorgan	11.0	0	68	1	1-40	68.00	0	0
G.A. Rogers	Scotland	51.0	0	274	4	2-55	68.50	0	0
R.A.G. Cummins	Northamptonshire	14.0	0	70	1	1-28	70.00	0	0
W. Lee	Kent	6.0	0	71	1	1-71	71.00	0	0
M.H. Yardy	Sussex	42.0	0	213	3	1-5	71.00	0	0
J.D. Nel	Scotland	64.0	5	357	5	3-62	71.40	0	0

A LAST ENGLISH SUMMER

		Overs	Mdns	Runs	Wkts	Best	Avge	5w	10w
M.T.C. Waller	Somerset	12.0	0	72	1	1-46	72.00	0	0
H. Riazuddin	Hampshire	34.0	3	147	2	1-17	73.50	0	0
M.M. Ali	Worcestershire	12.2	1	74	1	1-23	74.00	0	0
G.T. Park	Derbyshire	30.0	1	152	2	1-23	76.00	0	0
N.J. Dexter	Middlesex	45.4	0	235	3	2-28	78.33	0	0
J. Needham	Derbyshire	20.0	0	82	1	1-28	82.00	0	0
M. van Jaarsveld	Kent	28.0	0	169	2	2-25	84.50	0	0
M.S. Panesar	Northamptonshire	33.0	0	170	2	1-38	85.00	0	0
R.M. West	Ireland	33.0	1	177	2	1-23	88.50	0	0
A.J. Hall	Northamptonshire	36.2	3	181	2	1-38	90.50	0	0
S.P. Crook	Northamptonshire	15.0	1	93	1	1-31	93.00	0	0
R.N. ten Doeschate	Essex	49.0	0	283	3	1-28	94.33	0	0
G.M. Andrew	Worcestershire	24.1	2	123	1	1-42	123.00	0	0
M.A. Parker	Scotland	18.4	0	126	1	1-57	126.00	0	0
P.J. Franks	Nottinghamshire	31.2	0	150	1	1-30	150.00	0	0
S.J. Cliff	Leicestershire	25.0	0	157	1	1-69	157.00	0	0

The Twenty20 Cup

South Division

	P	W	L	D	T	NR	RR	Points
Kent	10	7	2	0	0	1	0.64	15
Sussex	10	7	3	0	0	0	0.32	14
Hampshire	10	6	4	0	0	0	0.85	12
Essex	10	5	4	0	0	1	0.15	11
Surrey	10	2	8	0	0	0	-0.66	4
Middlesex	10	2	8	0	0	0	-1.19	4

North Division

	P	W	L	D	T	NR	RR	Points
Lancashire	10	8	1	0	0	1	1.11	17
Durham	10	5	4	0	0	1	0.16	11
Leicestershire	10	5	5	0	0	0	-0.04	10
Nottinghamshire	10	4	6	0	0	0	-0.01	8
Yorkshire	10	4	6	0	0	0	-0.48	8
Derbyshire	10	3	7	0	0	0	-0.61	6

Midlands/Wales/West Division

	P	W	L	D	T	NR	RR	Points
Northamptonshire	10	7	2	0	0	1	0.58	15
Warwickshire	10	7	3	0	0	0	0.24	14
Somerset	10	6	3	0	0	1	0.42	13
Worcestershire	10	5	5	0	0	0	0.58	10
Glamorgan	10	2	8	0	0	0	-1.03	4
Gloucestershire	10	2	8	0	0	0	-0.66	4

Quarter-finals:

Kent v Durham at Canterbury
Kent won by 56 runs

Sussex v Warwickshire at Hove
Sussex won by 38 runs

Lancashire v Somerset at Old Trafford
Somerset won on a bowl out

Northamptonshire v Hampshire
Northants won by 13 runs

Semi-finals

Northamptonshire v Sussex
Sussex won by 7 wickets

Kent v Somerset
Somerset won by seven wickets

Final

Somerset v Sussex at Edgbaston
Sussex 172 (Smith 59)
Somerset 109 (Trescothick 33, Kirtley 3-9)
Sussex won by 63 runs

Batting averages

		Mtchs	Inns	NO	Runs	Best	Avge	100	50	Ct	St
G.P. Swann	Nottinghamshire	2	2	1	96	90*	96.00	0	1	2	
R. Clarke	Warwickshire	5	5	4	95	51*	95.00	0	1	3	
V.V.S. Laxman	Lancashire	3	3	1	159	78*	79.50	0	2	0	
I.J.L. Trott	Warwickshire	11	11	3	525	86*	65.62	0	5	2	
D.J. Hussey	Nottinghamshire	2	2	1	63	55	63.00	0	1	1	
S.D. Peters	Northamptonshire	2	2	1	61	61*	61.00	0	1	1	
D.I. Stevens	Kent	11	11	5	356	77	59.33	0	4	4	
Z. de Bruyn	Somerset	12	10	3	391	83*	55.85	0	3	4	
A.G. Prince	Lancashire	6	6	3	159	44	53.00	0	0	2	
R. McLaren	Kent	10	6	4	100	31	50.00	0	0	5	
M.J. Brown	Surrey	2	2	0	100	77	50.00	0	1	0	
A.C. Voges	Nottinghamshire	6	6	2	198	82*	49.50	0	1	1	
A. Flintoff	Lancashire	2	2	0	98	93	49.00	0	1	0	
G.J. Muchall	Durham	5	4	2	98	50*	49.00	0	1	4	
P.D. Trego	Somerset	12	8	3	241	58*	48.20	0	1	3	
A.N. Cook	Essex	8	8	1	337	100*	48.14	1	2	1	
J. Allenby	Leicestershire	10	10	1	432	110	48.00	1	3	4	
M.J. Wood	Nottinghamshire	4	4	1	137	45	45.66	0	0	0	
M.J. Lumb	Hampshire	11	11	1	442	124*	44.20	1	3	4	
C.D. Nash	Sussex	10	8	3	216	56*	43.20	0	1	2	
W.W. Hinds	Derbyshire	10	10	3	299	66	42.71	0	1	1	
A.W. Gale	Yorkshire	10	10	1	383	91	42.55	0	3	4	
A.U. Rashid	Yorkshire	3	3	2	42	28*	42.00	0	0	2	
D.G. Cork	Hampshire	9	5	4	41	18*	41.00	0	0	0	
J.L. Sadler	Derbyshire	9	8	5	123	29*	41.00	0	0	1	
N.J. O'Brien	Northamptonshire	5	5	1	150	48*	37.50	0	0	2	
M.L. Pettini	Essex	10	10	1	334	87	37.11	0	2	3	
G.K. Berg	Middlesex	6	6	3	111	33	37.00	0	0	1	
S.J. Croft	Lancashire	9	9	2	259	83*	37.00	0	1	6	
M. van Jaarsveld	Kent	12	10	1	326	75*	36.22	0	3	5	
C.M.W. Read	Nottinghamshire	9	6	2	144	58*	36.00	0	1	7	
O.A. Shah	Middlesex	6	6	1	180	61*	36.00	0	1	3	
T.C. Smith	Lancashire	6	6	2	143	57*	35.75	0	1	3	
J.J. van der Wath	Northamptonshire	12	10	5	176	29*	35.20	0	0	2	
G.J. Kruis	Yorkshire	10	3	2	35	22	35.00	0	0	4	
D.M. Benkenstein	Durham	10	10	2	276	53	34.50	0	1	4	
N. Pothas	Hampshire	10	7	4	103	26*	34.33	0	0	1	
M.W. Goodwin	Sussex	10	10	2	273	80*	34.12	0	2	4	
D.R. Smith	Sussex	13	13	3	338	69*	33.80	0	3	6	
H.H. Dippenaar	Leicestershire	10	8	3	167	63	33.40	0	1	3	
H.D. Ackerman	Leicestershire	4	4	1	100	66*	33.33	0	1	0	
G.P. Hodnett	Gloucestershire	4	4	0	133	60	33.25	0	1	2	
C.P. Murtagh	Surrey	2	2	1	33	28	33.00	0	0	0	
S.C. Moore	Worcestershire	10	10	1	294	62*	32.66	0	1	0	
M.E. Trescothick	Somerset	12	11	1	323	69*	32.30	0	3	1	
M.R. Ramprakash	Surrey	8	8	1	225	73	32.14	0	2	1	
J.W.M. Dalrymple	Glamorgan	10	10	0	318	63	31.80	0	3	3	
U. Afzaal	Surrey	9	9	1	251	98*	31.37	0	2	0	
I.J. Harvey	Northamptonshire	10	10	1	279	64	31.00	0	1	7	
C. Kieswetter	Somerset	12	11	3	248	84	31.00	0	2	8	
W.I. Jefferson	Nottinghamshire	10	9	2	216	75	30.85	0	1	2	
M.A. Carberry	Hampshire	11	10	0	307	62	30.70	0	2	7	
A.D. Mascarenhas	Hampshire	7	7	2	153	45*	30.60	0	0	0	
B.J. Wright	Glamorgan	8	8	2	179	55*	29.83	0	1	2	
J.W.A. Taylor	Leicestershire	10	10	3	205	41*	29.28	0	0	2	
M.H. Wessels	Northamptonshire	12	11	2	261	66*	29.00	0	2	2	

STATISTICS OF SUMMER

		Mtchs	Inns	NO	Runs	Best	Avge	100	50	Ct	St
/.T. Key	Kent	9	9	2	202	58*	28.85	0	1	1	0
1. Smith	Derbyshire	10	10	1	259	56	28.77	0	2	4	0
. Ervine	Hampshire	11	11	3	230	53	28.75	0	1	7	0
Westwood	Warwickshire	11	8	3	143	49*	28.60	0	0	2	0
. Newman	Surrey	8	8	1	200	81*	28.57	0	1	3	0
.. Warner	Durham	4	4	0	113	50	28.25	0	1	0	0
). Jones	Kent	12	10	2	216	56	27.00	0	1	7	5
. Botha	Warwickshire	11	7	4	81	35*	27.00	0	0	7	0
leer Ali	Gloucestershire	4	4	1	81	33	27.00	0	0	0	0
Solanki	Worcestershire	10	10	0	269	100	26.90	1	1	3	0
Boje	Northamptonshire	9	6	1	134	45	26.80	0	0	5	0
1. Yardy	Sussex	13	8	4	107	26*	26.75	0	0	6	0
. Bopara	Essex	4	4	0	107	53	26.75	0	1	2	0
. Nixon	Leicestershire	10	9	1	208	53*	26.00	0	1	9	0
1. Davies	Worcestershire	10	10	0	259	73	25.90	0	2	3	2
L. Rogers	Derbyshire	10	10	0	256	58	25.60	0	3	10	0
Troughton	Warwickshire	11	11	0	280	62	25.45	0	4	8	0
). Brown	Gloucestershire	4	4	0	101	56	25.25	0	1	3	0
). Brown	Nottinghamshire	10	10	0	251	72	25.10	0	3	2	0
.W. Silverwood	Middlesex	6	4	3	25	18*	25.00	0	0	0	0
. Smith	Worcestershire	10	10	3	171	44	24.42	0	0	3	0
. Joyce	Sussex	13	11	4	169	41*	24.14	0	0	3	0
Nel	Surrey	9	6	4	48	19	24.00	0	0	2	0
J. ten Doeschate	Essex	7	6	1	119	43	23.80	0	0	2	0
?. Vaughan	Yorkshire	9	9	1	188	41*	23.50	0	0	1	0
i. Law	Derbyshire	10	9	1	184	59	23.00	0	1	1	0
. Cosgrove	Glamorgan	6	6	0	136	52	22.66	0	1	4	0
1. Toit	Leicestershire	8	7	3	90	39	22.50	0	0	7	0
.W. Flower	Essex	10	8	1	157	61	22.42	0	1	4	0
Langer	Somerset	12	9	1	179	44	22.37	0	0	2	0
.H. Marshall	Gloucestershire	9	9	0	201	42	22.33	0	0	4	0
. Wright	Sussex	9	9	0	199	58	22.11	0	1	3	0
1. Powell	Glamorgan	10	10	2	176	39*	22.00	0	0	4	0
K.H. Mitchell	Worcestershire	10	8	3	110	35	22.00	0	0	2	0
McGrath	Yorkshire	7	7	1	132	34	22.00	0	0	5	0
u. Plessis	Lancashire	8	8	1	153	78*	21.85	0	1	0	0
A. White	Northamptonshire	12	12	1	240	59	21.81	0	1	2	0
R. Patel	Nottinghamshire	10	7	1	130	37	21.66	0	0	1	0
G. Wakely	Northamptonshire	6	5	1	86	29*	21.50	0	0	1	0
M. Ali	Worcestershire	10	10	0	214	46	21.40	0	0	2	0
Henderson	Middlesex	10	10	2	170	32	21.25	0	0	0	0
. Coetzer	Durham	8	8	1	148	39*	21.14	0	0	3	0
A. Noffke	Worcestershire	10	10	2	169	34	21.12	0	0	3	0
L. Brophy	Yorkshire	4	3	1	42	26	21.00	0	0	0	1

Bowling averages

		Overs	Mdns	Runs	Wkts	Best	Avge	5w	10w
S.G. Law	Derbyshire	0.5	0	6	2	3.0	2-6	0	0
J. Needham	Derbyshire	4.0	0	21	4	5.25	4-21	0	0
D.A. Burton	Middlesex	4.0	0	13	2	6.5	2-13	0	0
P. Chawla	Sussex	4.0	0	17	2	8.5	2-17	0	0
S.J. Walters	Surrey	1.0	0	9	1	9.0	1-9	0	0
R.J. Sidebottom	Nottinghamshire	16.0	3	86	8	10.75	3-16	0	0
R.J. Kirtley	Sussex	27.0	2	185	17	10.88	3-9	0	0
D.J. Willey	Northamptonshire	22.0	0	113	10	11.3	3-9	0	0
I.J. Harvey	Northamptonshire	22.0	0	138	12	11.5	4-18	0	0
R.J. Hamilton-Brown	Sussex	16.0	0	108	9	12.0	4-15	0	0
A.C.F. Wyatt	Leicestershire	7.0	1	36	3	12.0	3-14	0	0
B.W. Harmison	Durham	24.0	0	180	14	12.85	3-20	0	0
R.N. ten Doeschate	Essex	3.0	0	26	2	13.0	2-26	0	0
N. Boje	Northamptonshire	27.0	0	159	12	13.25	3-14	0	0
Yasir Arafat	Sussex	34.3	3	210	15	14.0	2-13	0	0
D.J. Malan	Middlesex	19.0	1	99	7	14.14	2-10	0	0
Naved ul-Hasan	Yorkshire	27.1	0	159	11	14.45	4-23	0	0
T.C. Smith	Lancashire	14.0	0	74	5	14.8	3-20	0	0
J.W.M. Dalrymple	Glamorgan	19.1	0	164	11	14.9	2-17	0	0
M.E. Claydon	Durham	37.2	0	254	17	14.94	5-26	1	0
T. Lungley	Derbyshire	12.3	0	122	8	15.25	5-27	1	0
S.P. Kirby	Gloucestershire	29.1	1	214	14	15.28	3-29	0	0
G.W. Flower	Essex	20.0	0	139	9	15.44	3-25	0	0
M.A. Carberry	Hampshire	2.0	0	16	1	16.0	1-16	0	0
R. Clarke	Warwickshire	17.0	0	166	10	16.6	3-20	0	0
G. Chapple	Lancashire	30.0	0	186	11	16.9	2-11	0	0
S.M. Ervine	Hampshire	29.0	0	220	13	16.92	4-16	0	0
K.J. O'Brien	Nottinghamshire	4.0	0	34	2	17.0	2-14	0	0
A.C. Thomas	Somerset	40.2	0	310	18	17.22	3-31	0	0
S.J. Croft	Lancashire	10.0	0	69	4	17.25	2-35	0	0
C.M. Willougby	Somerset	16.0	0	121	7	17.28	4-29	0	0
J.A.R. Harris	Glamorgan	16.0	0	105	6	17.5	4-23	0	0
A. Richardson	Middlesex	12.0	0	88	5	17.6	3-29	0	0
C.W. Henderson	Leicestershire	28.0	0	194	11	17.63	3-32	0	0
K.H.D. Barker	Warwickshire	35.0	0	283	16	17.68	4-19	0	0
A.V. Suppiah	Somerset	17.1	0	124	7	17.71	3-25	0	0
G.T. Park	Derbyshire	27.0	0	195	11	17.72	3-23	0	0
J.S. Patel	Warwickshire	37.4	0	270	15	18.0	3-15	0	0
A.J. Ireland	Gloucestershire	10.0	0	74	4	18.5	2-38	0	0
I.E. O'Brien	Leicestershire	14.0	0	113	6	18.83	5-23	1	0
P.D. Collingwood	Durham	4.0	0	38	2	19.0	2-38	0	0
A.J. Hall	Northamptonshire	41.1	1	267	14	19.07	4-19	0	0
A.D. Mascarenhas	Hampshire	28.0	0	172	9	19.11	2-14	0	0
D.I. Stevens	Kent	16.0	0	96	5	19.2	2-21	0	0
G.M. Hussain	Gloucestershire	25.0	0	193	10	19.3	3-22	0	0
R.E. Watkins	Glamorgan	30.0	0	214	11	19.45	5-16	1	0
I.D. Fisher	Worcestershire	17.0	0	117	6	19.5	3-16	0	0
M.J. Cosgrove	Glamorgan	6.0	0	39	2	19.5	2-11	0	0
M.H. Yardy	Sussex	47.1	0	254	13	19.53	3-21	0	0
A.J. Harris	Leicestershire	17.5	0	138	7	19.71	2-26	0	0
D.R. Smith	Sussex	23.2	0	159	8	19.87	3-19	0	0
G.R. Napier	Essex	22.2	0	179	9	19.88	3-21	0	0
O.A.C. Banks	Somerset	7.0	0	40	2	20.0	1-14	0	0
J.E.C. Franklin	Gloucestershire	14.0	0	100	5	20.0	2-21	0	0
Azhar Mahmood	Kent	45.1	0	328	16	20.5	3-16	0	0
R.H. Joseph	Kent	22.0	1	164	8	20.5	2-14	0	0

STATISTICS OF SUMMER

		Overs	Mdns	Runs	Wkts	Best	Avge	5w	10w
F.du. Plessis	Lancashire	17.0	0	103	5	20.6	1-4	0	0
M.T.C. Waller	Somerset	27.0	0	208	10	20.8	3-17	0	0
J.C. Tredwell	Kent	42.0	0	271	13	20.84	3-18	0	0
S.J. Mullaney	Lancashire	3.0	0	21	1	21.0	1-21	0	0
H. Riazuddin	Hampshire	19.0	0	148	7	21.14	3-15	0	0
G.J. Batty	Worcestershire	36.0	0	234	11	21.27	3-21	0	0
M.L. Turner	Somerset	15.0	0	128	6	21.33	2-20	0	0
M.A. Hardinges	Essex	5.0	0	43	2	21.5	2-12	0	0
D.G. Cork	Hampshire	32.0	1	237	11	21.54	3-30	0	0
Danish Kaneria	Essex	28.4	0	237	11	21.54	3-21	0	0
M.N.W. Spriegel	Surrey	32.5	0	263	12	21.91	4-33	0	0
W.B. Rankin	Warwickshire	4.0	0	22	1	22.0	1-22	0	0
S.I. Mahmood	Lancashire	34.0	1	242	11	22.0	4-29	0	0
B.J. Wright	Glamorgan	4.0	0	22	1	22.0	1-16	0	0
S.D. Parry	Lancashire	33.0	0	223	10	22.3	3-20	0	0
T.T. Bresnan	Yorkshire	23.0	0	157	7	22.42	3-26	0	0
A.A. Noffke	Worcestershire	35.0	1	250	11	22.72	2-25	0	0
Z. de Bruyn	Somerset	10.0	0	91	4	22.75	2-2	0	0
C.B. Keegan	Sussex	3.0	0	23	1	23.0	1-13	0	0
D. Evans	Middlesex	10.0	0	102	0	0.0	0-14	0	0
T.E. Linley	Surrey	5.2	0	42	0	0.0	0-17	0	0
T.J. Phillips	Essex	3.0	0	25	0	0.0	0-25	0	0
A.C. Voges	Nottinghamshire	4.0	0	44	0	0.0	0-13	0	0
G.G. White	Northamptonshire	3.0	0	21	0	0.0	0-7	0	0
S.P. Crook	Northamptonshire	1.0	0	16	0	0.0	0-16	0	0
E.C. Joyce	Sussex	0.4	0	6	0	0.0	0-6	0	0
M. van Jaarsveld	Kent	1.0	0	11	0	0.0	0-11	0	0
S.J. King	Surrey	3.0	0	28	0	0.0	0-28	0	0
D.M. Benkenstein	Durham	3.0	0	13	0	0.0	0-3	0	0
J. du Toit	Leicestershire	1.0	0	9	0	0.0	0-9	0	0
S.J. Cliff	Leicestershire	4.0	0	33	0	0.0	0-16	0	0
S.J. Harmison	Durham	4.0	0	31	0	0.0	0-31	0	0
R.S. Ferley	Kent	3.0	0	24	0	0.0	0-24	0	0
A. Roberts	Leicestershire	1.0	0	12	0	0.0	0-12	0	0
M.P. Vaughan	Yorkshire	1.0	0	9	0	0.0	0-9	0	0
K.W. Hogg	Lancashire	2.0	0	29	0	0.0	0-29	0	0
J.F. Brown	Nottinghamshire	5.0	0	49	0	0.0	0-24	0	0
J.L. Sadler	Derbyshire	1.0	0	15	0	0.0	0-15	0	0
L.E. Plunkett	Durham	6.0	0	57	0	0.0	0-21	0	0
C.D. Nash	Sussex	3.0	0	22	0	0.0	0-3	0	0
J.G.E. Benning	Surrey	2.1	0	14	0	0.0	0-14	0	0
W.W. Hinds	Derbyshire	3.0	0	26	0	0.0	0-10	0	0
J.A. Rudolph	Yorkshire	3.0	0	22	0	0.0	0-22	0	0

Nat West Pro40

Division One

	P	W	L	D	T	NR	RR	Points
Sussex	8	6	2	0	0	0	1.25	12
Somerset	8	5	2	0	0	1	1.14	11
Worcestershire	8	5	2	0	0	1	-0.33	11
Essex	8	5	3	0	0	0	0.33	10
Hampshire	8	4	4	0	0	0	0.23	8
Durham	8	4	4	0	0	0	-0.35	8
Yorkshire	8	2	5	0	0	1	-0.18	5
Gloucestershire	8	2	5	0	0	1	0.35	5
Nottinghamshire	8	0	6	0	0	2	-2.41	2

Division Two

	P	W	L	D	T	NR	RR	Points
Warwickshire	8	5	0	0	1	2	1.28	13
Middlesex	8	5	1	0	0	2	0.99	12
Kent	8	4	3	0	0	1	-0.63	9
Northamptonshire	8	3	2	0	1	2	0.6	9
Lancashire	8	3	3	0	0	2	-0.19	8
Glamorgan	8	2	4	0	0	2	-0.36	6
Derbyshire	8	2	4	0	0	2	-0.57	6
Leicestershire	8	2	5	0	0	1	-0.23	5
Surrey	8	2	6	0	0	0	-0.77	4

STATISTICS OF SUMMER

Division One batting averages

		Mtchs	Inns	NO	Runs	Best	Avge	100	50	Ct	St
A.V. Suppiah	Somerset	8	6	5	133	52*	133.00	0	1	1	0
J.S. Foster	Essex	8	6	3	279	83*	93.00	0	3	8	7
A.D. Mascarenhas	Hampshire	5	4	2	181	76	90.50	0	1	0	0
N. Cook	Essex	4	4	1	235	104*	78.33	2	0	1	0
D.K.H. Mitchell	Worcestershire	8	5	3	156	50*	78.00	0	1	3	0
A. Rudolph	Yorkshire	7	7	1	421	95	70.16	0	5	4	0
H.M. Amla	Essex	2	2	0	133	111	66.50	1	0	1	0
Z. de Bruyn	Somerset	8	8	3	324	109*	64.80	1	2	0	0
R.N. ten Doeschate	Essex	5	5	2	190	88	63.33	0	2	2	0
E. Root	Yorkshire	1	1	0	63	63	63.00	0	1	1	0
V. Chopra	Essex	5	5	1	231	101*	57.75	1	2	1	0
E.C. Joyce	Sussex	8	8	1	395	94	56.42	0	3	0	0
S.M. Davies	Worcestershire	8	7	0	390	106	55.71	2	1	6	1
J. Sayers	Yorkshire	1	1	0	55	55	55.00	0	1	0	0
K. Maunders	Essex	5	2	0	108	78	54.00	0	1	0	0
A.D. Hales	Nottinghamshire	5	5	1	215	150*	53.75	1	0	1	0
P. Mustard	Durham	8	8	0	416	102	52.00	1	4	6	3
M. Vince	Hampshire	6	6	1	257	93	51.40	0	2	1	0
M.A. Carberry	Hampshire	2	2	0	94	55	47.00	0	1	0	0
M.E. Trescothick	Somerset	8	8	1	318	80*	45.42	0	1	5	0
S. Gatting	Sussex	4	4	1	133	99*	44.33	0	1	0	0
G.J. Muchall	Durham	2	2	0	88	61	44.00	0	1	2	0
L.J. Wright	Sussex	4	4	1	125	95*	41.66	0	1	1	0
A.W. Gale	Yorkshire	7	7	1	245	83	40.83	0	2	0	0
K.J. Coetzer	Durham	8	8	3	198	63	39.60	0	1	3	0
M.W. Goodwin	Sussex	8	7	0	267	77	38.14	0	1	3	0
W.T.S. Porterfield	Gloucestershire	8	8	1	265	97*	37.85	0	2	2	0
J.E.C. Franklin	Gloucestershire	6	6	0	223	60	37.16	0	2	1	0
S.C. Moore	Worcestershire	8	7	1	220	87*	36.66	0	1	4	0
A. McGrath	Yorkshire	6	6	3	109	48*	36.33	0	0	4	0
D.R. Smith	Sussex	8	7	1	211	60*	35.16	0	3	1	0
M.J. Lumb	Hampshire	8	8	1	245	61	35.00	0	3	2	0
C. Kieswetter	Somerset	8	8	1	239	81	34.14	0	1	7	4
N. Pothas	Hampshire	4	4	2	67	36	33.50	0	0	1	0
S.M. Ervine	Hampshire	8	7	1	199	60*	33.16	0	1	0	0
V.S. Solanki	Worcestershire	8	7	1	199	82*	33.16	0	2	2	0
G.S. Ballance	Yorkshire	1	1	0	33	33	33.00	0	0	0	0
A. Lyth	Yorkshire	8	8	1	229	109*	32.71	1	0	1	0
G.W. Flower	Essex	5	4	1	94	43	31.33	0	0	1	0
Kadeer Ali	Gloucestershire	7	7	2	156	100*	31.20	1	0	3	0
J.H.K. Adams	Hampshire	8	8	0	248	79	31.00	0	2	3	0
B.W. Harmison	Durham	8	8	0	246	67	30.75	0	1	4	0
J.C. Hildreth	Somerset	8	8	1	213	62*	30.42	0	1	6	0
L.A. Dawson	Hampshire	8	7	2	149	69*	29.80	0	1	4	0
J. Lewis	Gloucestershire	6	4	1	86	54	28.66	0	1	2	0
M.L. Pettini	Essex	7	7	1	168	101*	28.00	1	0	2	0
S. Chanderpaul	Durham	3	3	0	82	54	27.33	0	1	1	0
H.J.H. Marshall	Gloucestershire	8	8	2	161	50	26.83	0	1	0	0
A.J. Hodd	Sussex	8	6	3	80	22	26.66	0	0	12	0
R.M. Pyrah	Yorkshire	7	5	2	80	27	26.66	0	0	1	0
M.A. Wagh	Nottinghamshire	4	4	0	106	56	26.50	0	1	0	0
D.M. Benkenstein	Durham	3	3	1	53	51*	26.50	0	1	2	0
I.D. Blackwell	Durham	7	7	0	182	59	26.00	0	1	2	0
R.J. Hamilton-Brown	Sussex	8	8	0	204	49	25.50	0	0	3	0
P.J. Franks	Nottinghamshire	4	2	1	25	23*	25.00	0	0	2	0
M.S. Westfield	Essex	6	2	1	25	17	25.00	0	0	1	0
L.J. Fletcher	Nottinghamshire	4	3	1	47	40*	23.50	0	0	0	0

A LAST ENGLISH SUMMER

		Mtchs	Inns	NO	Runs	Best	Avge	100	50	Ct	S
A. Patel	Nottinghamshire	4	4	0	92	41	23.00	0	0	1	
G.R. Breese	Durham	8	7	3	92	38*	23.00	0	0	3	
C.G. Taylor	Gloucestershire	8	6	1	113	44	22.60	0	0	3	
G.L. Brophy	Yorkshire	3	2	0	45	34	22.50	0	0	5	
M.J. Wood	Nottinghamshire	8	7	0	157	91	22.42	0	1	2	
B.F. Smith	Worcestershire	8	7	2	111	40*	22.20	0	0	1	
S.R. Patel	Nottinghamshire	8	7	0	151	58	21.57	0	1	3	
G.R. Napier	Essex	7	7	0	151	63	21.57	0	1	1	
T.J. Phillips	Essex	8	4	1	64	41	21.33	0	0	3	
Yasir Arafat	Sussex	6	4	2	42	15*	21.00	0	0	3	
Naved ul-Hasan	Yorkshire	2	2	0	42	42	21.00	0	0	1	
M.M. Ali	Worcestershire	8	7	0	145	51	20.71	0	1	3	
P.D. Trego	Somerset	8	6	1	101	28	20.20	0	0	5	
S.J. Adshead	Gloucestershire	8	5	0	98	34	19.60	0	0	6	
A.R. Adams	Nottinghamshire	2	1	0	17	17	17.00	0	0	0	
C.D. Nash	Sussex	5	4	0	68	29	17.00	0	0	1	
M.H. Yardy	Sussex	8	7	0	116	34	16.57	0	0	6	
P. Chawla	Sussex	2	2	0	32	32	16.00	0	0	1	
J.L. Langer	Somerset	6	5	0	77	45	15.40	0	0	2	
W.R. Smith	Durham	8	8	0	118	39	14.75	0	0	2	
C.C. Benham	Hampshire	8	7	1	87	42	14.50	0	0	2	
A.U. Rashid	Yorkshire	3	3	2	14	6	14.00	0	0	1	
I.D. Fisher	Worcestershire	6	3	1	28	12*	14.00	0	0	3	
A.D. Brown	Nottinghamshire	5	4	0	53	36	13.25	0	0	0	
K.J. O'Brien	Nottinghamshire	8	7	1	79	42	13.16	0	0	2	
G.M. Andrew	Worcestershire	8	5	1	51	27	12.75	0	0	3	
D.J. Wainwright	Yorkshire	8	3	2	12	10	12.00	0	0	2	
R.K.J. Dawson	Gloucestershire	8	5	0	59	31	11.80	0	0	2	
L.E. Plunkett	Durham	8	6	2	47	19	11.75	0	0	2	
R.S.C. Martin-Jenkins	Sussex	6	3	1	23	10*	11.50	0	0	3	
B.A. Stokes	Durham	1	1	0	11	11	11.00	0	0	0	
N. Killeen	Durham	2	2	1	11	11*	11.00	0	0	0	
W.R.S. Gidman	Durham	8	4	1	31	11*	10.33	0	0	4	
G.J. Batty	Worcestershire	8	5	0	50	21	10.00	0	0	4	
T.T. Bresnan	Yorkshire	4	4	1	29	8*	9.66	0	0	2	
L.J. Hodgson	Yorkshire	4	1	0	9	9	9.00	0	0	1	
R.J. Kirtley	Sussex	8	4	3	9	5*	9.00	0	0	5	
B.M. Shafayat	Nottinghamshire	4	3	0	25	22	8.33	0	0	1	2
O.A.C. Banks	Somerset	3	2	0	16	10	8.00	0	0	0	
R.S. Bopara	Essex	1	1	0	8	8	8.00	0	0	2	
A.P.R. Gidman	Gloucestershire	7	7	1	46	16*	7.66	0	0	0	0
D.O. Brown	Gloucestershire	5	3	0	23	19	7.66	0	0	3	0
W.A.T. Beer	Sussex	4	1	0	7	7	7.00	0	0	0	
A.C. Voges	Nottinghamshire	2	2	0	14	13	7.00	0	0	0	0
M.J. Walker	Essex	5	4	0	27	21	6.75	0	0	0	0
C.M.W. Read	Nottinghamshire	6	5	0	31	11	6.20	0	0	3	1
I.D. Saxelby	Gloucestershire	4	4	1	18	6*	6.00	0	0	0	0
C.D. Whelan	Worcestershire	4	2	0	11	11	5.50	0	0	0	0
J.M. Bairstow	Yorkshire	8	5	0	26	20	5.20	0	0	4	0
D.J. Pattinson	Nottinghamshire	6	4	2	10	5	5.00	0	0	0	0
T.G. Burrows	Hampshire	4	2	0	8	6	4.00	0	0	3	0
A. Carter	Nottinghamshire	6	5	0	20	12	4.00	0	0	2	0
M.E. Claydon	Durham	6	3	0	6	4	2.00	0	0	0	0
G.J. Kruis	Yorkshire	4	2	0	4	3	2.00	0	0	1	0
R.A. Jones	Worcestershire	2	1	0	2	2	2.00	0	0	0	0
S.P. Kirby	Gloucestershire	5	3	1	3	3	1.50	0	0	0	0
C.B. Keegan	Sussex	1	1	0	1	1	1.00	0	0	0	0
M.S. Mason	Worcestershire	3	2	1	1	1	1.00	0	0	0	0
C.E. Shreck	Nottinghamshire	2	1	0	1	1	1.00	0	0	0	0

STATISTICS OF SUMMER

Division One bowling averages

		Overs	Mdns	Runs	Wkts	Best	Avge	5w	10w
D.A. Griffiths	Hampshire	8.0	1	29	4	4-29	7.25	0	0
G.M. Hussain	Gloucestershire	5.0	1	17	2	2-17	8.50	0	0
A.C. Voges	Nottinghamshire	8.0	0	36	4	3-25	9.00	0	0
D.A. Payne	Gloucestershire	13.0	1	74	6	3-10	12.33	0	0
B.J. Phillips	Somerset	47.0	3	196	14	3-24	14.00	0	0
A. Shahzad	Yorkshire	15.0	1	44	3	2-19	14.66	0	0
A.C. Thomas	Somerset	37.1	3	194	13	4-18	14.92	0	0
P. Chawla	Sussex	9.3	1	45	3	2-10	15.00	0	0
D.R. Smith	Sussex	33.0	3	143	9	6-29	15.88	1	0
M.M. Ali	Worcestershire	15.0	0	66	4	3-32	16.50	0	0
J.E. Lee	Yorkshire	17.4	0	116	7	3-43	16.57	0	0
A. Patel	Nottinghamshire	5.0	1	34	2	2-34	17.00	0	0
I.D. Blackwell	Durham	33.0	1	173	10	4-36	17.30	0	0
C.M. Willoughby	Somerset	42.4	1	211	11	3-36	19.18	0	0
M.L. Turner	Somerset	23.0	1	145	7	3-27	20.71	0	0
T.J. Phillips	Essex	45.0	0	252	12	5-38	21.00	1	0
R.J. Kirtley	Sussex	51.0	3	299	14	5-26	21.35	1	0
A.J. Ireland	Gloucestershire	14.0	4	65	3	3-10	21.66	0	0
A.V. Suppiah	Somerset	12.2	0	90	4	2-12	22.50	0	0
Naved ul-Hasan	Yorkshire	13.4	0	91	4	3-44	22.75	0	0
G.M. Andrew	Worcestershire	54.0	1	331	14	5-31	23.64	1	0
G.R. Napier	Essex	46.2	2	286	12	4-33	23.83	0	0
W.R.S. Gidman	Durham	32.0	1	144	6	2-23	24.00	0	0
A. Carter	Nottinghamshire	31.0	0	169	7	3-32	24.14	0	0
S.P. Kirby	Gloucestershire	21.0	2	145	6	4-32	24.16	0	0
M.T.C. Waller	Somerset	28.0	1	147	6	2-34	24.50	0	0
C.B. Keegan	Sussex	4.0	1	26	1	1-26	26.00	0	0
J. Lewis	Gloucestershire	25.3	3	130	5	2-20	26.00	0	0
S.A. Patterson	Yorkshire	14.3	0	80	3	3-35	26.66	0	0
Yasir Arafat	Sussex	44.0	5	243	9	3-30	27.00	0	0
L. Evans	Durham	10.0	0	82	3	2-53	27.33	0	0
G.R. Breese	Durham	48.0	1	246	9	3-34	27.33	0	0
Z. de Bruyn	Somerset	32.4	1	170	6	4-20	28.33	0	0
Imran Tahir	Hampshire	45.4	0	228	8	3-30	28.50	0	0
Danish Kaneria	Essex	47.4	1	263	9	3-28	29.22	0	0
R.K.J. Dawson	Gloucestershire	27.4	0	148	5	2-39	29.60	0	0
H.J.H. Marshall	Gloucestershire	13.1	1	60	2	2-21	30.00	0	0
R.M. Pyrah	Yorkshire	19.0	0	151	5	1-16	30.20	0	0
W.A.T. Beer	Sussex	19.0	0	92	3	2-17	30.66	0	0
R.S.C. Martin-Jenkins	Sussex	35.0	2	130	4	1-9	32.50	0	0
J.T. Ball	Nottinghamshire	6.0	0	33	1	1-33	33.00	0	0
A.U. Rashid	Yorkshire	20.5	0	102	3	2-12	34.00	0	0
R.J. Hamilton-Brown	Sussex	27.0	0	175	5	2-58	35.00	0	0
R.S. Bopara	Essex	6.0	0	35	1	1-35	35.00	0	0
B.V. Taylor	Hampshire	10.0	0	72	2	1-27	36.00	0	0
D.O. Brown	Gloucestershire	3.0	0	36	1	1-36	36.00	0	0
Azeem Rafiq	Yorkshire	5.0	0	36	1	1-36	36.00	0	0
B.W. Harmison	Durham	37.0	1	253	7	2-29	36.14	0	0
I.D. Saxelby	Gloucestershire	15.0	0	111	3	3-20	37.00	0	0
D.K.H. Mitchell	Worcestershire	33.0	0	188	5	1-11	37.60	0	0
I.D. Fisher	Worcestershire	31.5	0	191	5	3-18	38.20	0	0
D.R. Briggs	Hampshire	13.0	0	78	2	2-36	39.00	0	0
D.G. Cork	Hampshire	29.5	0	157	4	2-34	39.25	0	0
L.J. Wright	Sussex	27.0	1	161	4	2-46	40.25	0	0
S.M. Ervine	Hampshire	46.0	1	282	7	3-23	40.28	0	0
G.J. Kruis	Yorkshire	26.3	1	162	4	2-34	40.50	0	0

A LAST ENGLISH SUMMER

		Overs	Mdns	Runs	Wkts	Best	Avge	5w	10w
D.J. Balcombe	Hampshire	16.0	0	122	3	2-56	40.66	0	0
L.E. Plunkett	Durham	39.1	2	245	6	2-29	40.83	0	0
M.S. Westfield	Essex	35.0	1	205	5	2-32	41.00	0	0
M.J.Hoggard	Yorkshire	21.0	0	83	2	1-25	41.50	0	0
H. Riazuddin	Hampshire	31.0	0	168	4	2-47	42.00	0	0
J.D. Shantry	Worcestershire	34.0	2	212	5	2-43	42.40	0	0
S.G. Borthwick	Durham	20.0	0	178	4	2-11	44.50	0	0
L.J. Fletcher	Nottinghamshire	25.0	0	179	4	2-59	44.75	0	0
C.T. Tremlett	Hampshire	26.0	2	136	3	2-39	45.33	0	0
C.J.C. Wright	Essex	41.2	0	274	6	2-35	45.66	0	0
L.A. Dawson	Hampshire	27.3	0	139	3	1-15	46.33	0	0
S.R. Patel	Nottinghamshire	42.0	1	285	6	2-37	47.50	0	0
D.J. Wainwright	Yorkshire	49.0	2	197	4	2-29	49.25	0	0
C.G. Taylor	Gloucestershire	16.2	0	99	2	1-13	49.50	0	0
Imran Arif	Worcestershire	22.0	1	154	3	2-51	51.33	0	0
C.D. Whelan	Worcestershire	30.0	2	158	3	1-30	52.66	0	0
L.J. Hodgson	Yorkshire	18.0	0	108	2	2-44	54.00	0	0
D.J. Pattinson	Nottinghamshire	30.0	0	175	3	1-25	58.33	0	0
T.T. Bresnan	Yorkshire	29.0	2	176	3	2-47	58.66	0	0
J.F. Brown	Nottinghamshire	31.0	0	177	3	2-36	59.00	0	0
G.J. Batty	Worcestershire	62.0	2	297	5	3-45	59.40	0	0
R.N. ten Doeschate	Essex	25.3	0	180	3	1-34	60.00	0	0
A.R. Adams	Nottinghamshire	8.0	0	60	1	1-30	60.00	0	0
G.W. Flower	Essex	10.0	0	63	1	1-33	63.00	0	0
P.D. Trego	Somerset	49.0	0	258	4	2-29	64.50	0	0
J.E.C. Franklin	Gloucestershire	17.0	1	134	2	1-27	67.00	0	0
M.H. Yardy	Sussex	36.0	0	216	3	1-27	72.00	0	0
K.J. O'Brien	Nottinghamshire	11.0	0	72	1	1-14	72.00	0	0
C.E. Shreck	Nottinghamshire	9.5	0	83	1	1-47	83.00	0	0
N. Killeen	Durham	13.0	1	84	1	1-42	84.00	0	0
M.E. Claydon	Durham	33.0	1	171	2	1-20	85.50	0	0
A.D. Mascarenhas	Hampshire	34.0	2	173	2	1-34	86.50	0	0
O.A.C. Banks	Somerset	13.0	0	92	1	1-45	92.00	0	0
P.J. Franks	Nottinghamshire	14.1	0	106	1	1-51	106.00	0	0

STATISTICS OF SUMMER

Division Two batting averages

		Mtchs	Inns	NO	Runs	Best	Avge	100	50	Ct	St
J.L. Trott	Warwickshire	7	5	2	275	86	91.66	0	3	0	0
.R.D. Compton	Middlesex	8	8	3	458	121	91.60	2	2	5	0
.A. Shah	Middlesex	5	4	1	266	130	88.66	1	1	1	0
. Clarke	Warwickshire	8	4	3	88	33*	88.00	0	0	6	0
R. Bell	Warwickshire	6	5	1	313	105	78.25	1	2	2	0
.J.L. Rogers	Derbyshire	5	5	1	287	111*	71.75	1	1	2	0
L. Denly	Kent	1	1	0	66	66	66.00	0	1	0	0
.M.J. Smith	Surrey	2	1	0	65	65	65.00	0	1	0	0
I.J. O'Brien	Northamptonshire	5	5	1	254	82	63.50	0	3	4	2
.L. Maynard	Glamorgan	7	6	1	315	108	63.00	1	2	1	0
'.E.J. Thompson	Leicestershire	3	3	2	56	39*	56.00	0	0	1	0
L. Clare	Derbyshire	2	2	1	56	34	56.00	0	0	1	0
I.H. Gibbs	Glamorgan	2	2	1	54	47*	54.00	0	0	1	0
.D. Groenewald	Derbyshire	3	2	1	53	31*	53.00	0	0	0	0
..J. Hall	Northamptonshire	5	4	1	140	104*	46.66	1	0	2	0
4.B. Loye	Lancashire	3	2	1	44	25*	44.00	0	0	1	0
1.J. Brown	Surrey	7	7	0	305	87	43.57	0	4	1	0
4.J. Cosgrove	Glamorgan	2	2	0	87	73	43.50	0	1	0	0
.C.P. Smith	Lancashire	1	1	0	43	43	43.00	0	0	0	0
R.A. White	Northamptonshire	6	5	1	171	70*	42.75	0	1	2	0
W.A. Taylor	Leicestershire	8	8	1	296	95	42.28	0	3	0	0
N.M. Carter	Warwickshire	8	6	1	201	103*	40.20	1	1	0	0
5.O. Jones	Kent	4	4	0	155	73	38.75	0	2	2	0
D.I. Stevens	Kent	7	7	1	231	75*	38.50	0	2	1	0
C.P. Schofield	Surrey	8	7	2	192	66	38.40	0	1	2	0
.E. Goodman	Kent	2	2	1	38	26*	38.00	0	0	1	0
G.M. Smith	Derbyshire	6	6	1	186	77	37.20	0	1	2	0
I.H. Dippenaar	Leicestershire	6	6	1	185	49	37.00	0	0	4	0
3.J.M. Scott	Middlesex	6	2	1	37	30	37.00	0	0	2	2
'. Henderson	Middlesex	8	5	2	108	55	36.00	0	1	2	0
5.J. Croft	Lancashire	7	5	1	143	70	35.75	0	2	3	0
'.J. Horton	Lancashire	7	6	0	213	84	35.50	0	2	4	0
G.P. Rees	Glamorgan	5	5	0	176	73	35.20	0	2	1	0
.L. Sadler	Derbyshire	5	4	1	105	38	35.00	0	0	0	0
.G.E. Benning	Leicestershire	6	6	0	205	89	34.16	0	2	0	0
M.N.W. Spriegel	Surrey	8	7	2	167	81*	33.40	0	1	2	0
T.C. Smith	Lancashire	2	2	0	65	54	32.50	0	1	0	0
?.G. Dixey	Kent	3	3	2	32	16	32.00	0	0	1	0
.V.D. Bragg	Glamorgan	6	6	0	190	78	31.66	0	1	0	0
. Allenby	Glamorgan	5	5	0	157	60	31.40	0	1	1	0
.J. van der Wath	Northamptonshire	5	3	1	61	35*	30.50	0	0	1	0
S.J. Walters	Surrey	8	8	1	212	67*	30.28	0	2	2	0
I.O. Troughton	Warwickshire	8	5	1	119	53	29.75	0	1	4	0
S.D. Peters	Northamptonshire	6	6	1	146	69	29.20	0	1	2	0
G.D. Cross	Lancashire	7	4	1	87	34	29.00	0	0	3	3
P.A. Nixon	Leicestershire	5	5	1	116	44*	29.00	0	0	2	0
G.G. Wagg	Derbyshire	2	2	0	56	35	28.00	0	0	0	0
U. Afzaal	Surrey	7	7	1	166	44	27.66	0	0	1	0
A.G. Botha	Warwickshire	8	4	2	55	32*	27.50	0	0	4	0
D.J. Malan	Middlesex	8	8	1	192	60	27.42	0	2	0	0
I.B. Hockley	Kent	5	5	0	137	55	27.40	0	1	3	0
T.J. New	Leicestershire	8	8	1	190	50	27.14	0	1	7	2
I.E. Ord	Warwickshire	2	1	0	27	27	27.00	0	0	0	0
V.V.S. Laxman	Lancashire	5	4	1	80	38*	26.66	0	0	1	0
T.J. Poynton	Derbyshire	5	3	1	52	24	26.00	0	0	3	1
P.W. Harrison	Northamptonshire	2	1	0	26	26	26.00	0	0	0	0

		Mtchs	Inns	NO	Runs	Best	Avge	100	50	Ct	S
G.T. Park	Derbyshire	6	5	0	128	64	25.60	0	1	0	
P.M. Borrington	Derbyshire	1	1	0	25	25	25.00	0	0	0	
S.A. Northeast	Kent	6	6	0	144	69	24.00	0	1	1	
M.R. Ramprakash	Surrey	2	1	0	24	24	24.00	0	0	0	
D.J. Redfern	Derbyshire	5	4	0	95	32	23.75	0	0	0	
A.J. Blake	Kent	7	6	0	142	80	23.66	0	1	6	
J.C. Tredwell	Kent	6	6	2	94	45	23.50	0	0	1	
N.J. Dexter	Middlesex	4	4	0	94	31	23.50	0	0	1	
H.M.R.K.B. Herath	Surrey	2	2	0	47	39	23.50	0	0	0	
J.J. Cobb	Leicestershire	3	3	0	69	43	23.00	0	0	1	
W.A. White	Leicestershire	8	7	3	92	46*	23.00	0	0	2	
E.J.G. Morgan	Middlesex	5	3	1	46	22	23.00	0	0	1	
J.M. Kemp	Kent	6	6	1	114	44	22.80	0	0	4	
G.C. Wilson	Surrey	7	4	0	91	42	22.75	0	0	3	
J.W.M. Dalrymple	Glamorgan	5	5	1	90	39	22.50	0	0	4	
M.J. Chilton	Lancashire	7	4	1	67	24	22.33	0	0	2	
T.R. Ambrose	Warwickshire	8	4	0	89	46	22.25	0	0	3	
J.A. Simpson	Middlesex	6	5	0	108	32	21.60	0	0	3	
D.J. Willey	Northamptonshire	6	4	2	43	21	21.50	0	0	1	
Azhar Mahmood	Kent	6	6	0	128	51	21.33	0	1	1	
W.L. Madsen	Derbyshire	2	2	0	42	42	21.00	0	0	1	
N.L. Buck	Leicestershire	4	1	0	21	21	21.00	0	0	1	
S.J. Cook	Kent	1	1	0	21	21	21.00	0	0	1	
N. Boje	Northamptonshire	7	5	0	101	44	20.20	0	0	5	
T.J. Lancefield	Surrey	1	1	0	20	20	20.00	0	0	1	
J.A.R. Harris	Glamorgan	2	1	0	19	19	19.00	0	0	0	
M.A. Wallace	Glamorgan	7	6	2	73	42*	18.25	0	0	4	
M.A.G. Boyce	Leicestershire	5	5	0	82	32	16.40	0	0	1	
J.W. Dernbach	Surrey	7	2	1	16	8*	16.00	0	0	3	
R.D.B. Croft	Glamorgan	4	2	1	16	10*	16.00	0	0	1	
D.J. Pipe	Derbyshire	1	1	0	16	16	16.00	0	0	0	
J.K.H. Naik	Leicestershire	6	5	2	44	18	14.66	0	0	0	
D.S. Harrison	Glamorgan	6	4	2	29	12*	14.50	0	0	2	
B.J. Wright	Glamorgan	3	3	0	41	26	13.66	0	0	0	
M. Kartik	Middlesex	1	1	0	13	13	13.00	0	0	1	
R.E. Watkins	Glamorgan	3	3	1	26	12*	13.00	0	0	0	
J. du Toit	Leicestershire	6	6	0	77	31	12.83	0	0	3	
A.G. Wakely	Northamptonshire	5	5	2	37	12	12.33	0	0	1	
F. du Plessis	Lancashire	6	4	1	37	30	12.33	0	0	1	
C.F. Hughes	Derbyshire	4	3	0	34	27	11.33	0	0	1	
K.W. Hogg	Lancashire	7	4	1	34	28*	11.33	0	0	1	
D.A. Cosker	Glamorgan	7	4	1	33	27	11.00	0	0	4	
P.S. Jones	Derbyshire	2	2	1	11	11*	11.00	0	0	0	
M.H. Wessels	Northamptonshire	6	6	1	53	17	10.60	0	0	5	
S.J. Mullaney	Lancashire	2	1	0	10	10	10.00	0	0	3	
M. van Jaarsveld	Kent	1	1	0	10	10	10.00	0	0	1	
J.A. Brooks	Northamptonshire	3	1	0	10	10	10.00	0	0	0	
I.J. Westwood	Warwickshire	7	4	0	40	22	10.00	0	0	0	
R.I. Newton	Northamptonshire	1	1	0	9	9	9.00	0	0	0	
G.K. Berg	Middlesex	8	5	1	34	16*	8.50	0	0	1	
R.A. Whiteley	Derbyshire	3	2	0	17	17	8.50	0	0	1	
K.S. Toor	Middlesex	2	2	1	8	5	8.00	0	0	0	
C.J. Jordan	Surrey	2	2	1	8	7	8.00	0	0	0	
J.N. Batty	Surrey	1	1	0	8	8	8.00	0	0	3	
B.H.N. Howgego	Northamptonshire	1	1	0	7	7	7.00	0	0	0	
G.G. White	Northamptonshire	2	2	1	7	4*	7.00	0	0	1	

STATISTICS OF SUMMER

		Mtchs	Inns	NO	Runs	Best	Avge	100	50	Ct	St
C.P. Ashling	Glamorgan	3	2	1	7	6*	7.00	0	0	0	0
J. Roy	Surrey	1	1	0	6	6	6.00	0	0	0	0
R.S. Ferley	Kent	7	3	1	12	9*	6.00	0	0	3	0
. Needham	Derbyshire	4	3	1	10	5	5.00	0	0	4	0
S.I. Mahmood	Lancashire	6	3	2	5	3*	5.00	0	0	0	0
R.J. Logan	Surrey	2	1	0	5	5	5.00	0	0	0	0
M.P. Coles	Kent	3	1	0	5	5	5.00	0	0	0	0
N.A. James	Glamorgan	2	2	0	10	6	5.00	0	0	0	0
M.T. Coles	Kent	1	1	0	5	5	5.00	0	0	0	0
W.W. Hinds	Derbyshire	3	3	0	15	7	5.00	0	0	0	0
C.P. Murtagh	Surrey	3	3	0	14	8	4.66	0	0	1	0
T. Lungley	Derbyshire	3	3	0	13	10	4.33	0	0	1	0
S.D. Parry	Lancashire	7	3	0	13	12	4.33	0	0	1	0
R.W.T. Key	Kent	1	1	0	4	4	4.00	0	0	1	0
G. Chapple	Lancashire	1	1	0	4	4	4.00	0	0	1	0
S.A. Piolet	Warwickshire	8	1	0	4	4	4.00	0	0	1	0
T.J. Murtagh	Middlesex	7	2	1	4	3*	4.00	0	0	1	0
C.W. Henderson	Leicestershire	7	4	2	7	6	3.50	0	0	0	0
P. Edwards	Kent	7	3	2	3	2*	3.00	0	0	0	0
G. Keedy	Lancashire	7	3	0	7	4	2.33	0	0	1	0
K.H.D. Barker	Warwickshire	6	2	1	2	2	2.00	0	0	1	0
H.T. Waters	Glamorgan	1	1	0	2	2	2.00	0	0	0	0
P.T. Collins	Surrey	3	1	0	2	2	2.00	0	0	1	0
D.A. Burton	Middlesex	3	1	0	2	2	2.00	0	0	1	0
L.A. Proctor	Lancashire	1	1	0	2	2	2.00	0	0	0	0
D.H. Wigley	Northamptonshire	1	1	0	2	2	2.00	0	0	3	0
M.J. Powell	Glamorgan	2	2	0	2	1	1.00	0	0	0	0
G.P. Smith	Leicestershire	1	1	0	1	1	1.00	0	0	0	0
G.J.P. Kruger	Glamorgan	4	1	0	1	1	1.00	0	0	0	0
T.M. Jewell	Surrey	2	2	1	1	1	1.00	0	0	0	0

Division Two bowling averages

		Overs	Mdns	Runs	Wkts	Best	Avge	5w	10w
O.A. Shah	Middlesex	3.2	0	11	4	4-11	2.75	0	0
H.H. Dippenaar	Leicestershire	2.0	0	5	1	1-5	5.00	0	0
W.L. Madsen	Derbyshire	4.0	0	18	2	2-18	9.00	0	0
M. Kartik	Middlesex	8.0	1	19	2	2-19	9.50	0	0
J.J. Cobb	Leicestershire	1.0	0	12	1	1-12	12.00	0	0
G.G. White	Northamptonshire	15.5	0	72	6	3-30	12.00	0	0
N. Boje	Northamptonshire	35.0	2	164	13	3-49	12.61	0	0
W. Lee	Kent	7.3	1	39	3	3-39	13.00	0	0
D.J. Redfern	Derbyshire	6.2	0	39	3	2-10	13.00	0	0
D.S. Lucas	Northamptonshire	24.0	1	122	8	4-28	15.25	0	0
S.J. Mullaney	Lancashire	11.0	1	61	4	3-36	15.25	0	0
J.B. Hockley	Kent	8.0	0	32	2	2-32	16.00	0	0
I.J.L. Trott	Warwickshire	25.0	0	132	8	3-36	16.50	0	0
T.J. Murtagh	Middlesex	32.2	0	156	9	3-43	17.33	0	0
S.D. Parry	Lancashire	49.1	0	197	11	2-12	17.90	0	0
G.K. Berg	Middlesex	36.0	3	163	9	3-18	18.11	0	0
R.D.B. Croft	Glamorgan	21.0	0	92	5	4-43	18.40	0	0
S. Sreesanth	Warwickshire	36.3	3	174	9	3-36	19.33	0	0
S.A. Piolet	Warwickshire	31.5	0	186	9	3-34	20.66	0	0
H.T. Waters	Glamorgan	7.0	0	42	2	2-42	21.00	0	0
C.W. Henderson	Leicestershire	43.0	2	190	9	3-30	21.11	0	0
N.M. Carter	Warwickshire	39.0	4	171	8	3-18	21.37	0	0
T.C. Smith	Lancashire	14.0	0	65	3	2-37	21.66	0	0
T.C.P. Smith	Lancashire	3.0	0	22	1	1-22	22.00	0	0
M.J. Cosgrove	Glamorgan	6.0	0	44	2	2-44	22.00	0	0
M.S. Panesar	Northamptonshire	25.1	1	132	6	2-27	22.00	0	0
M. van Jaarsveld	Kent	4.0	1	22	1	1-22	22.00	0	0
S.D. Udal	Middlesex	46.0	0	220	10	2-31	22.00	0	0
K.H.D. Barker	Warwickshire	21.5	0	115	5	3-23	23.00	0	0
W.B. Rankin	Warwickshire	12.0	1	47	2	1-16	23.50	0	0
A. Nel	Surrey	8.0	1	47	2	2-47	23.50	0	0
D.I. Stevens	Kent	14.0	0	96	4	2-25	24.00	0	0
J.J. van der Wath	Northamptonshire	33.0	2	152	6	3-55	25.33	0	0
S.I. Mahmood	Lancashire	37.2	2	181	7	2-14	25.85	0	0
S.C. Meaker	Surrey	23.0	0	130	5	2-21	26.00	0	0
T.M.J. Smith	Surrey	9.0	0	52	2	1-25	26.00	0	0
M.P. Coles	Kent	14.0	0	105	4	3-50	26.25	0	0
C.P. Ashling	Glamorgan	20.0	0	107	4	2-33	26.75	0	0
J.K.H. Naik	Leicestershire	35.2	0	188	7	3-21	26.85	0	0
G. Keedy	Lancashire	49.0	0	217	8	2-23	27.12	0	0
C.R. Woakes	Warwickshire	22.0	4	83	3	2-28	27.66	0	0
W.A. White	Leicestershire	38.5	1	230	8	4-36	28.75	0	0
T.D. Groenewald	Derbyshire	22.0	0	116	4	3-33	29.00	0	0
A.J. Shantry	Glamorgan	8.0	2	29	1	1-29	29.00	0	0
T. Henderson	Middlesex	37.4	2	176	6	2-19	29.33	0	0
A.G. Botha	Warwickshire	45.0	0	211	7	3-72	30.14	0	0
D.A. Cosker	Glamorgan	40.0	1	211	7	2-26	30.14	0	0
D.S. Harrison	Glamorgan	37.0	4	215	7	3-55	30.71	0	0
S.T. Finn	Middlesex	17.0	0	94	3	1-21	31.33	0	0
L.M. Daggett	Northamptonshire	42.0	1	251	8	3-44	31.37	0	0
G.M. Smith	Derbyshire	43.0	0	253	8	2-34	31.62	0	0
K.S. Toor	Middlesex	4.0	0	32	1	1-25	32.00	0	0
Azhar Mahmood	Kent	43.4	4	262	8	4-41	32.75	0	0
G.G. Wagg	Derbyshire	15.0	0	66	2	1-24	33.00	0	0
K.W. Hogg	Lancashire	46.0	1	201	6	3-18	33.50	0	0
P. Edwards	Kent	34.0	1	241	7	3-57	34.42	0	0

STATISTICS OF SUMMER

		Overs	Mdns	Runs	Wkts	Best	Avge	5w	10w
G. Chapple	Lancashire	7.0	0	35	1	1-35	35.00	0	0
N.A. James	Glamorgan	6.0	0	35	1	1-35	35.00	0	0
J. Needham	Derbyshire	26.0	0	144	4	2-39	36.00	0	0
S.J. Walters	Surrey	4.0	0	36	1	1-36	36.00	0	0
J. Allenby	Glamorgan	19.0	0	109	3	2-23	36.33	0	0
P.S. Jones	Derbyshire	14.0	0	73	2	2-37	36.50	0	0
N.L. Buck	Leicestershire	25.0	2	151	4	2-38	37.75	0	0
D.H. Wigley	Northamptonshire	5.0	0	38	1	1-38	38.00	0	0
S.J. Croft	Lancashire	11.0	0	77	2	1-8	38.50	0	0
M.N.W. Spriegel	Surrey	47.0	2	232	6	2-23	38.66	0	0
M. Hayward	Derbyshire	16.0	1	84	2	1-34	42.00	0	0
J.C. Tredwell	Kent	36.0	0	176	4	2-28	44.00	0	0
G.T. Park	Derbyshire	28.5	1	176	4	2-40	44.00	0	0
J.G.E. Benning	Leicestershire	34.2	1	183	4	1-24	45.75	0	0
S.J. Cook	Kent	8.0	0	46	1	1-46	46.00	0	0
D.A. Burton	Middlesex	15.0	0	94	2	1-26	47.00	0	0
R.S. Ferley	Kent	44.4	0	235	5	2-42	47.00	0	0
D. Masters	Leicestershire	7.4	0	49	1	1-49	49.00	0	0
D.J. Malan	Middlesex	24.2	0	149	3	1-1	49.66	0	0
C.E.J. Thompson	Leicestershire	6.0	0	51	1	1-22	51.00	0	0
C.P. Schofield	Surrey	42.4	0	266	5	2-36	53.20	0	0
J.W. Dernbach	Surrey	47.1	1	295	5	2-46	59.00	0	0
J.A.R. Harris	Glamorgan	10.4	0	60	1	1-38	60.00	0	0
G.J.P. Kruger	Glamorgan	16.0	0	122	2	2-54	61.00	0	0
A.J. Hall	Northamptonshire	25.0	1	125	2	1-21	62.50	0	0
H.F. Gurney	Leicestershire	32.3	0	189	3	1-16	63.00	0	0
T.E. Linley	Surrey	48.0	0	253	4	2-38	63.25	0	0
J.M. Kemp	Kent	7.0	0	67	1	1-11	67.00	0	0
I.E. O'Brien	Leicestershire	17.0	0	70	1	1-31	70.00	0	0
A. Khan	Kent	12.0	1	74	1	1-47	74.00	0	0
F. du Plessis	Lancashire	13.5	0	75	1	1-45	75.00	0	0
M.A.K. Lawson	Derbyshire	11.0	0	91	1	1-64	91.00	0	0
J.W.M. Dalrymple	Glamorgan	15.4	0	118	1	1-35	118.00	0	0
C.F. Hughes	Derbyshire	21.0	0	119	1	1-34	119.00	0	0

Overall MVP

	Player	County	Pts
1	Trescothick, Marcus	Somerset	632
2	Blackwell, Ian	Durham	582
3	Kieswetter, Craig	Somerset	537
4	Davies, Steven	Worcs	508
5	Hall, Andrew	Northants	486
6	Yardy, Michael	Sussex	486
7	Patel, Samit	Notts	477
8	Ervine, Sean	Hants	474
9	Tredwell, James	Kent	468
10	Trott, Jonathan	Warks	461

LV=CC MVP 2009

	Player	County	Pts
1	Blackwell, Ian	Durham	353
2	Trescothick, Marcus	Somerset	339
3	Di Venuto, Michael	Durham	333
4	Tredwell, James	Kent	311
5	Hall, Andrew	Northants	301
6	Croft, Robert	Glamorgan	280
7	Kaneria, Danish	Essex	279
8	Nash, Chris	Sussex	278
9	Read, Chris	Notts	269
10	Suppiah, Arul	Somerset	267

Twenty20 MVP 2009

	Player	County	Pts
1	Stevens, Darren	Kent	143
2	Harvey, Ian	Northants	142
3	Trott, Jonathan	Warks	137
4	Allenby, James	Glamorgan	133
5	Smith, Dwayne	Sussex	130
6	Yardy, Michael	Sussex	122
7	Dalrymple, James	Glamorgan	119
8	Lumb, Michael	Hants	119
9	de Bruyn, Zander	Somerset	112
10	Ervine, Sean	Hants	107

Friends Provident MVP 2009

	Player	County	Pts
1	Joyce, Ed	Sussex	120
2	de Bruyn, Zander	Somerset	120
3	Schofield, Chris	Surrey	114
4	Trego, Peter	Somerset	112
5	Trescothick, Marcus	Somerset	111
6	Kieswetter, Craig	Somerset	109
7	Yardy, Michael	Sussex	108
8	Patel, Samit	Notts	106
9	Cork, Dominic	Hants	104
10	Pyrah, Richard	Yorks	101

NatWest Pro40 MVP 2009

	Player	County	Pts
1	Mustard, Philip	Durham	115
2	Davies, Steven	Worcs	108
3	Foster, James	Essex	101
4	Rudolph, Jacques	Yorks	95
5	Smith, Dwayne	Sussex	94
6	Compton, Nicholas	Middx	92
7	de Bruyn, Zander	Somerset	88
8	Trescothick, Marcus	Somerset	88
9	Blackwell, Ian	Durham	84
10	Carter, Neil	Warks	82

Lancashire League

	P	W	T	L	NR	BatBP	BowBP	Adj	Pts
Accrington	26	17	0	8	1	4	36	0	213
Haslingden	26	16	0	8	2	11	32	0	209
Todmorden	26	15	1	8	2	11	29	0	203
East Lancashire	26	12	1	9	4	11	37	-1	186
Nelson	26	13	0	11	2	7	28	0	171
Church	26	12	0	12	2	8	34	-1	167
Enfield	26	13	0	10	3	2	25	0	166
Burnley	26	12	0	11	3	5	29	-1	162
Ramsbottom	26	10	0	12	4	18	23	0	153
Colne	26	10	0	12	4	7	30	-4	145
Lowerhouse	26	9	0	14	3	12	36	-3	144
Rishton	26	9	0	15	2	10	31	0	137
Bacup	26	8	0	16	2	12	23	0	121
Rawtenstall	26	7	0	17	2	3	27	0	106

Worsley Cup:

Winners: Ramsbottom (beat Todmorden by 5 runs)

Twenty20 Cup

Winners: Burnley (beat Nelson by 14 runs)

1st Test – Cardiff

July 8-12

England won toss and decided to bat

England First innings

			Runs	Balls	4s	6s
*A.J. Strauss	c Clarke	b Johnson	30	60	4	0
A.N. Cook	c Hussey	b Hilfenhaus	10	25	0	0
R.S. Bopara	c Hughes	b Johnson	35	52	6	0
K.P. Pietersen	c Katich	b Hauritz	69	141	4	0
P.D. Collingwood	c Haddin	b Hilfenhaus	64	145	6	0
+M.J. Prior		b Siddle	56	62	6	0
A. Flintoff		b Siddle	37	51	6	0
J.M. Anderson	c Hussey	b Hauritz	26	40	2	0
S.C.J. Broad		b Johnson	19	20	4	0
G.P. Swann	not out		47	40	6	0
M.S. Panesar	c Ponting	b Hauritz	4	17	0	0
Extras	(b 13, lb 11, nb 12, w 2)		38			
Total	(All out, 106.5 overs)		**435**			

Fall of wickets: 1-21 (21 Cook, 31 mins), 2-67 (46 Strauss, 59 mins), 3-90 (23 Bopara, 17 mins), 4-228 (138 Collingwood, 150 mins), 5-241 (13 Pietersen, 29 mins), 6-327 (86 Flintoff, 66 mins), 7-329 (2 Prior, 4 mins), 8-355 (26 Broad, 22 mins), 9-423 (68 Anderson, 43 mins), 10-435 (12 Panesar, 15 mins)

Bowling	O	M	R	W	Extras
M.G. Johnson	22	2	87	3	–
B.W. Hilfenhaus	27	5	77	2	(4nb, 1w)
P.M. Siddle	27	3	121	2	(5nb, 1w)
N.M. Hauritz	23.5	1	95	3	(3nb)
M.J. Clarke	5	0	20	0	–
S.M. Katich	2	0	11	0	–

Australia First innings

			Runs	Balls	4s	6s
P.J. Hughes	c Prior	b Flintoff	36	54	5	0
S.M. Katich	lbw	b Anderson	122	261	12	0
*R.T. Ponting		b Panesar	150	224	14	1
M.E.K. Hussey	c Prior	b Anderson	3	16	0	0
M.J. Clarke	c Prior	b Broad	83	145	9	1
M.J. North	not out		125	242	13	0
+B.J. Haddin	c Bopara	b Collingwood	121	151	11	3
Did not bat: M.G. Johnson, P.M. Siddle, B.W. Hilfenhaus, N.M. Hauritz						
Extras	(b 9, lb 14, nb 7, w 4)		34			
Total	(6 wkt declared, 181 overs)		**674**			

Fall of wickets: 1-60 (60 Hughes, 61 mins), 2-299 (239 Katich, 264 mins), 3-325 (26 Hussey, 24 mins), 4-331 (6 Ponting, 24 mins), 5-474 (143 Clarke, 151 mins), 6-674 (200 Haddin, 200 mins)

Bowling	O	M	R	W	Extras
J.M. Anderson	32	6	110	2	(1w)
S.C.J. Broad	32	6	129	1	(2w)
G.P. Swann	38	8	131	0	–
A. Flintoff	35	3	128	1	(7nb, 1w)
M.S. Panesar	3	5	4	115	1
P.D. Collingwood	9	0	38	1	–

England Second innings

			Runs	Balls	4s	6s
*A.J. Strauss	c Haddin	b Hauritz	17	54	1	0
A.N. Cook	lbw	b Johnson	6	12	1	0
R.S. Bopara	lbw	b Hilfenhaus	1	3	0	0
K.P. Pietersen		b Hilfenhaus	8	24	0	0
P.D. Collingwood	c Hussey	b Siddle	74	245	6	0
+M.J. Prior	c Clarke	b Hauritz	14	32	1	0
A. Flintoff	c Ponting	b Johnson	26	71	3	0
S.C.J. Broad	lbw	b Hauritz	14	47	1	0
G.P. Swann	lbw	b Hilfenhaus	31	63	4	0
J.M. Anderson	not out		21	53	3	0
M.S. Panesar	not out		7	35	1	0
Extras	(b 9, lb 9, nb 11, w 4)		33			
Total	(Close, 105 overs)		**252**			

Fall of wickets: 1-13 (13 Cook, 17 mins), 2-17 (4 Bopara, 4 mins), 3-31 (14 Pietersen, 20 mins), 4-46 (15 Strauss, 37 mins), 5-70 (24 Prior, 37 mins), 6-127 (57 Flintoff, 89 mins), 7-159 (32 Broad, 61 mins), 8-221 (62 Swann, 80 mins), 9-233 (12 Collingwood, 37 mins)

Bowling	O	M	R	W	Extras
M.G. Johnson	22	4	44	2	(1nb, 4w)
B.W. Hilfenhaus	15	3	47	3	(4nb)
P.M. Siddle	18	2	51	1	(2nb)
N.M. Hauritz	37	12	63	3	(2nb)
M.J. Clarke	3	0	8	0	–
M.J. North	7	4	14	0	–
S.M. Katich	3	0	7	0	–

Match drawn

Umpires: A. Dar, B.R. Doctrove

2nd Test – Lord's

July 16-20

England won the toss and decided to bat

England First innings

			Runs	Balls	4s	6s
*A.J. Strauss		b Hilfenhaus	161	268	22	0
A.N. Cook	lbw	b Johnson	95	147	18	0
R.S. Bopara	lbw	b Hilfenhaus	18	19	4	0
K.P. Pietersen	c Haddin	b Siddle	32	42	4	0
P.D. Collingwood	c Siddle	b Clarke	16	36	1	0
+M.J. Prior		b Johnson	8	10	2	0
A. Flintoff	c Ponting	b Hilfenhaus	4	10	1	0
S.C.J. Broad		b Hilfenhaus	16	26	2	0
G.P. Swann	c Ponting	b Siddle	4	6	1	0
J.M. Anderson	c Hussey	b Johnson	29	25	5	0
G. Onions	not out		17	29	2	0
Extras	(b 15, lb 2, nb 8, w 0)		25			
Total	(All out, 101.4 overs)		**425**			

Fall of wickets: 1-196 (196 Cook, 191 mins), 2-222 (26 Bopara, 20 mins), 3-267 (45 Pietersen, 38 mins), 4-302 (35 Collingwood, 43 mins), 5-317 (15 Prior, 10 mins), 6-333 (16 Flintoff, 12 mins), 7-364 (31 Strauss, 56 mins), 8-370 (6 Swann, 5 mins), 9-378 (8 Broad, 1 min), 10-425 (47 Anderson, 59 mins)

Bowling	O	M	R	W	Extras
B.W. Hilfenhaus	31	12	103	4	(4nb)
M.G. Johnson	21.4	2	132	3	–
P.M. Siddle	20	1	76	2	(4nb)
N.M. Hauritz	8.3	1	26	0	–
M.J. North	16.3	2	59	0	–
M.J. Clarke	4	1	12	1	–

Australia First innings

			Runs	Balls	4s	6s
P.J. Hughes	c Prior	b Anderson	4	9	1	0
S.M. Katich	c Broad	b Onions	48	93	6	0
*R.T. Ponting	c Strauss	b Anderson	2	15	0	0
M.E.K. Hussey		b Flintoff	51	91	8	0
M.J. Clarke	c Cook	b Anderson	1	12	0	0
M.J. North		b Anderson	0	14	0	0
+B.J. Haddin	c Cook	b Broad	28	38	3	0
M.G. Johnson	c Cook	b Broad	4	11	1	0
N.M. Hauritz	c Collingwood	b Onions	24	36	4	0
P.M. Siddle	c Strauss	b Onions	35	47	5	0
B.W. Hilfenhaus	not out		6	14	1	0
Extras	(b 4, lb 6, nb 2, w 0)		12			
Total	(All out, 63 overs)		**215**			

Fall of wickets: 1-4 (4 Hughes, 6 mins), 2-10 (6 Ponting, 20 mins), 3-103 (93 Katich, 109 mins), 4-111 (8 Hussey, 16 mins), 5-111 (0 Clarke, 6 mins), 6-139 (28 North, 24 mins), 7-148 (9 Johnson, 13 mins), 8-152 (4 Haddin, 16 mins), 9-196 (44 Hauritz, 37 mins), 10-215 (19 Siddle, 28 mins)

Bowling	O	M	R	W	Extras
J.M. Anderson	21	5	55	4	–
A. Flintoff	12	4	27	1	(2nb)
S.C.J. Broad	18	1	78	2	–
G. Onions	11	1	41	3	–
G.P. Swann	1	0	4	0	–

England Second innings

			Runs	Balls	4s	6s
*A.J. Strauss	c Clarke	b Hauritz	32	48	4	0
A.N. Cook	lbw	b Hauritz	32	42	6	0
R.S. Bopara	c Katich	b Hauritz	27	93	4	0
K.P. Pietersen	c Haddin	b Siddle	44	101	5	0
P.D. Collingwood	c Haddin	b Siddle	54	80	4	0
+M.J. Prior	run out (North)		61	42	9	0
A. Flintoff	not out		30	27	4	0
S.C.J. Broad	not out		0	0	0	0
Did not bat: G.P. Swann, J.M. Anderson, G. Onions						
Extras	(b 16, lb 9, nb 5, w 1)		31			
Total	(6 wkt declared, 71.2 overs)		**311**			

Fall of wickets: 1-61 (61 Cook, 52 mins), 2-74 (13 Strauss, 9 mins), 3-147 (73 Bopara, 124 mins), 4-174 (27 Pietersen, 26 mins), 5-260 (86 Prior, 50 mins), 6-311 (51 Collingwood, 42 mins)

Bowling	O	M	R	W	Extras
B.W. Hilfenhaus	19	5	59	0	(3nb)
M.G. Johnson	17	2	68	0	(1nb, 1w)
P.M. Siddle	15.2	4	64	2	–
N.M. Hauritz	16	1	80	3	(1nb)
M.J. Clarke	4	0	15	0	–

Australia Second innings

			Runs	Balls	4s	6s
P.J. Hughes	c Strauss	b Flintoff	17	34	2	0
S.M. Katich	c Pietersen	b Flintoff	6	5	1	0
*R.T. Ponting		b Broad	38	69	6	0
M.E.K. Hussey	c Collingwood	b Swann	27	63	3	0
M.J. Clarke		b Swann	136	227	14	0
M.J. North		b Swann	6	25	1	0
+B.J. Haddin	c Collingwood	b Flintoff	80	130	10	0
M.G. Johnson		b Swann	63	75	9	0
N.M. Hauritz		b Flintoff	1	5	0	0
P.M. Siddle		b Flintoff	7	13	1	0
B.W. Hilfenhaus	not out		4	4	0	0
Extras	(b 5, lb 8, nb 8, w 0)		21			
Total	(All out, 107 overs)		**406**			

Fall of wickets: 1-17 (17 Katich, 15 mins), 2-34 (17 Hughes, 30 mins), 3-78 (44 Ponting, 57 mins), 4-120 (42 Hussey, 43 mins), 5-128 (8 North, 23 mins), 6-313 (185 Haddin, 186 mins), 7-356 (43 Clarke, 61 mins), 8-363 (7 Hauritz, 5 mins), 9-388 (25 Siddle, 18 mins), 10-406 (18 MG Johnson, 10 mins)

Bowling	O	M	R	W	Extras
J.M. Anderson	21	4	86	0	–
A. Flintoff	27	4	92	5	(8nb)
G. Onions	9	0	50	0	–
S.C.J. Broad	16	3	49	1	–.
G.P. Swann	28	3	87	4	–
P.D. Collingwood	6	1	29	0	–

England won by 115 runs

Umpires: B.R. Doctrove, R. Koertzen

See p211 for 3rd Test statistics

4th Test – Headingley

August 7-9

England won the toss and decided to bat

England First innings

			Runs	Balls	4s	6s
*A.J. Strauss	c North	b Siddle	3	17	0	0
A.N. Cook	c Clarke	b Clark	30	65	3	0
R.S. Bopara	c Hussey	b Hilfenhaus	1	6	0	0
I.R. Bell	c Haddin	b Johnson	8	26	2	0
P.D. Collingwood	c Ponting	b Clark	0	5	0	0
+M.J. Prior	not out		37	43	5	0
S.C.J. Broad	c Katich	b Clark	3	12	0	0
G.P. Swann	c Clarke	b Siddle	0	15	0	0
S.J. Harmison	c Haddin	b Siddle	0	6	0	0
J.M. Anderson	c Haddin	b Siddle	3	10	0	0
G. Onions	c Katich	b Siddle	0	1	0	0
Extras	(b 5, lb 8, nb 3, w 1)		17			
Total	(All out, 33.5 overs)		**102**			

Fall of wickets: 1-11 (11 Strauss, 16 mins), 2-16 (5 Bopara, 9 mins), 3-39 (23 Bell, 39 mins), 4-42 (3 Collingwood, 11 mins), 5-63 (21 Cook, 30 mins), 6-72 (9 Broad, 12 mins), 7-92 (20 Swann, 20 mins), 8-98 (6 Harmison, 7 mins), 9-102 (4 Anderson, 6 mins), 10-102 (0 Onions, 1 min)

Bowling	O	M	R	W	Extras
B.W. Hilfenhaus	7	0	20	1	(2nb)
P.M. Siddle	9.5	0	21	5	(1nb)
M.G. Johnson	7	0	30	1	(1w)
S.R. Clark	10	4	18	3	–

Australia First innings

			Runs	Balls	4s	6s
S.R. Watson	lbw	b Onions	51	67	9	0
S.M. Katich	c Bopara	b Harmison	0	4	0	0
*R.T. Ponting	lbw	b Broad	78	101	12	1
M.E.K. Hussey	lbw	b Broad	10	10	2	0
M.J. Clarke	lbw	b Onions	93	138	13	0
M.J. North	c Anderson	b Broad	110	206	13	1
+B.J. Haddin	c Bell	b Harmison	14	23	1	0
M.G. Johnson	c Bopara	b Broad	27	53	5	0
P.M. Siddle		b Broad	0	1	0	0
S.R. Clark		b Broad	32	22	1	3
B.W. Hilfenhaus	not out		0	3	0	0
Extras	(b 9, lb 14, nb 3, w 4)		30			
Total	(All out, 104.1 overs)		**445**			

Fall of wickets: 1-14 (14 Katich, 7 mins), 2-133 (119 Watson, 111 mins), 3-140 (7 Ponting, 9 mins), 4-151 (11 Hussey, 4 mins), 5-303 (152 Clarke, 190 mins), 6-323 (20 Haddin, 24 mins), 7-393 (70 Johnson, 72 mins), 8-394 (1 Siddle, 1 min), 9-440 (46 Clark, 24 mins), 10-445 (5 North, 7 mins)

Bowling	O	M	R	W	Extras
J.M. Anderson	18	3	89	0	(1w)
S.J. Harmison	23	4	98	2	(1w)
G. Onions	22	5	80	2	(2nb, 1w)
S.C.J. Broad	25.1	6	91	6	(1nb, 1w)
G.P. Swann	16	4	64	0	–

England Second innings

			Runs	Balls	4s	6s
*A.J. Strauss	lbw	b Hilfenhaus	32	78	4	0
A.N. Cook	c Haddin	b Johnson	30	84	4	0
R.S. Bopara	lbw	b Hilfenhaus	0	1	0	0
I.R. Bell	c Ponting	b Johnson	3	12	0	0
P.D. Collingwood	lbw	b Johnson	4	10	0	0
J.M. Anderson	c Ponting	b Hilfenhaus	4	10	1	0
+M.J. Prior	c Haddin	b Hilfenhaus	22	29	3	0
S.C.J. Broad	c Watson	b Siddle	61	49	10	0
G.P. Swann	c Haddin	b Johnson	62	72	7	1
S.J. Harmison	not out		19	28	4	0
G. Onions		b Johnson	0	7	0	0
Extras	(b 5, lb 5, nb 11, w 5)		26			
Total	(All out, 61.3 overs)		**263**			

Fall of wickets: 1-58 (58 Strauss, 99 mins), 2-58 (0 Bopara, 1 min), 3-67 (9 Bell, 13 mins), 4-74 (7 Collingwood, 9 mins), 5-78 (4 Cook, 16 mins), 6-86 (8 Anderson, 1 min), 7-120 (34 Prior, 39 mins), 8-228 (108 Broad, 53 mins), 9-259 (31 Swann, 44 mins), 10-263 (4 Onions, 8 mins)

Bowling	O	M	R	W	Extras
B.W. Hilfenhaus	19	2	60	4	(9nb)
P.M. Siddle	12	2	50	1	(1nb, 1w)
S.R. Clark	11	1	74	0	(1nb)
M.G. Johnson	19.3	3	69	5	–

Australia won by an innings and 80 runs

Umpires: A. Rauf, B.F. Bowden

5th Test – The Oval

August 20-23

England won the toss and decided to bat

England First innings

			Runs	Balls	4s	6s
*A.J. Strauss	c Haddin	b Hilfenhaus	55	101	11	0
A.N. Cook	c Ponting	b Siddle	10	12	2	0
I.R. Bell		b Siddle	72	137	10	0
P.D. Collingwood	c Hussey	b Siddle	24	65	3	0
I.J.L. Trott	run out (Katich)		41	81	5	0
+M.J. Prior	c Watson	b Johnson	18	33	2	0
A. Flintoff	c Haddin	b Johnson	7	19	1	0
S.C.J. Broad	c Ponting	b Hilfenhaus	37	69	5	0
G.P. Swann	c Haddin	b Siddle	18	28	2	0
J.M. Anderson	lbw	b Hilfenhaus	0	6	0	0
S.J. Harmison	not out		12	12	3	0
Extras	(b 12, lb 5, nb 18, w 3)		38			
Total	(All out, 90.5 overs)		**332**			

Fall of wickets: 1-12 (12 Cook, 20 mins), 2-114 (102 Strauss, 108 mins), 3-176 (62 Collingwood, 89 mins), 4-181 (5 Bell, 25 mins), 5-229 (48 Prior, 54 mins), 6-247 (18 Flintoff, 23 mins), 7-268 (21 Trott, 24 mins), 8-307 (39 Swann, 42 mins), 9-308 (1 Anderson, 6 mins), 10-332 (24 Broad, 14 mins)

Bowling	O	M	R	W	Extras
B.W. Hilfenhaus	21.5	5	71	3	(5nb)
P.M. Siddle	21	6	75	4	(4nb)
S.R. Clark	14	5	41	0	–
M.G. Johnson	15	0	69	2	(8nb, 3w)
M.J. North	14	3	33	0	(1nb)
S.R. Watson	5	0	26	0	–

Australia First innings

			Runs	Balls	4s	6s
S.R. Watson	lbw	b Broad	34	69	7	0
S.M. Katich	c Cook	b Swann	50	107	7	0
*R.T. Ponting		b Broad	8	15	1	0
M.E.K. Hussey	lbw	b Broad	0	3	0	0
M.J. Clarke	c Trott	b Broad	3	7	0	0
M.J. North	lbw	b Swann	8	17	1	0
+B.J. Haddin		b Broad	1	9	0	0
M.G. Johnson	c Prior	b Swann	11	24	2	0
P.M. Siddle	not out		26	38	5	0
S.R. Clark	c Cook	b Swann	6	8	1	0
B.W. Hilfenhaus		b Flintoff	6	21	1	0
Extras	(b 1, lb 5, nb 1, w 0)		7			
Total	(All out, 52.5 overs)		**160**			

Fall of wickets: 1-73 (73 Watson, 94 mins), 2-85 (12 Ponting, 17 mins), 3-89 (4 Hussey, 6 mins), 4-93 (4 Clarke, 6 mins), 5-108 (15 North, 26 mins), 6-109 (1 Katich, 21 mins), 7-111 (2 Haddin, 1 min), 8-131 (20 Johnson, 34 mins), 9-143 (12 Clark, 13 mins), 10-160 (17 Hilfenhaus, 18 mins)

Bowling	O	M	R	W	Extras
J.M. Anderson	9	3	29	0	–
A. Flintoff	13.5	4	35	1	–
G.P. Swann	14	3	38	4	–
S.J. Harmison	4	1	15	0	(1nb)
S.C.J. Broad	12	1	37	5	–

England Second innings

			Runs	Balls	4s	6s
*A.J. Strauss	c Clarke	b North	75	191	8	0
A.N. Cook	c Clarke	b North	9	35	0	0
I.R. Bell	c Katich	b Johnson	4	7	1	0
P.D. Collingwood	c Katich	b Johnson	1	7	0	0
I.J.L. Trott	c North	b Clark	119	193	12	0
+M.J. Prior	run out (Katich)		4	9	1	0
A. Flintoff	c Siddle	b North	22	18	4	0
S.C.J. Broad	c Ponting	b North	29	35	5	0
G.P. Swann	c Haddin	b Hilfenhaus	63	55	9	0
J.M. Anderson	not out		15	29	2	0
Did not bat: S.J. Harmison						
Extras	(b 1, lb 15, nb 9, w 7)		32			
Total	(9 wkt declared, 95 overs)		**373**			

Fall of wickets: 1-27 (27 Cook, 49 mins), 2-34 (7 Bell, 13 mins), 3-39 (5 Collingwood, 6 mins), 4-157 (118 Strauss, 155 mins), 5-168 (11 Prior, 13 mins), 6-200 (32 Flintoff, 24 mins), 7-243 (43 Broad, 43 mins), 8-333 (90 Swann, 57 mins), 9-373 (40 Trott, 36 mins)

Bowling	O	M	R	W	Extras
B.W. Hilfenhaus	11	1	58	1	(4nb)
P.M. Siddle	17	3	69	0	(2w)
M.J. North	30	4	98	4	(1w)
M.G. Johnson	17	1	60	2	(5nb, 2w)
S.M. Katich	5	2	9	0	–
S.R. Clark	12	2	43	1	–
M.J. Clarke	3	0	20	0	–

Australia Second innings

			Runs	Balls	4s	6s
S.R. Watson	lbw	b Broad	40	81	6	0
S.M. Katich	lbw	b Swann	43	68	7	0
*R.T. Ponting	run out (Flintoff)		66	103	10	0
M.E.K. Hussey	c Cook	b Swann	121	263	14	0
M.J. Clarke	run out (Strauss)		0	4	0	0
M.J. North	st Prior	b Swann	10	24	2	0
+B.J. Haddin	c Strauss	b Swann	34	49	6	0
M.G. Johnson	c Collingwood	b Harmison	0	5	0	0
P.M. Siddle	c Flintoff	b Harmison	10	14	1	0
S.R. Clark	c Cook	b Harmison	0	1	0	0
B.W. Hilfenhaus	not out		4	8	1	0
Extras	(b 7, lb 7, nb 6, w 0)		20			
Total	(All out, 102.2 overs)		**348**			

Fall of wickets: 1-86 (86 Katich, 100 mins), 2-90 (4 Watson, 4 mins), 3-217 (127 Ponting, 153 mins), 4-220 (3 Clarke, 4 mins), 5-236 (16 North, 27 mins), 6-327 (91 Haddin, 97 mins), 7-327 (0 Johnson, 5 mins), 8-343 (16 Siddle, 14 mins), 9-343 (0 Clark, 1 min), 10-348 (5 Hussey, 26 mins)

Bowling	O	M	R	W	Extras
J.M. Anderson	12	2	46	0	(1nb)
A. Flintoff	11	1	42	0	(1nb)
S.J. Harmison	16	5	54	3	(4nb)
G.P. Swann	40.2	8	120	4	–
S.C.J. Broad	22	4	71	1	–
P.D. Collingwood	1	0	1	0	–

England won by 197 runs

Umpires: A. Rauf, B.F. Bowden

TEST MATCH AVERAGES: ENGLAND

Batting and Fielding

Player	Mat	Inns	NO	HS	Runs	Ave	100	50	Ct/St
I.J.L. Trott	1	2	–	119	160	80.00		1	1
A.J. Strauss	5	9	–	161	474	52.67	3	1	4
K.P. Pietersen	2	4		69	153	38.25	1		1
G.P. Swann	5	8	1	63	249	35.57	2		1
A. Flintoff	4	7	1	74	200	33.33	1		1
M.J. Prior	5	9	1	61	261	32.62	2		11 /1
S.J. Harmison	2	3	2	19*	31	31.00			
S.C.J. Broad	5	9	1	61	234	29.25	2		1
I.R. Bell	3	5		72	140	28.00	2		1
P.D. Collingwood	5	9		74	250	27.77	3		4
A.N. Cook	5	9		95	222	24.67	1		7
J.M. Anderson	5	8	2	29	99	16.50			2
R.S. Bopara	4	7		35	105	15.00			3
M.S. Panesar	1	2	1	7*	11	11.00			
G. Onions	3	4	2	17*	19	9.50			

Bowling

Player	Overs	Mdns	Runs	Wkts	Best	Ave	5w	10wM
S.C.J. Broad	154.1	25	544	18	6-91	30.22	2	–
G. Onions	77.4	11	303	10	4-58	30.30	–	–
S.J. Harmison	43.0	10	167	5	3-54	33.40	–	–
G.P. Swann	170.2	30	567	14	4-38	40.50	–	–
J.M. Anderson	158.0	38	542	12	5-80	45.17	1	–
A. Flintoff	128.5	18	417	8	5-92	52.12	1	–

Also bowled: R.S. Bopara 8-1-44-0; P.D. Collingwood 18-1-76-1; M.S. Panesar 35-4-115-1.

TEST MATCH AVERAGES:
AUSTRALIA

Batting and Fielding

Player	Mat	Inns	NO	HS	Runs	Ave	100	50	Ct/St
M.J. Clarke	5	8	1	136	448	64.00	2	2	8
M.J. North	5	8	1	125'	367	52.42	1	2	3
R.T. Ponting	5	8	–	150	385	48.12	2	1	11
S.R Watson	3	5		62	240	48.00	3		2
B.J. Haddin	4	6	–	121	278	46.33	1		15
S.M. Katich	5	8	–	122	341	42.62	1		6
M.E.K. Hussey	5	8	–	121	276	34.50	2		6
N.M. Hauritz	3	3	1	24	45	22.50			
G.A. Manou	1	2	1	13'	21	21.00			3
B.W. Hilfenhaus	5	6	4	20	40	20.00			
P.J. Hughes	2	3		36	57	19.00			1
P.M. Siddle	5	6		35	91	18.20			3
M.G. Johnson	5	6		63	105	17.50			
S.R. Clark	2	3		32	38	12.67			

Bowling

Player	Overs	Mdns	Runs	Wkts	Best	Ave	5w	10wM
B.W. Hilfenhaus	180.5	40	604	22	4-60	27.45	–	–
P.M. Siddle	161.4	24	616	20	5-21	30.80	1	–
N.M. Hauritz	103.2	17	321	10	3-63	32.10	–	–
M.G. Johnson	162.1	15	651	20	5-69	32.55	1	–
S.R. Clark	47.0	12	176	4	4-131	44.00	–	–
M.J. North	67.3	13	204	4	4-98	51.00	–	–

Also bowled: M.J. Clarke 19-1-75-1; S.M. Katich 10-2-27-0; S.R. Watson 8-0-49-0.

ICC Twenty20 World Cup

Group A

	Mat	Won	Lost	Tied	N/R	Pts	Net RR
India	2	2	0	0	0	4	+1.227
Ireland	2	1	1	0	0	2	-0.162
Bangladesh	2	0	2	0	0	0	-0.996

Group B

	Mat	Won	Lost	Tied	N/R	Pts	Net RR
England	2	1	1	0	0	2	+1.175
Pakistan	2	1	1	0	0	2	+0.850
Netherlands	2	1	1	0	0	2	-2.025

Group C

	Mat	Won	Lost	Tied	N/R	Pts	Net RR
Sri Lanka	2	2	0	0	0	4	+0.626
West Indies	2	1	1	0	0	2	+0.715
Australia	2	0	2	0	0	0	-1.331

Group D

	Mat	Won	Lost	Tied	N/R	Pts	Net RR
South Africa	2	2	0	0	0	4	+3.275
New Zealand	2	1	1	0	0	2	+0.309
Scotland	2	0	2	0	0	0	-5.281

Super Eights

Group E

	Mat	Won	Lost	Tied	N/R	Pts	Net RR
South Africa	3	3	0	0	0	6	+0.787
West Indies	3	2	1	0	0	4	+0.063
England	3	1	2	0	0	2	-0.414
India	3	0	3	0	0	0	-0.466

Group F

	Mat	Won	Lost	Tied	N/R	Pts	Net RR
Sri Lanka	3	3	0	0	0	6	+1.267
Pakistan	3	2	1	0	0	4	+1.185
New Zealand	3	1	2	0	0	2	-0.232
Ireland	3	0	3	0	0	0	-2.183

Semi finals

Pakistan v South Africa at Trent Bridge
Pakistan won by 7 runs

Sri Lanka v West Indies at The Oval
Sri Lanka won by 57 runs

Final

Pakistan v Sri Lanka at Lord's
Sri Lanka 139 (Sangakkara 64 not out, Razzaq 3-20)
Pakistan 139-2 (Afridi 54 not out)
Pakistan won by eight wickets

Man of the Match: Afridi

BIBLIOGRAPHY

BIBLIOGRAPHY

Books

Anstey, J. and Silverlight, J., *The Observer Observed*, Barrie & Jenkins, 1991

Arlott, J., *Concerning Cricket*, Longmans, 1949
How to Watch Cricket, Collins, 1983
On Cricket: His Writings on the Game (ed. David Rayvern Allen), Collins, 1984
The Essential Arlott (ed. David Rayvern Allen), Collins 1989
The Vision Sings: John Arlott, The Voice of Cricket (collected by Alex Murphy) Toilet Books, 2007

Atherton, M., *Atherton's Ashes: How England Won the 2009 Ashes*, Simon and Schuster, 2009

Bailey, T., *Sir Gary*, Collins, 1976

Bannister, J. and Graveney, D., *Durham CCC: Past, Present and Future*, Lennard Queen Anne Press, 1993

Birley, D., *The Willow Wand: Some Cricket Myths Explored*, Simon and Schuster, 1989

Booth, L., *What are the Butchers For?*, A & C Black, 2009

Bowen, R., *Cricket: A History of Its Growth and Development throughout the World*, Eyre and Spottiswoode, 1970

Brearley, M., *The Art of Captaincy*, Hodder, 1985

Bright-Holmes, J. (ed.), *The Joy of Cricket*, Peerage Books, 1986

Brookes, C., *English Cricket*, Weidenfeld, 1978

Cardus, N., *The Playfair Cardus*, The Dickens Press, 1963
Cardus on Cricket, Souvenir, 1977
Play Resumed with Cardus, Souvenir, 1979
The Roses Matches 1919–1939, Souvenir, 1982

Constantine, L. and Batchelor, D., *The Changing Face of Cricket*, Eyre and Spottiswoode, 1966

Cox, P., *Sixty Summers: English Cricket since World War 2*, Cox, 2006

Cozier, T., *The West Indies, Fifty Years of Test Cricket*, Angus and Robertson, 1978

Darwin, B., *W. G. Grace*, Duckworth, 1978/1934

Duckworth, L., *Holmes and Sutcliffe: The Run Stealers*, Hutchinson, 1970

Edmundson, D., *See the Conquering Hero: The Story of the Lancashire League 1892–1992*, Lancashire League, 1993

Eliot, T. S., *Collected Poems*, Faber and Faber, 1962

Engel, M. (ed.), *The Guardian Book of Cricket*, Pavilion, 1986

Fingleton, J., *Four Chukkas to Australia*, Heinemann, 1959

Foot, D., *Wally Hammond: The Reasons Why*, Robson, 1998
Fragments of Idolatry, Fairfield Books, 2001

Frewin, L. (ed.), *The Boundary Book*, Macdonald, 1962
The Poetry of Cricket, Macdonald, 1964

Frith, D., *Silence of the Heart*, Mainstream, 2001
The Golden Age of Cricket, 1890–1914, Omega 1983

Frindall, B., *The Wisden Book of Test Cricket, 1876–77 to 1977–78*, Macdonald and Jane's, 1980

Gale, F., *Echoes from Old Cricket Fields*, SR Publishers, 1972/1871

Graveney, T. and Seabrook, M., *Fine Glances, A Connoisseur's Cricket Anthonology*, Simon and Schuster, 1990

Green, B. (ed.), *Cricket Archive*, Pavilion, 1977
The Wisden Book of Cricketers' Lives, Queen Anne Press, 1986
The Lord's Companion, Pavilion, 1987

Haigh, G. (ed.), *Mystery Spinner, The Story of Jack Iverson*, Aurum, 2000
Endless Summmer: 140 Years of Australian Cricket in Wisden, Hardie Grant, 2002
The Ultimate Test, The Story of the 2009 Ashes Series, Aurum, 2009

Hall, W., *Pace Like Fire*, Pelham, 1965

Hamilton, D., *Sweet Summers: The Classic Cricket Writing of J. M. Kilburn*, Great Northern, 2008
Harold Larwood, The Authorised Biography

BIBLIOGRAPHY

of the World's Fastest Bowler, Quercus, 2009

Hart-Davis, D., *Pavilions of Splendour: An Architectural History of Lord's*, Methuen, 2004

Hayes, D., *The War of the Roses, A History of Lancashire v Yorkshire*, Parrs Wood Press, 2000

Hayter, R., *The Best of the Cricketer, 1921–1981*, Cassell, 1981

Heald, T., *The Character of Cricket*, Pavilion, 1986
Village Cricket, TimeWarner, 2004

Hodgson, D., *The Official History of Yorkshire County Cricket Club*, Leeds Carnegie, 2009

Hopps, D., *A Century of Great Cricket Quotes*, Robson Books, 1998

Hoult, N. (ed)., *The Wit and Wisdom of Cricket*, House of Raven, 2006
The Daily Telegraph Book of Cricket, Aurum, 2007

Howat, G., *Village Cricket*, David and Charles, 1980

Hughes, S., *And God Created Cricket*, Doubleday, 2009

Hutton, L., *Just My Story*, Hutchinson, 1956

James, C. L. R., *Beyond a Boundary*, Century, 1963

Kay, J., *Cricket in the Leagues*, Eyre and Spottiswoode, 1970

Kay, J. and Prittie, T. C. E., *Second Innings: The Revival of Lancashire Cricket*, Sherratt, 1947

Kilburn, J. M., *The Scarborough Cricket Festival*, The Yorkdale Press, 1948

Kilburn, J. M. and Yardley, N., *Homes of Sport: Cricket*, Peter Garnett, 1952

Langer, J., *Seeing the Sun Rise*, Allen and Unwin, 2008

Lemmon, D., *Cricket Mercenaries: Overseas Players in English Cricket*, Pavilion, 1987
Len Hutton: A Pictorial Biography, Collins and Brown, 1990
Changing Seasons: A History of Cricket in England 1945–1996, Andre Deutsch, 1997

Lillywhite: Scores and Biographies, Lillywhite, various editions

MacDonnell, A. G., *England, Their England*, Macmillan, 1933

Martin-Jenkins, C. (ed.), *The Spirit of Cricket, A Personal Anthology*, Faber and Faber, 1994
The Top 100 Cricketers of All Time, Corinthian Books, 2009

Marshall, J., *Headingley*, Pelham Books, 1970

Mason, R., *Sing All a Green Willow*, Epworth, 1967

Melford, M. (ed.), *Pick of the Cricketer*, Hutchinson, 1967
Fresh Pick of the Cricketer, Hutchinson, 1969

Meynell, L., *Famous Cricket Grounds*, Phoenix House, 1951

Mills, R., *Field of Dreams, Headingley 1890–2001*, Great Northern, 2001

Moorhouse, G., *The Best Loved Game*, Hodder, 1979
Lord's, Hodder, 1983

Murphy, P., *The Centurions: From Grace to Ramprakash*, Fairfield Books, 2009

Peebles, I., *The Watney Book of Test Match Grounds*, 1967
Woolley, The Pride of Kent, Hutchinson, 1969

Peskett, R., *The Best of Cricket*, Hamlyn, 1982

Plumptree, G., *Homes of Cricket*, Queen Anne Press, 1988

Rae, S., *W. G. Grace: A Life*, Faber and Faber, 1998

Ramprakash, M., *Strictly Me: My Life Under the Spotlight*, Mainstream, 2009

Robertson-Glasgow, R. C., *Crusoe on Cricket*, ed. Alan Ross, 1966
46 Not Out, Hollis and Carter, 1948

Robinson, D., *A Legend Dies, The Story of a Tree with a Cricketing History*, 2006

Robinson, R., *On Top Down Under*, Cassell, 1975

Ross, A., *Collected Poems*, Harvill, 2005

Rushton, J., *Ramsbottom Cricket Club 1845–1995: A Sesquicentenary Celebration*, Elland, 1995

Simons, G., *Lillywhite's Legacy: A History of the Cheltenham Cricket Festival*, Wisteria Books, 2004

BIBLIOGRAPHY

Sobers, G. and Barker, J. S., *Cricket in the Sun*,
  Barker, 1967
Sutcliffe, H., *For England and Yorkshire*,
  Edward Arnold, 1935
  How to Become a First Class Batsman,
  Herbert Sutcliffe Ltd, 1949
Swanton, E. W., *Cricket From All Angles*,
  Michael Joseph, 1969
  Kent Cricket, A Photographic History,
  1744–1984, Brillings, 1984
Thomas, E., *The South Country*, Hutchinson,
  1984/1910
Thomson, A. A., *The Great Cricketer:
  A Biography of W. G. Grace*, Robert Hale,
  1957
  Cricket Bouquet, Museum Press, 1961
  Cricket: The Golden Ages, Stanley Paul, 1961
  The Wars of the Roses, Pelham, 1967
Thomson, J., *Thommo*, Angus and Robertson,
  1980
Trescothick, M., *Coming Back to Me*,
  HarperCollins, 2008
Vaughan, M., *Calling the Shots*, Hodder, 2005
  Time to Declare, Hodder, 2009
Wellock, T., *Summers with Durham*, Caboodle
  Books, 2009
Williams, M., *Double Century, 200 Years of
  Cricket in the Times*, Collins, 1985
Wisden, various editions
Wynne-Thomas, P., *The History of
  Nottinghamshire County Cricket Club*,
  Christopher Helm, 1992

Newspapers and Magazines
*The Accrington Observer, The Australian,
The Birmingham Mail, The Birmingham Post,
The Brighton Argus, The Cricketer,
The Daily Mail, The Daily Telegraph,
The Derby Telegraph, The Evening Standard,
The Gloucestershire Echo, The Guardian,
The Jamaican Gleaner, The Kent Messenger,
Kent on Sunday, The Leicester Mercury,
The Liverpool Daily Echo, The Liverpool Daily
Post, The Manchester Evening News,
Melbourne Age, The Newcastle Journal,
The Northampton Chronicle and Echo,*

*The Northern Echo, The Nottingham Evening
Post, The Observer, Playfair Cricket Monthly,
The Rossendale Free Press, The Scarborough
News, The Somerset County Gazette,
The Southern Daily Echo,
The Sunday Telegraph, The Sunday Times,
Sydney Morning Herald, The Times,
The Wakefield Express, The Western Daily Press,
The Western Mail, Wisden Cricket Monthly,
Wisden Cricketer, The Worcestershire Evening
News, The Yorkshire Evening Post,
The Yorkshire Post*

DVDs, Videos, Audio
100 Years of Headingley (BBC)
20th Century Cricket (Classic Pictures)
The Ashes 2005: The Greatest Series (Sunset
and Vine)
Australian Summer (BBC)
Bodyline – It's Just Not Cricket (ABC)
Bradman: Reflections on a Legend (ABC)
Classic One Day Finishes (BBC)
Cricket, The Golden Age (BBC)
Cricket: The 1960s (BBC)
Cricket: The 70s (BBC)
Cricket's Entertainers (BBC)
Don Bradman Recalls (ABC)
The Final Test (1953)
Golden Greats of Cricket: Batsmen (Benson and
Hedges)
Golden Greats of Cricket: Bowlers (Benson and
Hedges)
Great Days in Test Cricket (ABC)
History of the Ashes (Green Umbrella)
A History of Trent Bridge (BBC)
John Arlott Early Memories (BBC)
John Arlott: Voice of Summer (BBC)
John Arlott's Vintage Cricket (BBC)
Lord's: The Home of Cricket (BBC)
Playing Cricket the West Indies Way (Apex)
*The Official History of Yorkshire County
Cricket Club* (Watershed)
*Twenty Five Not Out, A Cricketing Celebration
of Richie Benaud's 25 BBC Years* (BBC)
Working Spaces: Michael Vaughan (Sky Arts)

INDEX

INDEX

INDEX

INDEX

INDEX

All images courtesy of the author except
p11© Matt Bright, p23 © Getty, p27 © Getty, p37, © PA, p43 © The Roger Mann Collection,
p52 © Nottingham Post, p61 © The Roger Mann Collection, p68 © PA, p77 © PA, p84 © PA,
p91 © The Roger Mann Collection, p99 © PA p107 © PA, p119 © PA, p134 © Getty, p139 ©
Getty, p148 © Getty, p161 © Martin Bennett, 167 both images © The Roger Mann Collection,
p173 © The Roger Mann Collection, p181 © PA, p188 © PA, p207 © PA, p213 © PA, p227 ©
Vaughn Ridley/SWpix.com, p235 © Vaughn Ridley/SWpix.com p241 left © Getty, right © PA,
p247 © Getty, p253 © Alistair Cowe, p262 © Getty, p267 © PA, p272 © Getty, p281 © The
Roger Mann Collection, p289 © Getty

Excerpts from 'Test Match at Lord's' by Alan Ross taken from *Alan Ross Poems* and reproduced
by kind permission of the estate of Alan Ross.

Excerpts from 'Cricket at Worcester 1938' by John Arlott reproduced by kind permission of the
estate of John Arlott